Primo Carnera

ALSO BY JOSEPH S. PAGE

*Pro Football Championships Before the Super Bowl:
A Year-by-Year History, 1926–1965*
(McFarland, 2011)

Primo Carnera

*The Life and Career
of the Heavyweight
Boxing Champion*

Joseph S. Page

McFarland & Company, Inc., Publishers
Jefferson, North Carolina, and London

LIBRARY OF CONGRESS CATALOGUING-IN-PUBLICATION DATA

Page, Joseph S.
Primo Carnera : the life and career of the
heavyweight boxing champion / Joseph S. Page.
    p.   cm.
Includes bibliographical references and index.

ISBN 978-0-7864-4810-4
softcover : 50# alkaline paper ∞

1. Carnera, Primo, 1906–1967. 2. Boxers (Sports)—Italy—Biography. I. Title.
  GV1132.C28P34   2011   796.83092—dc22   [B]   2010046635

British Library cataloguing data are available

© 2011 Joseph S. Page. All rights reserved

*No part of this book may be reproduced or transmitted in any form
or by any means, electronic or mechanical, including photocopying
or recording, or by any information storage and retrieval system,
without permission in writing from the publisher.*

On the cover: Photograph of Italian boxer Primo Carnera

Manufactured in the United States of America

*McFarland & Company, Inc., Publishers
Box 611, Jefferson, North Carolina 28640
www.mcfarlandpub.com*

To Kevin and Brian — my undisputed heavyweight champions...

Table of Contents

Acknowledgments ix
Introduction — Primo Carnera: The Ambling Alp 1

1. Young Primo of Sequals, 1906–1928 — 5
2. Early Boxing Days in Europe, 1928–1929 — 8
3. To the United States, 1930 — 25
4. The Battle of the Cracked Rib and Other Tales, 1931 — 64
5. Making His Case, 1932 — 79
6. The Death of Ernie Schaaf, 1933 — 100
7. "A Right Uppercut": The Championship, 1933 — 110
8. Title Defenses, 1933–1934 — 121
9. Max Baer, 1934 — 135
10. After the Title, 1934–1935 — 148
11. The Joe Louis Fight, 1935 — 157
12. After Louis, 1935–1939 — 166
13. The War Years, 1939–1945 — 181
14. The Comeback/Wrestling, 1945–1962 — 185
15. The Films — 189
16. Boxing Ability — 192
17. The Fix Question — 200
18. Primo Carnera: The Man — 209

Appendix I: Ring Record 219
Appendix II: Undercards 225
Chapter Notes 234
Bibliography 241
Index 243

Acknowledgments

I have discovered that writing a book is a lot of work and a lot of fun, but also a collaborative effort. While the author is fully engaged, many different people step in and help throughout the process. During the course of my work, my family and friends have provided editorial support and listened to me ramble on about Primo Carnera, boxing, and the 1920s and 1930s, all the while remaining interested and supportive. Librarians across the country, and far too numerous to remember, have helped me access material. Of those, I especially want to thank Tracey Howerton, Sally Raye, and Pat McGee at the Nashville Public Library; Deirdre Schmidel, James Lewis, Willis Taylor, and Susan German at the Newark Public Library; Mary Plazo of Akron-Summit County Public Library; Lynn Sullivan of the Omaha Public Library; Jeff Brophy of the International Boxing Hall of Fame; Melissa and the librarians at the Saint Paul, Minnesota, Public Library; Tina Russo, principal librarian at the Hillsborough County Public Library (Tampa); Sam and the librarians at the San Francisco Public Library; Francis and Lou and company; Barbara Scheibel at the Onondaga County Public Library in Syracuse, New York; the librarians at the Minneapolis Central Hennepin County Library; the librarians at the New York Public Library; Rubin and Annette Ratkin-Rubin (thank you more than I can say for sharing over 90 years of memories of New York sporting events and venues, including many of the old Madison Square Gardens); David and Ellen Levy; Robin Rose; Loretta Thompson; Sandy Reagan of Sandra Reagan Photography; Father Charley Giacosa; Len and Jean Lepore and Rose Werner for sharing Newark memories; my brother Jim, who probably never thought he would look at microfiche of 75-year-old newspapers, and the rest of my family, friends and colleagues, who have been very patient and put up with me during the writing of this book.

Introduction
Primo Carnera: The Ambling Alp

For entirely too long, Primo Carnera has been on the butt end of boxing lore. Since he first landed on American soil, he was, for various reasons, a person at whom ridicule, jest, and contempt were frequently directed. More often than not, because of his good nature, he simply ignored or put up with it. Much of Carnera's boxing life is open to debate, but there can be no question as to his character and his basic goodness.

In North America, reporters and promoters regularly typecast him as a fool, an oaf, and a clown. Sometimes he was painted as the monstrous and villainous foreign intruder on the American scene, a puppet of Mussolini's Black-Shirted fascists, and a symbol of Il Duce's expansionist policy in Africa. In Italy, during Carnera's rise to the heavyweight title, Achille Starace and his fascist propaganda machine portrayed him as a heroic symbol of Italian virility and supremacy. In truth, Primo Carnera was none of these things. Primo was a respectable fighter with a strong left jab, a notable right uppercut, and an occasional right cross. He was a good but simple man with a modest education, who was easily taken advantage of. The world during Carnera's ring career was a volatile place in which clashing ideologies and territorial expansion was sending humanity hurdling towards the Second World War. The symbolism of this massive foreigner from Mussolini's Italy was too much for many in the journalistic world to ignore. Against the backdrop of Mussolini's African invasion and Hitler's Germany, when Primo met fighters of African or Hebrew heritage, the imagery was palpable. At times, what happened in the ring was almost a sideshow in comparison to the buildup in the press.

I have been fascinated with Primo Carnera since I was a child. While growing up in New Jersey, Len Lepore, my best friend Lenny's father—whom I've always thought of as my second father—told me stories of how when he was a boy, he would carry professional wrestlers' gym bags into the arena in Newark. He and his friends slipped in with the wrestlers because they couldn't afford a ticket, and probably, knowing Mr. Lepore, because it was more adventurous that way. He spoke of the different wrestlers—Mike Mazurki, Jimmy Londos, Ed "Strangler" Lewis, Sandor Szabo, and Primo Carnera. Mr. Lepore would tell these tales with an almost boyish exuberance, but when he spoke of Carnera, it was with a special tone, almost with a notable reverence. He spoke of the night in November 1947 when Carnera was in Newark to wrestle another former heavyweight boxer named "Two Ton" Tony Galento. Even years later, he spoke of Carnera's enormous stature, his giant hands, and his kindness. To this day, he always reminds me when we speak of Primo, that he was the heavyweight-boxing champion of the world. The stories of fixed fights and mob payoffs didn't resonate. They didn't matter. This man, this enormous man, had knocked out Jack Sharkey to win the crown. He held onto it for a year and did not sit idly by, but successfully defended his title twice—as many times as Gene Tunney. Carnera deserved some measure of respect for that alone. Through these memories I became fascinated by Primo, and I was, from that time on, hooked.

I'll not argue that he was a great fighter, but he was adequate and at times very good. I'll not argue that he was a top-flight champion, but he did hold the title for a full year, defending his belt successfully against two creditable fighters. Primo's two successful defenses are more than Max Schmeling, Jack Sharkey, Max Baer, and James J. Braddock—all the other heavyweight champions between Gene Tunney and Joe Louis—had in total, during all their years as champions. During the six years of those combined championship runs, only Schmeling, with his 1931 victory over Young Stribling, ever successfully defended his crown. And one cannot make any realistic claim that Carnera's defenses were setups or easy fights. After Carnera knocked out Jack Sharkey in the sixth round to take the title in 1933, he won title defenses over Paolino Uzcudun and Tommy Loughran, two very noteworthy fighters from that era.

Was he on par with Joe Louis or Rocky Marciano or Muhammad Ali over the course of his career? Of course not, but neither were Jess Willard, Jimmy Braddock, Buster Douglas, Leon Spinks or a slew of other fighters who got their shot and made the most of it. Like Carnera, they were probably not the world's greatest fighters, but each was a good fighter who had his sterling moments, and no matter what, each will always hold the title of world champion.

Primo's reputation was also hurt by his management team. Financial shenanigans and rumors of fixed fights hurt him during his lifetime and have continued to dog him to this day. He was poorly educated, highly ignorant of financial matters, and perhaps he was a simple and naive man, but he was not the fool that many have portrayed him to be. Most of Carnera's handlers were greedy cheats at best and organized crime thugs at worst. Men such as Owney Madden, Billy Duffy, and Luigi Soresi leeched off Primo during his rise as a professional fighter and were nowhere to be found after he was broken down—they had bled him dry, and he was no longer of any value to them.

Were his fights fixed? Sure, it's possible that some may have been, but on that we can only speculate and in doing so, we only guess and tarnish. And certainly, this is nothing new to the fight game. Professional boxing has long been the subject of speculation around fixed fights; this is nothing unique to Primo Carnera. Fighters such as Jack Johnson, Gene Tunney, Young Stribling, Jake LaMotta, Kid McCoy, and hundreds of others have had questions raised around the outcomes of fights in which they have participated. Actually, a detailed and reasonable analysis of Carnera's career suggests persuasively that at least most of his fights, if not all of them, were on the level.

Yes, Carnera fought a lot of hand-picked backbenchers, but he also fought a high percentage of quality fighters, many of whom were listed in *The Ring* magazine's annual top 10 heavyweights for periods of time. He was very busy in the ring, fighting an average of almost once a month for his entire career—an enormous burden for a heavyweight. Given the level of his activity, not everyone he fought could realistically have been of top quality. Furthermore, when did it become uncommon for promoters and trainers to pad their fighters' records with some easier opponents?

He was undeniably tough—getting up three times against the crushing blows of Joe Louis; 11 times under the hammer of Max Baer; entering the ring for his return bout against Jim Maloney with cracked ribs, and taking a 10-round decision against that formidable and seasoned opponent; reentering the ring after an 8-year retirement and short one kidney, for an ill-advised, but financially necessary, five-fight comeback.

He had a glass jaw that sometimes enabled opponents to score quick knockdowns, but he always got up. For his size, his punch was never as powerful or savage as it might have been, but at 6'7" and averaging 270 pounds of solid muscle, the man could hit. Just ask any of the 72 men he knocked out.

His is a legacy of ambiguity. Even his nickname, "The Ambling Alp," is ambiguous. Ambling can refer to Primo's kind, gentle, easy personality, or it can be defined as slow, tentative, cautious, even reluctant, which many would claim that he was in the ring. But he was a tall and powerful man who fought like a tall and powerful man. He used his great reach to land repeated jabs and came inside when an opportunity arose for his right uppercut. His style of fighting was much like that of Vitali Klitschko, who also has his share of detractors, but who also wears the heavyweight crown.

I believe it a mistake to write Primo Carnera off as a third-rater, a mob tool, and a foolish oaf who didn't belong in the ring. He may not have been a natural in the ring, but he worked as hard as any boxer could to learn his craft, to be in top condition, and he repeatedly showed that he was tougher than nails. Aided by God-given size and a self-taught work ethic, he became a respectable fighter—flawed, yes, but still a good fighter.

I was inspired to write an even-handed treatment of Carnera's career because of the treatment he usually receives in today's press and in other works. One example is a 2004 article in which the author indicts Primo as a stumblebum and a fool, claiming with little or no evidence that Primo stopped Jack Sharkey in 1933 with "a powder puff punch"; that "Sharkey got a bundle to take a dive"; and that "most of the sports writers wrote scathing articles on the fight in disbelief of Jack's integrity and the fight business."[1]

Those claims are utterly without merit. I've watched that fight repeatedly and seen Sharkey's head snapped back again and again by a solid right uppercut, and I've read a great many press reports from the era. In all, I don't see any overwhelming support for the author's sentiment. Yes, some pundits from the day declared Primo unworthy, but no more than claimed that Braddock or Douglas or Willard or Leon Spinks were undeserving of the title. That's boxing.

Blatant smears and the piling on by the uninformed has been the norm in works addressing the career of Primo Carnera. A fresh examination of both his career and his life are long overdue. In this book, I intend to reconstruct Carnera's career and to evaluate it fairly, without the negative bias and unwarranted assumptions that have clouded it for over 80 years.

1

Young Primo of Sequals, 1906–1928

Of all of the places Primo Carnera traveled in his life, of all of the places he lived, Sequals, Italy, was always his home. Primo's love of his hometown and the citizens of Sequals was returned manyfold by his family and neighbors, who adored him.

Sequals rests in the northeast part of the country in the foothills of the Italian Alps, just north of Venice, in the Province of Pordenone, in the region of Friuli-Venezia Giulia. The name Sequals is actually a Friulano corruption of the Italian words for seven hills— *sette colli*. It is a town known for its stonecutting laborers and mosaicists. The town had a population of about 3,200 at the turn of the Twentieth Century, but after cresting at 3,722 in 1921, it fell notably by half and leveled to 2,122 as of 2001. Of that number, eight Carneras are still listed in the Sequals phone book.

It is a picturesque town full of white painted buildings with red and orange tiled roofs that are set amongst lush pastures and the green, forested foothills. The church in the town square is named after the town's patron saint, St. Andrew the Apostle (Chesa di San Andrea a Sequals).

Primo was born in this small Friulian town on October 26, 1906. He was the first child of Sante and Giovanna Mazziol Carnera. The couple gave Primo two brothers: Secondo, who was born in 1908, and Severino, who followed in 1912. Three other siblings died in infancy.

Not surprisingly, Primo was reportedly large at birth, weighing 15.5 pounds. He continued to grow at an amazing rate, standing more than five feet tall at age nine and achieving his full 6-foot, 7-inch height by his mid-teens. As tall as Primo was, he was never thin or lanky. Instead, he was always large, muscular, and strong.

Life was quiet in Sequals while Primo was a young boy and the family got along well enough with Sante working as a stonecutter on building projects around Europe. All of that began to change, however, on May 23, 1915, when Italy entered the First World War on the side of the Triple Entente, by declaring war on the Austrian–Hungarian Empire. The Italians had originally determined to remain neutral during the conflict. The nation had been allied with the Central Power states of Austria-Hungary and Germany in the Triple Alliance, but border disagreements with the Austrians led to a breach in the agreement. While war was not a wildly popular option with the general public, secret negotiations with England and France and offers of Austrian territory in the Alps and down the Dalmatian coast induced Italy to betray her alliance with the Central Powers. Shortly after the signing of the Treaty of London, formally aligning Italy with the French, British, and the Russians, Italy was at war.[1]

With the commencement of hostilities, Sante Carnera was forced to return to Italy from Germany, where he had sought work. He enlisted in the Italian army, where his primary responsibility was to dig trenches along the Carso, a barren limestone plateau of about 50 square miles, located between Trieste and Gorizia. "The troops hated the area, describing the Carso as 'a howling wilderness of stones sharp as knives.' The summer wind was crushing and the winter featured a bitter wind they called the 'Bora.' It was through the Carso, however, that the Italian Army had to advance to capture its objective of Trieste. Many of the eleven battles of the Isonzo—all Italian offensives—had the Carso as a primary focus or a diversion."[2]

Without Sante's income, money was tight and Primo's mother was forced to sell her wedding ring just to feed her children. As the oldest son, Primo had to help his mother by gathering what food he could from the local forests—mostly roots, berries, and nuts. Due to his size and already burgeoning strength, he was also able to do odd jobs and pick up loose change or food from the local troops and townspeople.

After the war, Sante came home to Sequals, but finances were still meager for the people of the village. Now 12 years old, Primo continued to work odd jobs to help the family make ends meet.

Stories of Primo's legendary feats abound in Sequals, many from before his days in the ring. From his protecting his playmates from a rabid dog, to helping to carry the new bell to the top of the church tower, his strength and fearlessness have long been a source of wonder and pride in the small Friulian town. One story stands out. During the winter that Primo was 13, a fire broke out in the middle of the night in a nearby farmhouse. People saw the flames, heard the commotion, and began to gather at the flaming building. The parents, who had barely gotten out of the house themselves, were frantic because their baby was still inside. Upon hearing this news, young Primo, without hesitation, covered his mouth with a handkerchief and forced himself into the burning farmhouse. Several minutes later, he emerged with the baby—safe and sound—in his arms.[3]

Primo's enormous hands were simply not suited for the mosaic trade, so after four years of formal education in the local schools, the young man started to work as a carpenter's apprentice with his uncle Bonaventura Mazziol. At 6' 5" tall, Primo's uncle was one of the few people he knew who was as large as him. Bonaventura was a former grenadier who had lost a leg during his military service. The work with his uncle was good, but Primo wanted more opportunity. In 1923, he decided to move to Le Mans, France, to live with his aunt Antonia Mazziol and her husband Anselmo Cecconi. Anselmo also worked in the carpentry business, and Primo was excited about the opportunity to make more money than he could in Sequals. Wearing clothes borrowed from his family, the 16-year-old started the long journey to France. This departure was a watershed event in Primo's life. While he would return to Sequals time and again for the rest of his life, even building his dream home there, he would never again fully be a resident of the small town that was, more than any other, his home.

In 1932, Primo built his dream home on property he acquired on the Via Roma. The home is just a three-minute walk from the Piazza Cesarina Pellarin, the main downtown square. The villa is a beautiful, two-story building, exquisitely outfitted with floors decorated by local mosaicists and walls with frescoes. Large windows, porches and patios surround the home. The grounds are manicured with gardens and green lawns. The property is surrounded with a fence and an iron gate. Next to the villa there is a large, one-story building that houses a garage and a gymnasium, where Primo trained while at home. Across

1. Young Primo of Sequals, 1906–1928 7

Primo at Villa Carnera with his father Sante and mother Giovanna in January 1937. While Carnera was swindled out of much of his prizefighting earnings, he was able to build the villa, his dream home, in his hometown of Sequals in Italy, in 1932. (London Express/Hutton Archives/Getty Images)

the front of the gym is a sign that reads, *Mens sana in corpore sano*, Latin for "A healthy mind in a healthy body." Villa Carnera is the home to which he brought Pina, his new bride in 1939, and the home that his two children first knew. Primo returned here when he fell ill from liver disease and complications from diabetes and died here on June 29, 1967.

Another short walk from the Piazza is Primo's favorite bar, the "Cantina al Bottegon." A few minutes farther down the road and you will reach Primo's parents' home where Primo was born. The citizens of Sequals honored the town's favorite son by renaming a street Via Primo Carnera. The town was his home and his sense of being. He built his permanent home there and returned to Sequals when he knew that he was dying. When things were looking down, he was always welcome in Sequals.

2

Early Boxing Days in Europe, 1928–1929

According to Carnera's children, Primo first entered a boxing ring in 1924 while he was working as a bricklayer in France. The 17-year-old Primo was encouraged by a heavyweight fighter and fellow Italian emigrant named Amilcare Piana to join him in training at the Le Mans Sporting Association, where young men from various backgrounds gathered to share their love of boxing. Association president Fred Legros commented that young Primo worked diligently, but with mixed results. His great natural strength was tempered somewhat by his poor diet. He was slow in the ring, but even early on, he learned to use his left jab effectively.

One night in the central French town of Chateauroux, a heavyweight was needed to fill out a fight card and Legros decided to let Primo enter the ring against a French military heavyweight champion named Baronnet. Primo apparently did quite well in the first round, poking his opponent with repeated jabs and making a good impression on the crowd. He was, however, already tired while Baronnet entertained the crowd between rounds. The minute between rounds helped Primo only briefly. Having caught his breath, Primo came out of his corner looking sharp, but by mid-round, he was once again winded. With his arms feeling like lead weights, the tired and inexperienced bricklayer dropped his guard and began to take a beating. At the end of the round, Legros saw that his young fighter was in big trouble. He threw in the towel to prevent Primo from taking certain and unnecessary punishment.

Enjoying the companionship and the camaraderie with the other young boxers, Primo continued to train at Le Mans through 1926. By that time, however, he was bored with his work, tired of having no money, and continually hungry. One night Primo was spotted by the owner of a traveling carnival and asked to go to work for the man with the promise of better pay and enough food for him to eat properly. Anxious to leave bricklaying, carpentry and hunger behind, Primo jumped at the chance and thus became a strongman and wrestler in the small circus that traveled throughout France.

Billed as "Juan the Invincible" and "Juan the Guadalajara Terror," Primo lifted weights, and also wrestled or boxed all comers. The men in the audience were tempted by the promise of a 1,000 franc prize should they defeat the giant in the ring. The colossal Italian who had by now grown to his full size was encouraged by the show's owner to glare at the crowd and flex his huge muscles to frighten off some of the more intrepid men in the crowd. Many of the matches were actually prearranged events against other circus employees who were planted in the crowd and "volunteered" to face the Friulian giant. Primo did not love the work, but it paid better than carpentry, it allowed him to travel, and for perhaps the first time in his life, he was not continually hungry.

2. Early Boxing Days in Europe, 1928–1929

Primo's professional boxing career was conceived on the night of March 15, 1928. On that night, the circus had stopped for shows in the French seaside town of Arcachon, and Primo met a legitimate challenge from a strong and very determined young man. Primo defeated him in two rounds by landing a hard left to his jaw, but more significantly, former French heavyweight Paul Journee, who lived in town and ran a local gymnasium, was in the crowd and witnessed Carnera's rough but rugged performance.

The 35-year-old Journee had fought professionally throughout the decade of the 1920s, but his success in the ring was fleeting at best. The 6'1", 201-pound Journee fought 35 times, posting only a 6–28–1 record, but twice fighting for the French heavyweight title against Marcel Nilles.

Journee was Georges Carpentier's main sparring partner during the Orchid Man's preparations for the championship bout with Jack Dempsey at Boyle's Thirty Acres in Jersey City, New Jersey, on July 2, 1921. Journee challenged Carpentier more than any other opponent in camp. "The French heavyweight, with his long left jab and spirited attack, forcing Carpentier to retreat several times under attack and at close quarters got past the challenger's arms with rights and lefts for the stomach."[1]

He took a break from Carpentier's camp on June 20, when he traveled to Brooklyn's Ebbets Field to face Charley Weinert (52–12–3) in his first American appearance in a 15-round bout. Weinert made short work of Journee, dropping him 10 times before the fight was halted in the fifth round by referee Johnny Haukop.[2] Journee spent the remainder of the summer in the United States, working with Carpentier and preparing for an August 9th bout with Al Reich (28–13–1) at Queensboro Stadium in Long Island City, New York. This fight went even worse for Journee as Reich dropped him for the count in the first round of a scheduled 12. Journee then returned to Europe where he lost 21 of his final 24 fights over the next five years. After a second-round loss to Irish heavyweight Con O'Kelly in February 1926, Journee finally had had enough. With his ring career behind him, Journee retired to his hometown of Arcachon, a coastal village near Bordeaux. He opened a gymnasium there and had settled into a quiet life.

Journee first saw the massive 21-year-old, while attending the traveling circus that night in Arcachon. He watched as "Juan the Unbeatable Spaniard," defeated the strapping local youth. Upon inquiry, Journee discovered that "Juan" was actually Primo Carnera of Sequals, Italy. He arranged to meet with Primo the next day. During that meeting Journee talked with Carnera about considering professional boxing.

Primo was game, so Journee prepared a contract committing himself to train the young man and provide him room and board, in return for 35 percent of all monies earned by Primo in the ring. Carnera paused when he first saw the contract. When Journee asked him why he seemed hesitant, Primo responded, "Will I really have enough to eat?" Journee laughed and assured the young man that he would, and with that, Primo signed his first professional boxing contract. According to *The Ring* magazine in April 1930, Journee "discovered" Primo Carnera and owned a 25 percent cut, part of which he split with a Paris businessman (promoter Leon See): "Paul's personal cut to date on Carnera's takings is about a quarter of a million francs."[3]

Primo stayed in Journee's home and found a day job as a carpenter in Arcachon. He put his carpentry skills to good use making himself a bed large enough for his now 6-feet 7-inch frame. After work each afternoon, Primo would head over to Journee's gym and train with the former heavyweight for several hours.

In time, Journee introduced Carnera to See. See had trained Journee and Paul wrote to his former mentor, "I have found an interesting Italian boy, come and see him." Initially, See was uninterested in pursuing another fighter. He was content instead to concentrate on his journalism, but at the insistence of Journee, he finally traveled the 400 miles to Arcachon to evaluate the young man. He took one look at the enormous and heavily muscled Italian and shook his head, stating to Journee, "No, he is too big, he is not right for boxing." See told Journee that it would take too long to turn Primo into a boxer. See then returned to Paris, putting Journee's prospect out of his mind. Despite See's initial reaction, neither Carnera nor Journee was willing to give up and they kept working hard to improve Primo's skills in the ring.

In his memoirs, Carnera recalled, "I became Journee's trainee while going on working as a carpenter in Arcachon in order to earn my living. After the first month in the gym, my body changed: I weighed less, I was less slow and had started to make a lot of progress in my boxing technique."[4]

After a couple of more months, Journee felt that Primo had made enough progress to try See again. After Journee convinced See to come back and have a second look at his prospect, See was amazed at his progress. Primo was more agile and self-assured. His conditioning was much improved and he seemed ready to become a real heavyweight fighter. See exclaimed, "That is not the same boy, that is a different person!" Finally convinced that Carnera could be a fighter, the now intrigued See stated, "What a pity! We have lost some precious time." It was agreed that he would fight. See, a dapper little Frenchman with a moustache who barely came up to Primo's shoulders, would be his manager, and Maurice Eudeline and Journee would train him and teach him to box.

Leon See was born in the northern French city of Lille in 1877. His father was a successful businessman, but Leon showed no inclination to follow in his father's footsteps. Instead, after graduating from university, Leon became a journalist. While in school, he boxed as an amateur, but he met with limited success and determined to hang up his gloves and continue his involvement with the sport, outside of the ring.

See arranged for Carnera to come to Paris and train under his tutelage. A short time later, Primo and Journee arrived at Paris's Montparnasse Station, where they were met by Eudeline. The three proceeded to the Saint-Germaine-en-Laye gym, where Primo would train. Eudeline and Journee worked Carnera hard from morning to night, running, jumping rope, hitting the bags, and sparring. After working with Carnera for a month, Eudeline reported to See that Primo was "...very clever. He learns quickly all what I teach him. He is very strong and really willing to fight in a boxing ring. I am sure he will make it."[5] See was ready to start marketing his charge.

* * *

See went first to visit an American in Paris, promoter Jeff Dickson. Jefferson Davis Dickson, Jr., was a native of Natchez, Mississippi. He had served as a photographer and filmmaker in the U.S. Army during World War I and remained in France following the armistice. He showed no fear of battle as he set up cameras close to the action — so close in fact that he was injured during the St. Mihiel offensive. Dickson drifted around Europe and Africa where he continued his work as a photographer by taking both stills and moving pictures throughout those continents. He returned to Paris in the early 1920s and began selling automobile bumpers as well as promoting shows and athletic events — including prizefights.

He became the owner of the Salle Wagram in Paris and promoted fights throughout

2. Early Boxing Days in Europe, 1928–1929

the large cities of Europe. The Salle Wagram is one of the most famous and beautiful public venues in Paris. A short walk from the Arc de Triomphe, the neo–Classical facility is splendidly adorned with grand chandeliers, hardwood floors, and spectacular, hand-carved, decorative woodwork. The building has hosted parties, auctions, parliamentary receptions, concerts, exhibitions, fashion shows, sporting events, conventions, and more.

Dickson also tried his hand at promoting other events such as figure skating, tennis, ice hockey, bullfights, and bicycle racing. One noteworthy event promoted by Dickson was an indoor "lion hunt" with 100 lions, and a show called "The Jungle at Midnight." Those attending were able to view the wildlife under floodlights. The event was so successful that Parisian authorities thought that the more than 300,000 people who visited Dickson's Jungle might make the animals nervous. The officials decided to close the show after just eight nights. Dickson was now a promoter of legendary reputation, but his greatest fame came from his association with boxing.

In 1931, Dickson built his Palais des Sports on the site of the old Velodrome d'Hiver, using Madison Square Garden as his model. He had been named as a member of the boxing boards of both England and France. According to *Time* magazine, "He acquired boxing rights at London's Royal Albert Hall and White City Stadium, two bullfight arenas in Madrid and Barcelona which he uses for boxing and wrestling, and became sports Tsar of the Continent."[6] It's no wonder that he was known as the "Tex Rickard of Europe."

Dickson was a hard-nosed businessman, but he was well loved by many throughout the continent. He had a soft side that was evident in the annual Christmas parties he threw for orphaned and disadvantaged children. At these events celebrities and sports stars mixed with the children and handed out candy and toys.

On the day Dickson was scheduled to meet Primo, See took an elegantly dressed Carnera to the promoter's office. When Dickson saw Primo duck his head to avoid hitting the door frame leading into Dickson's office, the American was awestruck. He got up and eyed the Italian giant from head to toe and asked, "Can he box?" See responded, "Well, nothing special, you know." See reported that Dickson then stated, "My God, he is two heavyweight boxers together. If he could make it in the boxing ring, he would be a big attraction."[7] Dickson then offered the pair 1,000 francs for Primo to meet heavyweight Leon Sebilo at the Salle Wagram the next week. See was amazed that an untried fighter in his maiden appearance could command 1,000 francs. He was also a bit hesitant to put Primo in the ring with Sebilo, who had a dismal record but still had the experience of two years and nine professional fights under his belt. A loss to Sebilo could hurt Primo's self-confidence and his chances of landing other fights. Primo and Dickson urged See to sign the contract and after weighing the pros and cons, See agreed to the match after convincing himself that Sebilo would be an easy opponent to break Primo in and build his confidence.

* * *

On the evening of September 12, 1928, Carnera entered the ring for the first time as a professional, to fight against Leon Sebilo, at the Salle Wagram in Paris. See's decision to let Primo face the French heavyweight proved to be a correct one. Sebilo entered the fight with a notably poor 1–8 record, not having won since his debut in 1926. Sebilo won his very first professional bout, defeating Swedish journeyman fighter Joe Sylvain by way of TKO in six rounds in Paris. He should have stopped while he was ahead. He lost his next fight by disqualification, and it never got any better from there. He closed out his professional career by dropping 12 bouts in a row. His losses included a second-round knockout by Max

Schmeling in 1927. On this late summer evening, the crowd watched French middleweight Felix Sportiello outpoint Arthur Vermaut, and then cheered wildly as the Italian colossus was announced. The fans and perhaps Sebilo were awestruck as the massive fighter climbed into the ring. Carnera listened carefully to advice from Journee, Eudeline, and See and met his opponent head on, throwing an assortment of left jabs and right uppercuts. Primo scored an easy second-round knockout over Sebilo, who would drop three more fights in a row before retiring from the ring in 1930. See later claimed this fight was fixed for 1,500 francs, but against such a poor fighter, why would he have bothered to waste the money? Why would he have paid such a sum to assure a win against a 1–8 fighter who had been kayoed in each of his last six fights?

* * *

Two weeks later, Primo met Joe Thomas at the Cirque de Paris. Thomas was an aspiring heavyweight who was entering the professional ranks for the first time on this late September evening. In the second bout of a four-fight undercard, Primo finished off the 190-pound Thomas in three rounds. Like the Sebilo bout and many of Primo's early contests, this was among the fights that See alleged to be fixed. Frederic Mullally has suggested that half of Primo's 3,000-franc purse was given over to Thomas to take a dive.[8] Here's another classic example of a ridiculous allegation. Why on earth would See feel compelled to give 1,500 francs to a rookie fighter who was almost 90 pounds lighter than Primo? Thomas also proved to be a bust as a professional. He fought six bouts over the next couple of years, losing all but one, including another loss to Primo in their 1929 return bout.

* * *

On October 30 Primo met Salvatore Ruggirello, a 6'1" 215-pound fighter from Italy, who had posted a 7–7–0 record in two years in the ring. The fight was part of a three-bout card at the Cirque de Paris, and it is alleged that Ruggirello had imbibed a bit too much prior to the fight, thus helping Primo to stop his fellow countryman in the fourth by way of a technical knockout. Regardless of what Ruggirello's condition may or may not have been during the fight, Primo's great size and his knockout victories were beginning to draw attention from the French press and beyond. He was easy to recognize in a crowd and it was becoming common for fans and autograph seekers to approach him in public.

* * *

For his next fight, Primo would travel home to his native Italy for a bout at the Palazzo dello Sport in Milan. Italian promoter Giuseppe Carpegna contacted See and offered 12,000 francs for Carnera to come back to Italy in late November to meet aspiring Argentine fighter Epifanio Islas. Noting the Argentine's size at 6'4" and 225 pounds, See countered that he wanted 25,000 francs, an amount he felt that Carpegna would balk at and therefore the fight could be avoided. When the Italian promoter agreed to the amount, See hesitantly agreed and the fight was scheduled for November 25. Because Islas was big and an unknown quantity, See was a bit reluctant to put Carnera in the ring with him. Islas was fighting only his second professional bout, having lost on points in 10 rounds to Jose Santa in Rio de Janero 14 months earlier. While Islas was big, he never met much success in the professional ring. He retired in 1933 with a 2–12–2 record and finished 0 for his last 11 fights.

Press reports indicated that Primo looked good in training and was easily handling his

2. Early Boxing Days in Europe, 1928–1929

sparring partners, including "the Black boxer Bassin [French middleweight Claude Bassin?] with some champion-like feints."[9]

After six years away, Primo was excited to be returning home to his native Italy. He arranged to have his mother come to Milan by train. When Giovanna Carnera arrived at the Grand Hotel Agnelli and asked for Primo, she was at first denied. The hotel staff, assuming she was a fan, attempted to send her away, saying that the boxer had left instructions not to be disturbed. The travel-weary Giovanna, her eyes welling up with tears, asked the desk clerk, "May a mother hug her son after six years?" After establishing that this was indeed Primo's mother, Giovanna was taken to a lavish room and made comfortable while Primo was summoned. Soon a smiling and well-dressed Primo entered the room, opened his arms and exclaimed, "Mum!" The two embraced and cried tears of happiness at the reunion. They spent the rest of the day together catching up and laughing.[10]

That evening, Primo kissed his mother goodbye, left the hotel and headed for the Sports Palace. At 9:00 P.M. the fighters entered the ring. Primo was proud to be fighting in his home country and even more proud at the warm reception he received from the crowd. Carlo Lomazzi, one of the original founders of the Italian Boxing Federation (FPI) in 1916 and a man who had officiated at the 1924 and 1928 Olympics, was the referee.

Overall, the fight buildup was more exciting than the fight, which was a rather boring affair with the two men mostly circling each other and trading largely ineffective blows. The only real excitement came when Islas went down in the fifth as the result of a Carnera right cross. Lomazzi insisted Islas get up and fight, which he did, but the rest of the contest proved no better. Carnera defeated Islas by receiving a 10-round unanimous decision, but the crowd and the press were unhappy with the performance. In a rather harsh assessment, journalist Nino Cappelletti reported in the *Gazzetta della Sport* the day after the fight that Primo's reputation was merely fluff generated by his managers and the French media. He opined that in a couple of months, the only options open to Carnera would be to return either to the circus or to carpentry. Most accounts in the Italian press indicate that Carnera did not look very good against Islas, but given both fighters' inexperience and very large size, you really might not expect this to have been a particularly good fight.

See told the press that Primo was also influenced by his mother's gentle and calming presence, which is not exactly the right prescription for getting a fighter ready to knock another man out.

The fight was also a financial bust for Carpegna who, facing bankruptcy and ruin, committed suicide a few months later. The kind and generous Primo persuaded See to send money to Carpegna's family to help them out.

After putting his mother on the train back to Sequals, Primo and his entourage left Milan to return to the welcoming climes of Paris.

* * *

Anxious to get Carnera back into the ring quickly and distance their fighter from the Islas fight, See and Dickson arranged a bout at the Velodrome d'Hiver in Paris for December 1. Primo was to anchor a 3-fight card with a match against Constant Barrick of Marseilles. Barrick seemed to See and Dickson a perfect antidote to the mediocre showing in Milan. Barrick had been knocking around the European fight game since 1919 and lost virtually every fight he climbed into the ring for. He had won only one of his 17 bouts, while serving as cannon fodder for many of the big names of Europe including, among others, Battling Siki, Paolino Uzcudun, Piet van der Veer, Rudi Wagener, and "The Iron Man of France"

Moise Bouquillon. Barrick's one victory had come two years before, by disqualification, against Ernst Rosemann in Paris.

The press and the crowd were anxious that Primo show well against Barrick and expunge any lingering doubt set forth in Milan. They were not disappointed. Dickson and See had chosen wisely, as Primo easily handled the Frenchman. The spectators cheered as Carnera dispatched Barrick by way of a third-round knockout, while hardly breaking a sweat.

Barrick would fight just once more. His ignominious career would end as it had begun, with a loss by way of knockout, the following April, this time to the enormous Portuguese fighter Jose Santa in Lisbon. His final record was a weak 1–15–3.

* * *

On December 8 Primo fought an exhibition bout against Paul Journee in the city of Bordeaux just 30 miles from Arcachon, where the two had met the previous March. Journee was happy to have a chance to get back into the ring in front of his family and friends. The gym was sold out and a good time was had by the capacity crowd as the seasoned Journee and his eager pupil sparred for several rounds. Following the exhibition, Primo and his party spent several days by the sea before returning to Paris to ready themselves for his next fight in January.

* * *

As the new year began, See scheduled a potentially dangerous bout for Primo against the German heavyweight Ernst Rosemann. Rosemann was coming to the end of his once promising 8-year career. After posting an 11–3 record over his first three years in the ring, Rosemann had met with spotty success thereafter, winning only six of his 21 remaining fights, including a first-round knockout over Journee in 1925. While his record had slipped in the past several years, Rosemann was nonetheless a formidable opponent for the young Carnera. He was a veteran of 31 professional fights and had boxed over 130 rounds against a good number of seasoned opponents. This would not be an easy victory for Carnera. Even See never claimed this to be a set-up, and he and Eudeline spent the weeks leading up to the fight preparing their man by improving his defense and his punching power.

On the night of the five-bout card, Primo waited patiently in the locker room of the Sportpalast in Berlin as the first three fights went the distance. He was, as usual, confident while his managers and trainers were concerned. They knew that their fighter could win, but they also knew how difficult a loss would be to deal with. Finally, Rosemann and Carnera were called.

Primo fought perhaps his best fight yet. He handled Rosemann easily for five rounds until the referee called a halt to the bout to stop the German from taking any more unnecessary punishment. See, Dickson and company were elated, as Primo had stood up to and taken the fight to a seasoned, rough-and-tumble heavyweight. He had won a decisive victory and shown significant improvement in doing so.

* * *

For his seventh fight, Primo faced Franz Diener as part of a four-fight card in Leipzig, Germany, on April 18. In Carnera's toughest test so far, he faced a German heavyweight who brought a respectable 19–7–3 record into the bout. Diener was the former holder of both the amateur and professional German heavyweight titles. Diener's record boasted creditable bouts against Jim Maloney, Knute Hansen, Rudi Wagener. He also made a strong

2. Early Boxing Days in Europe, 1928–1929

showing in a tenth-round knockout loss to Larry Gains in 1924, and another in a 15-round loss to Max Schmeling in 1928, in a fight for the open–German heavyweight title. Franz fought Paolino Uzcudun to a ten-round draw in 1926. By 1929, Diener was having problems with his eyesight. He was looking to fight a few more good fights, put some more money in the bank, and then hang up his gloves and open a butcher's shop in his hometown of Charlottenburg, near Berlin.

See had instructed Carnera to use his most potent weapon — his long left jab — to keep Diener at a distance and wrack up points. Primo did so by continually landing the jabs in and around his opponent's eyes, causing the German's sight in his bad eye to blur. Irritated by his opponent's tactics, Diener landed a ferocious left hook to Primo's groin. Primo went down like a rock and had to be helped to his feet and guided back to his corner. The local referee claimed that he saw no foul, but still granted Carnera five minutes to gather himself. Primo was still in such agony after those five minutes had passed that he could not even stand. The referee offered to extend the time another five minutes, but it was obviously pointless. Amazingly, the referee then disqualified Carnera for being unwilling to fight and declared Diener the winner in the first round.

* * *

Shaking off the bogus first-round disqualification loss to Diener, Primo won his next eight bouts against a mix of novice and experienced fighters. In the first of these, Primo met the 1927 French National Heavyweight champion Moise Bouquillon at the Salle Wagram on May 22. Bouquillon, the 195-pound "Iron Man of France," had a solid record of 25–5–0 and had won both the French light heavyweight and heavyweight championships in 1927. Primo outweighed his opponent by nearly 80 pounds. In a strong showing, Carnera outpointed Bouquillon for a 10-round decision. It was a win, but most importantly, it was another win against a respectable fighter.

* * *

Primo next faced Marcel Nilles, another mediocre fighter reaching the end of his career. The fight was scheduled for May 30 in the Cirque de Paris as part of a two-bout card that also highlighted a 10-round heavyweight contest between Maurice Griselle and Knute Hansen in the opening contest. Griselle defeated Hansen by way of TKO in the fifth round.

Marcel Nilles had been fighting since 1919 and like so many other fighters had started with a string of victories and the lure of hope. His career, however, also finished like those of so many other fighters. Once he stepped up to face the next rung of competition, he became just another average fighter with a dream. After a 10–1 start, he won only 4 of his next 31 bouts. After nine straight losses stretching back to 1926, Nilles had defeated Leon Sebilo by knockout in three rounds and hoped that he could make it two in a row against Carnera. The result was indeed another third-round knockout, but the similarities ended there. This time it was Nilles lying on the canvas and Primo raising his massive arms in victory. Nilles hung up his gloves after the Carnera defeat, but resurfaced in Sao Paulo, Brazil, in 1934 when he fought Italian heavyweight Erminio Spalla in a return bout for both fighters. Spalla, who himself had not fought since being knocked out by Riccardo Bertazzollo in Milan in 1927, dropped Nilles for a knockout victory in the second round. Both men retired for good after this one-fight comeback.

* * *

On June 26 Primo took on 220-pound Jack Humbeeck in Paris. The Belgian, who owned a 36–31–12 record, was fresh off a rare victory, having received a points decision over Ernst Rosemann in Leipzig on June 7. He had not won regularly since 1924 and although Humbeeck would fight 17 more times, the victory over Rosemann was his last. Primo would start Jack's 0–17 drought by taking this fight by a sixth-round TKO.

* * *

On August 14, Primo traveled to the city of San Sebastian in Spain to meet the hard-hitting Basque heavyweight Jose Lete. Lete had started fighting professionally earlier in the year with three fights in New York City, winning the first two and earning a draw in the third. He then traveled back to San Sebastian where he defeated Chilean heavyweight Quintin Romero Rojas by way of a second-round knockout on August 4. Off to a great start, Lete was full of hope when he met Primo for what even See admitted was a genuine bout. Lete was a solid 205 pounds and by many accounts, he punched like a freight train. Primo had, however, improved to the point where he was able to hold off the powerful Basque and deal out enough damage to win an easy unanimous points victory over 10 rounds.

For whatever reason, the loss to Carnera spelled the beginning of the end for Lete's career. He next met Guillermo Silva in Montevideo, Uruguay, on January 4, where he was knocked out in just two rounds. Lete would then not return to the ring professionally until 1932 when he lost his final bout also by knockout to Jose La Roe in La Roe's debut in Barcelona. At that point, Lete ended his short career with a 3–3–1 record.

* * *

On August 25, Primo met Joe Thomas in a return match. Thomas was 1–1 since his third round knockout loss to Primo the previous September. The two met at the Prado in Marseilles. The outcome was much the same, as Carnera commanded the fight, winning by TKO in four rounds.

* * *

On August 30 Primo made short work of Russian heavyweight Feodor Nikolaeff in Dieppe with a first-round knockout against the novice fighter. The background is a bit sketchy on Nikolaeff, but it appears that he had last fought professionally in 1924, losing on points in eight rounds. After his loss to Primo, he would fight just once more, being knocked out in the fifth round by Harry Persson at the Circus in Stockholm.

* * *

Another tune-up fight was scheduled for September 18 at the Salle Wagram against German heavyweight Hermann Jaspers. The 185-pound Jaspers was 0–1 as he walked to the ring that September evening having lost his first fight to Hans Schonrath in Berlin in April. Twenty minutes later, he would be 0–2 as he was helped out of the ring and back to his dressing room. Primo knocked out the German in the third round of a scheduled ten. Jaspers went on to win his next two fights, but after a two-year layoff, lost his final three and ended his career at 2–5–0 in 1933.

The win was not a difficult one for Primo, but it was decisive and brought his record to an impressive 13–1–0. Leon See and Jeff Dickson now decided it was time to cross the channel and introduce England to their giant.

2. Early Boxing Days in Europe, 1928–1929

* * *

On October 17 Primo fought British heavyweight Jack Stanley at the Royal Albert Hall in London in the middle contest of a five-fight card. While not consistent, Stanley was a decent fighter who had posted a 10–17–3 record over the previous nine years. He fought almost exclusively against local boxers in London during the first half of his career, but by 1925 broadened his resume by accepting challenges from bigger-name fighters and moving beyond London. Primo won their October night's battle at 1:45 of the first round after dropping Stanley three times. The fight was over so quickly that the promoters called upon local heavyweight Pat Tarling to fight a couple of exhibition rounds against Primo to give the crowd their money's worth. Tarling had a limited professional record and Primo knocked him out within two rounds.

Stanley was somewhat amazing in the fact that he fought from 1920 until 1948 and only won two contests after 1926. In reality, Stanley retired after losing to Pierre Charles in Brussels on April 16, 1932, but he continually came back for "one more fight." He made a brief comeback to fight Reggie Meen twice in 1936 and 1937. Eight years later, he was coaxed back into the ring for a pair of fights against Charlie Collett. In 1948, Stanley, now straddling 50, put on the gloves one more time to meet Doug Mansfield on November 5. Stanley lost all five of these comeback fights, four by knockout, but he did look sharp in the first Collett fight, taking him the full eight rounds and losing a close decision on points. He finished his career with an 11–28–5 record.

In early November, Primo traveled north to Glasgow for a series of exhibition matches before returning to London. In both Glasgow and Edinburgh, Primo was met by raucous crowds who wanted to get a look at the famous Italian. The exhibitions and other public appearances were hugely successful and helped to set up a bout with one of the busiest fighters in ring history — Young Stribling.

* * *

William Lawrence "Young" Stribling, Jr., was a terrific athlete and a popular fighter who was well loved by many in his native Georgia. Stribling was a solid citizen who was involved in various civic groups, from the Elks to the Kiwanis to the Masons. He also worked with the less fortunate and was active in his church, where he taught Sunday school. Young served as a lieutenant in the Army Reserve Air Corps where he earned his pilot wings.

Stribling fought almost 300 professional contests between 1921 and 1933, building both an interesting and impressive fight resume. According to Stribling's son Guerry Boone Stribling, legendary sportswriter Damon Runyon "derisively dubbed Stribling as the 'King of the Canebrakes,' because he chalked up the boxer to being little more than a barnstormer who fought anyone, anywhere."[11] "Pa" Stribling, who managed his son's career, fostered that reputation. Between 1921 and 1925, Pa scheduled his son to fight an amazing 157 times in venues large and small. In 1925, they criss-crossed the nation, as only two of Stribling's 33 fights were held consecutively in the same state.

On July 3, 1931, Stribling fought Max Schmeling for the heavyweight title. Young lost the championship bout by way of TKO after 15 grueling rounds at Municipal Stadium in Cleveland, Ohio. For the first five rounds, Young acquitted himself very well, scoring against Schmeling with heavy and rapid combinations. Starting in the sixth round, however, Max began a systematic destruction of his foe. While Stribling continued to fight reasonably well through the ninth, he was absorbing more punishment than he was delivering, and it was simply a matter of time. Early in the tenth round Max landed a right to the jaw that shook the Georgian to his feet, and Stribling never really recovered. As a credit to his toughness, Stribling continued to hold on for the next six rounds, refusing to go down. In the 15th and final stanza, although he was on his last legs, Stribling reached deep into his reserves and unloaded on the German with a right uppercut to the jaw that rocked Schmeling, but the champion shook it off and moved in for the kill. Late in the round, Schmeling floored Stribling with a hard, sweeping right to the jaw that dropped the challenger in the corner. Stribling struggled to his feet at the count of nine, obviously in bad shape. Schmeling looked to referee George Blake to see if he was going to stop the fight, but when Blake made no motion for stoppage, Max began to rain a flurry of lefts and rights on his opponent. With only 14 seconds remaining on the clock, Blake stepped in and raised the champion's hand, giving Schmeling a successful, if somewhat difficult title defense.

On February 27, 1929, Stribling fought Jack Sharkey in a heavyweight championship elimination fight in Flamingo Park in Miami. After an eight-fight undercard, Sharkey outpointed Stribling in 10 rounds.

Stribling split a pair of fights with Paul Berlenbach, including a 15-round unanimous decision defeat in a fight for the light heavyweight championship, in front of 50,000 fans at Yankee Stadium in 1926. While he went the distance, Stribling, over-trained and worn-out from Pa Stribling's relentless barnstorming schedule, "lost the decision in what then–*Macon Telegraph* sports editor Bobby Norris described as 'the worst fight of his long career.'"[12]

Stribling knocked out Al Nelson twice in the same night on May 17, 1923. After controversy surrounded referee Bill Kaliska's decision in favor of an obvious knockout by Stribling, Nelson's seconds revived him and a short while later Nelson re-entered the ring for a second fight in which he took a terrible beating at the hands of the annoyed Stribling. Young, who was determined to make this outcome stand, battered his opponent around the ring and finished him off with a clean second-round knockout to win the southern middleweight title.

In another bizarre ending, Young apparently won the world's light heavyweight championship from Mike McTigue on October 4, 1923, in Columbus, Georgia. Stribling held the championship only briefly, however. Referee Harry Ertle, claiming that he felt threatened at the end of the fight by the angry mob of 10,000 fans, awarded the fight to the local favorite, Stribling. Once Ertle was safely out of the arena, however, the referee changed his ruling and called the fight a draw, thus enabling McTigue to hold onto his crown. The following March, Stribling gained a measure of justice when he floored McTigue in the tenth round of a rematch and then received a 12-round newspaper decision in Newark, New Jersey.

Stribling undeniably fought a lot of nobodies as he traveled the back roads of the boxing world as a sideshow fighter early in his career. That said, Strib also met a who's who of talent from his era. During his 12 years in the ring, Young fought Tommy Loughran to two wins and a loss, lost by TKO to Schmeling in the 15th and final round of their heavyweight championship bout, and lost to Sharkey by decision. He split with Carnera and McTigue, defeated Jimmy Slattery, Battling Levinsky, Big Boy Peterson, Maxie Rosenbloom twice, Phil Scott, KO Christner, Tuffy Griffiths, Jack Renault, and Chuck Wiggins in two of their three fights with the first ending in a draw. "When a sportswriter once told him he fought a lot of bums, Strib replied, 'Maybe, but I never lost to one.'"[13]

After decisioning the equally assiduous Maxie Rosenbloom in 10 rounds in Houston, Texas, on September 22, 1933, "The King of the Canebrakes" returned to his home in Macon,

2. Early Boxing Days in Europe, 1928–1929

Georgia, to await the birth of his next child. Guerry Boone Stribling was just a week old when his father, riding his motorcycle after a round of golf at the Idle Hour Country Club, was struck by a car. The badly injured fighter was taken to the same hospital in which his son had just been born. He died two days later on October 3. Stribling was just 28 years old and ended his career with an amazing 257–15–15 record.

* * *

On November 6 Young Stribling fought Maurice Griselle in Paris. Stribling took a 12-round points decision, but the outcome was never in doubt as the Georgian floored Griselle three times in the first round. Immediately, Pa Stribling began looking for another European opponent with drawing power. He contacted Leon See and found a willing opponent in Primo Carnera. In an interesting turn of events, Carnera and Stribling exchanged disqualification wins, with Carnera winning the first in four rounds, and Stribling winning the rematch in seven.

The first fight was held at the Royal Albert Hall in London on November 18, 1929, when a crowd of 10,000 — that included the Prince of Wales — saw what appeared to be a fairly evenly matched battle. Interest in the bout was high as fans were anxious to see if Stribling's vast experience could match "Carnera's colossal bulk and merciless uppercuts." Sportswriter Robert Edgren, writing about Stribling shortly after the bout, stated that Carnera was a dangerous fighter "who had demonstrated that he could punch, even if he didn't know much about boxing."[14]

The Associated Press reported, "Stribling gave the Italian giant a terrific body beating in the first two rounds."[15] "For two and a half rounds, Stribling looked like Jack the Giant Killer. He danced rings around Carnera, jabbing repeatedly with lefts and rights and making the big Italian look like a novice."[16] Primo, wary of his opponent's skills and vast experience, kept his distance from Stribling. But perhaps too much so as his repeated left jabs fell short by as much as a foot. Stribling took advantage of Primo's lapses to land shots of his own. He repeatedly hammered Carnera with shots to the head and digs to the body.

Stribling set an even more furious pace in the second round. He used his superior speed and powerful right hand to keep Carnera on the defensive.

Both fighters went to the mat in a thrilling third round. The Macon heavyweight dropped Primo with a heavy right to the jaw. Primo fell flat on his back with a thunderous crash. The punch came as the fighters were backing away from a clinch and Primo was not fully defending himself. Enraged, Carnera climbed to his knees, not waiting for the referee's count to reach eight or nine. He hopped to his feet and charged his opponent, shooting a powerful right to the cheekbone and then a left to Stribling's jaw that sent the American down for a count of nine. The *New York Times* described it this way: "Up he (Carnera) jumped at the count of four, glowered down at Stribling and rushed him like an infuriated bull. He packed such a punch into his huge right arm that Stribling did not have a chance to defend himself, then he crossed his left to the chin and Stribling went down for the count of nine, and the crowd went into a frenzy of cheering."[17] Stribling staggered back to his feet and simply lasted to the end of the round.

As the fourth round began, Stribling, thinking that he had better end this thing quickly, rushed Carnera. He determined to work on Primo's midsection, but things suddenly went wrong for the Georgian. "The fourth round had barely started when Stribling sent home a left and a right low on Carnera's body. The Italian went down, writhing, and Stribling was disqualified."[18] The referee stopped the fight, awarding Primo a disqualification victory. The crowd booed both Stribling and the stoppage, lustily.

Regardless of the reason for the win, newspapers reported that Carnera enthusiasts in his native district of Friuli in Italy and his adopted home of Paris gathered outside of newspaper offices and cheered the victory.

Defeating Stribling by way of disqualification did not prove Carnera a good boxer. The faster and much more experienced Stribling had outfought Primo most of the way, but Carnera's punches proved deadly when they landed. In the third round, Primo had gotten really angry and had shown the sheer power that he possessed. See had to be wondering how he could bottle that fury for future fights, and especially for their upcoming tour of the United States.

After the fight, His Royal Highness Edward, the Prince of Wales, attended a gathering of fans to honor Carnera. The prince, a passionate boxing fan, sat in his front row seat during the bout, and urged Primo on. He was a confirmed fan of the Italian Man Mountain and during the post-fight gathering, he sat at Primo's right hand. Later Primo commented that he felt ashamed because he was dressed in an ordinary lounge suit and his eye was a bit swollen and black and blue. Primo was quoted as saying, "The Prince did not talk much about the fight, but about my father, mother, and brothers. He said I was lucky being so young and with a chance of winning the championship."[19]

Following the fight, rumors circulated about a Carnera–Schmeling contest in Atlantic City, New Jersey, on February 22. This was high praise for Carnera's drawing power and possibly his improving talent, but Primo's managers knew that he still needed work before meeting a fighter of Schmeling's quality.

* * *

In the return bout, held at the Velodrome D'Hiver in Paris on December 7, the two fighters were anxious to climb back into the ring and finish what they started three weeks earlier. After Bob Carvill knocked out Joe Thomas in the second round of a scheduled 10 in the preliminary, Carnera and Stribling headed from their dressing rooms and out into the smoke-filled arena.

This much-anticipated rematch also ended early and on a sour note, as it was Carnera who this time was disqualified after he struck Stribling from behind after the bell ending the seventh round.

"Stribling easily out boxed his giant opponent in the first two rounds, but his blows did not seem to worry Carnera."[20] In the third, Primo rushed Stribling, firing a barrage of punches, but the quicker American was able to avoid most of them. He countered with hard blows to Primo's head and stomach that Primo felt, but refused to acknowledge. Primo used his bulk to continually work his way to the inside where he could land short shots and wear his opponent down. He landed a terrific wallop against the side of Stribling's head just as the round was about to end.

The fourth round was fairly even, but Stribling landed one powerful blow that sent Carnera into the ropes. The fifth was also close, with each fighter landing numerous shots to his opponent's head and body. In one exchange, Stribling cracked a straight left to Carnera's jaw, but a clearly agitated Primo countered with a series of rapid, hammer-like punches that had the American backing up into the ropes and searching for cover.

Overall, Stribling appeared to be winning a close fight. While Primo was acquitting himself well throughout, he simply was not as quick or skilled as the smoother and well-experienced Stribling.

With Carnera frequently leaving himself open to Stribling's left, the Georgian launched a missile that caught Primo in the pit of his stomach in the sixth. Primo fell to his knees, but very characteristically was back on his feet in an instant. The rest of the round was again fairly even, but with Stribling beginning to show some fatigue.

Throughout the fight, Primo's size helped to wear Stribling out, as the American frequently clinched to avoid Primo's powerful punches. Primo battered Stribling's arms and Stribling would attach himself to Carnera's waist, frustrating the Italian.

Stribling continued tiring in the seventh and appeared to be reserving his strength in order to muster enough for a knockout punch. At mid-round he caught Primo with a painful body blow, and again late in the round as the bell was sounding Stribling connected with a hard combination to Primo's mid-section. A frustrated, and uncharacteristically angry Primo, lost control and rushed Stribling, striking him in the head and dropping him to the canvas well after the bell had sounded ending the round. The crowd booed lustily and the referee immediately disqualified Carnera, awarding the fight to Stribling.

Primo claimed that he didn't hear the bell ending the round. Reports, however, state, "Even after officials and seconds swarmed into the ring together with the Stribling family troupers, the giant Italian continued to try to get at his opponent."[21] The news reports commented that Primo lacked aggressiveness until he was aroused. A study of Carnera's career shows that he often got sloppy and frustrated when his opponents controlled the fight, and by all reports, Stribling was controlling this fight. Additionally, while not a typically dirty fighter, Stribling, like many fighters, was known to skirt the edges of the rules when it was to his advantage. Sportswriter Robert Edgren, writing shortly after the second bout, stated, "It may be said that with his boxing style Stribling could easily lose on a foul in England, where all the rules of boxing are enforced."[22] A logical conclusion is that Carnera simply got frustrated at Stribling's control of the fight, and after receiving a final hard body blow at the bell, an agitated Carnera snapped at the end of the seventh. "It was a disappointing ending to a fight in which Stribling found the big carpenter no set-up to be brushed aside when he pleased. Carnera went down for a short count in the sixth round, but otherwise just about held his own with his American rival," reported the Associated Press.[23]

These two fights were among those rumored to be fixed, by See in his grousing book, *Le Mystere Carnera*. Again, the question, why fix two fights — one registering a win for your fighter and one a loss, when your goal is to pad his record. Neither a .500 record nor a low-blow disqualification victory does much to build the image of a fighter as an up-and-comer. Victories from getting hit in the groin don't make you a championship contender.

The back-to-back disqualifications were disappointing to all concerned and they were certainly not good for the fight game. When Phil Scott defeated Otto Van Porat at Madison Square Garden on December 9, in a fight that also ended in a second round disqualification, R.E. Middleton, chairman of the British Boxing Control Board, expressed his concern over the frequency with which disqualifications were occurring: "Fouling apparently is increasing in the present time. If it isn't checked great harm will come to boxing. The public cannot be expected to go on paying for boxing contests which end so wretchedly. Drastic measures must be taken quickly."[24]

For all of the hoopla made of the low blow, the late punches, nothing came of it. Most people simply forgot about it and while it was disappointing, it was simply part of the fight game. Willie Ratner, writing in the *Newark Evening News*, noted that much was being made of a problem that really did not exist. He stated, "As one reads the reports of the final scene, as penned by the experts of the daily papers, one would imagine that no boxer of any note had ever struck another after the bell."[25]

* * *

During his time in London, Primo spent a great deal of time at his favorite restaurant in the city: Molinari's in Soho. Molinari's was located between Leicester Square and Soho Square in the Hotel d'Italie on the corner of Old Compton and Frith streets.[26] It is hard to say whether Primo loved Molinari's Italian food or their young Italian waitress more. During his frequent visits there, Primo had become smitten with the restaurant's vivacious brunette waitress Emilia Tersini.

The British-born daughter of Italian immigrants, Emilia was a petite 19-year-old who was equally taken by the enormous boxer with the indefatigable appetite. Emilia's parents had met and approved of Primo, and See and Dickson chose not to interfere in the relationship. In the years to come, both men would regret their decision.

* * *

Before the year was out, Carnera had some unfinished business with Franz Diener to address. On December 17, Primo sought to avenge his bogus disqualification loss to Diener from the previous April. After Maurice Griselle TKO'ed Bob Carvill in the third round of the preliminary, the 8,000 assembled patrons cheered wildly as Primo entered the ring at the Royal Albert Hall in London, a man on a mission. The steely-faced Primo stared down Diener as the two met in the middle of the ring. During the fight, the German was clearly outboxed. Primo started early and used his left with quickness and precision. He sent Diener to the canvas in the first minute of the second round with a deadly, piston-like, straight left. Soon after Diener got to his feet, Primo struck again with the same punch. Diener was rocked to his core, but managed to keep on his feet.

Throughout the bout Diener's attempts to land shots to Carnera's body had all of the effect of rubber balls being thrown at a tank. Over and over, the German would throw a shot to the body and Primo would counter with a piercing blow to Diener's head.

By the third round, Diener was obviously tiring, staying up only through his rugged determination. In the fifth round Primo began landing punches at will and he fully sensed the end was near. During that round Carnera landed three straight lefts and a wicked right hook that dazed the German.

By the sixth round Diener could barely see, and Primo, big-hearted and lacking the killer instinct, began to look at the referee to call it off. Primo continued to toy with his badly beaten opponent until the arbiter had finally seen enough. Over the course of six rounds, a determined Primo dropped his opponent 10 times and clearly outboxed Diener who, without the benefit of his friendly hometown arbiter, was unable to finagle a decision. The German was ruled unable to defend himself by the referee and the fight was stopped. That satisfying victory was Primo's last bout before he headed to America to expand his fistic horizons. Later that month, sporting a 16–2–0 record, Carnera and his entourage sailed for New York.

This was also the final fight of Diener's professional career. After back-to-back TKO losses to Pierre Charles and Carnera, as well as losses in four of his last six fights, Diener finally determined that it was time to hang up his gloves. The former German amateur heavyweight champion left the ring with a decent, if not fabulous record of 20–9–3, but impressive showings in most of his fights. He was the victim of only one true knockout

2. Early Boxing Days in Europe, 1928–1929

and that came early in his career in the tenth round, at the hands of Larry Gains in Frankfurt in 1924.

Diener returned to Berlin and happily ran his butcher shop for many years, until the Second World War and the later Soviet occupation put a crimp in his freedoms. *Time* magazine resurrected Diener's memory in a short paragraph in May 1954 that read as follows:

Primo reading the headlines. (Chicago History Museum)

> In West Germany, onetime (1930–32) World Heavyweight Boxing Champion Max Schmeling heard that Franz Diener, the man he beat for the German boxing crown in 1928, had landed in a Soviet-zone jail. Diener's crime: while chief butcher in an East German sausage factory, he got caught passing out state-owned Bratwurst to hungry friends. Schmeling wrote to East Germany's Puppet President Wilhelm Pieck and got Diener pardoned by the Russians. Last week, after refusing a job as East Germany's commissar of boxing, Franz Diener fled to West Berlin and gratefully awaited a reunion with Old Opponent Schmeling.[27]

After returning to Charlottenburg in West Berlin, Diener opened a pub and restaurant that still remains open, nearly 40 years after his death. While few patrons remember Franz Diener the boxer, his authentically old-style Berlin pub near Savignyplatz is still extremely popular.

That evening, after his victory over Diener, Carnera and See were invited to dine with the Prince of Wales and his party at the home of one of the Prince's friends, Lord Birkenhead. The future King Edward, an avid boxing fan, had long admired Carnera. Primo joked to the court dignitary who delivered the invitation to the fighter in his dressing room, "Tell the Prince that I did not eat much for lunch and therefore I will be very hungry!"[28]

Those guests who expected to meet an illiterate and socially inept pug and his cigar-chomping manager that night were in for a pleasant surprise. Primo, neatly groomed and suitably outfitted in his Savile Row dinner jacket, was by all accounts charming. See had tutored Primo in manners and carriage, and Primo pulled the evening off beautifully. Seated next to the prince and displaying impeccable manners, he was every bit the refined gentleman. "When it became clear that the boxer was more fluent in French than in English, the entire company immediately switched to French."[29] By all accounts it was a marvelous evening for everyone present. After the meal, the prince had Carnera and See delivered back to their hotel in his chauffer-driven Rolls-Royce.

Soon after the Diener fight and his elegant dinner with the Prince of Wales, Primo traveled back to Sequals for Christmas. He would return to Italy, visit with family and friends for a week, and then meet up with See, Eudeline, and several others in Cherbourg, France, to board the Cunard liner *Berengaria* bound for New York. The lure of fame and fortune in America was calling.

3

To the United States, 1930

On December 24, 1929, Primo sailed for the United States, where plans were made for him to tour and box extensively throughout the country to make a name for himself and to hone his skills against a spate of relatively easy rivals. With less than a year and a half of boxing under his belt, Primo was still a novice and needed time to learn the skills of a seasoned fighter.

The crossing was well covered by the press. The Man Mountain was a great curiosity and everything was of interest, from the great quantities of food laid in for his Christmas dinner to the eight-foot berth built especially for his mammoth frame.[1]

Traveling with Primo on the voyage aboard the *Berengaria* were former and future South African Prime Minister Jan Christian Smuts, writer Hugh Walpole, and world-renowned pianist Sergei Rachmaninoff.

There was much excitement and press coverage surrounding Primo's stateside arrival. While he was green, he showed the toughness and underlying signs of a good boxer. The *New York Times* reported that "despite his short career, Carnera has turned in several performances that cause boxing followers in this country to consider him a serious threat for the heavyweight honors ... the fact that he has coped with [Young] Stribling on such even terms has made boxing experts revise their early opinions that the newcomer was merely a freak."[2] The *Times* also pointed out that Primo had the recent knockout victory over Franz Diener to his credit.

Primo's size was still the subject of much discussion by journalists and the fight crowd. Legendary New York sportswriter John Kieran, on the eve of Carnera's first U.S. fight, wrote a rather nonsensical piece about Primo's great size and a history of medical science involving giants, acromegaly[3], and pugilism.[4] Kieran implies that Primo suffered from acromegaly, which he most probably did not, but amazement at the sheer size, mass, and strength of Carnera captivated many sportswriters and legions of fans.

The traveling Carnera entourage included Leon See; Walter Friedman, who would with Billy Duffy help manage — or mismanage — Primo in the United States; two French fighters — featherweight Jean Boireau and welterweight Yvan Laffineur — Primo's trainer Maurice Eudeline, and cartoonist Louis Berings. See knew that he would need an in to the American boxing scene and Friedman was it. Shortly after their New York arrival, Friedman would introduce See to a number of his associates, who would buy See out but ultimately muscle the Frenchman out of his share of Carnera's future earnings.

Arriving at New York's West 14th Street pier onboard the *Berengaria* on December 31, Primo made an immediate impression on those present. As the well-dressed giant disembarked the liner, he cut quite an image. Press reports said, "A greyhound, named Primo II, was another member of the party, and in addition to a collection of trunks and bags Carnera sported a walking stick weighing 32-pounds, with a handle measuring 15½ inches, and with the appearance of a sapling."[5] In attendance at his arrival was former heavyweight champion Gene Tunney, who was at the pier to meet British novelist Hugh Walpole, but he made time to greet the massive Italian.

The *New York Times* reported that Carnera "made the ocean voyage on the A deck equipped with an especially constructed bed and will have an especially constructed bed to accommodate his huge frame in his suite at the Piccadilly Hotel where he is to make his headquarters."[6]

The United Press ran this January 1930 headline: "Giant Italian to Tour Country and Take Things Easy for About Six Months."[7] For the most part he did, easily winning his first 17 bouts in the U.S. by knockout.

* * *

Soon after their arrival in New York, See met Friedman's associates at Bill Duffy's restaurant at 158 48th Street, between Broadway and 6th Avenue. The restaurant was in actuality a speakeasy, one of several owned and operated by Duffy and his old friend and partner Owney Madden. Friedman's associates included Madden, Duffy, George "Big Frenchy" de Mange, and Frank Churchill, each of whom had strong underworld ties.

See "had experiences with American ring finances when he was piloting Gorgeous Georges Carpentier during the Dempsey epidemic, so when M. See got hold of Carnera, he knew enough to cable Duffy."[8]

Duffy and Madden were, respectively, products of Brooklyn's Gowanus section and the Hell's Kitchen section of Manhattan in the days before organized crime Dons "civilized" criminal activity in the city.

Madden was born in England in 1891 and arrived in New York with his father when he was 11 years old. Soon thereafter Madden joined the Gophers, a local gang, and before he was 20 he controlled the gang. He proved his loyalty, tenacity, and toughness repeatedly, and along the way he earned the nickname "Clay Pigeon of the Underworld," a title he received when he took a dozen bullets in a dance hall one night and survived.

By the age of 23 he was directly responsible for the death of at least five men, thus earning the nickname "Owney the Killer." Madden's ability to avoid charges for his actions failed in 1915 when he was convicted of manslaughter for the death of a fellow gangster, "Little" Patsy Smith, the year before. While in prison, Madden had acquired the well-known nightspot the Cotton Club. After serving eight years of a 10–20-year sentence, he was paroled, but during his time in the lockup, the rules had changed. Madden found himself entering a new world of organized crime and Prohibition. He began to re-establish himself starting as a hit man and enforcer for Dutch Schultz and Jack "Legs" Diamond, but he quickly rose in the syndicate and became a full partner in their breweries and speakeasies scattered around the New York area. Over the next 10 years the smallish and dapper Madden would increase his holdings to include nightclubs, hotels, and prizefighters.

William Duffy was a restaurant and nightclub owner, and a fight manager, but most of all he was a hoodlum. Like Madden, Duffy had a long history of run-ins with the law. He was first arrested in 1901 for burglary at the age of 17. Duffy was later sentenced to Sing Sing for 10 years after being convicted for armed robbery. It was during his time in prison that he first met Madden. While in Sing Sing, Duffy impressed the warden with his tenacity and organizational skills. The warden arranged for "Big Bill" to be released from prison to join the U.S. Navy, from which he was honorably discharged as a Chief Petty Officer. Once out of the Navy, Duffy fell back in with Madden and Schultz by opening a series of speakeasies named Club de la Vie, The Silver Slipper Cabaret, and the Rendezvous. The clubs were outlets for Madden's and Schultz's bootleg beer and liquor.

Duffy also managed a number of restaurants—most notably Keen's Chop House at 107 West 44th Street. A favorable review of the place was included in Rian James' *Dining in New York* in 1930. Keen's was described as "satisfying in both quality and quantity" and a hangout for celebrities. "Around and about you, you'll find artists, actors, and plain ordinary epicures—sportsmen of this day and of a day that is gone; prizefighters building up energy with the good food, and their hangers-on, watching them with awe and admiration."[9] Characteristically, Duffy also had several brushes with the law during this period. Most notably he was picked up on suspicion of murdering a Brooklyn nightclub singer—when he was picked up, he had a bullet wound in his shoulder—and also on suspicion of involvement in a jewelry store robbery.

Duffy was, however, more than just a body that Madden put in place to watch over Carnera; he knew boxing and Primo was only one of several fighters that Duffy managed. In addition to Primo he handled former Golden Gloves heavyweight champion Otis Thomas, long-time middleweight Phil "KO" Kaplan, and welterweight and middleweight champion "Irish" Mickey Walker in 1934–35. Duffy was also reportedly a good friend of heavyweight champion Jack Dempsey.

George "Big Frenchy" De Mange was a hoodlum and bootlegger and later a millionaire Broadway restaurateur running such venues as The Club Argonaut, Park Avenue, and The Silver Slipper. In 1931 Madden paid $35,000 to ransom Big Frenchy when itchy-fingered Vincent "Mad Dog" Coll kidnapped him and threatened his life.[10] "Mad Dog" Coll combined a lethal mix of violence and ineptitude. He received his moniker from New York Mayor Jimmy Walker after he mistakenly killed a 5-year-old boy and injured several other children in a botched 1931 gangland hit. He also went on a wave of additional kidnappings including that of Billy Warren, a banker to organized crime figures in New York, for whom he received over $80,000 in ransom. Tired of Coll's carelessness and eager to get even for the De Mange kidnapping, Madden paid $50,000 to hire freelance hitmen Leonard Scarnici and Anthony Fabrizzo to murder Coll in 1932. After one unsuccessful attempt, the gunmen found Coll making a call in a Manhattan drug store where they pumped at least 15 rounds into the Mad Dog. No one was sorry that Coll was gone, but the New York police determined to rid themselves of Madden as well. They hounded Madden for the next three years, first picking him up for a parole violation and then pestering him repeatedly until he eventually had had enough. Madden packed up and moved to Hot Springs, Arkansas, where he married and ran a hotel and casino for the next 30 years.

Walter "Good Time Charlie" Friedman was a longtime associate of gambling kingpin Arnold Rothstein. Friedman had his hands in a number of legitimate and illegitimate business ventures and also fronted as a talent scout and promoter. He would help schedule and promote Carnera's fights in America.

Frank Churchill was a longtime trainer and promoter. He did much to promote prizefighting in the Philippines, bringing along numerous fighters including flyweight champion Pancho Villa. Churchill also managed numerous other fighters including former junior lightweight champions Mike Ballerino and Tod Morgan. He died at his ranch in La Habra, California, on March 30, 1933, at the age of 59 after suffering from a weakening heart for several years.

At the meeting See was offered a buyout of his interest in Carnera. It was agreed, perhaps with a good bit of push from Friedman and his friends, that See would sell his interest in Carnera's U.S. fights to the syndicate headed by Friedman and retain rights along with Journee and Jeff Dickson to Primo's fights in Europe. See would stay on in America and help continue to train and tutor his pupil. Rumor had it that the "push" was insurance against accidents detrimental to his health.

Ultimately the syndicate would also include Luigi Soresi. Soresi was an Italian national with New York banking connections who would look out for the syndicate's financial affairs.

* * *

"Primo Carnera will be built up into the biggest fistic attraction since Jack Dempsey's hay-day by touring the country and fighting more or less easy opponents, the United Press learned from the giant Italian's crafty board of managers." The news agency went on to report, "Under no circumstances will Carnera be allowed in the ring with ... any formidable heavyweight until he gains experience and is taught to box by Abe Attell, former featherweight champion."[11]

The association with Attell is another point to which the "fixed fight" crowd looks to back their claims. "The Little Champ" was a known gambler with strong underworld ties. Boxing historian Bert Sugar stated, "As slick in the ring as the brilliantine which coated his hair, Attell was equally slick outside where he continually waited for a scam like an old taxicab waiting in line for whatever designation came along. Attell was fond of cards, horses, fights, whatever, and they were reciprocally affectionate."[12] He was known to bet with regularity on himself in his own fights. While this was not a particularly uncommon practice at the time, his gambling was to adversely affect his boxing reputation and tarnish his memory.

Attell, a known associate of Rothstein, was named by several Chicago White Sox baseball players as a conspirator in the 1919 World Series fix. The allegations resulted in an indictment by an Illinois grand jury. Ultimately, the charges were dropped when the prosecution was unable to produce enough evidence to maintain the charges. Attell always maintained his innocence, but the stain remained on his already blemished reputation.

Attell was also rumored to be involved in numerous other illegal actions, including the attempted arson of his nearly bankrupt women's shoe store "The Ming Toy Bootery" in 1922; operating "The Peacock Club," a Manhattan speakeasy on West 48th Street during prohibition; and several fight fixes, including rumors about the first Jack Dempsey–Gene Tunney fight in 1926.

Attell fought his first professional bout in his hometown of San Francisco on August 19, 1900, at the age of 16, knocking out Kid Lennett in the second round. The 5'4", 122-pound Attell was a terrific fighter with excellent defensive skills. A talented, sinuous boxer with a hard punch, Attell knocked out 22 of his first 29 opponents. Abe was the Featherweight Champion in 1903, 1904 and again from 1906 to 1912, defending his crown successfully a record 21 times before losing it to Johnny Kilbane on February 22, 1912. Attell's brother Monte won the bantamweight title in 1909, marking the first time brothers held world titles simultaneously. Abe retired from the ring for good in 1917. He finished his professional career with a record of 125 (51 by KO), 17 (5 by KO) and 21, with 7 no-contests, in 170 bouts. Despite his shady reputation, Attell was elected as a member of the Boxing Hall of Fame in 1955 and to the International Boxing Hall of Fame in 1990.

How much time Attell actually spent tutoring Carnera is not well chronicled, but the mere mention of an association was enough to keep pundits guessing on the legitimacy of the big man's record.

3. To the United States, 1930

Primo being tutored by former featherweight champion Abe Attell. Attell was a legendary fighter, but he tainted himself with the stain of scandal through his actions and association with several well-known gamblers and mobsters. (Chicago History Museum)

* * *

The America in which Primo landed on December 31, 1929, was a far cry from the one he would have found just a few months earlier. The boom of the 1920s had come to a screeching halt. Beginning with Wall Street's collapse, the book had closed on the decade of optimism. For many, the 1920s had been a time of excess. Automobiles and radios became necessities. The stock market became a playground for the masses. "Athletes became idols. Booming business became the national religion and buying on credit the universal pastime."[13] The Dow Jones Industrial Average rose from 88 in 1924 to a high of 381.17 on September 3, 1929. But it ended with a crash.

On October 23 and 24, a huge market sell-off began a slide that would end with calamitous results. Stock prices fell sharply on a record volume of 13 million shares. Major stocks began plummeting in value. Leading the way were such corporate luminaries as RCA, Woolworth, and Montgomery Ward, each posting losses between 30 percent and 50 percent. On October 24, "Richard Whitney, vice president of the New York Stock Exchange, armed with $240 million from a banking pool, marched across the panicky exchange floor buying big blocks to restore a measure of confidence."[14] The Hoover administration tried to calm fears by calling the crash nothing more than a needed adjustment.

The temporary respite ended in a train wreck on "Black Tuesday," October 29, when the market crashed. A record 16.4 million shares were traded, but mostly at a loss. That day, the Dow Jones Industrial Average fell more than 11 percent. "By November, everyone knew the worst. American Can, 181 in September, stood at 86; General Motors had dropped from 72 to 36; Union Carbide from 137 to 59; Electric Bond & Share from 186 to 50. The boom was dead, buried in paper capital and unfounded credit."[15]

There were warning signs of the impending downfall, but few paid much attention. Just a week before the collapse in October, noted economist Irving Fisher of Yale was assuring his audiences that the stock market gains appeared real and permanent.

"Super-speculator Joseph P. Kennedy, founding father of the clan, took his money and ran when he heard his bootblack passing out stock tips. Bernard Baruch obeyed his instincts and cashed in. Charles Merrill of Merrill Lynch had warned off his customers a year before."[16] But for most Americans the crash marked the beginning of a downward spiral into personal financial uncertainty. The Hoover administration continued to claim that the economy was fundamentally sound and "Recovery would be natural and would come soon. Meanwhile, no federal action of any kind was needed. Surprisingly, most Democrats agreed. In the congressional elections of 1930, the Democrats made prohibition as big an issue as the depression."[17]

In time, however, the cautious optimism waned. The stock market continued its slide, with the Dow finally hitting bottom in July 1932 falling 89 percent below its 1929 peak. A flood of bank failures and bankruptcies helped cause the nation's money supply to drop 27 percent from 1929 to 1933. Living standards dropped for most Americans and unemployment rose from 1.5 million in 1929 to over 12 million — 25 percent of the workforce — by 1932. Cardboard and tin shantytowns housing the unemployed and homeless sprang up in cities across the land. They would be named "Hoovervilles" after the man that many blamed for ignoring their plight. "Wall Street and President Hoover would be targeted as the culprits in the huge depression that followed. The aftershocks of October 1929 would put Franklin Roosevelt in the White House and federal watchdogs permanently on Wall Street."[18]

Against the backdrop of the deepening Great Depression, the public needed diversions and entertainment provided that. The burgeoning motion picture industry, popular music, radio, and sports were ready-made outlets for such departure from their personal anxieties.

* * *

Primo was big news as he prepared for his first American fight. Both the press and the public continued their fascination with the Italian colossus. Although his fights with Stribling both ended in disqualifications, the fact that Carnera had held his own against the Georgian and then dispatched Diener so handily had caused many in the fight business to revisit their earlier prognostications that Primo was nothing more than a flash in the pan, a curiosity, and a sideshow freak. Interest in the big Italian was running at a fever pitch. Legendary trainer Angelo Dundee tells the story of the crowds that gathered at Stillman's Gym when De Preem worked out there in 1930.

Located at 919 Eighth Avenue in Manhattan, Stillman's was, along with Madison Square Garden, the focal point of boxing in New York City. The gym was run by the cantankerous Lou Stillman. Stillman, who was born Lou Ingber, was hired by the founders of the original Marshall Stillman Athletic Club to oversee the facility when it was located in Harlem. When the founders got out of the business in the late 1920s, a new facility was identified near the old Madison Garden. The two-ring gym became the training home of boxing celebrities and unknowns alike and its stale air and grimy windows and walls only made it more loveable to its patrons. Stillman's has been known by many nicknames; perhaps none, however, is so apt as "the University of Eighth Avenue."

Stillman's was accessible to the general public for a small entrance fee that was advertised on a simple sign above the non-descript doorway. The sign read, "Stillman's Gym: World's Leading Boxers Train Here Daily." The crowds ebbed and flowed depending on which fighters were training that day. According to Dundee, "Perhaps the biggest day in the history of Stillman's came with the first New York appearance of the most ballyhooed fighter in the history of boxing ballyhoo: Primo Carnera. According to Stillman, more than 2,000 of Carnera's Italian fans and fellow countrymen, along with the usual curiosity seekers, crowded Eighth Avenue, all the better to witness the man billed as "the Ambling Alp," and forcing the cops to come and clear the area."[19]

Crusty old Lou Stillman once said, "When Carpentier was in training, the place was always crowded with Broadway chorus girls, while when Carnera trained, the gallery was packed with Italian women carrying their babies. I liked them better than the chorus girls, so I always let the babies in for free."[20]

* * *

On January 7 the New York State Athletic Commission voted not to permit Primo to meet local heavyweight Carl Carter. The fight was proposed by promoter Jess McMahon and was to be held at the Coliseum on January 15, but the commissioners determined that it would be an uneven contest. Carter was coming to the end of a career that had started in 1924 and at the dawn of 1930, he owned a professional record of 14–16–2. He would fight four more times, losing the first two, but ending his career on a positive note with a first-round knockout over Jack Taylor in 1931 and a six-round decision over Chester Matan in 1932 to end his career at 16–18–2.

Primo visited the Commission during the meeting and the sheer size of the Italian heavyweight caused a stir. Accompanied by Leon See, Bill Duffy, and Walter Friedman, Carnera met with commissioners James A. Farley and William Muldoon, while See filed a contract with the commission as Carnera's manager of record.

* * *

On January 25, 1930, Primo fought his first contest on American soil. He would square off against Clayton "Big Boy" Peterson in a packed Madison Square Garden.

Manhattan's Madison Square Garden has long been a Mecca for sports fans and especially for the fight crowd. The first and second Gardens were located on Fifth and Madison Avenues between 26th and 27th Streets. They were built in 1874 and 1890, respectively. This third incarnation of the Garden was built in 1925. The original Garden site was sold to developers and the new site selected for the third Garden was Eighth Avenue between 49th and 50th Streets. The new structure was palatial and had three tiers of seats that could hold as many as 18,500 fans for boxing events. Upon hearing that a new Garden would be built, legendary boxing promoter Tex Rickard, knowing the value that a large, state-of-the-art facility would provide to boxing and other events, helped raise money for the project.

A raucous, curious, and near-capacity crowd filed into the Garden on that cold midwinter Friday night, paying either $1.05 for general admission or $2.10, $3.15, $4.60, or $5.74 for a reserved seat. The four-fight preliminaries included a seventh-round knockout of Fred Lenhart by Chicago's hard-hitting heavyweight Larry Johnson. By the end of the fourth fight, the crowd was ready to see the Man Mountain from Italy in action. "Despite the fact that Primo hasn't completed an elementary course in boxing, he is regarded as a sure winner tonight by those who have seen him in his daily stunts at Stillman's, where he has been for two weeks. There he has been schooled by Prof. Abe Attell, and the aptitude of the foreigner is shown in his improved boxing form. Primo takes to things he wants to learn very quickly."[21]

As the fighters for the main event entered the ring, they towered over their corner men. While Peterson stood 6'5", the Minnesotan tipped the scales at just 205 and was therefore relatively thin in build. Primo, standing two inches taller and weighing 65 pounds of solid muscle more than Peterson, made short work of his opponent — just one minute and 10 seconds into the first round. United News Service Sports Editor Davis J. Walsh reported that Primo "proved to be remarkably fast on his feet."[22]

The bout began with the two fighters rushing towards each other ready for action. After Peterson landed an early left jab to Primo's face, it was all Carnera. "Pirouetting as lightly as a ballet dancer, Carnera opened up a rain of blows which fell upon 'Big Boy' like driven snow from Primo's native Alps."[23] Primo put Peterson on the canvas four times during the 70 seconds of action. The first was the result of a sweeping hook from the Venetian's strong left arm. Peterson rose quickly as Referee Arthur Donovan tolled off "three." The United Press described the punch that floored Peterson as one "which would have shaken the Statue of Liberty." The second knockdown came from a strong right uppercut that caught Big Boy on the chin. The United Press described this shot as one "which would have tunneled the Eighth Avenue subway."[24] Still trying to shake off the cobwebs, Peterson was wobbly, but on his feet at eight. Another thundering left caught the Minnesotan square in the face and dropped Big Boy for the third knockdown. Peterson squatted for four seconds before rising once more. The fourth and final knockdown came when Carnera caught Peterson with a prodigious overhand right to the side of his head. "His last punch was the only really hard blow he landed."[25] Big Boy dropped to his hands and knees and hit himself in the head several times apparently in an attempt to rally himself. Peterson tried to get up at the count of nine, but was too late as Donovan tolled off the fateful "ten" that ended the one-sided affair. The Garden crowd went wild. "The action and the finish provoked delirium among Carnera's enthusiastic admirers in the gallery and the mezzanine."[26] Those closer in also delighted in seeing the colossal Italian carry himself "so lightly about the ring, charging joyously and nimbly and bludgeoning his blows rapidly."[27]

While Peterson sat on a stool in his corner partaking of a liberal dose of smelling salts, the capacity crowd milled about the arena not particularly anxious to leave. Fire Department officials ordered the fighters to remain in the ring while the crowd dispersed and the aisles were cleared. The press noted, "Primo obliged with a little grand opera over the radio during the interval." Eventually, the crowd of 18,000 reportedly left the Garden pleased and "gibbering out into the night."[28]

Of Primo's performance, it was said, "It can not be denied Carnera has some promise as a fighter. Not alone does his tremendous size recommend him, but he was remarkably fast last night and fought with a reckless abandon which foreshadows an advance beyond the average when and if Carnera gets some more schooling. This he needs of course. Until the Venetian shows against a more formidable foe, however, it is wise to withhold judgment."[29]

Legendary fight managers Leo P. Flynn and "Dumb" Dan Morgan attended the fight and were impressed with the young, raw fighter. After the fight, Morgan stated of Primo, "He's your next million dollar gate." Flynn, who had trained Jack Dempsey and would die of pneumonia just four months later, went a step further, claiming, "He's the next world champion."[30]

Primo's dressing room was a who's who of celebrities after the fight: "There you found William Bolitho, the literary gentleman who writes on profound topics for the *New York World*; Maurice Chevalier, French movie idol; Jack Johnson, Johnny Dundee, Matchmaker Tom McArdle, Assistant District Attorney Gene Finnegan and a host of others. It was the kind of dressing room gathering reserved for a Dempsey."[31]

Primo celebrated his first U.S. victory by spending the rest of the evening at Duffy's Silver Slipper Cabaret. He consumed a large meal, three glasses of champagne, and a bottle of ale. He didn't turn in until almost dawn.

* * *

Moving on to Chicago, Primo was scheduled to meet French Canadian lumberjack Elzear Rioux in Chicago Stadium on January 31. The 210-pound Rioux had a 29–14–4 record, but had dropped four of his last six bouts. He would retire with an overall record of 41–18–4, but other than Primo, Jim Maloney (with whom he earned a draw), and maybe Joe Monte (to whom he lost by TKO in the fifth round of a scheduled 12), he never really fought anyone of note. On July 18, 1922, Rioux had faced Jack Dempsey in Montreal in a one-round exhibition match.

The International News Service reported, "Carpenters went to work Friday strengthening the Chicago Stadium ring to make sure the boards will support the two behemoths whose combined weight is nearly a quarter of a ton."[32] The ring stood up during the fight much better than Rioux.

A strong undercard included a heavyweight battle in which King Levinsky defeated Jack Barry and bantamweight Ray McIntyre outpointed Irish Mickey Gill. "In the semi-final, King Tut, Minneapolis lightweight, defeated Bruce Flowers, New Rochelle, NY, in ten rounds, flooring him twice for counts of nine in the seventh."[33]

The 17,500 fans who paid a collective $59,625.28 to watch the fights had seen three very good contests leading up to the main event. They might as well have left after the third bout, for in the final battle they were treated to the ridiculous spectacle of Rioux diving to the canvas and rolling to avoid Carnera's swings. Once, when Primo launched a ponderous right, Rioux ducked and landed on the canvas, rolling back up to his feet at the count of one. He repeated this "defensive" tactic several times. Rioux went down for the final time when Primo caught the lumberjack on the chin with a flailing right. This time Rioux had

Elzear Rioux affixes himself to Primo's waist and hangs on for dear life as Primo begins to dismantle his opponent. Referee Dave Barry looks on. (Chicago History Museum)

had enough and stayed down as referee Dave Barry counted him out at 47 seconds of the first round. The sellout crowd was unamused by Rioux's unique maneuvers, and boos and shouts of "fake" filled the arena.

Commissioner Frederick Gardner of the Illinois State Athletic Commission was in the crowd that night and immediately called for both fighters to be suspended and their purses withheld pending an investigation of the fight. Fellow commissioner George Getz seconded Gardner's call for investigation. The Commission determined to meet the following Tuesday afternoon to consider the affair.

Primo answered the commissioner's questions at a special Saturday hearing since he was scheduled to meet Cowboy Billy Owens in Newark, New Jersey, the following Thursday. He testified that he believed that Rioux was frightened and acting irrationally during their brief encounter.

On Tuesday afternoon Rioux, his representative Charles Turner, his manager Dr. J. P. Gadbois, fight referee Dave Barry, the fight judges W. A. Batty and E. L. Cook, and Walter Friedman, who stayed behind to represent Carnera's team for the hearing, met at the Commission's offices to sort out the details of the spectacle.

Barry testified that he believed the big Canadian was simply the victim of fright due to Carnera's reputation and huge size. He saw nothing that made him suspicious of a fight fix and stated that even before the fight Rioux had acted fearful. "Even before he entered the ring," Barry said, "Rioux appeared rigid with fear and when the bell clanged for the

Rioux sits on the canvas as referee Dave Barry counts him out at the 47-second mark of the first round. (Chicago History Museum)

start of the match, Rioux stood in the center stunned and too frightened to lift his hands for defense."[34]

Cook and Batty agreed with Barry and further pointed out that Rioux fell to the canvas repeatedly "Without being hit hard enough to topple over a bantamweight." The final knockdown they judged as legitimate, but "The punch that sent him to the floor, flat on his face, for the sixth and final count was described by them as well directed, but not hard enough to produce drowsiness."[35]

Warren Brown, sports editor of the *Chicago Herald and Examiner*, also testified to the Commission that "he did not think Rioux was a fit opponent and that the bout shouldn't have been sanctioned or promoted."[36]

During the Commission hearing, Rioux admitted to being "very scared" and claimed that his fear and apprehension over fighting the man mountain had left him disoriented in the ring from before the first bell. While speculation has remained in some circles that Rioux took a dive in this fight, the participants and objective, expert eyewitnesses from the day — the most qualified to judge on the matter — ruled that the fight, while a spectacle, was on the level.

The commissioners ruled that Rioux was indeed the victim of fear and that his actions that night proved him unfit to enter the ring again in Illinois. His state boxing license was immediately and indefinitely revoked and he was fined $1,000. The Commission recommended that other state bodies follow suit, but shortly after the ruling, Rioux headed east and was back in the ring by mid–April for three fights in Massachusetts. He then spent the next year fighting a string of mediocre fighters in Britain before returning to the United States and Canada to finish his pugilistic career with three more fights. After dropping a 6-round decision in Toronto to Buffalo native Joe Doctor,[37] Rioux defeated two ring novices and finally hung up the gloves on his dubious career. In all, Rioux fought professionally another 15 times after the Chicago Stadium fiasco before retiring in 1932.

The Associated Press relayed the Commission's findings under a headline that screamed, "Declare Rioux a Victim of Fright — Referee and Attendant Testify That Canadian Feared 'Big Boogey Man' Carnera."[38] Primo was held blameless and exonerated of all charges. The Commission awarded him his $16,000 share of the gate.

* * *

Getting on with his career, Primo met Cowboy Billy Owens in front of 8,000 fight fans at the 113th Infantry Regiment Armory in Newark, New Jersey, on Thursday February 6. This fight actually made it into the second round, but just barely.

The good-sized crowd predicted by promoter Harry Mendel was treated to three interesting preliminaries in which heavyweight Buck Weaver TKO'ed Jack Shaw in four and Primo's shipmates Jean Boireau and Yvan Laffineur won and lost third- and eighth-round TKOs, respectively. Boireau had little difficulty finishing off local novice Jack Pelecos, but Laffineur's bout was stopped in the eighth by referee Hyman Kugel after a vicious gash was opened over his left eye by New York welterweight Charlie Rosen, who was already ahead on points.

After the preliminaries, Owens and Carnera climbed through the ropes to a thunderous ovation. In the first, Owens caught Carnera with a wild swinging left to the head, to which Primo responded with two straight lefts that must have cleared Owens' sinuses. As a result, Owens spent the rest of the round clinching, ducking, and countering Primo's hefty blows. He was able to land several good shots to Carnera's ribs, but these did little more than rile a sleeping giant.

At the start of the second round, the combatants rushed towards each other from their respective corners. Immediately, Carnera landed several rapid-fire rights to the head and a left uppercut to Owens' jaw that rocked the Oklahoman to his feet. Primo, sensing victory, landed two more quick and powerful blows — one a stinging right cross, the other a straight, ponderous right to Cowboy Billy's chin that dropped the 220-pound Owens to the floor, where he lay motionless on his back as he was counted out by referee Gene Roman. "After playing with Cowboy Billy, hailed as a Cherokee Indian from Guthrie, Okla., through the first round, experimenting, taking a punch or two and dancing violently to display his speed, Carnera turned vicious at the opening gong for the second session and wiped the Indian out of there in 23 seconds."[39]

United News Service Sports Editor Davis J. Walsh, no fan of Primo's, may have said it best when he stated, "Primo did more than knock Owens out, he demolished him."[40]

* * *

Carnera's next stop was St. Louis, where Primo met another Oklahoma heavyweight in the form of Tulsa policeman Buster Martin. Martin lasted three minutes and 56 seconds before becoming Primo's fourth knockout victim in four American appearances. Twelve thousand fans paid their way into the St. Louis Arena to see if the Tulsan could have any effect against the Italian giant. But this fight ended rapidly as well.

Martin, who could move ably about the ring, was in the last bout of an undistinguished six-fight professional career. At the bell, he danced and weaved, keeping his distance in the opening moments of round one. Primo found the quick and distant gendarme a difficult target as he missed on a number of punches. Martin landed one hard right cross to Primo's jaw that Carnera chiefly ignored. It may have been at this precise moment that Buster began to rethink the virtues of the fistic life.

As Primo began to reset his coordinates and land some blows, Martin changed his tactics and now found refuge in draping himself around Primo's waist and hanging on to Carnera like a man clutching his hat on a windy day. Press reports described Martin as "diving for the big boy's abdomen and hanging on until Primo wrestled free."[41] Carnera staggered the 209-pound Tulsan with several left hooks late in the round, but Martin managed to hold on — quite literally — until the bell.

In the second stave, after several more clinches, Martin, fully sensing the gravity of his situation, decided to go for it all. Summoning up all the power that he could muster, the constable tried to tag Primo with a powerhouse right that was aimed at the giant's head. Carnera sidestepped the blow and countered with an ominous, straight right to Martin's jaw. Like a rock, the policeman hit the canvas hard and lay prostrate and motionless as the referee counted out what proved to be the final 10 seconds of his professional ring career. Always magnanimous in victory, Primo helped Martin's seconds carry his woozy opponent out of the ring.

* * *

On Valentine's Day, Primo had a date in Memphis, Tennessee, with Jim Sigmund, who'd lost 18 of his 26 professional fights.

Primo had a grand time in Memphis, where he was well received by the city's thriving Italian community. Upon his arrival, he was met at the train station by several hundred enthusiastic fans who escorted Carnera to his hotel. That afternoon he dined at the home of a prominent member of the Italian community, where he consumed vast quantities of ravioli and three whole chickens. Prominent Memphians also arranged for a special 12-foot bed to be placed in Primo's hotel room.

While in Memphis, Leon See was quoted as saying, "Carnera would remain in the United States until he 'is either champion or is eliminated.'"[42]

In the fight, which had almost become secondary to the circus surrounding the man mountain, Primo wasted little time in dispatching the 235-pound Sigmund. Moments after the opening bell, Carnera staggered his opponent with a hard shot to the chin. Sigmund was able to land a couple of non-damaging punches on Primo, but each time he did so, Carnera countered with several hard retorts to the head and body. Finally, in the middle of round one, Primo let loose a thunderous straight right that sent Sigmund through the ropes and on to his stomach, where he was counted out. In all Sigmund landed two punches to Carnera's nine. Only 7,000 fans showed up for the one-sided affair.

Sigmund would lose his next three fights and mercifully retire from the ring in 1932 with a 7–22–1 record. He had not recorded a win since January 9, 1928.

* * *

On February 17, Primo kayoed 6'4", 227-pound John Erickson at the Coliseum in Oklahoma City in the second round. Like Primo, Erickson was later a professional wrestler and was also known as "Man Mountain." The United Press reported, "Carnera toyed with his opponent throughout the first round, but opened the second with a rush and flattened Erickson with a left hook to the body and another left to the chin."[43]

Erickson fought hard and hung in during the first round, gaining the approval of the 6,000 fans. "However, Carnera grew furious in the second round after his opponent stung him on the jaw with a right and floored Erickson twice before the latter took the count."[44] The fight ended at 1:45 of the second round.

* * *

Over the next few weeks, newspapers around the nation began running a number of speculative stories confirming that Jack Dempsey was considering a ring comeback and thought that Primo might provide a good point of re-entry. From Dallas, Texas, Leon See was quoted as saying, "We are negotiating for the fight and feel reasonably sure that it will go through. Dempsey told me in Chicago that if Carnera went through with all his bouts in America unbeaten he would stage a comeback, because he figured that such a bout would draw the greatest gate in the history of boxing."[45]

Indeed, Dempsey, while visiting Minnesota's Mayo Clinic in March, stated that he would start intensive training in Ensenada, Mexico, in May for a comeback planned for late summer or fall. No opponent was named by the Dempsey camp, but Chicago fight promoter Mique Malloy said he was offering a million-dollar purse for a Dempsey–Carnera tilt and that Dempsey was said to be considering the offer contingent upon Primo remaining undefeated through the summer while Dempsey trained.[46]

* * *

Primo did his part a week later in New Orleans when he dropped St. Paul heavyweight Farmer Lodge in round two of a scheduled ten. Lodge had not won a fight since 1924, losing nine straight. In short order, Primo made it ten. According to the Associated Press, the "gigantic Italian pushed Farmer Lodge, ponderous Minnesotan, about the ring like a child and then knocked him out in the second round tonight."[47]

Primo knocked Lodge down in the first round for a short count. Carnera floored him again early in the second, but Lodge staggered to his feet just before the referee got to ten. Seconds later Primo hit Lodge with a quick right uppercut that dropped the Minnesotan to the canvas for the third and final time. Both Lodge and his career were counted out at 1:22 of the second round.

Always the gentleman, Primo assisted his victim back to his corner before celebrating. It was the last fight of the 235 pound Lodge's 11-year career. He finished with an overall record of 12–21–2.

* * *

On March 3, Primo faced 6'5", 235-pound Roy "Ace" Clark at the Arena in Philadelphia. Despite losing three times for every one win, Clark regularly fought big-name fighters and refused to lie down. After a four-fight undercard, a crowd of 11,000 fans saw local fighter Clark hold his own for six rounds before succumbing to Carnera.

The first round was largely uneventful, but Clark came alive in the second and third, taking a lead on the judge's cards. Early in the fourth stanza Clark battered Primo with repeated shots to the head and body. After that, Carnera figured out his more experienced opponent's style and ended Clark's control by putting him on the canvas twice in that round.

Carnera continued to control events in the fifth, but Clark, making good use of his left jab, had almost shut Primo's left eye due to swelling. As the round ended, the eye was swollen to the point that Carnera's corner felt real fear that Referee Tommy Reilly might stop the bout. Reilly looked at the swollen eye and "appealed to Carnera, who said he would try one more round."[48] Knowing that he had better end it quick, Carnera took matters in hand and dropped Clark with a shot to the midsection for the KO at 2:14 of the sixth. Clark, doubled over on the ground and bleeding from the mouth, looked to his corner for assistance while Reilly counted him out.

Clark went on to fight for another five years, retiring for what appeared to be for good after losing to Al Walker in Galveston, Texas, on January 7, 1935. But like many fighters, he was not really done — it just took Ace longer to climb back through the ropes than most. Gene Engel reported in the April 1950 issue of *The Ring*, "after 'Lashane Clarkell,' West Indies, threw a few harmless blows, veterans recognized him as being none other than Ace Clark, long time retired heavyweight."[49] Clark lost by knockout to Leon McClinton.

* * *

By March some of the immediate interest and curiosity in Carnera seemed to be waning. The constant parade of mediocrity was beginning to wear thin. According to Robert Edgren, writing for the Bell Syndicate in March 1930, "Instead of making a reputation for Carnera, this picking of 'suckers' to use in showing him off before the American public has just about destroyed interest in him. Perhaps Carnera can fight, but he isn't given a chance to prove it."[50]

Much has been said about Primo's fighting easier opponents with limited skills — many of whom went down in a single round — but since when has that been a unique way to build up ring experience and a record? Primo's managers arguably overdid it, but the technique is nothing new. Only four of Jack Dempsey's first 22 opponents had winning records and many had almost no record at all. Only six of those first 22 opponents had ever entered the ring professionally when they climbed in with the "Manassa Mauler."

Gene Tunney faced minimal opposition in his first 36 fights. Over that five-year period only five of his opponents had winning records. He didn't fight a man with a winning record until his ninth contest nor one with a notably winning record until his 11th bout, when he defeated journeyman Joe Borrell who, at just over 5'6" and 158 pounds, was a middleweight who had stepped up to light heavyweight. Tunney would climb into the ring 11 more times over the remainder of his career with men who had never won a professional fight. Twenty-three more of his wins came against men with losing ring records. As such, fully 43 — or half of Tunney's 86 fights—came against men with losing records, many of whom had little or no ring experience.

Only one of Joe Walcott's first 12 opponents had any real record. Only two of Archie Moore's first 26 professional bouts came against men with winning records. When in his 27th fight Moore faced his first heavily experienced fighter, he lost, dropping a 10-round decision to the southpaw Johnny "Bandit" Romero at Lane Field in San Diego. Mexican great Julio Cesar Chavez faced only five opponents with winning records in his first 30 fights and 17 of those had never won a professional fight when they met Chavez.

Even Joe Louis was not immune. Over a period spanning from December 1940 to May 1941, Louis fought regularly against a series of challengers who many sportswriters considered unworthy opponents for the champion. Rightly or wrongly, history has labeled this series of fights "The Bum of the Month Club."

One of the hardest things to do in the world of sports is climb into the ring knowing that you're about to get hit by a guy who is trying to knock you down if not out. Most fighters get used to it, but it's never easy. Legendary trainer Angelo Dundee, when talking about people who have the nerve to climb through the ropes, summed it up best when he stated emphatically, "I resent that ['Bum of the Month' label] because if a kid's a fighter, he can't be a bum. You've gotta be a special individual to be a fighter. I blow my stack when I hear that because it's one on one; anything can happen. Any bum can get lucky. There's no bum of the month."[51]

But with the hype and build-up surrounding Carnera, the press, the public, and boxing officials were demanding more from the Italian. By March, the National Boxing Association, with the help of some state commissioners, was trying to stop the carnage by either forcing Carnera to fight a better class of pugilists or prohibiting the Italian from fighting in the United States at all.

Officials in both the Illinois and New York State Athletic Commissions were working to assure that Primo face off against reputable opponents in their states in the future. Madison Square Garden was trying to set up a fight with the large and skilled veteran heavyweight George Godfrey. It was reported by the International News Service on March 14 that the Carnera camp had been offered a $100,000 purse to meet Godfrey in Philadelphia later that spring. "A privilege of taking forty-five per cent of the receipts was also proffered the Venetian man-mountain."[52]

That same day, the Associated Press announced that Chicago promoter Mique Malloy would offer $1,000,000 for a fight between Carnera and former champion Jack Dempsey, who continued to work out and fight exhibitions while making noise about a possible May comeback.

Even with the persistent Dempsey rumors, interest in Primo was lagging. Sportswriter John Kieran relayed the following story — apocryphal or not — that summed up some people's feelings: "At the ballgame yesterday somebody said, 'What's become of Carnera?' and the respondent answered, 'Who cares?' It was decided to let it go at that."[53] It was clearly time for Primo to step up in competition.

* * *

On March 10 Emilia Tersini told reporters in London that she and Primo were engaged to be married. The pretty, young Soho waitress stated that the couple were to be married in London upon Carnera's return from his current tour of America. This seemingly joyous revelation was instead to be the beginning of a long, drawn out, and expensive battle for Primo.

On the next day, Carnera fought the type of battle he preferred to fight and was much better prepared for — in the ring against Sully Montgomery in Minneapolis. While Montgomery was only a mediocre fighter, Primo had his work cut out for him. Montgomery was big and he was never known as the fairest of fighters. The Texan had been disqualified at least four times during his career. In a bout with George Godfrey in 1926, Montgomery was disqualified after fouling Big George at least a dozen times. Primo's trainers warned him to make short work of Montgomery.

The single-fight undercard featured St. Paul featherweight Paul Wangley scoring a first-round knockout over Bobby Laurent of Minot, North Dakota. In the main event, Montgomery came out all energy, but heeding his corner's advice, Primo wasted little time in taking the fight to his opponent. At the bell ending the first round, Montgomery was staggering and searching for his corner. Primo scored a second-round knockout after a cavalcade of rapid punches from the Italian dropped Montgomery twice in that round. The 6'2", 220-pound Texan couldn't rise after the second knockdown and was counted out at one minute and 15 seconds of the second stave. "For Carnera the encounter appeared to be a pleasant workout without the discomfiture of receiving any serious blows."[54] While the crowd of 14,000 had only seen a short three rounds of fighting over two contests, Primo was warmly received with cheers from the patrons.

This appearance turned out to be Montgomery's second-to-last fight. He retired a month later with a 38–33–1 record, after losing a bout by way of knockout to Tuffy Griffiths.

* * *

On March 17, Primo met Chuck Wiggins of Indianapolis in front of a crowd estimated at somewhere north of 20,000 persons at the Arena in St. Louis. This set a record as the largest crowd ever to see an indoor sporting event in the Gateway City. Wiggins had been a sparring partner as well as twice an opponent for Gene Tunney. Known as the "Hoosier Playboy," Wiggins was a rough-and-tumble sort in and out of the ring.[55] Standing just under 6 feet tall and weighing in at 207 pounds, the 32-year-old Wiggins entered the contest with an 87–45–19 record and a career that dated back to 1914, meaning that he had been fighting professionally for literally half his life.

Wiggins, who fought his first professional bout at 15, was no stranger to trouble. He always insisted that street fights as a boy had piqued his interest in boxing. A United Press report from October 21, 1930, stated that Wiggins was arrested for brawling in a restaurant. According to Boxrec.com quoting the UPI story, "Police said he gave them no trouble although on a previous occasion he soundly drubbed three officers who attempted to arrest him in a North Side hotel lobby. 'Just getting a little training, that's all,' Wiggins remarked as he climbed into the patrol wagon. After he had fought three prisoners in the city jail he was removed to solitary confinement." Wiggins' death in 1942 was violent as well. The Associated Press reported on May 18, "Charles F. (Chuck) Wiggins, veteran of hundreds of fights in and out of the ring, died yesterday in (Indianapolis) City Hospital of a fractured skull, which he apparently suffered in a fall down a stairway."[56]

In addition to Tunney, Wiggins fought many of the great fighters of his era, including Les Darcy, Theodore "Tiger" Flowers, Tommy Gibbons, Harry Greb, Leo Houck, Battling Levinsky, Tommy Loughran, Mike Gibbons, and Young Stribling. Several more than once.

Wiggins fought Harry Greb nine times from 1919 to 1922 and while Wiggins never defeated Greb, several of the fights were very close. Each fight went the distance and resulted in newspaper decisions. No longer in use, but common during the early 20th Century in North America, a "newspaper decision" might be made after a no-decision bout had ended. A "no decision" bout occurred when both boxers were still standing at the fight's conclusion and there was no knockout, no official decision was rendered, and neither boxer was declared the winner. But this did not prevent the pool of ringside newspaper reporters from declaring a consensus result among themselves and printing a newspaper decision in their publications. Officially, however, a "no decision" bout resulted in neither boxer winning or losing. Many of those sportswriters, however, gave Wiggins the nod on two of the Greb bouts, thinking him the victor. The two fought an amazing 86 rounds in nine fights, each bout going the distance. Greb and Wiggins each called the other the best fighter they had ever faced.

Primo entered the arena for the St. Patrick's Day contest appropriately clad in a Kelly green cap and jersey. Wiggins was considered by many to be a step up in competition for

Carnera, and a reported 25,000 fans packed the house hoping for a competitive match, but the result was anything but competitive.

During the first round, Primo battered his opponent with a steady barrage of destructive combinations to the head and body. The leather-tough Wiggins refused to lie down to Carnera as he waded into his larger foe, attempting to inflict damage. All he got for his trouble was frustrated and tired as he failed to land a solid shot. "The Indianapolis heavyweight, who has been in the boxing game sixteen years, appeared surprised by Carnera's speed and defense."[57]

Wiggins went through the ropes twice in the first 60 seconds of round two. He was helped back into the ring the first time, but was unable to get back to his feet the second. Wiggins was counted out by Referee Walter Heisner as he lay beside the ring, after one minute in the second of a scheduled 10 rounds. After being counted out, Wiggins had to be helped back to his dressing room where he complained of an injured back. Primo was unruffled as he left the ring.[58]

Before the fight, Wiggins was held up to be one of Carnera's toughest opponents to date, yet during the bout Primo was in command and "showered rights and lefts to the Hoosier's head and body in the first round, leaving the bald-headed veteran red in body and face. Wiggins failed to land a solid punch, although he was in there trying."[59]

It was estimated that after the Wiggins fight, Carnera had earned $103,391 in his 10 American appearances. This translated into nearly $5,000 per each of his 21 rounds.

* * *

On March 20 a small crowd of just a few thousand saw Primo make short work of Frank Zaveta, finishing the New Jerseyan in 1:51 of the first round in Jacksonville, Florida. Zaveta, from Newark, fought professionally only 12 times and all 12 of his fights ended in knockouts—unfortunately for Frank he was on the losing end of 10 of them. In his final fight he lost in two rounds to Ray Impelletiere in the latter's first professional appearance.

Those present in Jacksonville that night saw more in the prelims than in the main event. Jean Boireau knocked out local fighter Bill Temmes in the second round of their featherweight contest and New Jersey heavyweight Frank Montagna (a.k.a., The Madison Butcher Boy) dropped Tampa fighter Joe Smith in the first round.

Zaveta, who appeared nervous during the fight, rushed towards Carnera at the opening bell, but Primo decked him for a nine-count with a sharp, left uppercut. The boys sparred for the next minute or so until Primo dropped the hammer with a left to the head and a hard right to the body that finished the bout. The 235-pound Zaveta did not land a solid punch during the brief fight.

Again, the lack of a sound opponent was hurting Primo's reputation and his next fight would further damage him in the eyes of the press and boxing's governing bodies.

* * *

In late March, the Carnera entourage traveled to Kansas City to meet professional football player and erstwhile boxer George Trafton. Trafton was a terrific football player who would later be named as a member of the Professional Football Hall of Fame and voted to the NFL's 1920's All-Decade Team at center. Trafton was a roughneck on and off the gridiron. Since he refused to back down from a fight, he determined at the close of the 1929 football season that he should fight professionally. Beginning in December, Trafton beat four fighters who had a combined record of 2–1–0 when they climbed into the ring with him. At the end of their careers, those same four men had a combined record of 6–6–0 and Art Shires, his first opponent, accounted for five of those wins.

Trafton defeated Shires on points in a five-round contest in Chicago on December 16, 1929. Shires was a Chicago White Sox baseball player at the time. According to the January 9, 1930, *Seattle Daily Times,* "Shires had earned $8,000.00 for four bouts— more than the $2,900.00 he had made playing as a first baseman for all of 1929. That was 30 days of fighting versus five months of baseball."[60] When fighting, Shires appeared in garish trunks and a red robe that had "Art the Great" splashed across the back. He was unreserved, loud-mouthed, combative, irresponsible, and not well liked, all of which contributed to his short major league career. On January 10, 1930, Shires knocked out Boston Braves catcher Al Spohrer at the Boston Gardens. By then, baseball's imposing commissioner Kenesaw Mountain Landis, well known for his extreme solemnity, had had enough of "Art the Great" and his shenanigans. Landis intervened to stop a proposed fight between Shires and Cubs outfielder Hack Wilson, telling Shires to give up boxing or give up baseball.

The Trafton fight, like the Rioux fight, was a disaster. It took Primo less than a minute to cold-cock the gridiron star. Trafton failed to land a clean blow against Carnera. The 8,000 fans present at the event booed and jeered as Trafton alternately charged Carnera and dropped to the mat. Trafton landed on the canvas three times, the first time just seconds into the fight for a count of six. After the second knockdown, Primo was standing, frustrated at the lack of competition, with his hands on the ropes and surveying the crowd when Trafton, on his feet at the count of nine, charged Carnera and clubbed him in the back. Primo, now irritated, turned quickly and rained a flurry of lefts and rights on his opponent. A short right jab to Trafton's chin put the 229-pound gridiron star down for the count.

Following the fight, the Missouri Boxing Commission suspended Trafton indefinitely, "for failing to offer any semblance of fight in his 54-second swooning session." Commissioner Harry Davis, who was at ringside, said, "To me it looked as if Trafton went down both the first and second times without being hit."[61] Commissioner Davis, who proffered the announcement, was careful not to blame Primo for the outcome of the fight, but the Commission did rule that Primo would not be permitted to fight in Missouri again unless a "worthy opponent" was signed. Following the rulings, the fighters were awarded their purses with Primo receiving $5,100 and Trafton $2,500. It was George's last fight. He returned to the Bears that fall to continue his Hall of Fame career. He played for three more seasons before retiring from the gridiron for good after the 1932 campaign.

* * *

Patience among the governing bodies and the media with the Carnera traveling massacre was wearing thin. His next scheduled fight was set for March 28 in Denver against Canadian Jack McAuliffe. McAuliffe had been fighting professionally with moderate success since 1921, but had dropped his last six contests in a row and was clearly on his way out as a fighter. The Colorado Athletic Commission tried to halt the fight, claiming that McAuliffe was not a suitable opponent for Carnera. The West Side Athletic Club of Denver, which was sponsoring the fight at Denver's Stockyards Stadium, challenged the Commission in court and obtained a restraining order allowing the fight to continue as scheduled. District Judge Henry Bray ruled in favor of the club, determining that it "had gone to considerable expense and should be permitted to go through with the bout."[62]

In the fistfight that followed the legal fight, the Commission was shown to be correct as Carnera scored another first-round knockout. Greeting Primo as he entered the ring with cheers of "Viva Carnera," the 6,500 in attendance saw Primo drop McAuliffe three times. The first was ruled a slip by referee Dan Darnell, but the second brought a count of nine. After rising to his feet, a woozy McAuliffe wasted no time in leading with his chin and Primo landed a straight right that knocked his opponent partway out of the ring, where Darnell counted him out at 2:18 of the first round.

McAuliffe, born Henry Bussineau in Ontario, would fight just once more, losing in the third round by way of disqualification to journeyman Andy Shanks in Congress Stadium in Chicago on August 19, 1930.

* * *

On April 8 Primo stepped into the ring with one Cornelius N. Clisby at the Olympic Auditorium in Los Angeles. Clisby, a 26-year-old Californian better known as Neil, was a seasoned veteran of 68 professional fights and owned a 39–18–11 record. He was a respectable fighter who had lasted seven rounds with a top ten-ranked George Godfrey in 1927 and had TKO'ed Tony Galento in Boston just four months earlier. Galento never went down, but he took a savage beating from Clisby. The fight was stopped in the seventh round due to a severe cut over Two Ton Tony's right eye. In this bout, however, Clisby, 75 pounds lighter than the Preem, lasted just two rounds.

An enthusiastic throng of 12,000 fans jammed into the arena for the five-fight card. As the main event got underway, the crowd began to cheer for Carnera, but they grew impatient with his repeated punching while referee Larry McGrath separated the fighters from the frequent clinches used by Clisby to avoid Carnera's blows. Primo dropped Clisby once in the first round with a hard left hook to the neck, but beyond that Clisby mostly clinched or steered clear of the Italian. As the second round started, Clisby attempted to clout Carnera, but Primo swept away the punches and countered with a tremendous right to the jaw, "which lifted him off the floor"[63] and sent Clisby sprawling. He tried to rise, but collapsed again as McGrath counted him out at the 40-second mark of round two. It took three minutes to bring Clisby around to the point that he could walk to the dressing rooms. While the outcome of the fight was similar to 12 of the previous 13, the skill level was up. By the end of the fight, the cheers were again for Primo.

Like McAuliffe, Clisby fought just once more after meeting Carnera. He was knocked out in the third round by fellow Angelino Mack House in Pasadena on June 19 and decided to hang up the gloves on his seven-year career.

* * *

Next up was a stop at the Oaks Ballpark in Emeryville, California, on April 14 for a scheduled ten-round bout with Leon Chevalier. After the five preliminaries were decided by points, referee Toby Irwin called the fighters to center ring for the main event.

As the fight began, Carnera met his opponent at mid-ring and began pelting him with an array of rapid punches. The ring was wet from a rain that had been falling and Primo once lost his footing and slipped to his knees. He was up immediately from what was correctly judged a slip. Chevalier was able to connect on several clean shots. According to the Associated Press, Chevalier "stood up to his huge opponent and ringsiders believed he made an impressive showing, despite a nine-count knockdown in the sixth round."[64]

Chevalier rose at the count of nine, but as he got to his feet one of Chevalier's seconds, Bob Perry, tossed a towel into the ring. Immediately, there was an uproar from the crowd, most feeling that there was no reason to halt the fight, as it appeared to them that Chevalier

3. To the United States, 1930

was in no worse condition than Carnera. According to California boxing rules, Perry's action was illegal as only the chief doctor has the authority to stop the fight by throwing in the towel.

An angry demonstration followed the stoppage. The Associated Press reported that "the second, Bob Perry of Hollywood, immediately became the center of a milling mob, which handled him roughly and inflicted a gash over one eye." The report continued: "Fellow countrymen of Carnera's stood on chairs and shouted 'fake' and urged the huge Italian be made to fight over again."[65]

Members of the California State Athletic Commission started an immediate investigation to determine if the fight was legitimate and whether or not bettors had wagered excessively on the contest. On April 18, Commissioner Charles F. Truang recommended that the licenses of Carnera, See, Duffy, Friedman, and Churchill be revoked and that Primo not be allowed to box again in California. In addition, Truang called for the indefinite suspension of Chevalier's manager Tim McGrath and his seconds Perry and Robert Laga.

Concluding their investigation on April 21, the Commission adopted Truang's recommendations and revoked the licenses of Primo, See, Duffy, and Churchill. Receiving suspensions were Chevalier, McGrath, Perry and Laga.

According to the Associated Press, "Chevalier said Perry threatened him if he did not 'lay down' to Carnera, but Perry denied this, saying he intended to save the Negro from further punishment."[66] Chevalier's wife testified that her husband had been approached earlier to agree to a "fake fight," but that he had refused to discuss it, instead directing all business to his manager, McGrath. McGrath denied any knowledge that Perry was going to throw in the towel, and that the towel should not have been thrown in. When asked why he hadn't protested Perry's action, McGrath replied that he was so shocked by the turn of events that he had failed to protest to the referee.

The Commission did release both fighters' purses, ruling Chevalier and Carnera themselves were blameless for the stoppage. Primo received $13,239 and Chevalier $1,500 for their efforts.[67]

Leon's suspension didn't last long. He was fighting again in California by May 9 when he dropped a 10-round decision to Angus Snyder at the Dreamland Auditorium in San Francisco. He would continue to fight—chiefly in California and elsewhere on the West Coast through 1934. He ended his decade-long career with a 25–20–8 record after a ten-round draw with the notable light-heavyweight "Tiger" Jack Fox in Pocatello, Idaho.

Adding to Primo's woes, the New York State Athletic Commission after reviewing the California case to see if proper action was taken, determined on April 30th to follow suit and revoke Carnera's state license along with those of Chevalier and both fighters' management teams. This caused a bit of a domino effect of suspensions by other state commissions, effectively ending his ability to fight in many states. Even the British Boxing Control Board, which had a working agreement with NYSAC, was considering a ban on the Italian heavyweight. As legendary sportswriter Grantland Rice noted in his column "The Sportlight" on April 25, "That towel may be the most costly piece of tapestry ever known."[68]

* * *

Regardless of the California and New York commission activity, Primo was due the following Tuesday in Portland, Oregon, to meet Sam Baker of Los Angeles in the Ice Coliseum. Baker, who stood 6'4" and weighed 246 pounds, entered the fight with a mediocre

9–9–1 record and a waning career that ended in 1931 after consecutive losses to Carnera, Art Lasky and Jimmy Byrne.

Shortly after the opening bell, Carnera knocked Baker down for the first time. It was the first of many knockdowns by Primo as Baker was on the canvas at regular intervals for the remainder of the brief fight. "Carnera used a powerful, crushing right to excellent advantage."[69] Baker went down five times before Primo launched the knockout blow — a hard right to Baker's jaw that sent him crashing to the canvas where he lay dazed and helpless while being counted out.

* * *

Primo remained out West spending the month of May fighting exhibitions. Between May 1 and May 31, Carnera fought 13 exhibitions in Oregon, Utah, and Iowa. On May 1 Primo fought a total of five exhibition rounds against three men in Portland. Sequentially he knocked out Peter Jackson, Tom Moore, and Art Shearer. Jackson and Moore were light heavyweights nearing the end of lackluster careers and Shearer, who finished a 1–6–0 career in 1931, was a true heavyweight weighing in at 225. As with most exhibitions, these were little more than public sparring sessions with mediocre local fighters, but they accomplished the dual purposes of bringing in some money and giving Primo more time in the ring.

* * *

On May 7 and 8, the Pennsylvania and Michigan Boxing authorities bucked the trend of the other commissions and, respectively, each sanctioned a 10-round contest featuring Primo Carnera. Primo was to meet George Godfrey in Philadelphia on June 23 at Baker Bowl. The Michigan bout was against K.O. Christner and scheduled for May 31 at Floyd Fitzsimmons' outdoor arena at the Michigan State Fairgrounds in Detroit.

Before Primo could get to Detroit to fight Christner, he would have to fight outside the ring for his reputation. The United Press reported on May 14 that Carnera, See, Duffy, Friedman, and Churchill were to be suspended indefinitely by the National Boxing Association. A report issued by an investigative committee headed by Gen. John V. Clinnin of the Illinois Athletic Commission recommended action be taken against the Carnera camp. In what was described as "an exhaustive investigation," the group sought Carnera's suspension: "The committee believes there has been a definite conspiracy to defraud and recommends that for the best interests of boxing and the public that Carnera and his managers be suspended indefinitely."[70] The report was forwarded to National Boxing Association president Stanley Isaacs, who supported the suspension, making it effective in 28 states. New York, Pennsylvania, and Massachusetts were not affected, but New York had just placed Primo on suspension as well. Primo now felt he really had something to prove — something to show his critics.

* * *

Working back eastward, the Carnera troupe stopped off in Utah where Primo fought seven more exhibitions. On May 12 he fought Jack Silva, Al Dawson, and Ed Wilkes in Ogden. The next day in Salt Lake City he met Hyde Lyndell, Jack Lewis, Steve Strilich, and Tony Clawson. Each fight lasted one round and in each fight, Primo knocked out his opponent. Between May 19 and June 2 Carnera had six more exhibition bouts in Iowa. Noteworthy among his opponents were Jack McAuliffe, whom Carnera had defeated in Denver in a sanctioned bout earlier in the year, and Seal Harris, whom he would also defeat in a sanctioned bout in Sao Paulo, Brazil, in January 1935.

* * *

The NBA ruling was a problem for Carnera's next fight, scheduled for May 31 against K.O. Christner in Detroit where Primo was still licensed to fight. Longtime local promoter Floyd Fitzsimmons was backing the evening event. The powerful and well-connected Fitzsimmons was a smart dresser with a wide nose, deep-set eyes, and never a hair out of place. He had promoted fights in the Motor City for many notable fighters including Jack Dempsey, Young Stribling, and Harry Greb.

Primo set up camp in the Danceland Gymnasium where he trained in front of full houses of paying customers on a regular basis. The Carnera camp took in as much as $1,500 a day from fans watching the big man prepare for battle.[71] His sparring mates were Jack McAulliffe, Jack Lewis, Larry Creighton, and an unknown journeyman with the unlikely name of Jappo Moppo. Jappo's only known professional bout came in January 1931 when he was knocked out in the first round by the notable Mexican light heavyweight "Indian" Benny Deathpaine, "The Aztec Assassin."

Christner arrived in Detroit two weeks before the fight and trained at Sillman's Gym under the guidance of his manager Suey Welch. K.O. was known for taking his work seriously and always showed up in the ring in good condition. His stable of sparring mates included George Wilson, Tiny Herman, and Lynn Jordan. Welch told reporters in an interview days before the fight that, "Christner will go in with the opening bell to shoot for the knockout. We figure that his best chance lies in putting the big boy out before the bell calls them out for the fifth round. After that Christner's chances will diminish with each round."[72]

On the day before the contest, the fighters attended the Detroit Tigers vs. Washington Senators baseball game at Navin Field where each man reportedly took a turn at being the clubs' batboys. Christner was actually a ballplayer of note, having played semi-pro baseball in the Akron area before his fight days, but Primo, just arrived from Europe, was a baseball novice on whom the game was lost in 1930.

The bout was delayed from its original May 31 schedule until June 5, but on the newly appointed date, both men came to the Detroit Fairgrounds Arena ready to fight. The Fairgrounds Arena was a large outdoor venue with wooden bleachers. More than 18,000 fans crowded the Arena to watch the six-bout card headed by the Italian Man Mountain and the former tire maker from Akron, Ohio.

The fights on the undercard began at 8:30 P.M. local time with Detroit heavyweight Charley Retzlaff knocking out long-time ring veteran Tom Sayers in less than a round. The next three bouts totaled only a combined five rounds with each contest also ending in a knockout. The scheduled semi-final between Detroit heavyweight Bennie Touchstone and last minute stand-in Frankie Simms of Cleveland actually went the scheduled eight rounds and ended in a draw. But even with a five-minute delay while Jack Lewis' corner brought the fighter back to his senses after he was knocked out cold by Tiny Powell in the night's second bout, the undercard went so quickly that an emergency filler fight was arranged between George Wilson and Jack Silver. Silver was not the well-known California lightweight of the same name, but a journeyman light heavyweight from Portland, Oregon, who would fight on other Carnera undercards. Silver commanded the fight from the beginning, dropping Wilson to the canvas a half dozen times in as many rounds. Wilson, one of Christner's sparring mates, was, however, used to taking a beating for a living and got up every time.

He was still standing at the final bell and while he lost the fight, he won the adulation of the crowd for his toughness.

Before the featured bout Fitzsimmons protected his investment in the next fight he was promoting by introducing the participants from the ring. The fight was a featherweight elimination bout between Italian Earl Mastro and Bud Taylor. The winner of this fight was to meet Kid Chocolate for the featherweight championship.

Primo entered the ring first wearing a dark green sleeveless shirt and a taxi driver's cap. Christner then entered wearing a more traditional purple robe. Just before the fight, the fighters donned their gloves, but when Christner pulled his on, he found them several sizes too large. It was quickly discovered that the ring officials had picked up a pair of Carnera's back-up gloves by mistake. The fight was held up for several minutes while Christner's gloves were retrieved and brought to the ring.[73]

Christner carried through with his plan to rush Carnera at the opening bell and try to rack up some early damage to his opponent. Primo mainly used his trademark left jab in the early going, but also landed several notable rights to Christner's chin. Primo failed to connect on the heaviest swing of the round, "a short right uppercut, which would have torn Christner's head loose from its mooring mast had it connected."[74] Somehow Christner managed to get his chin out of the way of the rocket and the punch found nothing but air. The round was close with most observers calling it either even or awarding it to Christner for his level of busyness.

The second round was Primo's. While Christner kept up his charging style and worked on Carnera's mid-section, Primo peppered the Akron tire maker with lefts and rights to the head. By mid-round, the pace had slowed a bit and referee Slim McClelland had to break the fighters from clinches on several occasions. At the end of the stave, Carnera made a statement with his fists by battering Christner with three strong lefts to the jaw.

The third round was again fairly even with both fighters keeping busy. Carnera scored early with several hard shots to Christner's face, including a solid left that caused an immediate swelling around K.O.'s right eye. It was a good round for Primo, but again the scorecards were split with some observers picking Carnera while others believing that Christner took the round.

In the fourth, Primo sensed that Christner was tiring and he settled in to prepare for the finish. After just missing an early knockdown, Carnera watched for the right time to strike. Just past the 1-minute mark, that time came. Primo threw a left at K.O. and his left thumb caught the Akronite at the base of his already battered right eye. McClelland gave Carnera a warning, but waved the fighters on. With his right eye nearly shut, Christner took a hard swing at Primo, but left himself wide open. Carnera seized the moment, pounding his opponent with a hard right uppercut followed by a left hook that crashed into the side of Christner's head and a follow-up right that finished Christner. K.O. went down like a rock. The United Press reported, "The knockout came after 1:26 of the fourth round. As Christner went to the canvas, he rolled over on his back and blood trickled from his mouth, the result of a series of sledge-like rights to the jaw."[75]

Christner appeared unconscious as McClelland began the count. It was the first time in his 50-fight career that Christner had been knocked off his feet. Always the good sport, Primo waited for McClelland to call "ten," then went to his opponent's aid and helped him to his stool.

Time magazine reported in their June 16, 1930, edition, "Carnera fought in Detroit last week, where he has not been suspended. Opponent was K. O. Christner, tough Akron rubber maker, who fought well against Jack Sharkey and Tom Heeney. Carnera knocked Christner out in the fourth round."[76]

While the reports of the fight clearly show a bloody, swollen, and beaten Christner lying on the resin and being helped to his corner, the former tire maker was quoted by the *Omaha World Herald* in 1932 as claiming that he was threatened by gun-toting racketeers to take a dive or else. "I'm a peaceful man," Christner reportedly said on the eve of his 1932 rematch with Primo, "and I'm also a prudent man. And when I saw those gorillas at ringside with their hands stuck ominously in coat pockets, what could I do? They'd have shot me down if I hadn't carried out orders."[77]

Interestingly, Christner made no mention of this in 1930. His post-fight comments referenced only the eye gouging and his hopes for a rematch. In his dressing room and later back at his hotel, Christner commented, "If I were as big as he is, I could lick any heavyweight in the game with one hand tied behind me and I wouldn't have to blind them first either."[78] But stating a more reasoned view of the night's events, Lynn Wagner, sports editor of the *Akron Times-Press*, commented on Primo's performance by saying, "Don't let anyone tell you that Carnera can't fight. The knockout he registered under the glare of a flock of powerful lights here last night was the real McCoy. It was genuine and clean-cut, it was not an act."[79]

Is it possible that Madden's thugs were at ringside? Sure it is, but what would the mob have gained by knocking off Christner? If he had been told to take a dive and refused, shooting him would have blown the lid off Owney Madden's alleged scheme and ended it with the strong possibility of jail time for those involved. What would have been the point? It is just as likely that Christner, a man who fascinates me and whom I like a great deal, simply jumped on the then-current bandwagon to cover up the fact that he was beaten badly in a fair fight for the first time in his career. Wagner, commented from ringside: "Christner didn't hit the tank, didn't take a dive for the muscle man. He took a pair of the healthiest swats on the whiskers we have seen in many a year in that fourth round."[80] Author Michael DeLisa was probably on target when he wrote of the knockdown, "Under Bill Duffy's keen guidance, the lumbering Carnera was learning to fight."[81]

Meyer "KO" Christner led an interesting life. As a young man, he was sent to St. Mary's Industrial School in Baltimore where he played baseball and was the battery mate for a strong-armed young pitcher named George Herman Ruth. He served in the Army before and during World War I. His unit saw action during the Mexican border action against Pancho Villa in 1916. While he was stationed in Texas, he met and married his wife Elizabeth. Elizabeth Christner inherited an 1,800-acre ranch outside of San Antonio. After Meyer left the Army, the Christners relocated to Akron, Ohio, where the future heavyweight accepted a job at the Firestone Tire Plant.

He didn't start fighting professionally until he was 29 years old. According to his obituary, he got into an argument one day at the plant with a man who was trying to push him around. The situation soon escalated and Christner punched the bully, broke his jaw, and knocked him cold, thus earning his nickname. Coworkers soon suggested he enter an upcoming amateur boxing show. He did and a respectable boxing career was born.

To his credit, Christner knocked out fifth-ranked heavyweight Knute Hansen in 1928, took Jack Sharkey and Paolino Uzcudun 10 rounds each, losing both fights in close decisions in 1929, and split a pair with Ernie Schaaf in 1929–30. His first victory came in his very first professional fight in the form of a second-round knockout of Pete Rogers in February 1926. His last came in his final bout in May 1940 against Jack Owens, again in a second-round knockout. The 43-year-old Christner then hung up his gloves for good with a professional record of 56–48–4.

Prior to boxing, Christner had played semi-professional football with the Akron Indians. He also played semi-professional baseball, as a catcher, for various teams in and around the Akron area. After he left the ring, he opened a bowling alley in Cumberland, Maryland, which he ran until he and Elizabeth retired and returned to the Akron area in 1967. Christner passed away on November 1, 1979.

* * *

June 14 found Primo in the Upper Peninsula town of Ironwood, Michigan, where he fought two, 2-round exhibitions, against Larry Creighton of New York, who had been a talented amateur boxer but never saw much professional success, and an unknown from Detroit. Again, Carnera put both men away with ease.

* * *

On June 16 the French Army declared that Primo, whom they claimed was a naturalized French citizen, had been ordered to report to the Saint Germain City Hall several months earlier and serve up to one year in the peace-time reserves. Officials in Saint Germain had previously approved an application for naturalization for Carnera and determined that his age — 24 — did not preclude him from service. Primo, claiming that he was still an Italian citizen, refused to report.

The problem apparently dated back to the late 1920s when one of Primo's employers had encouraged him to sign a document and ensured him that it would alleviate his residency concerns. It did in fact provide alleviation, but the document turned out to be an application for French citizenship. Primo stated clearly to the press and the French authorities that he was and always had been an Italian national, that he had never renounced his Italian citizenship, and that he knew nothing of his being a French citizen. Seeing the futility in pressing their argument, the Republic let fall their claims to Monsieur Carnera.

* * *

While the French Army was fretting about military matters, Primo was concentrating on his next fight, scheduled for Monday June 23 at Baker Bowl in Philadelphia. On March 14 the International News Service had reported that the fight promoters in Philadelphia were guaranteeing a $100,000 purse for the Carnera–Godfrey bout in that city.[82]

Godfrey, who entered the ring with a strong 67–15–1 record, was nearly as big as Carnera. Godfrey stood 6'3" and weighed in at 250 solid pounds. Primo was a trim 262 for this fight, leaving one of the narrowest weight margins he had yet experienced. Godfrey was rated by many as the best heavyweight in the game in 1930 and it was said that no man could stand up to him if he really wanted to let himself go. Godfrey was listed in *The Ring* magazine Top 10 heavyweights six times from 1924 to 1930, peaking at number two in 1928. Godfrey has often been compared to another "Big George" from a different era — Big George Foreman. Going into it, none of Primo's critics could claim this was an easy fight.

Nonetheless, the United Press ran an article the day before the fight stating that Godfrey regularly carried fighters to make a bout look better, while Primo — whom they point out was guiltless of any shenanigans himself — was "accustomed to slapping almost playfully and seeing his man do a backward somesault [sic]."[83] I believe that any number of Primo's opponents might disagree with the description of his punches as playful slaps. Other sportswriters' descriptions of Carnera's punches, including "a tremendous

3. To the United States, 1930

right," "which would have shaken the Statue of Liberty," "which would have tunneled the Eighth Avenue subway," "blasting blows that were cruel in their power," and "a series of sledge-like rights to the jaw," were lost on that uncredited writer.

Anyway you cut it, this was no easy fight for Primo. *Time* magazine reported on June 16, "On June 23 in Philadelphia Carnera meets George Godfrey, 222-lb. Negro, whom white heavyweight challengers have consistently avoided."[84]

Chairman Frank Wiener of the Pennsylvania State Athletic Commission was promising a good fight and had taken precautions against an unsatisfactory outcome. "Seconds were forbidden to throw in the towel or to climb to the ring platform during the progress of the bout. The contest will be entirely in the hands of the referee on the staff of the Pennsylvania board."[85] The referee's identity was kept a secret until fight time.

The evening of June 23 brought mild summer weather and a perfect night to sit outside and watch an athletic event. The 35,000 fans were treated to a five-fight undercard featuring, most notably, local favorite Jack Gross and welterweights Billy Angelo and Gene Moretti. At ringside were Jack Dempsey, Gene Tunney, and Max Schmeling. Those present saw, in Davis Walsh's opinion, "a bruising, bone-crushing fight," at least for five rounds.[86]

Godfrey came out at the opening bell with the intention of seeing what Primo was really made of. He pummeled Carnera with a surge of vicious body shots that drove Primo quickly on the defensive. While he landed four lefts and three straight rights, Primo spent the bulk of round one unsure of how to react and on the run.

The first minute and a half of the second continued the same way with Godfrey landing savage and largely unanswered blows to the Italian's massive body and driving him to the ropes. But suddenly, in the final minute of the round Primo found himself and began to fight back. He fought back so well, in fact, that he came close to evening out the round on the judge's scorecards.

Round three began with the fighters rushing into a clinch. Godfrey landed a blasting left hook to Primo's body, but Carnera countered well with a strong right uppercut and several right crosses to Big George's jaw. Godfrey hooked a left to the body at the bell, but the tide was turning in Primo's favor.

Trying to regain the momentum, Godfrey started fast in round number four, but Primo responded well to several good Godfrey combos. Moving to the inside, Primo continued to hit and tie Godfrey up. Primo was able to push, pull, slug and wrestle with Big George for the remainder of the round and even up the fight on the judge's cards. Gaining control of the fight, Carnera was beginning to wear Godfrey down.

Round five started well for Primo, with the Italian using his rights effectively to his opponent's head and body, but after a minute, he was hit by a low blow from Godfrey and the mountain crumbled to the mat. Writhing in agony, he was attended by Dr. Vaughn Dever, State Athletic Commission physician, who determined quickly that Primo was unable to continue. Referee Tommy Reilly, who had also been the third man in the ring for the first Dempsey–Tunney contest in 1926, stopped the fight.

There is little doubt that the low blow genuinely debilitated Carnera. The United Press described the final punch: "A left hook to the body one minute and 13 seconds after the fifth round started Carnera to the canvas in obvious agony. A doctor examined him and declared the Italian had been incapacitated." "It took six men to drag Primo's huge bulk to his corner, while a crowd of 40,000 jammed into Baker Bowl roared its disapproval."[87]

The United Press lamented the fact that a good fight had ended under less than desirable circumstances, stating, "Until that time, the men had fought on comparatively even terms."[88]

Time magazine reported on June 30, 1930:

> In Philadelphia, Primo Carnera, Italian behemoth, stood up straight as his first dangerous U. S. opponent, George Godfrey, 249-pound Leiperville, Pa., Negro, wove toward him with a yellow smile, shuffling his feet and feinting in a manner to which he had been tutored by onetime Negro heavyweight Champion Jack Johnson. Carnera was puzzled in the first round, but thereafter held Godfrey's neck immovably in the clinches, jolted him with short rights, stung him with long lefts. In the fifth round Godfrey suddenly and apparently with deliberation hit Carnera low, followed the first bad blow with a long left below the groin. Carnera, writhing in agony, was declared winner on a foul.[89]

According to the *New York Times*, "George Godfrey, giant Negro heavyweight of Leiperville, after hammering Primo Carnera, mammoth Venetian, through four rounds of a scheduled 10-round battle which attracted 35,000 fans and about $160,000 in gate receipts, was disqualified on a foul in the 5th round amid scenes of wild disorder."[90]

Why a deliberate foul? The Pennsylvania State Athletic Commission wanted to know. The Commission held up Godfrey's purse pending a hearing scheduled for the day following the fight. At the hearing, Godfrey told the commission members that he never intended to foul Carnera intentionally. Rather, Godfrey testified that his fight strategy was to batter Carnera's body, weaken him, and then finish him off as his defenses dropped. In attacking the body, he indicated that several of his blows incidentally landed below the belt. Godfrey had also been warned for another low left just moments before the final blow.

It should also be noted that Godfrey often hit low as he worked the body and this was not the first time he had lost a fight by disqualification — it was in fact the eighth. In 1929, this same Pennsylvania Commission fined and suspended Godfrey after he was disqualified for hitting Al Walker low, and the year before that Godfrey was disqualified for a low blow in Toronto after hitting Larry Gains so hard that it dented the aluminum in Gains's protective cup.[91] In 1926, Godfrey peppered Chuck Wiggins with so many low blows over two rounds that Wiggins required an examination by the ringside physician between rounds seven and eight. When it was ruled that he could not continue, Wiggins was awarded the win by disqualification. And on it goes. Suffice to say, the fact that George Godfrey was hitting below the waist was nothing new.

During the hearing, referee Tommy Reilly told the commissioners, "My official slip, as you are aware, was marked Godfrey fouled deliberately. The first two rounds were won by Godfrey; the third, fourth, and fifth, as far as it was contested, were won by Carnera."[92] So why the foul? If it was deliberate, it was more likely frustration on the part of Godfrey than any kind of shenanigans. He had given Primo all he could dish out and Primo had taken it and was now, according to Reilly and most observers, in control of the fight. If a blow landed a bit low and he got away with it, it might give him an advantage as he pressed on. Most likely, Godfrey simply let a punch get too low as he pressed his fight to Primo's body. He had fought fiercely in the opening rounds, was getting tired, and a punch slipped. It's probably that simple, but the recent events from the Chevalier fight and others, brought this bout, too, under the cloud of suspicion.

The commission revoked Godfrey's license to fight in Pennsylvania and fined him half of his $10,000 purse. Godfrey's manager Jimmy Dougherty also received an indefinite suspension in the Keystone state.

In an interesting side note, the Pennsylvania commission also suspended Primo after the fight, but it was for something that happened outside the ring that he neither participated in nor had any knowledge of. He, his managers and his entire stable were suspended after a scrape that involved light heavyweight Jack Silver, one of the preliminary fighters. Silver apparently refused to follow commission rules that required fighters to wear "the regulation protective device" (boxing code for a cup). Primo's managers got involved by supporting Silver and then getting mixed up in an altercation that followed. Commission Deputy Inspector Francis Connelly suffered a cut lip and a loose tooth in the dressing room fracas. The *New York Times* reported that Billy Duffy struck Connelly on the jaw. All of this happened before Primo even arrived at the stadium. In the aftermath, Billy Jones knocked out Silver in the fourth round — perhaps Silver should have worn "the regulation protective device" on his head! Primo's ridiculous suspension was soon repealed.[93]

Primo, who did not appear before the commission, instead traveling to Atlantic City to rest, was absolved of any wrongdoing and was granted his entire $43,641.39 purse. The commission also reversed itself on its stand that Godfrey alone should be given the next heavyweight title shot. "The commission, which heretofore has ruled that it would never recognize anyone as champion of the world until Godfrey had been taken into account further decided his showing ruled him out of the championship contenders."[94]

Davis Walsh, never a great fan of Primo's, wrote a rather flattering piece in his June 24 International News Service fight recap. Walsh, who sometimes seemed to grudgingly warm to Primo, said, "They can take lots of things away from Godfrey's purse and maybe something from Godfrey's prestige, but they will take nothing away from the impression that Carnera left with the crowd by his performance last night." Walsh continued: "The mastodon proved himself to be a real heavyweight and a definite menace to any and all who may stand between him and the championship. He wasn't winning this fight when it ended, but he had lived down a savage beating in the first two rounds and was beginning to come on, a performance that savored of potential greatness."[95]

The Pennsylvania Commission's suspension had little effect on Godfrey. He was in the ring again two weeks later at the Taylor Bowl in Cleveland where he TKO'ed Frankie Simms in two rounds. He stayed on the road until 1932, when the suspension was lifted. Godfrey continued to fight through 1937 when, at age 40, he retired with a 99–20–2 record under his belt. Of his 99 victories, Godfrey won 81 bouts by knockout.

* * *

After the fight, Primo and his entourage headed to Leon Sée's Atlantic City home for some rest and some time to determine their next steps through the maze set before them by the myriad suspensions adopted by state sanctioning bodies throughout the country. Influential promoter Mique Malloy proposed an exhibition in Chicago set for sometime in July, but the Illinois State Athletic Commission upheld the suspensions. During their weekly meeting on July 1, the commission supported the National Boxing Association by refusing to sanction the fight.

Instead of the Windy City, Primo headed for Omaha, Nebraska, for his next fight, against Ed "Bearcat" Wright on July 17. Wright stood 6'1", weighed in at 218 lbs. and had an impressive ring record of 54–13–11. Wright was a solid fighter who usually battled from a crouch as he waded into opponents, throwing hooks and jabs. Once inside, he tried to soften up his opponent's midsection before landing uppercuts to the head and body. In his 10 years in the ring, he'd fought many big names, most notably former champion Jack Johnson, whom he KO'ed in five, and George Godfrey, whom he'd fight twice more before retiring in 1936, following a six-round points loss to Max Baer. Again, this was no easy opponent for Primo.

The fight moved fairly evenly through three rounds. "Early in the fourth round Carnera connected squarely with a straight right to the head that sent the Negro hurtling out of the ring. So terrific was the blow that Wright snapped the middle strand as he went down."[96] Bearcat landed hard but his fall was somewhat broken by the laps of several front-row spectators. He was given 10 seconds to get back into the ring. After doing so, he took an additional nine before rising to his feet. He might as well have not bothered. With Wright back on two legs, "Carnera plunged in and another powerful right, straight from the shoulder, put Wright down for the final count."[97]

* * *

The next few weeks held a number of outside-the-ring diversions that kept Carnera preoccupied. Squabbles among his fractured management team, more licensing maneuvers by the National Boxing Association, and immigration matters all took front stage.

In July, the association announced that it was lifting its ban on Carnera, but not on Leon See. See was becoming more and more frustrated with his American experience.

Fissures in the Carnera camp became evident when on the day of the Wright contest, See and Billy Duffy openly expressed their different plans for Carnera's future. Realizing that he was being squeezed out by Duffy, Madden, and company, See had announced on July 15 that Carnera and he would sail to Europe and not return until Primo—and perhaps See—could be assured of better treatment in America. The Frenchman was ready to take his fighter home to Paris where he hoped to regain control of Carnera's career and get a respite from American gangsters, the American press, and the various American athletic commissions. Co-manager Duffy announced a day later that he had signed a contract for Primo to fight a third time against Young Stribling in Atlantic City on August 30. As it turned out, both men were wrong in their projections, but the chaotic and splintered nature of Carnera's camp was obvious.[98]

Perhaps most disturbing of all, U.S. immigration officials ruled that Primo's six-month visa had expired on June 30 and he must now, along with See, immediately leave the country. Carnera's business manager, Frank Paccassi, "revealed the contents of a telegram forwarded here (Omaha, Nebraska) to See and Carnera from Byron H. Uhl, official at Ellis Island, New York, informing the pair that immigration officials had denied their request for a six months' extension of their legal stay in the United States which terminated recently."[99] Labor Department officials including Commissioner Uhl did commit, however, that if Carnera or See "cared to introduce further evidence a reconsideration might be given to him."[100]

Over the next week, the scenario haunted Carnera and See with a number of frustrating turns. On July 24 it was reported that Carnera was denied permission to enter Canada where he was to have appeared in an exhibition fight in Montreal. Carnera and See stated that the exhibition had been postponed and while they were in route to New York from Cleveland, they decided to visit Niagara Falls. According to See, "We started to the Falls, but we turned back when Canadian officials refused us entrance because of lack of passports. Returning, we were stopped by United States authorities, who believed we were attempting illegally to enter the United States."[101] After See showed the U.S. officials their railroad tickets from Cleveland to New York and explained that they had not entered Canada, they were allowed to be on their way.

At Primo's request, a hearing with the Labor Department Board of Review was set for August 1. Primo and his representatives traveled to Washington, D.C., for the meeting, during which Primo asked that the order that he leave be rescinded and that his original visa be extended for six months. Immigration officials stated that time extensions were commonly granted and since there were no objections to doing so, they granted six-month visa extensions to both Carnera and See.

On July 31, promoter Mique Malloy announced that a proposed "battle of vindication" between Carnera and Leon Chevalier had been approved and would be held on August 14. The still-suspended See was prohibited from participating in fight negotiations. Regrettably, this fight, like the proposed Stribling rematch, never occurred. Both the return bout with Chevalier and a rubber match with Stribling would have been interesting fights and perhaps cleared up some of the taint surrounding their earlier encounters.[102]

* * *

George Cook was next up. Cook had fought in over 80 professional fights, but had lost more than half of them. Despite his sub–.500 record, Cook claimed the Australian heavyweight championship. He met Primo in front of a crowd of 10,000 on July 29, 1930, at Taylor Bowl in Cleveland.

The first round was a fairly even trading of punches by both fighters. In the waning seconds of the stave, Primo caught Cook with three hard lefts to the jaw that forced the 201-pound Australian to fall into a clinch with Carnera and hang on till the bell.

The effects of those blows seemed to carry over into the second round and Cook continued to be on the receiving end of most of the punches thrown. "Cook went down for the count under a ponderous left to the jaw after 1 minute and 44 seconds of the second round had passed."[103]

Cook was out cold and it took a couple of minutes to bring him around. As was becoming a trademark, Primo helped carry his defeated opponent to his corner.

* * *

After defeating Cook, Carnera fought six more exhibitions in Indiana, Illinois, and Ohio—four of which were against his seemingly favorite foe Jack McAuliffe.

In mid–August while Primo was barnstorming his way through the Midwest, news out of New York announced that Jack Sharkey had been offered a flat guarantee of $125,000 to meet Carnera in Chicago in September. Promoter Mique Malloy, Sharkey's manager Johnny Buckley, and Carnera's representatives met to discuss the details. Buckley countered that Sharkey wanted the greater of a $100,000 guarantee or a 30 percent share of the gate. Also in New York, representatives of Madison Square Garden were trying to persuade Sharkey to meet Victorio Compolo in September instead. Neither fight ever occurred, but Sharkey would meet Carnera in Brooklyn in October 1931.[104]

On August 30 the United Press ran quotes from Jack Dempsey about his "impending" comeback. The former champion spoke positively, stating, "I feel I can get into shape since I'm going to make one more fight before I hang up the old gloves for good." The article stated that Dempsey "believed Young Stribling, Primo Carnera and Max Schmeling should stage an elimination tournament and that if he got into good shape, he would like to meet the winner."[105] Dempsey, even three years removed from his last fight, was such a name in boxing that he made headlines each time it was rumored that he would enter the ring again.

* * *

That night Primo met fellow countryman Ricardo Bertazzolo at the year-old Atlantic City Auditorium (now known as Boardwalk Hall). After New Jerseyan Gene Moretti finished off unknown Angelino Billy Murphey in the third round of their welterweight bout, the main event was ready to commence. The fight was scheduled for 15 rounds. Bertazzolo had a mediocre 16–7–2 record going into the fight and he was outgunned from the beginning.

Primo, with his almost 86" reach, kept Bertazzolo at bay most of the night. Bertazzolo was able to land only one solid punch in the first round. Carnera continually battered away at his opponent's chin. By the end of the first, Bertazzolo, his lip bleeding badly, was so groggy that he could barely find his way back to his corner after the bell.

At the start of the second frame, Bertazzolo, having gathered himself between rounds, rushed Carnera to fight him in close, but Primo worked his way free and continued his assault to Bertazzolo's head and body. "At the beginning of the third round it was obvious that Bertazzolo was in a trance and he swung wildly a few times before Primo rushed him to the ropes and battered him mercilessly until Referee Harry Ertle grabbed Ricardo by the arm and led him to his corner."[106] The fight was over in less than a minute of round three.

There has been blatant rumor that this fight was fixed and that Bertazzolo, refusing to take a dive, was crossed up by his manager Aldo Linz, who slit the fighter's eyebrow with a razor blade between the second and third rounds. Linz reportedly covered the cut with Vaseline which acted as a coagulant for the bleeding until one punch from Primo sent blood spurting from the wound. According to the story, this caused the referee to stop the fight and give Carnera a third-round TKO.[107] Where stories like this come from I cannot say, because it's clear from the eyewitness accounts that Primo controlled the fight from the opening bell on, requiring no help from Linz, and that Harry Ertle stopped the fight because of the cumulative damage Bertazzolo had suffered at the hands of the Italian giant and not because of an arranged cut over the fighter's eye. Also, if Bertazzolo had refused to take a dive, why would he have allowed Linz to slit his eyebrow with a razor blade? He never said a word about this and it's not logical that he would have failed to notice such a wound.

* * *

After his demolition of Bertazzolo, Primo finally took his delayed trip north of the border to fight a half dozen more exhibitions in Montreal. Most notably, he fought Jack McAuliffe, a Canadian by birth, for the seventh time, on September 2. That was the final time the two men would face each other in the ring. McAuliffe fought 39 professional bouts from April 18, 1921, to August 19, 1930. He finished up his ring career with a wildly average 17–16–6 record, but it was an interesting if not memorable one. Jack fought in the United States and Canada from coast to coast, in a great many famous venues (Madison Square Garden, Yankee Stadium, Boyles 30-Acres, Chicago Stadium), and against several notable fighters. In addition to Primo, Jack fought Luis Angel Firpo for the right to meet Jack Dempsey for the heavyweight crown, as well as Jack Gross, K.O. Christner, Battling Levinsky, and Pierre Charles twice. Suffice it to say, he had great memories and terrific stories to tell for the remainder of his life.

* * *

Primo's management agreed to have their fighter meet Boston's Pat McCarthy on September 8 at the Newark Velodrome. Thirteen thousand fans filled the Velodrome for a five-fight card that featured all heavyweight action.

In the semifinal, highly touted local fighter "Cowboy" Frank Willis beat up on periodic pugilist Borack Czirolnik. Willis grew arm weary from his continual assault before referee Hymie Kugel brought an end to the slaughter in the fifth round. The two had met a month earlier and fought to an eight-round decision in favor of Willis. Before that, there is no record of Czirolnik fighting even a round since his professional debut in 1922 when he lost by knockout to Otto Flint in his native Prague.[108] Including the defeat of Czirolnik, Willis, who owned an 18–5–0 record, was about to step up into the ranks of stiffer competition.

In his next fight — the very next day — he was kayoed in the first round by a young Jersey Joe Walcott in the latter's first professional bout. He didn't know what hit him and he never recovered. Over the next three years, Willis posted a 1–13–2 record, his only victory coming against a winless novice named Frankie Buzzoni. Each of the other bouts on the September 8 undercard resulted in early-round knockouts.[109]

In the main event, a scheduled 10-rounder, the story was much the same. The 214-pound McCarthy held a respectable 45–28–6 record going into the fight, but was clearly on his way down after a 15-year career. McCarthy had dropped his last two fights on points and, frankly, had posted a miserable record going back to 1927. Exploiting his opponent's weaknesses, Carnera "flattened Pat McCarthy of Boston after one minute and 16 seconds of fighting in the second round."[110]

After an uneventful first round, Carnera began to take charge. Early in the second, Primo, locked in a clinch with his opponent, clipped McCarthy on the jaw with a short but powerful right uppercut that dropped the Bostonian to the mat. McCarthy jumped up immediately, but visited the canvas again just moments later courtesy of a sweeping Carnera right to the head. Taking a count of nine from referee Hank Lewis, McCarthy gamely rose again. This time he walked directly into another powerful Carnera right that glanced off his shoulder and into his jaw, decking McCarthy for the final time. "The finish came after 1:16 of the second round and found McCarthy counted out after he had fallen flat on his back under a right to the jaw and had rolled over to pillow his head on his folded right arm. Referee Hank Lewis counted the prostrate Bostonian out amid the frantic 'vivas' of Carnera's superlatively thrilled countrymen."[111]

* * *

In his next fight Primo squared off against Jack Gross at the Chicago Stadium on September 17. Ten thousand fans paid a total of roughly $35,000 to watch a four-fight card. Each of the preliminaries went the distance, but the main event ended in four rounds. Gross, a 25-year-old southpaw, was a respectable fighter who had been ranked ninth in the heavyweight division by *The Ring* magazine in May 1929. The Philadelphian was a solid fighter who claimed the mythical "Jewish championship," but despite his 45–3–1 record, Gross had fought mostly moderate competition. In his few contests against top-notch talent he had been decisioned by Tommy Loughran in 1928 and TKO'ed in the fifth round by George Godfrey in Philadelphia the previous March.

This fight had a quick ending, with Gross on the losing end of a fourth-round knockout. "The fight ended amid a chorus of boos and jeers with Gross groggy, bleeding and on the floor. Gross was twice felled with heavy right hand blows to the head."[112] After being felled for the second time, Jack was counted out. It was Primo's 24th win of the year and the 23rd by way of knockout.

This was originally announced as Primo's last American bout before he would be sailing for Italy on October 11. That would change as an opportunity to square off with Boston heavyweight Jimmy Maloney was scheduled for early October.

* * *

On September 16, the National Boxing Association leadership, meeting in Omaha, Nebraska, passed a resolution trying to consolidate their control over boxing in every state. The resolution, sponsored by the association's former president Stanley Isaacs, provided for the suspension of fighters participating in contests held in states other than those affiliated with that organization.[113] Much of their angst was a direct result of not being able to control fighters in certain states (i.e., Carnera in Michigan and Pennsylvania, Godfrey in Ohio, or Rioux in Massachusetts). This resolution was still just as dependent upon the various state bodies supporting it as before, but the boxing association officials were trying to grab at mythical power.

* * *

On October 7 Primo met Jimmy Maloney in Boston for a scheduled 10-round affair. Carnera outweighed Maloney by 65 pounds, but again the competition had improved. Maloney entered the fight with 44 wins under his belt against 10 losses and 2 draws. He was admittedly a shade past his best days, but he was still a formidable opponent. As recently as 1928, Maloney had been a top ten–ranked contender and had experienced the carnage of 56 professional heavyweight bouts.

Twelve thousand fans packed the Boston Garden to root on local favorite Maloney. They got their money's worth. The four-fight undercard was busy and full of action. Two knockouts and two six-round decisions kept the crowd interested and often on their feet. The main event did not disappoint either. The Associated Press called the fight "a wild and furious 10-round bout."[114]

Carnera took the fight to Maloney in the first two rounds, savagely battering his opponent with a vicious flurry of shots to the head. According to the Associated Press, "Carnera spent most of the ten rounds clubbing Maloney's head and body with short blows in the clinches."[115]

Maloney fought Carnera on even terms in the third and took the middle rounds, landing 192 punches to 195 for Primo.

Primo came back in the ninth and tenth, but he had lost the middle five rounds and without a knockout, he stood no chance of winning. But he couldn't manage to land the devastating blow to finish Maloney. Primo suffered his first American loss in 23 bouts. The closest either fighter came to hitting the canvas in the entire affair was late in the bout when Maloney fell against the ropes after missing on a wild, roundhouse right. It was one of the last high points Maloney would know in the ring.

Earlier in the year Maloney had split a pair with California heavyweight Armand Emanuel. Maloney won the first fight, in Boston, by knocking out Emanuel in the second round. Maloney lost the return match in Los Angeles on points in ten. It was the beginning of his end. While he could still be dangerous, he was never again the same fighter. After coming back to outpoint Carnera in ten, Maloney would lose 9 of his last 13 fights and finally leave the ring for good in 1934.

In a classic case of biased journalism, one uncredited Associated Press reporter wrote that Primo showed little in a "Furious Bout"—I'm not sure how that is possible. A one-sided, furious fight would be a massacre, which this fight clearly was not. Logically, therefore it was a two-sided "Furious Bout" and Carnera, by default, had to be busy and must have shown something. He also wrote, "The Boston battler also proved that Carnera was easy to hit. Maloney scored 192 times to the head or body of his huge opponent and 90 per cent of them landed cleanly."[116] He did mention earlier in the piece that Primo landed three more blows than Maloney, but could only say that the punches were not powerful enough to drop his opponent. What he did not mention was that in 192 punches, Maloney never came close to putting Primo down either. No one would disagree that Primo was a fairly easy target. He was massive and did not have the world's best defense, but he proved again in the first Maloney fight that he was tough and wouldn't go down.

Carnera had fought a decent fight, but had still lost for the first time in America. He was anxious to go home to Europe after almost a year in the States and now seemed the appropriate time to do so. See was equally anxious to kick the dust of America and Owney Madden's thugs off his shoes. After the Maloney fight, Primo fought a series of exhibitions in Connecticut and New York before he and See finally returned to the refuge of Europe to map their next steps. See booked passage on the liner *Conte Grande* bound for Naples and Genoa.

In Naples, Primo disembarked long enough to be greeted by over 100 fans, photographers and reporters. After granting a brief press conference, Carnera and See returned to the ship and sailed for Genoa. As the ship docked the next day, a large crowd gathered, waiting for a chance to greet the fighter. Waiting at the bottom of the bridgeway was Giovanna Carnera, Primo's mother, who was anxious to see her son after a year's absence in America. Primo told the excited crowd that by June 15, 1931, there would be an Italian heavyweight champion of the world.

Immediately upon arrival, See set to work arranging a schedule of several exhibitions throughout Italy. While Primo made short work of his exhibition opponents, See looked to set up some sanctioned bouts. When a contest was arranged against Paolino Uzcudun in Barcelona, See cancelled an exhibition in Florence, leaving the promoters of that bout high and dry. When the promoters appealed to the Italian pugilistic federation for recompense, the commissioners listened intently and took the matter seriously. On January 6, 1931, the federation levied a fine of 22,000 lire ($1,200 U.S.D) against Carnera for breaking his contract with the Florence promoters. They also forbade Primo from fighting in all International Boxing Union countries until the fine was paid and warned Leon See not to treat a breach of signed contract so lightly again.[117]

It was apparently a bad day for fighters and commission rulings. This was the same day that the New York State Athletic Commission withdrew recognition of Max Schmeling and Mickey Walker as titleholders in their divisions for their refusals to accept fights with Jack Sharkey and Tommy Freeman, respectively.

* * *

The fight with Uzcudun was scheduled for November 23 at Montjuiche Stadium in Barcelona, Spain. The 207-pound Basque woodchopper was another legitimate contender with a 41–9–2 record and he spent four years in *The Ring*'s ratings of top 10 heavyweights.

On November 20, the provincial governor in Barcelona ordered a postponement of the bout due to political strife and severe strike conditions. Civil unrest was common in Spain in the autumn of 1930. The effects of the worldwide depression, anarchists, and a heavily devalued peseta were contributing mightily to the discreditation and unpopularity of the monarchy of King Alfonso XIII. The unpopular king's attempt to rule Spain through the appointment of strong-armed dictators was failing miserably. By February 1931, Alfonso would announce the restoration of the constitution and schedule limited local elections. Those "limited local elections" would quickly turn into a national debate on the direction of the country culminating in the 43-year-old king exiling himself to Italy and the Spanish

Republic being proclaimed on April 14.[118] In light of the civil unrest, the match was rescheduled for the following Sunday — November 30th.

During this time of extreme nationalism, the fight was not terribly popular with many Spaniards due to it being promoted by a foreigner, Jeff Dickson. Dickson, ever the showman, sought to strike at the heart of Spanish national pride by promoting a bullfight as well. To show his interest in the sport as well as his intrepid nature, Dickson himself entered the bullfight ring as the matador. His promotion obviously worked to eliminate any real opposition to his boxing card. It is estimated that between 75,000 and 90,000 fans jammed the huge bowl-like Montjuiche Stadium, setting a new record for a professional fight in Spain. The flags of many nations ringed the picturesque stadium. Given the recent civil unrest, tighter than usual security was evident. More than 1,000 armed troops occupied seats in the center of the stadium, while others were positioned strategically around the bowl.

After watching British welterweight Jack Kirby knockout local favorite Jose Girones and Spanish bantamweight champion Carlos Flix outpoint a Londoner named George Joseph Stockings — better known as Kid Socks — the main event was on.

As Primo entered the ring wearing his customary bright green robe, the Spanish crowd was struck by his enormity. They were used to the good-sized Uzcudun, but the large Basque was even dwarfed by Carnera.

Primo was handicapped by having to wear regulation-sized gloves, instead of his usual custom-fit gloves made especially to fit his enormous hands. The local boxing commission had custom gloves made for Primo, but in trying them on shortly before the fight, they fit so poorly that he almost refused to enter the ring. Primo agreed to fight wearing the smaller regulation-sized gloves, but they were quite small. "The Italian's hands stretched the regulation gloves so much that it made the padding ineffective."[119]

Primo's ability to make a tight fist was affected, but in spite of this, he rained thunder on Uzcudun. "It was just as well for Paolino that the gloves did not fit his opponent for his attempts to rip into Primo's mid-section were met by battering lefts and rights to the head that were powerful and damaging despite the ill-fitting gloves."[120]

The Associated Press stated, "Carnera, with his long arms and tremendous height, controlled the pace in practically every round. Only at intervals could Paolino duck in close where he does his most effective work. Most of the time, Carnera kept him off with jolting rights and lefts."[121]

While the huge facility brought in a tremendous crowd, it also presented a challenge for many to see the true fight. Fans who were sitting far back in the huge bowl and could barely see the fighters clearly generally believed that Uzcudun was winning the fight for the way he was carrying the fight, although ineffectually, to Carnera's body. "Those at ringside, however, could see that Carnera was brushing aside some of Paolino's punches and taking the others on his gloves. Meanwhile, Carnera's terrific lefts and only slightly less effective rights punished the Basque throughout all of the ten rounds."[122]

Knowing he was behind on points, Uzcudun made a valiant and desperate effort in the tenth round to turn the fight, but it was too little too late as Carnera again won that chapter.

The Associated Press scored the fight for Carnera with Primo taking the first, second, seventh, eighth, ninth, and tenth rounds; Paolino the fourth, fifth, and sixth; and round three even.[123] Neither fighter was badly marked at the end of the fight although Uzcudun had some bleeding from his nose and mouth. "Two judges disagreed after ten rounds of close battling and they stuck to their opinions Monday (the day after the fight). The Spanish judge, Casanovas, said that he believed Paolino should have been given the decision by a very slight margin, while the Italian judge Maggia, gave his opinion not only that Carnera had won, but that he should be matched with Young Stribling, Jack Sharkey, and Max Schmeling as foremost contender for the world's heavyweight championship."[124] English referee M. Moss Deyong broke the judges' tie and raised Primo's glove. Afterwards the 52-year-old arbiter said, "Uzcudun put up a good fight, but he was meeting the future world's champion in my opinion. Carnera's improvement was surprising."[125]

The United Press reported, "Although Carnera, in the eyes of most of the experts, won no less than eight of the ten rounds, Barcelona fans stoutly maintained that the Basque deserved at least a draw. The fight, which was held in the Montjuiche Stadium, was attended by 75,000 persons, the largest crowd ever to witness a sporting event in Spain. Paolino blamed the referee for his loss."[126]

Throughout Italy, a buzz of pride and enthusiasm filled the air as the greatly improved Carnera took on Uzcudun, another serious and talented fighter. In Rome, thousands of people stood outside newspaper offices where round-by-round updates were given as the fight progressed. At stadiums throughout Italy, updates were given at halftime of soccer matches. People were excited as one of their own countrymen was making a run at the big time.

*　*　*

Primo finished off 1930 with one more sanctioned fight. Traveling back to London, for his first fight in England in a year, he met 6'1", 203-pound British heavyweight Reggie Meen on December 18 at the Royal Albert Hall. Carnera, the heavy favorite, was in his usual dark trunks and Meen in white trunks with black trim. Meen was a competitive fighter who had a 26–12–2 record. He would later hold the British Heavyweight championship. While Primo was heavily favored, Reggie Meen was not a fighter to be overlooked.

A crowd of 10,000 saw a ten-fight card that featured nothing but heavyweights. The main event was the draw, however, and Primo was cheered wildly as he made a triumphant return to a city in which he had fought frequently during his earliest days in the ring. The attendance helped prove that Primo was truly one of the great fistic attractions of the era. When Primo entered the ring, he played up his size in front of Meen. Instead of climbing through the ropes as is normal, he stepped over the top rung. "From the moment the two heavyweights shook hands it was obvious to every one of the 10,000 spectators that Meen never had a chance against his more skillful opponent who towered over him."[127] But Meen was game to make it a fight.

At the opening bell, Meen pursued Carnera and landed a good left to the head. An irritated Primo responded by raining heavy blows upon his rival. Completely in control, Carnera bullied Meen around the ring for the remainder of the round, staggering his opponent with a crashing right hook that eventually dropped Reggie to one knee as the bell sounded the end of the first.

The second round was all Carnera. Backing his opponent against the ropes, Primo hit Reggie with a punishing series of blows to the head and body that when watched, even eight decades later, would still serve as a primer for any young fighter. The series started with a left jab followed by a hard overhand right, a punishing left uppercut, and another crushing overhand right. Primo then reached way down and launched a powerful uppercut. The punch caught Meen flush on the jaw, stood him straight up, and jolted his head back violently. Primo finished out the series with a roundhouse right that might have started some-

Primo Carnera stands with his manager Leon See (left) and promoter Jeff Dickson at London's Savoy hotel after his arrival in England in December 1930 for his upcoming fight with Reggie Meen. (Popperfoto/Getty Images)

where in Wales. That rocket jarred Meen's head sideways and grotesquely contorted the Briton's face. Primo then landed another hard left to Reggie's face and with that, Meen finally wilted to the bottom rope where he sat trying to gather himself.

Meen gamely rose at the count of nine, but was in serious trouble. His heart was willing, but after the second knockdown of the night, the fight was virtually over. Referee

Moss Deyong knew he had to stop it immediately, "to save the plucky young Desborough shoemaker from being beaten to a pulp."[128] "It was an intervention prompted by a sense of mercy for the Englishman who was hopelessly outclassed from the start. The four and a half minutes that he lasted against Primo were long enough to send him staggering from the ring with a badly beaten body and a sadly lacerated face."[129]

The Associated Press reported of the fight, "Carnera toyed with Meen for one round in Albert Hall last night and then settled down to the business in hand. Early in the second round he floored the Briton, but Reggie got up. Another powerful blow sent him to the canvas again and the referee mercifully stepped in and halted the bout."[130]

The wire service correspondents noted that Meen "went back to a north of England shoe factory today a sadder and wiser heavyweight. Reggie thought he could whip Primo Carnera, the Italian man-mountain, and discovered he was mistaken."[131] Reggie Meen continued to fight throughout the United Kingdom through 1938. He finished his 11-year career with a record of 57–44–3.

Between Christmas and New Year's, Carnera and his entourage traveled to the north of Europe, where Primo would spar 10 more exhibitions in Sweden, Denmark, and Norway with as many as four bouts in a single day.

These exhibitions, along with the Meen fight, put a wrap on what had been a long and turbulent but successful year in the ring for Primo. He had gotten a lot of exposure in both Europe and the United States—though not all of it good. But exposure is exposure and people throughout the world knew his name. He was a very marketable commodity whom people would pay to see. But most importantly, he had a built strong record and he had gained valuable ring experience. It was now home to Sequals for a family Christmas and some much needed rest and relaxation.

4

The Battle of the Cracked Rib and Other Tales, 1931

Some of 1930's headaches carried over into 1931. On January 31, General John V. Clinnin, president of the National Boxing Association, announced the suspension of Carnera in support of the Pugilistica Italiana and the International Boxing Union. The action was tied to the Italian body's January 6 suspension and $1,200 fine for breach of contract regarding the exhibition bout scheduled for Florence, Italy, the previous November. Clinnin went on to say that Carnera would be reinstated when the Italian commission was satisfied that the fine had been paid in full.[1]

After taking a couple of months off and relaxing in Sequals with family and friends, Primo returned to the United States to prepare for a ten-round rematch with Jimmy Maloney in Miami on March 5.

Carnera and his entourage were confident that with Maloney out of Boston, he was especially vulnerable. They agreed with John Kieran, who stated, "Maloney thrives and flourishes in the home town ring, but is not nearly so dangerous or destructive when waylaid and assaulted in distant territory."[2] Carnera's camp assured all who would listen that October's points decision would be reversed. "Last autumn with the aid of a hometown referee Maloney took a decision from Carnera in Boston. Carnera had to even the score if he was to get anything out of his proposed match with the winner of next summer's W. L. Stribling–Max Schmeling bout."[3] For his part Maloney just smiled and said modestly, "I licked him once. I'll do it again."[4]

Primo's legal and financial challenges were beginning to appear. The day before the fight Primo and managers See and Duffy were named in a lawsuit filed by fight promoter George A. Biener of Fort Wayne, Indiana. Biener was seeking $6,000 in damages alleging that Carnera failed to show up for a fight the previous June 9 in Fort Wayne.

On March 5, however, it was all boxing. The Thursday night crowd was anxious to see if Maloney could replicate his victory from October, or if Primo, after solid victories against Uzcudun and Meen, was back on track.

A week before the fight, it was announced that Carnera had broken a rib during training. Speculation arose that the fight would be postponed or even cancelled, but Primo put an end to the rumors by stating unequivocally that he would climb through the ropes to meet Maloney at the appointed hour. The fight was still on and it was one that many fight fans wanted to see, but unseasonably cool weather that threatened frost in the Everglades did little to help the already slow advance ticket sales. The chilly weather helped fuel fears that promoter Frank J. Bruen would lose money and added to the nagging postponement speculation.

4. The Battle of the Cracked Rib and Other Tales, 1931

The cold weather worked to keep the crowd down at the outdoor venue. Roughly 20,000 showed up, filling Madison Square Garden Stadium to less than half capacity. The smallish crowd was a bit surprising as six bouts were scheduled, three of them featuring notable fighters—a preliminary with light heavyweight champion Maxie Rosenbloom, who outpointed Marty Gallagher in eight; Carnera and Maloney in the main event; and then Jimmy Braddock knocking out Jack Roper in a walkout bout after the Carnera–Maloney affair.

Primo was the first of the combatants to climb into the ring at just before 10:00 P.M. In an attempt to protect his damaged ribs, Primo's right side was heavily taped for several inches above the waistband of his trunks. "He was shouting to an Italian compatriot when Maloney slipped over from the far corner and grasped his hand by way of welcome. Primo jumped up very politely and bowed deeply with a huge smile."[5] "Primo sat down on his stool while various brisk little men fussed around him. One of the men was a doctor, for Carnera was supposed to have cracked one of his lower right ribs in training. The doctor had authority to stop the fight at any time if the patient felt badly."[6]

Prior to the fight, there had been a disagreement as to which gloves Primo would wear. The pair provided by the Florida Boxing Commission was too small and Maloney's manager Dan Carroll immediately rejected the pair produced by Primo's managers. Eventually, the Commission produced a third pair that all agreed upon.[7]

As the main event began, Carnera went on the offensive, carrying the fight to Maloney through the early rounds. The Vast Venetian forged ahead, throwing ponderous punches and putting Maloney into a defensive retreat. In Primo's corner Leon See continually chattered at his protégé in French to throw his left jab and keep Maloney on the defensive.

Throughout the fight, Primo heeded See's advice and used his left jab regularly and effectively to keep Maloney at bay. Those strong lefts staggered his opponent in the first, second, eighth, and tenth rounds. Primo used his right hand sparingly, but he did hurt Maloney with a couple of hard rights to the head in the first round. Despite the effectiveness of his left, the Associated Press stated, "Primo showed no inclination or ability to use his right at all, except as a blocking instrument. For the most part he was out footed, out boxed, and out cuffed, especially in the latter part of the fight."[8] Given that Primo's broken rib was on his right side, it's fairly obvious that his hesitance to throw his right was a tactic to protect the injury. It's also difficult to breathe deeply with a cracked rib. Anyone who has suffered that injury, an asthma attack, or any other serious respiratory ailment would vouch for the fact that exertion when breathing is difficult, is laborious. With this injury, it's amazing that Carnera stepped into the ring at all on that cool, early March, Miami night.

In the end, it was a close fight on points and "The Battle of the Cracked Rib" ended with a split decision. The Associated Press reported, "Referee Elmer (Slim) McClelland of Detroit showed no hesitation in lifting Carnera's glove in token of victory, basing his decision on Primo's aggressiveness and more effective punching when the blows connected."[9] While each fighter slipped during the contest, there was no clean knockdown on either side. Maloney, however, was the worse for wear at the final bell with a face full of bumps and bruises.

Many in the crowd booed lustily for as much as 15 minutes after the announcement of Carnera's victory was made. Why, no one is quite sure. In the opinion of sportswriter John Kieran, "There was no great complaint about the justice of the decision; the spectators were simply disapproving of the contest as a whole. It was not a spirited battle nor an exhibition of boxing as an art."[10] The press corps was split, with some journalists giving the contest to each fighter. The Associated Press scoresheet gave Maloney five rounds, Carnera three, with two rounds even, but according to their own article, "The majority of the critics agreed with the official verdict."[11]

In a walkout bout, future heavyweight champion Jim Braddock flattened Californian Jack Roper with a short right cross at just 1:08 of the first round. The "Cinderella Man" was angry about having to fight after the main event and apparently decided to "walk out" of the stadium with the crowd and therefore made short work of his opponent. Roper had a 16-year career in the ring during most of which he supplemented his boxing income with bit parts in movies. He continued his acting throughout the 1950s and appeared in 79 films playing mostly fighters, thugs, and sidekicks.

Despite a strong fight card, promoter Frank J. Bruen did indeed lose money on the event. With fewer than 10,000 paid admissions at the Garden Stadium, the gross gate receipts totaled just $53,115.89. Bruen estimated that he would need to take in between $75,000 and $100,000 just to break even.

* * *

On April 1 the Pugilistica Italiana (Italian Boxing Federation) levied a further fine of 500 lire ($260) against Carnera for participating in the Maloney fight without paying the $1,200 Florence breach of contract fine as well as for ignoring its ban on his fighting before the fine was paid. The Federation announced its intention of levying an additional 500 lire fine each time he fought without its sanction.

As a show of the often conflicting, confusing, and self-serving nature of the various state, national, and international sanctioning bodies, James A. Farley, chairman of the New York State Athletic Commission, announced on April 17 that Carnera's license had been reinstated in that state. He had been under suspension in New York since the fallout from the "Bombo" Chevalier fight in California the previous April. This action opened the way for a rumored June 10 fight with Jack Sharkey. Bob Edgren of the California Athletic Commission declared, however, that despite New York's forgiveness, Primo's suspension was still in effect in the Golden State. The Italian Federation, supported by the International Boxing Union, was still awaiting payment on its fine and continued to uphold Carnera's suspension as well.

Just 10 days later, Carnera and Sharkey met at a luncheon at the Biltmore Hotel to sign a contract for a June 10 bout that the New York State Athletic Commission was ready to recognize as being for the world heavyweight championship. The boxing governing board had dethroned Max Schmeling in January due to the German's unwillingness to meet Sharkey. The fight, scheduled for Brooklyn's Ebbets Field, would shape up into a legal struggle between promoters Jimmy Johnston, Humbert J. Fugazy, and the Madison Square Garden Corporation and its Illinois subsidiary.

At the same time that Schmeling signed to fight Young Stribling in a Garden-sponsored bout in Cleveland on July 3, Carnera was signing a contract to fight the winner of that contest. The contract to fight the Schmeling–Stribling winner also had a clause that prohibited Primo from fighting Sharkey in the meantime. Shortly after the Sharkey–Carnera signing at the Biltmore, William V. Saxe, the president of the Madison Square Garden Corporation, stated that Carnera was contractually obligated to the Garden and could not therefore proceed with the scheduled June 10 fight with Sharkey. If the fight planning continued, Saxe said, "We are prepared vigorously to prosecute a suit for an injunction and damages."[12]

Johnston, See, and Duffy argued on the other side, stating that since Primo signed the

4. The Battle of the Cracked Rib and Other Tales, 1931

Garden's contract in New York while he was under suspension by the state athletic commission, the contract was void. Johnston intentionally had Carnera and Sharkey hold off on signing their contract until after Primo was reinstated by NYSAC, to avoid any questions regarding contractual legitimacy. On May 1, the commission determined to let the June 10 fight continue and also chose to recognize the bout as a world championship contest.

In the end, the fight date was postponed from June to October, making all of the saber rattling from the parties involved pointless. Since Carnera was already preparing for a mid-June bout, his management team determined to set up a contest. They found a willing opponent in "Irish" Pat Redmond.

* * *

Since Ebbets Field in Brooklyn was already booked for the Sharkey–Carnera fight on June 10, the bout with Redmond was planned for that date with Redmond simply taking Sharkey's place. The 6'3", 245-pound Irish fighter brought Carnera-like size and a 25–6–0 record into the event, but only a modicum of respect. Redmond's opponents had gotten better since his arrival from Australia and he was beginning to show that he could hold his own with more creditable fighters. Even so, Primo was the prohibitive favorite to drop his opponent in the early rounds. The fight was, however, a bit of a calculated risk for Primo, who was still under contract to meet the winner of the Max Schmeling–Young Stribling battle. While he was no longer at any risk for being held in violation of his Madison Square Garden contract, by fighting at all he risked his spot on the Schmeling–Stribling card. Tommy Loughran would replace him on the card if he were somehow to lose the Redmond fight.

Redmond was born Dick McRedmond in Curragh, County Cork, Ireland, in 1906, into a longtime farming family. Always athletic, Redmond excelled at the Irish sport of curling while in school. He emigrated to Australia in 1925 and settled first in Melbourne and then in Sydney. There he learned to box and had his first professional bout in 1927. He fought in Australia with some success through the summer of 1930 when he sailed for America with dreams of taking the heavyweight crown.[13] His time in America started well as he made his way to New York and rolled to five straight victories, but as the competition began to improve, the good times started to come to an end. On March 7, 1931, he met Ernst Guhring at the Ridgewood Grove Sporting Club in Brooklyn. While Redmond fought well, Guhring won on points in 10 rounds. He proceeded to win three of his next four fights, losing only on points to wily veteran Jack Renault in April 1931. Redmond had proven himself to be a good fighter and Carnera and his managers knew that Primo needed to be careful in the ring that night.

The Ebbets Field event, originally scheduled for Wednesday June 10, was delayed due to rain to the following Monday evening. The delay didn't help the situation much as the 15th also brought stormy weather to the New York area, but rain or no rain, the fights needed to go on. Pressure to get the fights in that evening was strong with the hometown Dodgers returning to Brooklyn to play the Chicago Cubs on the 18th in the opening game of a long home stand. The delay also put the Ebbets Field event up against a seven-card event being held indoors at Madison Square Garden that same evening with admittedly lesser names, but a warm and dry environment.

Despite a light rain falling off and on that evening and the threat of stronger showers lingering on the horizon, 25,000 spectators paid the price of admission. "Late-comers, delaying their plans for attendance until the last minute because of threatening, overcast skies, stormed the box office in long, unwieldy lines which gave mounted police and patrolmen a difficult time."[14] Notable celebrities in the crowd that evening included Gene Tunney, Floyd Gibbons, Sam Pryor, and mayors Jimmy Walker and Frank Hague of New York City and Jersey City, respectively.

The undercard featured three other heavyweight bouts with notable fighters. Ted Sandwina would face Tom Kirby; Harold Mays and Canadian Jack Renault were up next; and the main event was followed by a scheduled 10-round battle between heavyweights Ernie Schaaf and Jack Gagnon. Both the Sandwina–Kirby and the Mays–Renault bouts were scheduled for 10 rounds as well but were shortened to eight and six, respectively, probably due to the wet weather.

Neither Carnera nor Schaaf apparently wanted much to do with the life aquatic, as both fighters wasted little time in vanquishing their foes in the first round. Ernie, in a walk out bout, displayed strong punching power, finishing Gagnon off in just 46 seconds of the opening stave. In the main event, Primo took just a bit longer than Schaaf would, but he achieved the same result, sending Redmond to the resin twice in 2:24 of fighting. In the first half-minute of the match, Primo dropped his opponent with a clean right to the jaw. Taking full advantage of the count to gather himself, Redmond rose at the count of eight after the first knockdown. He wasn't so lucky the next time. At the 2:10 mark, Primo caught the Irishman with a looping left hook, square under the chin. Redmond crumpled to the canvas and was counted out by referee Billy "the Kid" McPartland. "Redmond rolled over on his back to take the count and when the fatal ten seconds had been tolled, he remained in a reclining position, until he was assisted to his corner, where he was quickly revived."[15] Primo was on his way back to his dressing room before Redmond's seconds were able to bring him around.

Primo was on the offensive — almost recklessly so — throughout the brief encounter, throwing and landing multiple punches against his opponent. Redmond, on the other hand, landed no more than a half-dozen blows, none of which registered significantly with Carnera. In an amusing comment, the *New York Herald Tribune* wrote, "Had Redmond weathered the first round he would undoubtedly have beaten Carnera."[16] Based upon the other ringside reports, Primo thrashed Irish Pat for two full minutes, so it is not clear how the fight would have suddenly turned in the second. The comment is therefore a bit like saying, "If he hadn't died, he'd still be alive," or "If the other runner hadn't run faster than me, I'd have won the race." After losing his next three bouts, to Carnera, Eddie Benson, and Guhring again in a rematch, Redmond dropped out of sight and stopped fighting, finishing up with a respectable record of 25–9–0. Redmond was always a good fighter whom an opponent dared not take for granted. He was a big and strong man with occasional flashes of power, but like so many hopefuls, he could never quite break through to the top.

* * *

Primo traveled upstate for his next fight, against Umberto Torriani at the Broadway Auditorium in Buffalo on June 26. After 12 months of relatively tough opponents, this fight once again pitted Carnera against a fair-sized hack. Torriani had an anemic 1–11–2 record. He had lost 10 of his first 11 fights, managing only a draw to break the string of losses. He won number 12, but promptly drew and lost his next two fights, respectively.

After a five-fight undercard, Carnera wasted little time in handing Torriani his twelfth loss. He was flattened by Carnera just 43 seconds into round two. The Associated Press reported, "That the bout went into the second round apparently was due to the desire of Carnera to give the crowd something of a show."[17] Torriani went down twice in the first round and was groggy and rubbery-legged when Primo finished him in the second with a short, right uppercut that caught Torriani on the chin.

Torriani finally had enough of the prize ring after being knocked out in the sixth round on October 23, 1932, in Lucca, Italy, by Roberto Roberti. He retired after that fight with a professional record of 1–14–2.

* * *

The next day Primo and his entourage left Buffalo and traveled the short distance across the Canadian border and around Lake Ontario to Toronto. There, 6', 223-pound Bud Gorman waited for a chance to square off with the big Venetian carpenter at the Arena Gardens on June 30. Gorman was born Earl M. Lovejoy in Chicago in 1897. His fighting career began in 1915 just short of his 18th birthday when he scored a third-round TKO over Billy Fraser in Oshkosh, Wisconsin. Sixteen years later, the now 34-year-old Gorman had not fought in 10 months and was carrying an extra 20 pounds over his usual fighting weight. Needless to say, Primo was the prohibitive favorite.

After four preliminary bouts, each of which went their scheduled distance, the mainliners climbed through the ropes. The sizable Gorman now lived in Kenosha, Wisconsin, and had won his share of fights, posting a 48–17–11 record. He would not win this one. The fight ended in just two rounds with referee Lou Marsh counting Gorman out towards the end of the second. According to the *New York Times*, "Gorman was down for two counts of nine and one of six before the finish came after two minutes and thirty-five seconds of the second round. A crowd of 5,000 gave Carnera an ovation after the battle."[18] It was Gorman's last recorded fight.

* * *

Heading back across the border, Carnera now made his way to Rochester, New York, and a date with 6' 4" Danish heavyweight Knute Hansen. The 27-year-old Dane was nearing the end of his professional fight career that had started in Milwaukee in 1922. A promising early career gave way — as do so many fighting careers — to frustration, as he stepped up to a better level of talent.

The mid-summer's night crowd of 5,000 saw two preliminaries that ended in sixth- and fourth-round knockouts, respectively. Each turned out to be considerably better fights than the headliner.

Rain postponed this event twice before Carnera and Hansen finally climbed through the ropes on July 24. And when the bout actually began, the rain had more resilience than Hansen. In 130 seconds of boxing, the big Dane visited the canvas four times. Primo was all over Hansen from the opening bell on, delivering a maelstrom of lefts and rights to the head and body. At the two-minute mark of the first round, Primo landed a sharp left to the body followed by a hard right to Hansen's jaw that finished him: "Knute landed face downward and rolled around several times while being counted out."[19]

Counting a December 1928 knockout loss to K.O. Christner in Cleveland, Hansen lost nine of his last 11 bouts. He would fight once more after the Carnera bout, but after dropping his last fight on points to Lucien Delleau in Paris in 1932, Hansen retired from the ring. On January 9, 1933, in his column "Today's Sport Parade," United Press writer Henry McLemore wrote, "Knute Hansen, once one of Boston's better trial horses, is now a Parisian painter, specializing in posies.... He quit the ring, he says, when he felt himself getting goofy.... Knute classes himself a 'neo-realist.'... Maybe he didn't quit soon enough."[20]

* * *

The storms once again seemed to be following Primo as he attempted to face off against Roberto Roberti at Dreamland Park in Newark, New Jersey. Rain postponed the fight from Monday to Tuesday night, August 4.

The weigh-in was held on Monday at the Newark City Hall, using the city's official scales. The weigh-in revealed that the scheduled 10-round battle would feature over 500 pounds of heavyweight. Primo tipped the scales at 274, and his fellow countryman Roberti at 234. The *New York Times* reported the following story that showed some of the raw power that Carnera possessed: "When Carnera weighed, photographers wanted the scales moved for better light and a half-dozen men tugged at the heavy machine only to discover that the base was nailed fast to the floor. With an exclamation of impatience, Carnera reached down with one hand, gripped an end of the machine and jerked it loose, nails and all, moving it to where the photographers wanted it."[21]

On Tuesday evening, 12,000 fans filled Dreamland Park. The night started out with five fights on the undercard, ending in four KOs and an eight-round decision as middleweight Al Rossi outpointed Lou Halper in the semifinal.

In the main event, Primo fought his way to an easy victory over Roberti, who boasted a 32–12–7 record going into the fight. The battle only lasted into the third stanza. Referee Gene Roman stopped the bout with 35 seconds remaining in the round and nothing remaining in Roberti's tank.

Roberti had fought a decent first round, reaching Primo several times with long-range shots. By the end of that round, however, Primo determined his strategy and took complete control of the fight. Midway through the second, Carnera dropped a tiring Roberti for the first time with a left-right combination to the head. Roberti climbed off the canvas, briefly rested on one knee, and rose as Roman counted off "seven," but walked right into another Carnera maelstrom that sent him to the lower rung of the ropes, for a count of six. Weakened, but refusing to quit, Roberti fought on, managing to land a left to Carnera's head just before the bell. "Roberti was rocky and bewildered as he limped to his corner."[22]

As the third round opened, Roberti caught Primo with a couple of lefts to the head, but Primo shook off the clouts and charged his opponent ferociously, landing a series of combinations that sent Roberti swooning for a third time, this time for a count of nine. Roberti was clearly in trouble now and Carnera smelled a knockout. The fourth knockdown came on a left to the jaw, but once again, Roberti was up at nine. Primo now decided to go to the body, and under the power of heavy, digging blows Roberti went down twice more. The sixth knockdown came with about 45 seconds remaining in the round. After being forced to retreat in an attempt to avoid the savage attack of Carnera, "Roberti reached the ropes, where he sank to the floor exhausted. He tried to rise, but the referee stepped in and stopped the bout, declaring Carnera the victor by a knockout."[23]

Anthony Marenghi described it this way: "There lurched Roberto Roberti towards the ropes, rosin on his trunks, blood smeared under his nose and spreading over onto his left cheek, showing up sharply under the white lights. He raised a feeble right hand as Primo Carnera stepped toward him, whereupon Referee Gene Roman strode between, threw an arm protectingly around Roberti's well-battered body and led him to his corner."[24]

4. The Battle of the Cracked Rib and Other Tales, 1931

* * *

On August 5, the Pennsylvania State Boxing Commission voted to conditionally reinstate George Godfrey, Primo Carnera, and their managers. They had all been suspended after Primo's disqualification victory over a year before. For reasons not explained, however, the commission reversed itself three weeks later and reinstituted the indefinite suspensions on all of the parties. In addition to Carnera and Godfrey, the commission's ruling made ineligible Leon See, Billy Duffy, Godfrey's manager Jimmy Dougherty, and all of the fighters in Dougherty's stable.[25]

* * *

On August 6, Carnera fought Armando De Carolis on a five-fight card at Shellpot Park in Wilmington, Delaware. Carnera, who had an 85-pound weight advantage over De Carolis, took it easy on his opponent early in the first round, but the massive Italian was eventually warned by referee Joe Denny to fight. He did, knocking De Carolis down as the bell tolled, ending the round. After the minutes' intermission, Primo wasted little time in dropping his opponent again and finishing De Carolis at 1:08 of the second.

De Carolis, a 187-pound Italian, had lost seven of his last eight fights before facing Primo, and he went on to lose his next three bouts after the Carnera contest. Those losses came from Steve Hamas, Don McCorkindale, and Arthur Huttick before Armando finally called it quits on his ring career. His loss to Huttick came on the undercard of Carnera's title defense over Paolino Uzcudun, in Rome in October 1933. He wound up with an 8–16–1 record.

* * *

On August 9, the International News Service reported that Carnera would meet Paolino Uzcudun again on September 3 at Yankee Stadium, with all proceeds benefiting the Bronx Cancer Hospital. The bout was still tentative, pending talks between New York Secretary of State Edward Flynn and William Carey of Madison Square Garden. Talks dragged on, stalled and eventually, a November 13 Madison Square Garden option was proposed. Ultimately, the talks fell through and the fight never came off.

* * *

Primo continued to garner interest in the media. He made the cover of *Time* magazine on Oct. 5, 1931, with the newsmagazine running a nice article on Carnera that was part biography, part look at the man, and part evaluation of his career and prospects. It was great publicity. Magazine covers and feature articles were not uncommon for Primo in the early to mid–1930s. In addition to *Time*, he was a regular in the pages of *Newsweek* and graced its cover several times.

* * *

Primo's next fight was the long-awaited 15-round meeting with Jack Sharkey, originally scheduled for June 10. Sharkey, who was born Josef Paul Zukauskas, left school in his early teens to work at a series of blue-collar jobs. He joined the navy and while serving, he talked his way onto a card for which he was paid $100 for four rounds. "I'd have fought the entire navy for a hundred dollars," said Sharkey.[26] He took the last name Sharkey from former sailor and heavyweight Tom Sharkey and turned professional in January 1924. A tribute to his time in the navy, Sharkey's nickname was the "Boston Gob," the term "Gob" meaning sailor.

Sharkey was a wildly talented fighter, possessing a short, vicious left jab and a deadly right, but he was also the king of inconsistency. While he had all of the physical ability in the world, the source of his inconsistency was to be found between his ears. New York State boxing commissioner William Muldoon described Jack this way: "Sharkey's the best fighter in the world—from the neck down."[27] When he was on his game, there was no stopping him, but from fight to fight, you never knew which Jack Sharkey was going to step into the ring. Some nights he might be fighting beautifully and suddenly lose his cool or pout over a foul or a disputed referee's call. Promoter Tex Ricard claimed that Sharkey was "the fastest heavyweight in the ring, with a left like a piston and a right straight and hard as a ramrod."[28]

Sharkey's head undoubtedly cost him an impressive win against Ritter's protégé Jack Dempsey, on July 21, 1927. Over the first six rounds, Sharkey was pounding the former champ with flurries of solid combinations that left Dempsey bewildered. Sharkey looked to be on his way to either a knockout or at least an easy decision. In the seventh round, a desperate Dempsey began digging shots to Sharkey's midsection and several were arguably low. Dempsey was getting a bit of a reaction from his opponent and decided to try a little gamesmanship by positioning himself between the referee and Sharkey. Now screening the view of the official, he punched Sharkey once on the leg and again just below the belt. He knew he'd get a reaction from his opponent. While Tunney and others had simply ignored this type of baiting from Dempsey, Sharkey reacted, as Dempsey knew he would — by standing up straight, dropping his guard, taking his eyes off Dempsey, and pleading with referee Jack O'Sullivan. Seeing his chance, the wily former champion sprung upon his opponent like a cat and knocked the unprepared Sharkey to the canvas for a count of ten. Sharkey later said, "I turned to the referee to complain I was getting hit low, and I got hit by a haymaker. That was that. I was out on the canvas."[29]

After getting the better of Max Schmeling for four rounds, Sharkey lost the heavyweight title to the German in 1930, on a fourth-round low blow. According to the *Baltimore Post*, "With but six seconds left to go in the fourth round of last night's spectacular fight in Yankee Stadium, Jack Sharkey, who had outclassed Schmeling in every way, whipped home a terrific left hook which landed below Max's belt."[30]

In his previous fight in July, Sharkey had fought former welterweight champion Mickey Walker to a disappointing 15-round draw. While standing only 5'7" and 170 pounds, Walker was a terrific fighter who regularly fought above his weight class and met a great deal of success in doing so. The New Jersey native established himself as a legitimate threat against much larger men. Walker's moderate size but great tenacity and courage earned him the sobriquet "The Toy Bulldog."

John Kieran wrote of Sharkey's temperament and amazing inconsistency: "He could have continued against Dempsey. Against Heeney and Risko he loafed himself out of a bout with Gene Tunney. He ruined bright chances for the title when he fouled Schmeling. He apparently removed himself from further serious consideration when he couldn't do any better than get a draw with Mickey Walker, a stylish-stout middleweight."[31]

The Carnera–Sharkey bout finally came about at Ebbets Field on October 12. After being delayed from its original June date, the fight was resurrected by Jimmy Johnston and the Dodger A.C. The new date was set for October 1st, but it was delayed again after Sharkey complained of swelling in his little finger. His physicians ordered X-rays, but they revealed no structural damage so the doctors determined that a few days' delay in the fight would right the wrong. *Time* magazine wrote the following: "Eight days before the fight, Sharkey inspected his left hand, discovered that his third and little fingers were slightly swollen at the knuckle. Convinced that such a hand was no fit instrument with which to assail the long lantern jaw of Primo Carnera, Sharkey called in four doctors to attest his injury, demanded a postponement. The postponement was first denied, then granted, to Oct. 12."[32] Many fight insiders, however, felt this to be an indication that Sharkey might be backing away from the Carnera fight.

Sharkey's apparent wavering hurt pre-fight wagering. Betting was also light for several other reasons. Following Sharkey's poor showing against Walker in July, many thought he was on his way down. Many were unsure that he could beat an improving Carnera. Others were uncertain of his resolve. And of course, there were the standard, seemingly obligatory rumors of a fix attempt.

Despite the delay and the questions about the fight, almost 30,000 patrons showed up at Ebbets Field on a chilly Monday night. While the crowd huddled in overcoats and blankets, they saw a well-fought bout which Sharkey clearly won, but in which Carnera definitely proved his mettle. Associated Press sports writer Herbert W. Barker spoke of it this way: "If this fight reinstated Sharkey to his position as a leading contender it served also to remove any lingering doubt as to Carnera's courage and stamina."[33]

The chilled patrons watched 21 rounds of undercard boxing with four of the five fights going their scheduled distance. When it came time for the main event, those present settled in for a war. They were not disappointed. Both fighters entered the ring bundled up against the cold. "Between rounds the ring men departed from custom by allowing their seconds to cover them with towels and robes before they sat down."[34]

Carnera fought extremely well through the first three and a half rounds. Barker reported that Primo "amazed Sharkey and the crowd with his speed and skillful boxing."[35] Carnera skillfully used his left jab to keep Sharkey off balance.

Midway through the fourth round, however, the fight changed rapidly. Carnera had been giving Sharkey a terrific beating in the clinches when the Bostonian, out of nowhere, launched a devastating left hook to the head that dropped Primo to the canvas like a rock. John Kieran recalled that when he hit the canvas, "The ring platform quaked and quivered under the terrific impact of that gross tonnage."[36] Kieran continued: "Doubtless the seismograph at Fordham University registered the shock on the revolving drum."[37]

Scrambling to his knees, Primo began pulling himself up on the ropes, as referee Ed "Gunboat" Smith reached the count of six. Carnera's corner had been exhorting him to stay down until the count of nine, to take full advantage of the break afforded by the count. As he stood, Primo finally heard his corner. He was on his feet briefly when he suddenly dropped again to one knee.

As soon as Carnera's knee hit the canvas, Sharkey ran across the ring screaming at Smith, "He went down without being hit, he's disqualified. Count him out."[38] Smith ignored Sharkey's pleas and, waving him aside, continued the count. Both Sharkey and Smith were right. New York State Athletic Commission rules at the time stated that if a fighter goes down, gets up, and then goes down again under his own power, the referee may use his judgment to either disqualify the fighter or resume the count. Rarely would a referee stop the fight if the combatant were still in shape to fight. At this point, Carnera was clearly able to continue, and when Smith hit nine, Primo hopped to his feet.

An incredulous Sharkey, after trying again, in vain, to change Smith's mind, ran across

Primo lands a left hook in his first bout with Jack Sharkey at Ebbets Field on October 12, 1931. The blow almost toppled Sharkey, but the Boston Gob kept his feet and went on to defeat Carnera on points in a hard-fought, fifteen round battle. (Bettmann/CORBIS)

the ring and began to climb through the ropes and out of the ring. His manager, Johnny Buckley, kept him from leaving by blocking his path and literally pushing Sharkey back into the ring. By this time, Primo was resting against the ropes, having received over 20 seconds to get his head back together. The extended rest period really didn't help, however. Primo was not the same for the rest of the fight.

Sharkey, with the exception of the 13th round, ruled the remaining action. He continually hammered away at Primo with sharp lefts to the head and body. In the 15th round, Sharkey hammered Carnera with left and right crosses that almost toppled the giant. At the end of 15 rounds, there was little disagreement as to the winner. Most observers were split over the first three rounds and scored the 13th even, but all of the others went to Sharkey. Smith and fight judges George Kelly and Charles Mathison were in agreement, giving Sharkey a unanimous decision. After the tabulation of the point totals, Smith returned to center ring and confidently raised Sharkey's hand.

Writing for the International News Service immediately after the fight, Carnera commented, "Though Sharkey staggered me a few times and hurt me often, I was never near a

4. The Battle of the Cracked Rib and Other Tales, 1931

knockout, I swear."[39] Any damage done to either fighter was no doubt assuaged by their take of the gate. It was a good night at the gate and each fighter pocketed around $27,000. Sadly, though, Primo undoubtedly saw little of the payout.

* * *

With the success of the Carnera–Sharkey fight, the Garden attempted to put together an all-heavyweight card for December 11, in its Manhattan arena. The event would be planned as the *New York American*'s annual Christmas Fund Benefit, and big names were being bandied about including Carnera, Sharkey, Mickey Walker, Tommy Loughran, and Ernie Schaaf. The press even reported once more on the rumors that Jack Dempsey would at last return to the ring to put an end to the mediocrity atop the heavyweight division. The event never occurred, so the Garden attempted instead to get Carnera into the ring with the 5'10" Basque heavyweight Paolino Uzcudun. The fight was proposed for November 13 at the Garden, but the New York State Athletic Commission refused to sanction the fight, due to the six-inch and 60-pound size disparity between the fighters. Speaking for the commission, William Muldoon denied Jimmy Johnston's plea that the fight be allowed. Johnston, not to be deterred, returned to his Garden office and conferred with Leon See and Andy Neidereiter to come up with a plan B. With Uzcudun out of the picture in New York, they instead scheduled Carnera for a late November bout with the equally massive Victorio Campolo.

* * *

On November 19 Primo was in the Windy City to square off with the old fishmonger, King Levinsky, at Chicago Stadium. Levinsky owned a record of 39–14–4 going into this fight and was ranked in *The Ring* magazine's Top Ten Heavyweights that year. He was, in fact, listed in *The Ring*'s Top 10 every year from 1931 through 1934, and was ranked as high as third in 1933. Even so, Carnera entered the fight as a 3-to-1 favorite over Chicago's fighting fish peddler.

Levinsky was a character who grew up on Chicago's west side as Harris Krakow. In 1930, the 20-year-old Harry took the nom-de-ring Kingfish Levinsky. The name was derived by combining the names of two of his favorite figures, the gravel-voiced "Kingfish" character from the *Amos and Andy* radio show and light heavyweight boxer Battling Levinsky. He was very popular in his hometown as he pieced together a strong record against mediocre competition during his first two years as a professional. But Levinsky made a real splash in the boxing world when he put the heavily favored Leo Lomski on the canvas five times in the first round and knocked him out in the fifth round of their bout in September 1930. The Kingfish was a wild and sloppy fighter who sometimes led with his face, but he brought to the ring a fast, furious and unorthodox style of attack that had made him a trial horse for up-and-coming heavyweights.

Levinsky's most potent weapon was a sweeping right that could devastate an opponent if it landed. It caught Tommy Loughran on the side of his head during the second round of their first meeting in 1930 and dropped him like a rock. Loughran recovered to take a ten-round decision. Tommy wasn't so fortunate 13 months later when Levinsky evened the score, taking a 10-round decision Fortunately for most opponents, the Kingfish usually telegraphed to everyone in the arena that the big right was on its way, giving even a mediocre fighter a chance to block it or step out of harm's way.

The Chicagoan was a popular draw for fight cards. "Kingfish Levinsky's earning power is due partly to an engaging slapstick manner in the ring, an engaging entourage which includes his sister Mrs. Lena ('Leaping Lena') Levy, famed for her loud voice and strong talk."[40] Lena received her nickname because it was said that she was continually up and down yelling instructions in her brother's corner.

The four-fight undercard on November 19 included Battling Battalino — the world's featherweight champion — and Bushy Graham of Utica, N.Y. The two had recently fought with Graham having won, but that bout, like this one, was a non–title fight, since weight limits were not being observed.

When the main bout began, Levinsky started off fighting very well over the first three rounds. The crowd was frenzied, sensing an upset, but from there on, it was all Carnera. Primo won the 10-round affair on a split decision, with referee Eddie Purdy and one fight judge calling the fight for the Italian. There were no knockdowns in the fight and while Levinsky fought admirably and landed many blows, none registered any damage on Carnera. Primo, too, did marginal damage with his punches, but he manhandled Levinsky throughout the fight. Primo leaned on his opponent in the clinches and mauled him with short hooks and uppercuts, registering enough points to take the victory.

After the fight, Carnera was tired, but ready to celebrate his victory. Instead of a night of celebration in Chicago, Primo and See were arrested after the fight, in connection with the $3,754 judgment filed against them by Indiana fight promoter George Biener on March 4. Biener was seeking damages, alleging that Carnera failed to show up for a fight the previous June 9 in Fort Wayne. Primo and See were soon released pending further review, but the officers in the Chicago precinct in which they were briefly detained had a great story to tell of their time spent cutting up with the Italian Giant.

* * *

Another Battle of the Behemoths was scheduled for November 27, between Carnera and an even taller Victorio Campolo, at Madison Square Garden in New York City. The card was a benefit for Jewish Philanthropic Societies charities with top tickets going for $15.

The 28-year-old Campolo, an Italian by birth, was now living in Argentina. Known as "El Gigante de Quilmes," Campolo had been a butcher in his father's meat shop in Argentina before becoming a professional boxer. Frenchman Gustavo Leneve, a mechanic in a Buenos Aires machine shop, became Campolo's manager. Campolo's reach was variably reported to be anywhere from 82 to 86 inches. While Victorio stood over two inches taller than Carnera, he was lighter by about 40 pounds. Campolo was 17–5–1 coming into this fight.

Campolo, considered by many to be a rising heavyweight star, was on the cover of the October 1931 edition of *The Ring* magazine, but his reputation had suffered badly after losing to both Tommy Loughran and Ernie Schaaf earlier in the year. He was looking to reestablish himself as a serious heavyweight contender.

On November 22, many Sunday papers carried a terrific photograph of the 6'9" Campolo and the 6'7" Carnera standing — each with an arm extended to the other's shoulder — on either side of the diminutive fight promoter Jimmy Johnston. The top of Johnston's head barely touched the fighters' outstretched arms. The headline over the photograph in the *Nashville Banner* read, "Brawn, Brains, More Brawn."[41]

Primo entered the contest as the 2-to-1 favorite to topple Campolo. The Associated Press wrote on the day of the fight: "Carnera, although beaten by Jack Sharkey in his last fight here (New York), showed unlimited courage if not much else. He was belted all around the place and floored into the bargain, but he was still in there trying at the finish."[42] Carnera was heavier and a better boxer, but Campolo was overall a stronger puncher.

Twelve thousand fans filled Madison Square Garden to watch a great night of fighting. On a card being fought for the benefit of Jewish Charities, eight well-known and respected heavyweights would be squaring off in the Garden ring on this late November Friday evening.

Starting things out, Walter Cobb dropped German fighter Ted Sandwina in the second of eight scheduled rounds. In the second bout Hurricane Steve Hamas outpointed Hans Birkie in eight rounds. In the final preliminary, Stanley Poreda won a seven-round technical knockout over Ralph Ficuello. Referee Johnny McAvoy called a halt to the fight after Poreda's powerful right had caused a serious laceration on Ficuello's left ear. Ficuello, the 1929 National AAU heavyweight champion, would recover from his damaged ear and fight through 1935, posting a notable 38–12–5 record in his professional career.

When it was time for the main event, the energized crowd was ready to watch the two mastodons mix it up. The referee for the bout was former heavyweight Gunboat Smith, who at 6'2" still stood half a foot shorter than the two participants.

It was a short but busy fight with plenty of action from both men. The first round saw the two fighters mix it up freely as "resin dust rose in clouds as the gigantic warriors tramped around the ring."[43] Campolo won the first round on many cards. He repeatedly fired his best shots at Primo and many of his powerful rights were true, but time and again, they garnered no reaction from Carnera.

Just a few seconds into round two, Primo went to work, unloading a volley of lefts and rights, each finding its target. One powerful right found Campolo's jaw and sent the Argentine crashing to the canvas. Campolo landed on his backside with his arms outstretched. Gunboat Smith ran over to the timekeeper to pick up the official count and then, leaning over the fallen fighter, he continued tolling off the numbers. Campolo, regaining his composure, took full advantage of Smith's count, rising just before ten.

After Campolo got to his feet, the two fighters met in the middle of the ring where a determined Campolo landed a clean left jab on Primo's nose. From then on, however, it was all Carnera. Primo landed a series of clean and hard combinations that forced Campolo to retreat into the ropes. Carnera then stepped forward with his left leg as he wound up, delivering a powerful right to the head, followed by another sweeping left. The heavy shots were beginning to take their toll, but Campolo was able to move away from the ropes and hit Carnera with a mostly ineffective overhand right. Primo then swept Campolo away from the ropes with his powerful right arm, and hit him with a left uppercut. Campolo, trying to survive, fell into a clinch. When Smith separated the two, Campolo retreated across the ring with Carnera in hot pursuit.

After another combination from Carnera, Campolo let go his final notable punch of the night, a sweeping right to Primo's ribs, fired off balance, as the Argentine was stumbling into the ropes. The lack of having his legs behind the punch cost Campolo any real power, and it failed to do much damage.

Carnera, sensing that Campolo was still unsteady, went for the kill. His punches were now coming rapidly, with almost machine-like precision — overhand right, left hook, right uppercut. Again and again, Carnera unleashed brutal attacks on his increasingly vulnerable opponent, landing repeated shots to the head and body. Finally, a left jab to the head, a right cross to the jaw, and one more sweeping left that caught Campolo flush on the jaw, sent the wounded warrior crashing down to the canvas for a second time. While Primo leaned with his arms on the ropes and Smith counted, a prostrate Campolo leaned on his left forearm and stared blankly at the canvas for several seconds. Campolo got to his knees by eight and was attempting to stand as Smith tolled ten, but he did not make it. Primo's last attack ended the evening as Smith counted Campolo out at 1:27 of the second round. As usual, Primo headed for his opponent to help him up, offer his "attaboys," and assist him to his corner. See then entered the ring and raised Carnera's right arm in victory.

The year 1931 ended on a positive note for Primo. He had posted a 9–1 record with seven wins coming by way of knockout. His only loss was a repectable loss to Sharkey. All in all, the year had gone reasonably well. He had put together convincing wins over several respectable fighters and made progress on his road to heavyweight title contention.

5

Making His Case, 1932

After fighting only 10 times in 1931—actually a very busy schedule for a heavyweight, but about half-pace for Carnera—Primo stepped up the tempo again in 1932. He fought 25 fights, going 23–2, with 17 knockouts. His two losses would come on 10-round decisions, the second of which was highly controversial, resulting in the suspension of the fight referee. He fought against a mix of good and mediocre competition.

Primo opened his schedule in Paris on January 25 against French heavyweight Moise Bouquillon in a scheduled 10-rounder at Jeff Dickson's Palais des Sports. Carnera and Bouquillon had met previously, on May 22, 1929, at the Salle Wagram in Paris, with Primo outpointing Bouquillon over 10 rounds. The 195-pound "Iron Man of France," who currently owned a 32-11-0 record, had been recognized as the French National heavyweight champion in 1927, after his second-round knockout of Francois Charles. Other than three fights in the United States in 1929 and 1930, he fought exclusively in Europe. He lost the three U.S. fights to Emmett Rocco, Jim Maloney, and Joe Monte, the first two on points, and the third on a TKO in the eighth, when referee Johnny Martin stopped the fight due to a deep cut that had opened up over Bouquillon's eye. Moise led easily on all cards at the time of the stoppage.

In their 1932 rematch, Primo, after sizing up his opponent in the largely subdued first round, set upon the Iron Man: "The big Italian swarmed all over the Frenchman and had him out on his feet soon after the second round began."[1] Employing a whirlwind of thunderous left-right combinations, Primo dropped Bouquillon to the canvas four times, each for a count of either seven or eight. On the verge of the fifth, the referee stepped in and ended the fight, an action that was lustily booed by the capacity crowd.

* * *

Rumors still persisted that Jack Dempsey was coming out of retirement. He was fighting exhibitions around the country, reportedly tuning up for an official return. On February 11 he fought a four rounder with Primo's former opponent K.O. Christner in Cleveland. Also that month, he met King Levinsky in a four-round barnburner in which the Kingfish reportedly gave the former champ all he could handle.

Dempsey's manager Leonard Sachs reportedly told the press that the former champion would meet anyone in the heavyweight division with the exception of Jack Sharkey. "Jack knocked out Sharkey. That settles it. I'll never let Sharkey make any money by fighting Dempsey."[2] Sachs may have been trying to avoid putting Dempsey back into the ring with Sharkey. That knockout came in their famous July 21, 1927, battle in which Dempsey was being thoroughly beaten by Sharkey for six rounds, before Dempsey, displaying a bit of gamesmanship, fouled Sharkey out of the referee's view. Dempsey then waited for the reaction that he knew would come and knocked Sharkey out after the Gob took his eyes off his opponent and turned to the referee to complain of the foul. It's certain that Sharkey would love a chance to even the score with Dempsey.

Primo was persistently included in the Dempsey comeback rumors. On February 4, news out of Berlin stated that Dempsey would meet Primo in Australia. Carnera's manager Leon See said that Australian promoter Hugh McIntosh was handling negotiations. See stated, "It's now all up to McIntosh. I believe he will succeed in arranging the fight. I have demanded a $90,000 guarantee. It will be a great fight. Dempsey's recent knockouts show he is staging a great comeback. He and Carnera are great drawing cards. With the whole world bidding for a match between them it makes it more difficult to bring them together."[3] Another article in March had the two heavyweights certain to get together in Reno, Nevada, on either July 2 or 4.[4] Once again, neither fight ever came off as, alas, Dempsey, who continued fighting regular exhibitions throughout the early 1930s, never "officially" came back to the ring.

See's comments regarding the Australian bout with Dempsey were made while he was with Carnera in Berlin, where Primo met German heavyweight Ernst Guhring. Guhring had a notable 29–2–9 record coming into the fight. The three-fight card was held at the Sportpalast in front of a large crowd that included the former German crown prince Frederick Wilhelm.

The first four of the scheduled 10 rounds were fairly even, but Primo began to come alive in the fifth. During that round, Guhring apparently turned his foot and was forced to withdraw because of an injury to his ankle. Primo took the 5-round TKO. Guhring fought for another couple of years, finishing up with a 31–9–10 record.

* * *

Next up was 215-pound Belgian Pierre Charles in Paris on February 29. Just shy of his 29th birthday, Charles had been fighting professionally for 10 years and owned a strong 52–19–8 record. The three-fight card held at the Palais des Sports featured all European heavyweights. Notable German fighter Walter Neusel kayoed Dane Soren Petersen in five for his 21st victory against one draw in 22 fights, and Italian Innocente Baiguera dropped Frenchman Marcel Moret in four.

In the main event, Primo had a tough time with European heavyweight champion Charles, who took Carnera the full 10 rounds. "The decision was awarded to Carnera whose 280-pounds were too much for Charles who weighed 215."[5] Primo won every round, but was still unable to put his opponent down for the count.

After losing to Carnera, Charles would post a 17–3–1 record over the next five years. When Charles walked away from the ring in 1937, he retired with a 69–23–9 record.

* * *

Primo met 187-pound Australian George Cook on Wednesday night March 23, at the Royal Albert Hall in London. Primo was down to around 250 for this fight. Cook was down in the first and third rounds for counts of three and six, respectively. After the first knockdown, Cook got up with fire in his eyes. Throwing rights and lefts in rapid fire, he drove Carnera into the ropes and left several bruises on the big guy. In the fourth, Primo caught the Australian's jaw with a right that dropped him for nine. Still, Cook wasn't finished, as he struggled to his feet and prepared himself for the onslaught to come. It came in the form of a Carnera right that sent Cook crashing through the ropes for a knockout. Apparently some in the crowd were not pleased with either the fact that the giant so thoroughly thrashed his much smaller opponent, or the fact that the referee didn't stop the bout earlier. A scattering of boos and shouts of "disgraceful" and "it's a shame" could be heard as the crowd filed out of the arena. The *New York Times* reported, "Cook was in bad shape after the knockout and it was some time before he recovered."[6]

* * *

On April 7, Primo was again at the Royal Albert Hall versus Don McCorkindale (14–5–3) of South Africa. McCorkindale represented South Africa in the 1928 Olympics in Amsterdam, where he came within a point's loss to winning a bronze medal, losing to Karel Miljon of the Netherlands. He also won the Amateur Boxing Association light heavyweight title in England in 1926.

Carnera took an early lead on points. He was especially strong in the second, when he floored his opponent twice, the second time dropping McCorkindale to his hands and knees, but Don was not through. Despite being knocked down once in the third, McCorkindale fought very well in rounds three and four, and opened a cut over Carnera's eye in the fifth round, but ultimately Primo's size and reach advantage were too much for the more-than-game McCorkindale to overcome. While McCorkindale was reportedly still fresh at the final bell, Primo won in a ten-round decision over the South African heavyweight champion.

McCorkindale continued fighting through 1938, ending his ring career with a 28–17–5 record. After hanging up his gloves, he went into acting. His son Don Jr. followed his father into the acting world and is a well-known actor in the United Kingdom.

* * *

On April 15, the London *Daily Mail* reported that Emilia Tersini had served a writ on Primo, charging him with breach of promise for breaking off their engagement. The report cited a London *Daily News* article from March 11, 1930, that stated that Primo and Emelia would marry upon Carnera's return to England from his first U.S. tour. At that time both Primo and Leon See denied that the story was true. This suit was to hang over Primo for the next several years.

* * *

Primo crossed the English Channel again in mid–April, to meet 211-pound Maurice Griselle in Paris on April 30. Like Primo, the Frenchman had been fighting professionally since 1928, but unlike his Italian opponent, he had met with more mixed results, giving him a moderate record of 16–13–1 as he entered the ring for his only fight with Carnera. While Primo failed to knock Griselle out, he did control the fight, taking a 10-round decision. The Associated Press, in its report on the fight, stated, "Primo Carnera, Italian heavyweight, easily outpointed Maurice Griselle of France in ten rounds tonight. Griselle was outpointed from the start."[7]

Griselle continued to fight through 1936, but his days of promise were behind him. He had at least one more bright moment, however, when he outpointed Don McCorkindale with a solid performance in their return bout in Paris in August 1932.

* * *

From Paris, Primo headed south across the Alps to his native Italy for a bout with 206-pound German heavyweight Hans Schoenrath in Milan, at the San Siro open-air stadium on May 15. The Associated Press reported, "A crowd of 20,000, many of them from Carnera's home village, cheered wildly as the giant punched Schoenrath all around the ring and battered him so badly the referee halted the unequal struggle shortly after the third round opened."[8]

After the fight Primo was quoted by the International News Service as hoping to meet Toronto heavyweight Larry Gains by the end of the month. He soon got his wish.

* * *

Heading back to England, Primo met the 200-pound Gains, the British Empire Heavyweight champion, on May 30, at White City Stadium in London. The multi-talented Gains owned a 72–12–4 record.

Lawrence Samuel Gains was born in Toronto, Ontario, Canada, in 1900. He was a good fighter who held the British Empire Heavyweight championship, but never received a shot at the world title. Despite this, Gains defeated a number of solid fighters including Carnera, Max Schmeling, George Godfrey, Phil Scott, Rudi Wagener, Jack Renault, Reggie Meen, Pierre Charles, Constant Barrick, Len Harvey, and Franz Diener. In an almost 20-year career, Gains would amass 114 victories and meet the bell for over 1,000 rounds.

Gains left Canada in 1923 to fight in Europe where he would begin to make his name. He sailed to Britain on a cattle ship and fought his first professional bout in London, in June of that year, losing by TKO in five rounds to the vastly experienced Frank Moody. A week after that loss, he was back in action in Paris, beginning an extended tour of Europe and North America, during which he would build an impressive 47–12–3 record before returning to England in 1929. After his return, he rarely fought outside of Britain — and he rarely lost a fight, twice going years without a loss. According to the *New York Times,* "A crowd of 70,000, setting a new all-time British record for boxing attendance, saw the Canadian outbox Primo all the way to win Referee Hart's decision at the finish."[9]

The pace of the fight was fast as Gains frustrated Primo time and again: "Carnera was at a loss after his blows failed to stop Gains, who wove in and out about Carnera's guard, hitting almost at will. Gains was fast and hit hard."[10] Throughout the fight, Gains was able to move in the inside and land hard, fast left hooks to Primo's body and then move away again before Carnera could respond. Only once did Primo ever really look hurt. Two powerful rights in the sixth from Gains plowed into Carnera's jaw and staggered Primo, but he quickly gathered himself and plowed on.

Primo looked his best in the seventh and tenth rounds. "In the seventh a hard left sent Gains back on his heels just before the bell and in the tenth the Canadian nearly went down when Primo connected with a right swing to the jaw."[11]

The bout went the scheduled 10 rounds, but despite going the distance, it was the Canadian's arm that referee Jack Hart held up as the decision was announced. Gains received a unanimous decision, taking eight rounds to Primo's two on most cards. This was the first loss Primo had suffered since the Sharkey fight the previous October.

The majority of the fans seemed thrilled with the outcome, elated that one of His Majesty's subjects had defeated the Italian Man Mountain. Gains' wife greeted him with a big hug after his seconds forced a path through the milling crowd, who were in no hurry to leave. The big Canadian and his entourage had to push their way through the crowd to Gains' dressing room as hundreds of spectators reached out to shake his hand and slap him on the back. Years later, Gains' manager, Harry Levene, blamed himself for not working with Madison Square Garden's Jimmy Johnston to arrange a fight for the world title after Johnston reportedly contacted Levene about such a bout.

Following the loss to Gains, Carnera and his management set sail for a return to the United States. This time, however, Leon See and Maurice Eudeline would not accompany him. Eudeline, Primo's good friend, who had trained him since 1928, saw Carnera off at the pier in Le Havre. The two friends, with heavy hearts, simply shook hands and Primo turned and walked up the ramp.

* * *

Upon his arrival in New York, Duffy put Primo under the tutorial eye of former featherweight Billy Defoe. William Henry Defoe began his professional boxing career at age 20 in 1913. When he finally retired in 1930 he owned a ring record of 68–37–12. In all he boxed over 1,100 rounds and his knowledge was crucial to Carnera's further development as a fighter. Defoe set up camp in Orangeburg, New York, where he tutored the Italian giant on his ring skills. Journalists and ring veterans visiting the camp were amazed by Carnera's progress. "His style of stepping off his toes has given way to a more flat-footed shuffle that is less spectacular to watch, but is far more effective. He has developed a snap to his heavy left jab and has learned to shoot a short right hand jolt to the body."[12]

In his return to Ebbets Field where he had lost to Sharkey, Primo met an old foe in southpaw Jack Gross of Philadelphia. Since his fourth-round knockout loss to Primo in 1930, Gross had only fought seven times including two losses to Tommy Louhgran and one to Ernie Schaaf. He had, on the other hand, defeated Roberto Roberti and fellow Philadelphian Big George Godfrey. Gross, now holding a 49–7–1 professional record, was another chance to show that Primo was still operating against a better class of fighter, but one that his managers believed he could defeat. The New York State Athletic Commission approved the 10-round fight, to be under the direction of promoter Humbert J. Fugazy. The bout was scheduled for July 20th.

A smaller than expected crowd of 5,000 came out to watch a five-bout card featuring four heavyweight fights and one welterweight contest. In the semi-final, Jack Redman (31–3–2) from South Bend, Indiana, knocked out Eddie Benson of New York in the seventh round of a scheduled eight. New Yorker Bob Olin outpointed Muggs Kerr of Oklahoma City.[13]

In the main event, the crowd saw a good if not great contest. In the early rounds, Primo had trouble hitting the quicker and elusive Gross from a distance. Remaining wary of the left-hander's style, Primo determined to move inside, where he launched series after series of rapid-fire combinations that began to weaken his opponent. While Primo controlled the fight throughout, Gross was able to land a fair number of shots to Carnera's jaw and body.

As the seventh round began, Primo decided to end it by cavalierly walking into Gross and forcing him into a corner where the Philadelphian received a two-fisted pummeling about the head. Gross worked his way out of the corner, but Primo pursued him, forcing him back to the ropes where he attacked Gross' body with relentless lefts and rights. Sensing victory, Primo raised his sights and sent another flurry of lefts and rights to Gross' head after which Gross quickly slumped to the canvas.[14]

With Gross weak and exhausted from the terrific beating he had been absorbing for seven rounds, referee Arthur Donovan stepped in and stopped the fight with ten seconds remaining in the round. "Just before Donovan led Gross to his corner the latter was on the floor for a count of seven, the result of absorbing a pair of heavy blows to the jaw."[15]

* * *

If the Gains and Gross fights were examples of Primo fighting a better class of fighter, his next bout against Jerry Pavelec was not. Pavelec, of Southhampton, New York, was 2–8–0 over the four years he had been fighting. His wins had been a four-round unanimous decision against Jack Saunders in 1929 — which Saunders rectified a month later by knocking Pavelec out in the third round of the rematch — and a second-round knockout of Artie Suess as part of the undercard at Ebbets Field eight days earlier. This was the first bout of Suess' four-fight professional career, but the last for the next three years. The three-year hiatus would make no positive contribution to his fight record as he would lose his next three fights and retire with an 0–4–0 record. Needless to say, Pavelec was not an A-teamer.

The fight was scheduled for the evening of July 28 at the West New York Stadium in West New York, New Jersey. On that night, nerves across the nation were frayed by the eerie news coming out of the nation's capital. Earlier that day D.C. city police and U.S. army troops had moved with lethal force against thousands of out of work veterans of the Great War and their families who had come to Washington in search of financial relief from the government. The story of the tragedy of the "Bonus Army" began in 1924 when Congress voted to give World War I veterans a bonus payable in 1945 as a tribute to their service. Each veteran would receive $1.50 for every active duty day spent overseas and $1.00 for each active duty day spent stateside. In the spring of 1932, with the nation in the grips of an ever-deepening Depression, Texas Representative Wright Patman introduced a bill in the House that would make the bonuses payable immediately.

Veterans from all over the country descended upon the nation's capital. The veterans began calling themselves the "Bonus Expeditionary Force." They were by and large an orderly group led by an unemployed cannery worker and veteran Walter W. Walters. Walters left Oregon in May with a band of around 300 unemployed veterans. By the time the "army" reached Washington, it had grown to an estimated 20,000 men, many of whom had brought along their families. Originally housed in vacant buildings along Pennsylvania Avenue, the veterans were asked to move and set up camps in fields and vacant lots in various parts of the city. Their largest camp was located along the swampy, muddy banks of the Anacostia River near the Capitol. Men, women, and children lived in makeshift shelters made from salvaged material found in dumps and junkyards. The marchers were largely ignored by official Washington; their only friend was D.C. police chief Pelham D. Glassford who helped arrange for lodging and field kitchens for the veterans and was known on more than one occasion to send them food and coffee from his own personal funds. Food, blankets and other supplies poured in from local charities and American Legion Posts.

Fears that the large mass of humanity would bring with it an undesirable element and crime were chiefly unfounded. By almost all accounts, the camps were kept neat and orderly with the men filing into formation each day; the city's crime rate actually fell during the army's stay. A lack of running water was the biggest obstacle.

The House passed the Patman Bill on June 15, and on June 17 the Senate was set to take up the vote. By the time of the vote, the Capitol grounds were awash with members of the veterans contingent, who waited anxiously for news of the final tally. Late in the day, Walters addressed the group with an anguished look on his face. He reported to his colleagues that the Senate had resoundingly defeated the bill by a vote of 62–18. Still, order was the call of the day as Walters told the crowd, "I have bad news. Let us show them we can take it on the chin. Let us show them we are patriotic Americans. I call on you to sing

'America.'"[16] Though discouraged and unsure of what was to come of them, the marchers sang and fell into formation as they headed back to their camps.

Over the next month, many veterans left the camps for home, but a number estimated at 8,600 stayed on with their families, having nowhere else to go. Frequent marches around the city and around the Capitol were common. They served as a regular reminder that the veterans were still there. Congress adjourned on July 17, but the marchers showed no signs of leaving. Finally on July 28, Attorney General William D. Mitchell ordered D.C. police to clear the veterans off all government property. The veterans offered some resistance, resulting in shots being fired. When the dust settled, two veterans lay dead. Fearing a full-scale riot, President Hoover ordered the Army to clear out all veterans from their camps that afternoon.

The Army forces—commanded by General Douglas MacArthur—were assembled from bases around the Washington area. Infantry, mounted cavalry, trucks and six tanks were dispatched. MacArthur's aide, Maj. Dwight D. Eisenhower, served as liaison with the local police while Major George Patton led the cavalry.

By late afternoon the troops were gathered on Pennsylvania Avenue near the Capitol while thousands of government workers on their way out of work paused to see what the troops were doing. At first, some people including the veterans cheered the troops, but suddenly a sickening reality of what was happening overcame the crowd. Patton's men, some on horseback, others on foot and wielding rifles with fixed bayonets, began to charge the unarmed veterans and their families.

MacArthur, who showed throughout his career that he had no respect for presidential orders, sent his men into the main camp, directly disregarding Hoover's command. MacArthur's men drove the bonus marchers out of their camps, scattering them along the streets and the muddy riverbank. In a short time, it was over. Thousands of veterans and their families were now even more homeless. Dust, the acrid smoke of adamsite gas, and smoke from the burned out shacks filled the air. Casualties from the raid rose to over 1,000. Most notably, two veterans had been shot to death; two infants died from asphyxiation from the tear gas and another went into shock; one veteran's wife suffered a miscarriage; an 11-year-old boy was partially blinded by gas; several people including a child were injured by bayonettes—that number included a veteran who lost an ear; one bystander was struck by a bullet in the shoulder; and local hospitals were filled with the injured. Later Eisenhower would write, "The whole scene was pitiful. The veterans were ragged, ill fed, and felt themselves badly abused. To suddenly see the whole encampment going up in flames just added to the pity."[17]

General Glassford had no compunction about sharing his first-hand view of what happened. He accused Hoover and others of overreacting and overstating the threat posed by the veterans. "The peacetime army of our present commander in chief drove from the National Capital at the point of the bayonet the disarmed, disavowed and destitute army of Woodrow Wilson."[18]

The routing of the Bonus Army is certainly one of the saddest and most disturbing tragedies of the Great Depression. The absurd spectacle of the government ordering the Army to attack its own unarmed and peaceably assembled veterans marked one of the most bizarre and regrettable episodes in American history. It proved to be one of the final missteps of the Hoover presidency. "His belief in voluntary cooperation, his constitutional scruples, his fiscal conservatism — these might be forgiven, but not sending tanks and cavalry against unarmed civilians."[19]

Against this backdrop of tragedy, the fight would hopefully serve as a way to take people's minds off of the ever-worsening economy.

A four-fight card was scheduled as a benefit for the West New York Milk Fund. The opening bout between Walter Cobb and Gene Stanton was ruled no contest in the second round. Jack Redman outpointed Pietro Corri in 10 rounds in the second fight and Tony Galento kayoed Charley Boyette in four in the final preliminary bout.

Before the fight, Carnera's corner filed an official objection to the selection of Jim Manley as referee. The objection was based on the outcome of a recent fight in which the New Brunswick native had intervened. The fight was hopelessly one-sided, but Manley stepped in, stopped the bout and ruled it a no contest. After discussion, state boxing commission representatives Ernest Masini and John Flood dismissed the objection, ruling that Manley would be the third man in the ring that night.[20]

In the main event, Primo, a prohibitive favorite, scored an easy fifth-round TKO. Primo controlled the fight throughout, but the 216-pound Pavelec refused to go down for the first three rounds. That changed markedly in the fourth when Primo began bombing Pavelec and floored his opponent six times for varying counts. The fight was stopped after 51 seconds of the fifth stanza by referee Jim Manley after Carnera decked Pavelec for the eighth time.[21]

* * *

Hans Birkie had a better record than Jerry Pavelec, but he too had been on the slide. After building up a 9–1–0 record in 1930, he had been a poster child for mediocrity. He'd lost seven of his last 10 fights, but interestingly during that stretch, he had floored Leo Lomski twice the previous January en route to a ninth-round TKO. Birkie had flashes of strength and was a hard man to finish, but he went downhill after his fast start and finished his career in 1939 with a final record of 36–41–8.

Primo met the 23-year-old German at the Queensboro Stadium in Long Island City, New York, on August 2. The undercard began at 8:30 P.M. with middleweight Tony Brescia of Harlem knocking out Joe Valenti in just over a minute of the second round. After three more heavyweight bouts, all of which went the scheduled distance, the crowd was ready for the main event.

Carnera controlled the fight from the beginning, registering left jabs with stunning regularity and peppering Birkie with blistering rights, but as was usual, Birkie refused to be dismissed. The fight went the distance, with the cards of referee Eddie Forbes and judges Jim Buckley and Bob Cunningham all registered in favor of Carnera. While no one really questioned the verdict, Primo received boos from many in the crowd for his inability to knock Birkie out.

* * *

Two weeks later Primo met 23-year-old Stanley Poreda in a six-fight card at Dreamland Park in Newark, New Jersey. The Jersey City native had built up a strong 25–5–0 record and a reputation for having a strong right hand, a weak chin, and few discernable boxing skills. He was a standup-type fighter who rarely bobbed or weaved, making him an easier target. Primo entered the fight a 7-to-5 favorite. The odds were certainly defensible. *Newark Star-Eagle* sports Editor Murray Robinson, frequently critical of Carnera, was beginning to see some promise in Primo. In his column, he mentioned several fights including the Sharkey and Gross fights, in which Primo began to show some skill and toughness. "Carnera,

5. Making His Case, 1932

it seems to me, is too big, tough, and courageous for Poreda to outpoint or knockout tonight. Primo has a pretty fair left, and his advantages in reach, height and bulk should more than offset the New Jersey favorite's speed and precision on the attack."[22]

The five-fight undercard started at 8:30 P.M. with three of the fights in advance of the main event going their scheduled distances. The main event got started close to 10:15 P.M.

Early in the fight, Primo was the aggressor and fought well, but was repeatedly warned for his rough tactics by referee Joe Mangold. Few in the crowd saw any reason for the warnings. Mangold claimed that Carnera used his elbows while attempting to uppercut Poreda in close. Carnera easily took the first three rounds, pounding the Jersey City heavyweight with massive lefts and rights to the body. Carnera worked his jab well, jerking Poreda's head back repeatedly.

At the start of the fourth round, Mangold again gave a warning to Carnera for no apparent reason. Primo protested vehemently. He then proceeded to take his frustration out on Poreda. Carnera hit Poreda with one right so vicious that it jerked Stan's head back over the ropes like it had been pulled back by a rope. Poreda fought back and this round was a draw in several sportswriters' eyes.

In the fifth, Poreda had his best round when he seemed to come alive, hurting Primo with a series of lefts and rights to the body. Carnera responded with a blistering right that spun Poreda into the ropes, but for busyness and number of shots landed, Poreda won the round.

The sixth round was slow, but Primo won primarily due to his effective jabs. The seventh began with Primo setting the pace, but Poreda then came alive, staggering Carnera with a left hook to the jaw followed by a combination of strong body blows. Poreda continued to land some hard, digging shots into the eighth and ninth rounds, "But against these punches of Poreda was Carnera's steady bombardment of stiff left jabs and cuffing left hooks at long range, and a barrage of lefts and rights to the body with which the Italian carried off the honors of infighting in every round."[23] The eighth and ninth rounds were more of the same with Carnera taking the eighth but Poreda doing enough in a come-from-behind role to get the nod from many in the ninth.

While Poreda made a late, desperate stand in the tenth stanza, Carnera again outfought his opponent, winning the round in virtually all observers' eyes. When the fight went to the cards, most officials, writers and fans gave Carnera at least seven of the 10 rounds and a definitive victory. Mangold didn't agree. The International News Service reported, "Joe Mangold of Atlantic City lifted Poreda's gloved right hand at the finish. The verdict didn't please the Carnera rooters one bit, and they booed long and loud."[24] That was perhaps a bit of an understatement according to James P. Dawson, writing for the *New York Times*. Dawson reported that Mangold's decision "almost precipitated a riot among some 10,000 fans. This writer thought Carnera won eight of the ten rounds."[25] The crowd booed and jeered the decision, showering the ring with an array of objects including hats. Calm was not restored until heavyweights Walter Cobb and Chester Matan entered the ring for the final fight of the evening.

According to Dawson, "Carnera outboxed and outfought Poreda, notwithstanding the New Jersey fighter's determined bid for victory. Carnera lost only the fifth round and the seventh."[26] Murray Robinson of the *Newark Star-Eagle* gave Carnera the first, second, third, sixth, eighth, and tenth, with the fourth a draw. The three rounds he scored for Poreda were close.[27]

After the fight, Robinson asked Mangold how he had scored the fight, but the referee refused to show anyone his scorecard. Refusing to explain his terrible decision, Mangold stated, "I thought Poreda won, and that's enough for me."[28]

State boxing commission auditor John Flood stated, "Before the fight it was impressed on Mangold that the crowd would be decidedly for Poreda and that he shouldn't permit their yells to sway him. But it seemed our warning went for naught."

New Jersey Boxing Commissioner George E. Keenen, at ringside during the bout, was incredulous over Mangold's decision. On Wednesday it was announced that the commission was suspending Mangold indefinitely for what Keenen termed an "unpardonable decision." John Flood, administrative agent for the New Jersey State Athletic Commission, announced the immediate suspension "pending further investigation of his decision in favor of Stanley Poreda over Primo Carnera in their fight in Newark last night."[29] Keenan was a bit more direct, going on record as saying, "The decision given by Mangold was the worst I have ever seen. He can't possibly have any excuse for his action, and I have decided to suspend him and keep him suspended until he learns how to judge a fight."[30] Mangold, who had also fought a handful of professional bouts, did not officiate another match for a year, but would then receive reinstatement and continue as a fight referee in New Jersey through 1957.

* * *

Three days later Carnera was in Tiverton, Rhode Island, to mix it up with 219-pound Canadian fighter Jack Gagnon. Gagnon had not won a fight since the fall of 1930, having dropped six straight fights, all by knockout. Clearly at the end of his seven-year career, Gagnon was serving as cannon fodder for a series of respected fighters. He was summarily knocked out by Larry Johnson, King Levinsky, Charley Retzlaff, Ernie Schaaf, Micky Walker, and Paolino Uzcudun. Primo Carnera would be added to that list before the clock ran out on August 19, and that clock ran out after just one minute and 35 seconds of the first round. Gagnon failed to make any offensive showing for himself, with Carnera landing virtually all of the punches during the half-round fight. "A crowd of 5,000 persons hooted while Gagnon lay on the mat after a stiff right under the heart."[31] Apparently in pain, Gagnon received medical attention in the middle of the ring before exiting to the boos of the crowd.

Gagnon would fight just once more professionally. He defeated "Two Ton" Tony Galento on December 12 in Philadelphia when Galento was disqualified. After being knocked out seven straight times, Gagnon no doubt decided that a win is a win and wisely decided to retire on a victory. His career record stood at 33–27–1.

* * *

Two weeks later on September 1, Primo met the immeasurably better Art Lasky in St. Paul, Minnesota. The 6'4" Minnesota native was born Arthur Lokofsky in 1909. Managed by his older brother Maurice, Lasky, in a fast professional start, had built an 18–1–0 record over the previous year and a half. "In his brief ring career, Lasky had never been knocked off his feet."[32] His only loss had come in January 1931 in a 10-round newspaper decision to Dick Daniels in Minneapolis. He'd also added to his stock when he fought Jack Dempsey toe to toe in a two-round exhibition the previous December. Even with Lasky's strong showing to date, Carnera entered the bout as the heavy favorite.

Having learned the value of mixing with the public before a bout, Primo visited several events in the area. On Tuesday he visited the Keller Country Club where the Professional Golfer's Association was playing that week. Carnera hobnobbed with local celebrities, fans, and golf's elite.[33]

Primo shows his size and strength by lifting up and holding three men in a Chicago hotel in 1930. (Chicago History Museum)

Nearly 4,000 persons paid their way into the St. Paul Auditorium to witness a night of boxing that included a strong seven-fight card. They got their money's worth that night as they were treated to 41 rounds of quality boxing. Four of the first five bouts went the their respective four- or six-round distances, with the third contest ending in a third-round TKO.

The semi-windup fight featured 1930 national Golden Gloves light-heavyweight champion Buck Everett and Larry Udell, a seasoned scrapper from Aberdeen, Kansas. Everett scored a bit of an upset after taking control of the fight in the third round. Everett nearly floored Udell in the seventh stave with a combination that included a sharp left hook that crashed into Udell's head and a follow-up right to the chin that sent the Kansan reeling into the ropes. Everett might have scored a knockout then and there had he remained collected, but sensing the knockout he began lobbing wild and inaccurate punches that missed their target badly and allowed Udell to fall into several clinches and last to the end of the round. Everett punished Udell severely in the eighth, but could not put across the finishing blow. The fight went the distance, but there was no question about the winner with Everett taking an easy decision.

In the main event Primo made effective use of his left arm jabbing and hooking Lasky throughout the fight. The Minnesotan was, however, no wilting flower as he absorbed the pounding and kept wading in on his foe. "While there were no knockdowns, the fight was exceptionally interesting to watch. There was a lot of punching and seldom did the pair come into a clinch."[34]

The headliner also featured Mike Gibbons as the third man in the ring. Of Irish heritage, Gibbons was a native of St. Paul and learned to box at a local YMCA. He was the older brother of light-heavyweight contender Tommy Gibbons. Mike turned pro at the age of 19, earning the nickname the "St. Paul Phantom." Gibbons was a defensive wizard with a punch. Following his boxing career, he became a successful businessman in St. Paul. During his 15-year ring career, Gibbons was a real crowd pleaser and a local fistic hero who was considered to be one of the best middleweights ever to come out of the Twin Cities. He won an amazing 112 fights, losing only 9 with 9 draws.[35]

The first round started fast as Primo rocked Lasky with a solid right to the jaw. Lasky quickly shook off the effects of that punch and made a strong comeback throwing flurries of punches that caught the big man and scoring enough points to take the round.

Primo took the second with crisp, clean and accurate punching. Each time Lasky would attempt to rush him, Carnera would repel the invader with hard, straight lefts and rights. The third was much the same with Primo opening a cut over Lasky's left eye.

In the fourth, Lasky was back on the prowl taking the round with rapid combinations that put Carnera on the defensive for the bulk of the stanza.

Twice in the middle rounds, Carnera sent Lasky spinning into the ropes with powerful shots to the head. The first came in the fifth stanza, after Lasky connected with a left hook that opened a small cut under Primo's right eye. Primo became enraged and "cut loose with a roundhouse right that caught Lasky back of the head and sent him floundering into the ropes."[36] After gathering himself, Lasky waded back in and the fighters continued their 18' × 18' war.

By the sixth round, Lasky, with his faced badly bruised and blood trickling from the cut over his left eye, was showing visible signs of fatigue. Carnera took full advantage of the fact by peppering him with a continual barrage of left jabs to the nose and mouth. Late in the round Primo launched a right-handed missile that caught Lasky flush on the jaw, again sending the Minnesotan into the ropes. The seventh was no better for Lasky as Primo kept pouring it on.

In the eighth round after several furious exchanges, Primo doubled up his opponent with a powerful right uppercut. Lasky cried foul, claiming that the blow landed south of his beltline, but referee Mike Gibbons saw it differently and instructed Lasky to fight on.

Fight on he did as Lasky staged a small comeback in the ninth. Knowing that Carnera had taken the last three rounds, Lasky realized that he had to make a showing now or the fight was lost for him. At the opening bell the Minnesotan energized the crowd as he charged

5. Making His Case, 1932

toward his opponent and powered two lefts to Carnera's body and fired a hard right to Primo's head. Carnera responded with several jabs to Lasky's mouth, but when he tried a left hook, Lasky slipped under it and buried his own left hook deep in the Italian's gut. This shot hurt Primo, who fell into a clinch for the first time in the fight. After Gibbons separated the men Carnera went on the defensive for the remainder of the round and Lasky earned the ninth.

In the tenth and final round Lasky was spent and Carnera knew it. Smelling blood he pursued Lasky around the ring trying to score the coup de grace, but Lasky had other ideas. Briefly he attempted to mix it up with Primo, but that ended when Carnera landed a sweeping left hook to Lasky's head that nearly dropped him. Again, Lasky kept his feet, but he was in survival mode. Backpedaling, he led Primo around the ring in a defensive effort to avoid more punishment and to watch for an opening that could turn the fight in his favor. It never came. Primo finally caught up with him and landed several hard shots to Lasky's head in the final seconds before the bell.

Both men fought well, but in the end it was all Primo, with the *Minneapolis Tribune* commenting that Carnera "boxed exceptionally well and amazed the crowd with the speed and grace with which he moved around the ring. Lasky is fast, but Carnera actually outspeeded his lighter opponent much of the time."[37]

Lasky would continue to fight, mostly on the West Coast, for the remainder of the decade, with the highlights of the rest of his career coming in his defeat of Hans Birkie at Madison Square Garden in 1933; a win and a draw in a pair against King Levinsky in 1934; and a 15-round upset decision loss to Jimmy Braddock in March 1935. Lasky retired in 1939 with a very good professional record of 45–9–5.

* * *

Once again the papers reported that a Baer–Carnera fight was in the offing. On August 31 Max had narrowly missed knocking out Ernie Schaaf in Chicago and with Primo's decision over the highly regarded Lasky, the fight between the heavyweight contenders seemed a natural. The day after the Lasky contest the *Minneapolis Tribune*'s fight recap was accompanied by a two-paragraph piece. The article stated that Brooklyn promoter Humbert Fugazy was conducting negotiations between the two camps for a fight to be held in Ebbets Field on September 28. The negotiations reportedly started in St. Paul and "were underway Thursday night and are expected to be completed in Chicago Friday."[38] Again, negotiations broke down over gate splits, but this fight, unlike the Braddock and Schmeling fights, would eventually occur.

* * *

Actually, Primo did fight a boxer named Max in New York on September 28. On that date Max Schmeling appeared at the New York County Courthouse for examination in a suit filed by Primo's managers against the former champion for breach of contract. The Carnera camp contended that Schmeling had broken a contract to meet Primo in September of 1931. Schmeling, who was being sued for $100,000, was deposed in private about the existence of a contract. Schmeling had failed to appear for examination the previous June and expunged a contempt charge and $250 fine leveled against him at that time. Eventually the charge was dropped and Primo and Max would appear to be on friendly terms.

* * *

On October 7 Primo fought 6'2", 207-pound Ted Sandwina in Tampa, Florida. Sandwina was a German Jewish fighter who began fighting in Europe before making his way to the United States in 1927 and settling in Sioux City, Iowa. Sandwina was big and powerful with a heavy punch. He registered 40 knockouts during his seven-year career. His mother Kate Sandwina was a noted circus strongwoman who traveled with the Ringling Bros. and Barnum Bailey Circus in the first half of the 20th century. The two were featured on the cover of *Boxing* magazine in February 1932. Sandwina had built a 48–25–6 record by the time he climbed in the ring with Carnera, but was clearly on his way down, having dropped eight points decisions in a row. Carnera won the first three rounds, battering his opponent all around the ring. Throughout the contest Primo wore Sandwina down with a series of furious attacks to the body before knocking the journeyman fighter out in the fourth with a right to the jaw. After the fourth-round loss to Carnera, Sandwina would go on to lose six more fights—all by knockout or TKO—before hanging up his gloves in August of 1933.

* * *

Six days later, Primo met Gene Stanton of Cleveland at the 114th Regiment Armory in Camden, New Jersey. With exception of a disqualification, the four-fight card had all of the possible outcomes. Billy Hendrie gained a TKO over Buddy Pierce in a welterweight opener, Greek middleweight champion Costas Vassis and Philadelphian Joe O'Neill fought to a no-decision over six rounds, and Jack Kilbourne, a.k.a. Herman Bundren, of Enid, Oklahoma, defeated Jack Mackaway by way of an eight-round decision in Mackaway's only professional fight.

A fun night of good boxing almost took a tragic turn. During the preliminaries, a temporary bleacher section collapsed, sending several hundred fans crashing to the floor. Providentially, only 12 spectators were injured, each receiving only slight cuts and bruises.

In the main event, Primo took command of the fight early, flooring Stanton 11 times and scoring a sixth-round knockout. Stanton, once called a great heavyweight prospect by Jack Dempsey, went on to fight for another couple of years, but never achieved the potential that the former champ saw in him. He retired in 1934 with a professional record of 14–29–1 and two no contests.

* * *

On October 17 Primo was in Louisville, Kentucky, to fight 220-pound Jack Taylor. The 33-year-old Taylor was on the butt end of a long but mediocre fistic career. He started as a promising young fighter out West and wound up fighting chiefly in Europe in the latter part of his career. He had, however, fallen on hard times in the boxing world with bouts becoming scarce and wins even scarcer. Taylor had not won a fight since 1929. Coming into this contest, the former Marine had lost six in a row including once to Primo's "old friend" the rolling and diving defensive genius Elzear Rioux in England in December 1930.

After Art Schultz defeated Al Hamilton in an eight-round newspaper decision, Primo scored an easy second-round kayo over Taylor.

After losing to Primo he fought twice more in the Netherlands, dropping two eight-round decisions before stepping away from the ring for good.

* * *

On November 4 Primo met 210-pound Les Kennedy of Los Angeles in the Arena in Boston, Massachusetts. After a four fight undercard, Primo toyed with Kennedy in the first two rounds before coming on with a barrage of powerful, short left and right hooks to his opponent's head and registering the knockout in the third stanza.

Kennedy was a streaky fighter who in addition to Carnera fought notables like Max Baer, Paulino Uzcudun, Mickey Walker, Steve Dudas, K.O. Christner, and Leroy Haynes. He had caught the attention of former champion James J. Jefferies who predicted big things for Kennedy. Like so many fighters, however, he never attained the status that others predicted. He retired in 1935 with a respectable professional record of 39–30–2.

* * *

On November 8 America went to the polls to elect a president. The electorate, having endured three years of a worsening economy, deepening unemployment, poverty, and bread lines, was ready for a change.

When the Democrats gathered for their national convention in Chicago in late June, they nominated second-term Governor Franklin D. Roosevelt of New York. Roosevelt secured the nomination on the third ballot, beating out his fellow New Yorker and the 1928 Democratic standard-bearer Al Smith and U.S. House Speaker John Nance Garner of Texas. The wheelchair-bound Roosevelt campaigned energetically to dispel any fears that the effects of his polio would interfere with his ability to govern the nation during the difficult times it faced. He began by flying to Chicago to accept the nomination in person. Both actions were unheard of in 1932, but Roosevelt knew that he must act decisively and boldly to win the election.

President Hoover was widely blamed for the Great Depression. Since the market collapse in the fall of 1929, Hoover had regularly been claiming that the worst was over. It never was and inevitably, the economic downturn worsened. The president was so unpopular by 1932 that he was often booed in public whether he was giving a speech, campaigning, or attending a baseball game. Despite his unpopularity, he chose to run for a second term and, holding the strings to the Republican Party Convention, he easily won re-nomination.

The campaign was long and acrimonious. Governor Roosevelt called for a New Deal for the American people and a period of fundamental change to get America working again. President Hoover attacked Roosevelt as a socialist whose policies would only make the Depression worse by raising taxes and increasing the federal debt to pay for a whole host of expensive welfare and social-relief programs. But, with one in four American laborers out of work and economic conditions worsening, Hoover's criticisms failed to gain traction with the public. On election day Roosevelt won the presidency in a landslide, receiving 57.4 percent of the vote to Hoover's 39.7 percent and Socialist Norman Thomas' 2.2 percent.

* * *

On November 18 Primo faced 6'9", 250-pound Portuguese heavyweight Jose Santa.

Santa was a decent fighter who faced many of the big names of the era, but who never could quite turn the corner to stardom.

Santa had a pretty good 1931, going 10–4–1. He also was involved in one no contest against Knute Hansen. The Santa/Hansen bout was stopped after referee Davey Miller declared that Hansen was felled by a phantom punch. Notable wins that year came over Rudi Wagener and Roberto Roberti, each of whom he edged on points, and a six-round TKO of Hans Birkie. But Birkie withdrew, claiming that he had broken his right hand, a claim supported by the fact that he had stopped throwing rights at some point in the second round.

Only 6,000 fans showed up that night at Madison Square Garden. During the first round, the two giants traded punches and Santa landed several good rights to the body. The rest of the fight, however, was Primo's.

After Primo had dropped Santa in the second, third and sixth rounds, referee Jed Gahan stepped in and stopped the carnage. The *New York Times* reported, "Needless to say Santa was relieved. He had been battered and hammered around the ring rather generously from the beginning and judging by his expression, was getting tired of the treatment."[39]

Referring to the third knockdown, the Associated Press reported that Santa "had visited the resin dust twice before but not quite so emphatically."[40] After watching Santa laboriously right his substantial frame at the count of nine, Gahan determined that Santa had had enough and the fight should not go on. Gahan stopped it and awarded Primo a TKO at 1:10 of the sixth round.

Santa would continue to fight actively through 1934, ending that year with a second-round knockout over Erwin Klausner in Brazil. He fought one fight each in 1935, 1936, and 1937, ending each one on his back no later than the third round. Finally convinced that he was through, Santa retired with a 45–18–4 record.

* * *

Traveling west, Primo met rising Missouri heavyweight John Schwake in St. Louis on December 2. Schwake turned pro in 1930 after winning the 1929 international A.A.U. heavyweight championship. He won 14 of his first 17 fights with two of the three non-wins coming by way of one no contest with K.O. Christner and one draw in his third professional bout, with another St. Louis fighter named Dave Knost. His only loss came by way of a sixth-round KO to unsung Canadian Angus Snyder in June 1931. Schwake avenged that loss seven months later when he outboxed Snyder and took a 10-round decision. After the second Snyder fight in January 1932, Schwake's career faded. He dropped his next fight in a rematch with the ever-colorful Chuck Wiggins. He then lost on points to journeyman Johnny Freeman and fought to a 10-round draw with Tom Heeney. Next up after Heeney was Carnera. With his record slipping towards mediocrity his loss to Primo would be his final fight.

Knowing that Schwake was dangerous, Primo felt his opponent out for the first few rounds. As the fight progressed, however, Primo wore the Missourian down with his persistent left jabs. In the seventh round Primo finished Schwake, registering yet another win by KO. Schwake left the ring that night for the last time as a professional with a career record of 14–4–2.

* * *

Primo rolled into Chicago the next week for a rematch with King Levinsky. Chicago's fighting fish peddler now owned a 43–19–4 record, having gone 4–4–0 since their last meeting in November 1931. The two met again at the Chicago Stadium on December 9 in front of 14,333. Primo gained the nod in the first bout with a 10-round decision. Levinsky had looked good early, leaving his hometown fans sensing an upset over Carnera who was installed as a 3–1 favorite, but Carnera battled back, taking rounds 4 through 10 and the decision.

In the first round, Levinsky came out swinging, trying to do some damage to the powerful Carnera early before the giant could wear him down. In the middle of the round,

5. Making His Case, 1932

Levinsky brought the crowd to their feet when he caught Primo with a wild, roundhouse right that caught Carnera flush on the jaw. Primo was rocked and almost went down, but at mid-squat he caught himself and Levinsky was unable to capitalize.

Levinsky believed that this time he could take Primo, but Primo looked sharp that night. The Associated Press reported, "The Italian giant, noticeably improved as a boxer, poked and clubbed out a ten-round decision over the pride of Chicago's ghetto last night in the Chicago Stadium, his second in a little more than a year, but as on the former occasion, Levinsky won the hearts of the customers."[41]

While Levinsky won the hearts of the Chicago faithful with his tenacity, Carnera outboxed his hard charging, but tiring opponent.

It was a split decision, with referee Ed Purdy and one fight judge choosing Carnera and the other judge handing a questionable nod to the kingfish. Levinsky's hometown crowd, full of emotions for their local hero, roared its disapproval.

* * *

In a rematch of his first fight on American soil, Primo met "Big Boy" Peterson (52–40–9) in Grand Rapids, Michigan, on December 13. This time Peterson lasted two rounds with the Italian mountain. Peterson showed notable aggressiveness in the first round, but in the second, Primo took control of the fight. The big Italian wasted no time in pummeling his opponent with combinations to the Minnesotan's head and body. After absorbing tremendous punishment throughout the second stanza, Peterson's handlers threw a towel in the ring as their man visited the canvas for the fourth time in the round.[42]

On December 14 the Associated Press reported that promoter Nate Lewis was making an attempt at setting up a match between Primo and Max Baer in Chicago Stadium on December 29. Unfortunately, the two camps couldn't get together. Instead of meeting for a fight in Chicago, Maxie enjoyed a quiet Christmas while Primo traveled to Texas for the holidays where he would fight three relatively easy opponents who served as tune-ups to keep him sharp for his run at the championship in 1933.

* * *

Before heading for the Lone Star state, Primo had some business to conduct with his old foe K.O. Christner (46–29–3) in Omaha, Nebraska, on December 15. In their previous meeting, Primo had knocked Christner out with a series of heavy rights in the fourth round at the Detroit Fairgrounds on June 5, 1930. After that encounter Christner, still smarting from a poke in the eye and his first visit to the canvas in his professional career, had pushed for a rematch with Primo, saying, "Just give me another shot at Carnera and I'll fight him for nothing and guarantee to knock him out."[43]

Christner was coming off a second-round knockout over novice Nick Nolan in Lima, Ohio 10 days earlier and had been fighting fairly well, having lost only once in his last 11 fights. That single loss came on points in October against Tiger Jack Fox over 10 rounds. The 37-year-old former rubber molder had fought in Omaha twice before, winning both matches, and he felt good about his chances against Carnera. He left his hometown of Akron, Ohio, telling the local press that he was "confident he was going to give the big Italian all he can take."[44] He told Howard Wolff of the *Omaha World-Herald*, "All I want is a clean shot at that dago's lug. And in 10-rounds I'll get it. And when I do, that mug is going down. And he's going to stay down."[45]

The bout was scheduled as part of a fundraiser for the local American Legion's Christmas Basket Fund, the Free Shoe Fund, and other local charities. A small crowd of around 1,500 braved the frigid night air, which registered a bitter two degrees below zero.

The undercard held five fights. Kid Glover took a 4-round decision over Jack Tottershaw of Montreal; Ray McMillan and Kid McCaffrey fought to a 6-round draw, as did Jimmy Wooten and Canada Lee; and Happy Jack Spurgin of Memphis scored a first-round knockout over Big Boy Sullivan in the only other heavyweight match of the evening. The semi-final bout featured Sonny Sofio and Buzz Smith in a lightweight battle. Smith, a last-minute replacement for Henry Falegano, gave a spirited account of himself, lasting the scheduled eight rounds. Smith was floored three times by the long power shots that Sofia fired off throughout the fight, but he stayed in for the duration and managed to land numerous rights to his opponent's head that gave Sofio pause. Sofio got the decision, but the crowd got on Smith's bandwagon. Sofio was a good local fighter from Omaha. In his brief career, he fought only eight times, but posted a 5–0–3 professional record. Smith actually lost a six-round newspaper decision to Falegano in Atlantic, Iowa, a week later, and continued to fight through 1938, leaving the ring with an 8–12–3 record.

The third man in the ring for all bouts that evening was Johnny Lee. Lee was a sometime heavyweight who had posted an 0–4–0 record as a professional. His most notable fight came in 1925 when he was knocked out in the second round in Salt Lake City by Young Stribling.

In spite of Christner's pre-fight prognostications, the night's bout ended much the same as the first, with Carnera again knocking out the tough Akron tire worker in the fourth round of a scheduled ten.

Christner battled Carnera gamely for the first three rounds, alternately providing a difficult target at long range and then wading into the giant to land several good pokes on Primo's chin. After wading in to deliver punches, he was quickly tied up by the massive Italian, who mauled and pushed Christner around the ring while landing stinging jabs and uppercuts.

By the fourth round, however, things began to change. Primo found his range and began landing mortar shots on the Ohioan. One caught Christner on the forehead and in the words of Omaha journalist Al Wolf, "shoved him halfway through the floor."[46] The tough tire maker caught himself and stayed on his feet in the wake of that pile driver, but Primo was heating up and it was now clearly just a matter of time. In the middle of the round Carnera "hit K.O. a terrible wallop to the pit of the stomach. The Buckeye doubled up like the interest on a year old debt."[47] With Christner clearly in trouble, Primo unloaded a heavy right that caught his opponent on the side of his head and a follow-up right to the ribs, putting him down for the first time in the fight. Christner "went down in a flurry of dust, staggered up at the count of nine and then toppled over like the last pin on a slow strike."[48] Christner was still groggy as referee Johnny Lee reached the count of nine, but he jumped up to beat the count and immediately threw a right that caught the surprised Carnera on the jaw.

While the punch surprised Primo, he was undeterred: "Like the hunting dogs sensing the kill,"[49] Primo became the aggressor tearing into his groggy opponent. Seconds later, Carnera dropped Christner again with a thunderous right to the chest. This time K.O. struggled to his feet, but was still up at nine. He need not have bothered. Once on his feet, he was so disoriented that he simply lunged at Primo and keeled over onto the canvas where Lee promptly counted him out.

Christner had again fought Primo valiantly, giving as good as he got for several rounds, but as in their Detroit battle in 1930, Primo found his opening and when he did, the end came quickly for Christner. He got flat-out beat and this time there were no claims of gun-toting gangsters at ringside.

K.O. would experience a dry spell, losing six of his next nine fights. At 36, he was clearly slowing down. Christner continued to fight for two more years, posting an 8–16–1 record for the rest of his career. He retired after defeating Ford Smith in an impressive showing in 1935. In 1940, K.O. made a brief two-fight comeback in which he defeated Fred Bozic and Jack Owens, both Akron amateurs, in second-round knockouts. After his retirement from the ring, Christner opened a bowling alley in Cumberland, Maryland. He operated it until he retired in 1967 and returned to the Akron, Ohio, area.

* * *

After defeating Christner, Primo left the frigid climes of Nebraska for Texas where he would fight several times over the next two weeks against a series of smaller-name locals. First up was Joe Rice at the North Side Coliseum in Ft. Worth on December 19. Rice, a local bus driver, owned a professional ring record of 4–2–0 before he entered the ring with De Preem. He was 4–3–0 when he left with the aid of his corner men. Primo finished Rice that evening with a second-round knockout.

Rice continued to fight for another two-and-a-half years and wound up his career with an 11–11–0 record. He retired after being knocked out in the second round by King Levinsky in Oklahoma City in April 1935.

* * *

The next day Primo met 6'2", 213-pound Oklahoman James Merriott (3–1–0) at the City Auditorium in the coastal city of Galveston. Merriott owned a verifiable ring record of 3–1–0 going into the fight, but newspaper reports indicated that it could be as high as 23–2–0. Either way, it didn't matter as Carnera made short work of the man with the mysterious record. After a three-fight undercard provided the audience with one knockout, two decisions, and 19 rounds of action, Primo took very little time to finish off his opponent by scoring a first-round knockout over the Oklahoman. Merriott continued to fight regularly through 1940 and made the usual comeback after World War II, dropping two more fights in Oklahoma and winding up his career at 6–20–1.

* * *

Arriving in Dallas on Friday December 23, Primo and his managers Walter Friedman and Mike Collins met with Dallas-based promoter Larry Meinert to set up a card to be held in Dallas in one week's time. Meinert, a long-time boxing promoter in the Dallas area, promised a multi-fight card to be held at Dallas' Fair Park Auditorium with a portion of the proceeds going to the Dallas area Community Chest.

* * *

Primo climbed into the ring for two exhibitions in San Antonio on December 29. The first fight was with a local fighter named Frank Malish. Primo finished Malish with a left hook to the Texan's jaw after just two minutes of fighting.

The second exhibition was with veteran Jack League. He was formerly a member of the Jack Dempsey stable and was a respectable fighter. League made a determined effort to take the fight to Carnera and move to his inside where the Texan believed that he stood a better chance of lasting with the Man Mountain. And last he did, through all three rounds. While League landed several good blows, Carnera was never hurt and controlled the fight from the first.

League, who hailed from El Paso, began his ring career in 1925, fighting mostly throughout the southern half of the United States from Florida to California. Other than Primo, League's most notable fights came against Young Stribling whom he fought twice — each fight ending in a knockout loss to the Georgian. Jack was on the undercard for Primo's Valentine's Day battle in Memphis in 1930 where he knocked out his opponent Paul Cannon in the second round.

League had a running battle with Carnera's next opponent, Young Spence, whom he fought five times. League was on the verge of retiring, but decided to pick up one more payday against the Italian Giant. League finished his career with a record of 16–12–2 with one no contest.

* * *

To end the year, Carnera fought one more time, this one in Dallas on December 30 against James "Young" Spence. The 11–8–1 Spence started fighting professionally in 1921 with a third-round TKO loss to Jack Tolar in Beethoven Hall, San Antonio, Texas. He continued to fight chiefly in and around Texas for the next 15 years. Spence fought Jack League five times, winning one, losing three and enduring one no contest ruling.

Clearly beginning to slide in the ring, 1931 did not start out kind to Spence as he dropped a 10-round decision to Jack League in the Plaza de Toros in Nuevo Laredo, Mexico, on February 23, 1931. The one "No Contest" on his record came in his next bout during his fifth meeting with League. It was part of a messy night of fighting at Beethoven Hall in San Antonio on April 1, 1931. According to Boxrec.com, "To the fans' disgust nearly all the fighters on this card, a benefit for the local Newsboys organization, stalled their way to draws. Midway through the main event the arena was almost empty."[50] The first four fights each actually ended in four-round newspaper decisions and the main event, the Spence–League fight, ended in the tenth with referee Mercy Montez calling for the no contest. Neither of the San Antonio dailies, the *Express* or the *Light*, apparently bothered to print the results of the main event.

After the debacle in San Antonio, Spence headed west to California where he met Primo's former nemesis Leon "Bombo" Chevalier, for a scheduled ten-rounder on October 14 at National Hall in San Francisco. This fight was not much of a contest either as Chevalier pounded Spence around the ring for a couple of minutes before landing a final pile driver that registered a quick, first-round knockout.

By the end of 1932 Spence owned a professional record of 11–8–1, but was beginning to consider turning out the light on his fight career. The promise of a decent payday against the towering Italian from Sequals enticed him into the ring that night in Dallas.

The card at the Fair Park Auditorium that night offered what the *Dallas Morning News* called "some of the classiest boxing seen here in many moons."[51] The evening featured several good fights including the semi-final between bantamweights Kid Granite and Bobby Fernandez. While Granite won on points, Fernandez refused to quit pressing and though battered by Granite's relentless left jab, he was still going strong at the final bell.

In the first fight featherweights Bobby O'Dowd and Joe Montana — no, not that Joe Montana — fought to a six-round draw. The evening's only knockout came in the second fight when Californian Frenchy LeFevre, who had been manhandled by his opponent Francis

Burke in the first round, caught Burke off guard with a haymaker to Burke's jaw that ended the affair quickly.

Primo took little time to eliminate Spence, finishing him with a first-round knockout. From the beginning it was obvious that the fight was to be a one-sided affair. "From the opening gong until he was counted out Spence looked like he was trying to find the easiest way out." The fight no doubt reminded Primo of his encounter with Elzear Rioux. Despite Carnera's best efforts to carry Spence for a while by pulling punches and even helping him up after the first knockdown, the fight ended quickly. Spence did not care to extend the bout. After a right from the Mountain grazed his head, the San Antonio heavyweight went down for the final time. The *Dallas Morning News* reported, "The Santone heavy didn't care to prolong the agony. He was eager to seek the solace of the canvas and after coming up from the first count he dropped again and stayed there when Carnera brushed him with a backhand pass."[52]

The *Morning News* continued, "The sorry showing wasn't Carnera's fault. As a matter of fact, the big Italian looked better than one would expect from one of his enormous size. He had speed, moved his gigantic dogs round in classy style, and there was little doubt that he packed dynamite of the sleep-producing variety in his pile-driving right."[53]

After the Carnera bout, Spence left the ring for three and a half years, fighting just once more in Dallas and losing by way of a fifth-round TKO to Tex Leavelle on May 21, 1936. It was Leavelle's only professional ring victory. Spence finished his prizefighting career that night at 11–10–1 and one no contest.

6

The Death of Ernie Schaaf, 1933

Ernie Schaaf died on Valentine's Day in 1933 at the age of 24, a few days after fighting Carnera. Ernie was a very good heavyweight prospect who fought in 75 professional bouts in his short but busy career. Ernie had all of the tools—he was a skilled boxer who could both give and take a hard punch. In his first 71 fights, he'd sent 23 men to the canvas, but had himself never been knocked out. From 1930 to 1932, he was ranked seventh, second, and fifth, respectively in *The Ring* magazine's Annual Heavyweight ratings. Ernie Schaaf was on his way up.

A myth has developed over the years and it asserts that when Schaaf died on February 14, 1933, it was a direct result of the beating that Max Baer gave him on August 31, 1932. Several factors play into this myth.

Much cited is the fact that West Coast heavyweight Frankie Campbell truly had died at the hands of Baer during a bout in San Francisco in August 1930, but in 1933, few in the press really believed this had any bearing on the Schaaf tragedy. One who did draw the correlation was journalist Tom Anderson. Writing in the days following Ernie's death, Anderson blamed the promoters whom he claimed knew of Schaaf's underlying encephalitis, thus of the danger to Schaaf. Anderson also claimed that Primo's shots hadn't been lethal and then brought up the Baer scenario. Anderson, writing under the headline "Tragic Outcome Does Not Prove Bout Was on the Level,"[1] stated that he thought the fight was fixed and that the proof lay in the fact that Primo couldn't hurt a flea and that the day before he fought Schaaf, Carnera had signed to fight Jack Sharkey in a championship bout. He also stated that athletic commissions accommodated fighters regularly by bending the rules to suit them. These charges are uninformed and ludicrous.

First, there are no fighters who would die to take a dive. Second, Primo most assuredly could hit with power. A quick read of the newspapers and magazines from the day reveal many journalists and other fighters who argued that point, and a viewing of Carnera's fight films shows plenty of hard shots tossed by the Italian man mountain. Third, while Primo and Sharkey did sign to fight on February 9, there is no reason to believe that it had anything more to do with the Schaaf fight. It may simply have been a way for each side to get a commitment from the other for what would undoubtedly be a fight with a very big gate. The signing was also no secret. The story of the signing was photographed and discussed by all of the wire services and therefore carried in newspapers worldwide — a strange way to keep a "fix" under their hats. Fourth, while the various boxing commissions did at times accommodate fighters and promoters they had been anything but Primo's friend since he arrived on American shores. So much for Tom Anderson's jaundiced view.

Other factors contributing to the myth are that the 23-year-old Baer was also considered to be an excellent prospect with improving skills and a powerful punch. This is an absolute fact. While some questioned Max's work ethic, his training regimen, his seriousness about his boxing career, and his morals, few would ever question his obvious talent, the power of his punch, or the sheer ferociousness of his attack. He had a killer-like instinct in the ring the likes of which Primo would never possess. He had in fact beaten Schaaf badly in August 1932, but this beating did not cause Ernie's death.

Finally and perhaps most notably in the public consciousness is the fact that two movies have squarely laid Schaaf's death at the feet of Max.

In the first, 1956's *The Harder They Fall*, Max himself makes the claim as his character says, "You know, I'm the guy who nailed Gus, murdered him for 15 rounds. Don't know what held him up, but when Gus left the ring that night he was a dead man. All your joker did was tap him. I did all the work and they gave your guy all the glory."[2] In this dark and thinly disguised telling of Primo's story, Baer basically plays himself, "Gus" is obviously Ernie Schaaf, and "your joker/your guy" is undeniably Primo Carnera. The movie was so far off on any number of points, but many forgot that it was just a Hollywood movie and heard what they wanted to hear.

The second was the 2005 movie *Cinderella Man*, the story of Jim Braddock's improbable rise to the heavyweight championship. As creditable as *Cinderella Man* was in so many ways, it gets Max Baer all wrong. Cocky and brash, yes, he certainly was, but remorseless, even proud of killing Campbell or claiming the death of Schaaf, no. The Campbell tragedy, in fact, so distressed Baer that he lost four of his next six fights. Baer's son, actor Max Baer, Jr., was furious with his father's portrayal in the movie. He states, "The portrayal of my father in *Cinderella Man* couldn't have been more wrong and inaccurate. They turned a good-hearted, fun-loving, friendly and warm human being who hated boxing into Mr. T from *Rocky III* with no redeeming characteristics."[3]

The fact is that the death of Campbell greatly affected Baer the fighter and Baer the man for the rest of his life. "Nothing haunted my father more than that fight," Baer Jr. said. "Nothing."[4] Baer would not return to the ring for another four months. Ironically, when he did climb through the ropes in Madison Square Garden, it would be for his first bout with Ernie Schaaf on December 19, 1930. Schaaf outboxed Baer for 10 rounds and received a unanimous decision.

Baer, Sr., later wrote, "Nothing that ever happened to me — nothing that can happen to me — affected me like the death of Frankie Campbell."[5]

Never again was Baer the same fighter. His fury was gone. His tenacity came and went. He often held back and even pulled punches on opponents he felt were beaten, as if he were afraid that he would hurt them. Many people, including Lou Nova himself, cite Baer's unwillingness to finish Nova off when he was wavering as the reason for his two wins over Max. More than once, it has been speculated that Baer's inability to fully put Campbell's death behind him caused Max to act erratically in the ring.

In 1935, Max raised over $15,000 for Campbell's widow Elsie and young son during a benefit exhibition in California.

Max Baer, Jr., has stated that his father had nightmares about the Campbell fight for the rest of his life. According to Max Jr., his dad would have a dream and "bolt awake at night, sweating and muttering, 'You're okay! Please be okay!'" Max's night terror always involved Campbell lying flat on the canvas and Max trying in vain to revive him.[6]

In other circles, it is said that Schaaf died from the blows he received over 13 rounds from Primo Carnera on February 10 at Madison Square Garden.

The former is totally fallacious and the latter only a small percentage of the story. It seems that many who speculate on either of these scenarios completely ignore the single most important testimony in the case — Ernie Schaaf's autopsy report.

According to the autopsy, the cause of Ernie's death was oedema — or swelling — of the brain. The report, referenced in the *New York Times*, clearly states, "Ernie Schaaf ... was suffering from an inflammation of the brain before he entered the ring." And it continued by stating, "Schaaf's condition probably was owing to an attack of influenza he suffered some weeks before the fight. According to the report, Schaaf's condition was aggravated during the bout by blows not in and of themselves dangerous, and his condition made him less able to avoid blows."[7] This supported the previous day's comments by brain surgeon Dr. Byron Stookey, who had just operated on Ernie to relieve pressure on the brain from swelling.

After examining Schaaf's body during the autopsy, Dr. Charles Norris, Chief Medical Examiner of the City of New York revealed that the examination of Schaaf's head and brain showed no fracture of the skull and no signs of long-standing injury or hemorrhage. Norris said that Schaaf had swelling in the brain, the cause of which could not be known for sure, but it may have been logically referred to Ernie's recent attack of influenza with a reasonable degree of probability.

Given the strength of Schaaf's two performances in the months preceding the Carnera fight it would seems less likely he had this inflammation at that time. It was only after he contracted influenza that Ernie gave the poor showing and looked so sluggish as he did

Ernie Schaaf drops Salvatore Ruggirello at Madison Square Garden on February 5, 1932. Referee Arthur Donovan is about to step in and call the fight. Schaaf had battered Ruggirello throughout the fight. Ruggirello was a late replacement for Paulino Uzcudun, who had fractured a rib in training. (*New York Daily News*)

against Carnera. As Dr. Norris indicated, it seems to be fairly cut and dried; there is, however, no absolute certainty.

In December 1930, Schaaf defeated Baer by decision. In their 1932 bout in Chicago Stadium, both fighters fought cautiously for the first eight rounds. The referee twice warned both men to fight. In the ninth round, Baer took charge of the fight, driving Ernie into the ropes with a powerful two-fisted assault. In the final round Baer pummeled Schaaf savagely about the head and body. The *New York Times* reported that only the bell saved Ernie from being kayoed. Schaaf was cold-cocked by Baer and knocked flat on his face with just two seconds remaining in the fight. At the bell, Ernie was dragged to his corner. It took several minutes before his seconds were able to bring him around.

To add to the evidence against the "Baer killed Schaaf" theorists, five and a half months passed between the Baer fight in August and the Carnera fight the following February. During this time Schaaf fought three times for a total of 22 rounds, losing one on a close, 10-round split decision, but scoring knockouts in the two victories.

In his first fight after his loss to Baer, Ernie faced Hartford heavyweight Ed "Unknown" Winston. The two fighters had met at the Eastern States Coliseum in West Springfield, Massachusetts, on May 16. In that fight, Schaaf had KO'ed Winston in the fifth. The rematch was scheduled for October 20 at the Boston Arena as part of a four-fight card and a capacity crowd of 12,000 fans showed up. In a close, hard-fought, ten-round contest, Winston took a split decision.

With each fighter having taken one contest, a rubber match with Winston was scheduled for December 12, again at the Boston Arena. This fight, scheduled for 12 rounds, was determined to be for the New England heavyweight championship. A crowd of 10,000 showed up to see if Schaaf could avenge his October loss and Ernie did not disappoint, looking very sharp throughout the contest. According to the *New York Times,* "Winston won the first round, but from there on his rival, who had the expert counseling of Jack Sharkey, drove ahead at a pace that earned him one of the most impressive victories he has registered in a local ring."[8]

Ernie began his dominance in the second round, attacking Winston with series after series of hard shots to the head and body and he drove his opponent to all corners of the ring. At 2:45 of the sixth round, referee Johnny Martin counted Winston out. Always the gentleman, Schaaf helped carry the groggy fighter to his corner where it took several minutes to fully revive him. Winston continued to fight through 1945 when he retired after 100 professional bouts with a record of 51–42–5 and two no contests.

Three and a half weeks later on January 6, 1933, Schaaf squared off in a rematch against Stanley Poreda, who had previously decisioned him. This time Ernie was in command, putting Poreda on the canvas three times and knocking him out in the 6th round. The *New York Times* reported, "Poreda was down twice in the 2nd and had to be carried to his corner. He was down again in the 4th and for the fourth and final time in the 6th."[9] Referee Arthur Donovan stopped the bout at 28 seconds of the sixth round. Poreda, a one-time prospect, was never the same. After being whipped by Schaaf, Poreda would lose five of his next six fights and retire in 1935.

On January 10th, Schaaf and Carnera met at the Madison Square Garden offices of Jimmy Johnston to sign for a fight scheduled for February 10th.

With a February bout against Carnera up next, some press reports widely picked the much-ballyhooed Schaaf to defeat Primo. Many news stories followed lines such as this: "Schaaf Superior to Carnera — Anyone who saw last night's bout can easily visualize Schaaf battering down the Italian man mountain if the former fights in the manner he did last night."[10]

Early in the week before the fight, odds makers unaware of Schaaf's condition installed Ernie as a 2-to-1 favorite to beat Carnera. Later in the week, the odds tightened and Carnera was even a 6-to-5 favorite on many cards. Primo had been promised a shot at Jack Sharkey and the championship if he were to dispatch Schaaf. Schaaf had been promised nothing but his end of the purse. Since Sharkey and Johnny Buckley were his managers, a championship fight between Schaaf and Sharkey was impossible.

The five-fight card drew a crowd that filled Madison Square Garden to near capacity on that cold and fateful February night. Three of the four fights on the undercard went the distance, keeping the fans well entertained as they anxiously awaited the headliner in which the 4th- and 5th-ranked heavyweights in the world would mix it up. Schaaf entered the fight with an impressive 59–13–2 record and Carnera 74–6–0. Both fighters stood legitimate shots at the heavyweight crown.

Jimmy Johnston had specifically chosen William J. "Billy" Cavanaugh as the third man in the ring for the main event to further assure people the fight was on the level. Cavanaugh was a veteran of the fight game, a respected arbiter, and the long-time boxing instructor at the United States Military Academy at West Point.[11]

In Ernie's corner were his managers, trainers, and close friends Johnny Buckley and Jack Sharkey. In Primo's were Duffy, Defoe, and Soresi. Soon after Cavanaugh yelled, "Seconds out," the bout began.

The fight started with both fighters feeling each other out and initially nothing seemed amiss. As the fight wore on, however, it was clear that Schaaf was in no shape to have entered the ring to fight Primo or anyone else that night. Reports of the bout reveal that Schaaf made a mediocre showing. Press reports show that Schaaf "had been dangled, figuratively, on the end of Carnera's long left jabs, sent off balance not infrequently with Carnera's ponderous hooks, and smashed by the giant's awkward right crosses and uppercuts. In every round of the twelve that were completed Carnera held the upper hand."[12] A simple review of the fight films shows this to be absolutely true.

In the 13th round, the boxers met at center ring. After landing a solid left early, Schaaf only pawed at Carnera while Primo landed consistently sturdy shots. Still in the center of the ring, Carnera landed a solid, straight left that snapped Ernie's head back and sent him backwards near the ropes where Ernie went down hard on his left side. When Carnera dropped Schaaf that final time, Ernie lay on his left elbow with a dazed look on his face. He was not quite prostrate and he grasped the bottom rope with his right hand, but was clearly unable to rise. Cavanaugh sent Primo to a neutral corner and began the count. At three, Schaaf's right hand slipped from the ropes. At four, he fell forward and completely collapsed. At five, Cavanaugh waved him out and the fight was over. Within three seconds Primo was back across the ring to offer assistance to his clearly troubled opponent. Ernie lay closer to Carnera's corner and Primo's seconds arrived first, followed immediately after by Sharkey and the rest of Schaaf's corner.

As fight announcer Joe Humphreys lifted Primo's right arm and proclaimed him the victor, Schaaf lay struggling for his life on the Garden canvas. All through the fight, Ernie presented a porous defense, leaving himself open and even walking into Carnera's punches. At times he seemed almost trance-like as he sat on his stool between rounds with Sharkey and Buckley animatedly instructing him on how to attack Carnera. Instead of acknowledging his friends, he simply stared ahead at the canvas.

6. The Death of Ernie Schaaf, 1933

As the decision was announced, many in the crowd of 20,000 yelled "fake" and booed lustily. They could not believe that Carnera's final punch was of the knockout variety and on this point they may have been right. But Schaaf was much more seriously injured than anyone in the crowd realized. There had been no setup as rumored before the fight; rather, Ernie was simply too ill to have been in the ring that night and he was slugging it out with a fighter against whom he couldn't hide that fact and simply outlast.

The final punch was simply the last in a 13-round series of punishment suffered by Schaaf that night that ultimately caused him to fall. His brain was swelling and his body giving out. The crowd simply did not realize that Ernie had done all he could that night and that the life was now ebbing out of his limp body.

After several minutes of feverishly trying to revive Schaaf, Sharkey grabbed him under the arms and dragged him across the ring to his corner where he was set upright, but still unconscious on his stool. After several more minutes, Sharkey and five other men helped pass Ernie through the ropes and out of the ring for the last time — his body was as limp as a rag doll.

In Schaaf's dressing room, medical personnel desperately attempted to revive the stricken fighter. After 20 minutes of respiratory work, New York State Athletic Commission physician Dr. William H. Walker ordered Schaaf be taken to the hospital.

Shortly after 11:00 P.M., Ernie was carried out of the Garden and across the street to the Polyclinic Hospital where Dr. Walker announced that Schaaf was suffering from a concussion.

While Schaaf gave it all he had, he was no match for Carnera throughout the fight. Michael Hunnicutt of the International Boxing Research Organization sums up Schaaf's performance nicely: "Perhaps, most importantly, Ernie seemed in this bout not able to ride or roll with virtually any of the punches that he received. His head was continuously being pushed, jerked, and snapped back through the 12 rounds as it was when the final jab in the 13th snapped his head back and Ernie collapsed. Under his condition of meningitis at that time, it is remarkable he did not collapse much sooner. Ernie was more than game, he was heroic in his final bout."[13]

Schaaf remained at the Polyclinic Hospital for several days clinging to life and going into and out of a coma. His left side showed signs of paralysis and he had difficulty recognizing visitors when he was conscious. Ernie's devoted mother Lucy and his sister May Daly hurried down from their home in Massachusetts to be at his side at the hospital. Ernie was very close to his mother. After every ring victory he would send her rose carnations. Also there throughout the long vigil was his friend and manager Johnny Buckley.

On Monday afternoon, Schaaf underwent three hours of surgery. A team of four noted neurologists[14] worked carefully to relieve swelling from a deep-seated intra-cranial hemorrhage. A hospital bulletin stated, "The patient stood the operation well and afterwards moved his left arm which had been paralyzed. The patient's condition however, is still critical."[15] The brain specialist in charge of the operation, Dr. Byron Stookey, stated that Schaaf "must have been knocked out on his feet," and that there was no doubt that the injury had been suffered in the Carnera fight.[16]

Buckley told the press that due to Schaaf's battle with influenza just a few weeks earlier, he had only trained for 10 days prior to the Carnera fight. The level of training is not in and of itself a big problem given the fact that Ernie was 24 years old, in fine condition, and had fought 26 rounds over the past three months against quality opponents, but it does show the severity of the illness. While training for the fight, Ernie was stricken, but stubbornly refused all advice to postpone the bout. This was typical of Schaaf's no worries mentality. Long-time friend and former manager Phil Schlossberg commented, "Schaaf only has one fault as a boxer. He is too game. He takes too many unnecessary punches. He is too confident that nobody can hurt him."[17]

By midnight, the doctors knew that Ernie was fading and there was nothing they could do. Once, Ernie awoke briefly from his coma. Asked by his mother how he was, Ernie replied weakly, "I'm okay, Mom." He then slipped back into a coma and never regained consciousness. His close friend Father Remi B. Scheuver, who had come down from Boston, was called to administer the last rites of the Catholic Church. Ernie Schaaf drew his last breath at 4:10 A.M. on Tuesday, February 14, 1933. His mother, his sister, and Jack Buckley were with him when he died.

Sharkey had left for Miami shortly after the fight to vacation with his family. He was to cut his trip short and board a train back to New York on Tuesday morning to visit Schaaf. Instead, he headed back to Massachusetts for his funeral.

Shortly after Schaaf's death, orders were given to pick up Primo on a technical charge of manslaughter. This order was quickly changed from an arrest to an interrogation at the district attorney's office. Carnera, his managers and trainers, Schaaf's team, referee Billy Cavanaugh, and members of the state boxing commission were all present. After a brief conversation, Assistant DA James P. Daly announced that no evidence of any criminal negligence could be found, but a final determination would be made following the official autopsy. Later that day, the New York City Medical Examiner's office released their report. As stated, their findings and the signed autopsy certificate gave the cause of death as "cerebral hemorrhage and cerebral compression. The cause of the inflammation cannot be known with certainty, but it may be referred to the recent attack of influenza with a reasonable degree of probability."[18] In other words, Ernie Schaaf shouldn't have climbed into the ring that night against Primo or anyone else.

The same afternoon, politicians and governing bodies all did what they do in these situations. New York Governor Herbert Lehman ordered a thorough investigation of the Schaaf–Carnera affair, the state legislature looked into more stringent regulation if not a downright ban on boxing in the state, and members of the New York State Boxing Commission announced that they had been against this fight and that they would no longer sanction Carnera to fight anyone under 6' 2" tall or weighing less than 220 pounds. This would limit Primo to fewer than 10 known opponents, all but one of whom he had already defeated.

In an afternoon news conference, New York State Boxing Commissioners William Muldoon and General John J. Phelan announced they would attempt to reestablish the "super-dreadnaught" class for over-sized heavyweights like Carnera. Muldoon had first pushed the new weight class in 1931 as a reaction to the huge weight disparities in many of Primo's fights. If successful, Muldoon and Phelan's action would force Carnera to choose opponents from only within this super-sized weight class. Muldoon was quoted as saying, "Carnera is a great athlete from the feet up. He has the speed and agility of a middleweight and as far as punching is concerned he needs no snap to his blows. His weight is enough. He is the greatest physical specimen I have ever seen."[19]

This move was a huge potential problem for Madison Square Garden promoter Jimmy Johnson, who was attempting to match Primo against Jack Sharkey for the heavyweight championship in the Garden later that year. To cover his bets, Johnson began looking at alternative venues in other states in which to hold the bout including the MSG Corporation's

6. The Death of Ernie Schaaf, 1933

subsidiaries. Most prominently mentioned were the Boston Garden and Miami's Madison Square Garden Arena.

Not everyone in a position of authority found it necessary to overreact. National Boxing Association President James M. "Bingo" Brown commented that he thought that Muldoon's motion was a bad idea and completely out of order. Pack McFarland of the Illinois Boxing Commission decried Muldoon's proposal, stating, "The New York Commission may be going a little too far if they permit Carnera to fight only men such as Vittorio Campolo."[20] Commissioner McFarland continued his comments by pointing out that while heavyweights like Sharkey, Baer, and Schmeling would all be significantly outweighed by Carnera, each could give him a busy evening in the ring. New York State Athletic Commission Chairman James A. Farley, a close confidante of President-elect Roosevelt's and the recently named Democratic Party Chairman, commented with a cooler head that, while Schaaf's death was to be deplored, it in no way should be construed as a reflection on boxing. The wrangling continued for the next few days. It was, however, now time to bury Ernie Schaaf.

* * *

On the day before the funeral, Lucy Schaaf, Ernie's mother, consoled Carnera with a soothing note: "Kindly be assured that I do not consider you in any way responsible for the death of my boy. I feel toward you like I would have wished your mother to have felt toward my Ernie if you had met with some misfortune during your bout with him. I thank you for your offers of sympathy and for your kind expressions of admiration for Ernie."[21] Primo, upon receiving the telegram, was moved to tears by the gesture.

On Friday morning family and friends gathered at Schaaf's home in Wrentham, Massachusetts, to escort his body to St. Mary's Catholic Church in nearby Sheldonville. It was Schaaf's intent to go into the Catholic priesthood upon retiring from boxing. When at home, Ernie regularly attended mass at St. Mary's and spent time at the Passionist Monastery in Brighton.

It was a cold, gray morning and the late winter snow lay all around. The funeral was set for 10:00 A.M. Father Walter J. Mitchell, Father James J. Walsh, and Father Scheuver celebrated High Mass. "The town's highways were choked with traffic and public buildings flew flags at half staff as the funeral cortege of the dead boxer slowly wended its way from the Schaaf home to the church and thence to the cemetery."[22] Legionnaires lined the steps of the church as Ernie's flag-draped gray casket was carried up the steps. After the Mass, Ernie's casket was placed back in the hearse for a final trip to the cemetery in Foxboro. Flag bearers, members of the Navy firing squad detail, and members of Wrentham's Fire Department preceded his hearse.

It is estimated that a crowd of 3,500 mourners stood quietly during the brief graveside service. As Ernie's body was lowered into the grave, the naval escort fired three volleys into the air followed by taps being sounded by a U.S. marine bugler.

Flower arrangements filled five automobiles. Tributes had been sent by a variety of notables including Sharkey and Max Schmeling. Primo sent a $150 cross—six feet high and four feet across—adorned with roses, orchids, lilies and violets, bearing a satin ribbon inscribed "with the deepest of sympathy—Primo Carnera." A blanket of roses and carnations from Ernie's grieving mother covered his grave.

As a show of respect to Schaaf, Madison Square Garden was dark that evening and its card of fights featuring Johnny Risko and King Levinsky was postponed one week.

* * *

It seems to be all but certain that Max Baer had nothing more to do with the death of Ernie Schaaf than any of the other fighters whom Ernie met in the ring during his career. In all the deluge of press coverage after Schaaf's death, few writers considered the Baer fight newsworthy.

According to Michael Hunnicutt, it was influenza that really killed Schaaf, "as noted in the autopsy and Ernie's obituary 'just before his bout with Carnera, Schaaf went into reclusion in a religious retreat near Boston to recuperate from an attack of influenza that produced the meningitis and then fighting with this condition.'"[23]

During a 2005 interview Ernie's sister-in-law Anita Schaaf told reporter Alan Tays that while she enjoyed *Cinderella Man*, she was very disappointed with the implication that Ernie had died from injuries received during the Baer fight. Director Ron Howard implied this and, "They even showed Ernie being dragged to the side and saying that was from the Max Baer fight. It isn't; it's from the Carnera fight. That's when I really got upset."[24]

Ms. Schaaf also points to the influenza and meningitis as the real culprit in her brother-in-law's death. "What weakened him," she said, "two or three weeks before he fought Carnera, he was in the hospital for four days with the flu. He should have never boxed."[25] She also points out that Ernie received a number of beatings in his final year in the ring. In addition to the Baer fight, Ernie took a severe beating in a victory over Tony Galento. An article from a 1972 copy of *The Ring* points out that "some experts insist that Ernie began to die on June 7, 1932, when he fought Two Ton Tony Galento.... Though Ernie won a 10-round decision, he absorbed a great deal of punishment.... From then on, it seems, Schaaf was never the same."[26]

* * *

In time the fallout over Schaaf's death blew over. It was a busy news week and other stories took its place. Soup kitchens were still in full operation and nearly 25 percent of the eligible workforce was unemployed. On Monday, *Newsweek* Magazine appeared on the newsstands for the first time. A massive earthquake in northwest China killed an estimated 70,000 people.

In Miami, a naturalized Italian bricklayer named Giuseppe Zangara unloaded his pistol at President-elect Roosevelt in Bayfront Park on February 15. Zangara aimed his gun carefully, but as he pulled the trigger spectators who saw the weapon forced his arm up. Roosevelt was unharmed, but Chicago Mayor Anton J. Cermak and four bystanders were hit. Zangara was immediately wrestled to the ground and arrested. Overriding a Secret Service order, Roosevelt directed his driver to pick up Cermak and the other injured and take them to the nearest hospital. During the drive Roosevelt cradled Anton Cermak's head on his shoulder and continually talked to the mayor, saying, "Tony, keep quiet, don't move, Tony." The doctors later credited Roosevelt with keeping Cermak alert and from going into shock. The president-elect remained at the hospital for over four hours until the wounded were stabilized. Despite the best efforts of surgeons, Cermak's wounds proved fatal as he finally succumbed to his injuries on March 6. The other injured bystanders all made full recoveries.[27]

On February 17, the Blaine Act was passed in the United States Senate, spelling the beginning of the end of Prohibition in the United States by allowing for the sale of beverages containing up to 3.2 percent alcohol by weight.

6. The Death of Ernie Schaaf, 1933

* * *

Primo, who was in so many ways a gentle giant, was greatly upset by Ernie's death. After receiving the news of his passing, the powerful titan reportedly sat and sobbed for hours in his rooms at the Hotel Victoria. He arranged for a large floral arrangement to be sent to the Schaaf home and sent a wire to Ernie's mother expressing his condolences and begging her forgiveness. He sent a priest, Father Delerole, to represent him at the funeral and arranged for a mass to be said in memory of Ernie after his return to Sequals. There is even an unsubstantiated story that Primo turned over his purse from the fight to Ernie's mother Lucy to help cover funeral costs and other needs in the coming years. While the story has never been verified as fact or fiction, the act would fall into the category of something those who knew Primo could easily see him doing.

Primo even briefly considered leaving the ring. Ironically, Primo's trainer Billy Defoe proved to be uniquely prepared to offer Primo counsel in this time of grief and self-searching. The former featherweight notable had fought Dominick Tippero on September 7, 1925, in Great Falls, Montana. On that Labor Day afternoon both men fought well, but Tippero built up an early points lead. In the later rounds Defoe began landing powerful punches to his opponent's head and body. Tippero absorbed a tremendous amount of punishment. With Tippero beginning to show signs of distress it appeared as if the fight might be stopped, but he refused to quit and he ordered his corner not to throw in the towel. Defoe begged for his opponent to quit and even began to lay back a bit. Somehow Tippero had managed to hold enough of a point lead from the early rounds to eke out a close decision, but after being helped from the ring, he collapsed in his dressing room. After being partially revived Tippero began showing signs of paralysis and was hospitalized. He died on September 11 from a brain concussion sustained in the fight. As a result of this tragedy, Defoe knew firsthand the frightening realities of death in the ring. Defoe's perspective and Lucy Schaaf's forgiveness helped Carnera decide to continue fighting, but from that point on whenever he fought, Primo "had to face two opponents: the boxer and Schaaf's ghost."[28]

In late February Primo sailed for Italy where it was felt that some time at home would do him some good in putting the tragedy in the past. Like Max Baer with Frankie Campbell, however, Primo Carnera would forever be haunted by his vivid memories of that cold February night and the death of Ernie Schaaf.

7

"A Right Uppercut": The Championship, 1933

Primo sailed for Italy in late February, anxious to get away from the specters haunting him in New York. He wanted to go home to Sequals and surround himself with the familiarity and comfort of his home, family, and friends. Arriving in Italy on March 4, Primo made his way to the warmth of Sequals and hopefully, a chance at some peace and distance from the requiem for poor Ernie Schaaf.

While in Sequals, Primo found some solace in being able to host friends and family in his newly completed home built on the Via Roma, on the outskirts of the downtown area. The home still stands and is a beautiful 2-story Italian villa with large rooms, impressive gates, and a formal front garden. A one-story building at the end of the driveway and to the left of the main house was built as a garage and houses a fully equipped gymnasium where Primo exercised and sparred while in Sequals. Above the gymnasium door is a large mosaic sign that spells out a quote in Latin, from the Roman poet Juvenal. The passage reads, "Mens sana in corpore sano," which translates roughly in English to, "A sound mind in a sound body." The home, which he named very simply the "Villa Carnera," was his sanctuary of which he was very proud and it proved to be one of the few sound investments made during his boxing career.

Back in Manhattan, at its March 14 meeting, the New York State Athletic Commission approved a fight for the heavyweight championship between Primo and reigning champ Jack Sharkey. It was established that the fight would be held at the Madison Square Garden Bowl in Long Island City, N.Y. The Madison Square Garden Corporation built the open-air arena in 1932, to accommodate larger crowds than could fit into the indoor Garden in Manhattan. The Bowl, located at 48th Street and Northern Boulevard in Long Island City, could hold upwards of 72,000 spectators.[1]

During the meeting, the commission also gave permission to Tim Mara to promote a 15-round bout between former world champion Max Schmeling and Max Baer. Mara, in association with Jack Dempsey, planned to schedule the battle for June 1. Mara, founder and owner of the National Football League's New York Football Giants, held the rights to promote boxing events in both the Polo Grounds and Yankee Stadium, which assured that the fights would be held in either of those large venues.[2]

Coincidentally, on the same day that the commission was approving the biggest fight of Carnera's life, the morning news reports out of Italy announced that Primo had suffered injuries when a racing car that he was driving had overturned near Udine. Primo and a companion, Bruno Rapieri, were taken to the hospital in nearby San Vito. Rapieri was in serious condition, and required a lengthier hospital stay, but Primo suffered only a laceration on the back of his head and a cut on his left temple. He was released from the hospital and returned to Sequals on March 15.[3]

On March 30, the wire services reported that Carnera's Western "manager" Frank Churchill had died of heart failure at his home in La Habra, California, at the age of 59. Churchill had been involved in arranging Primo's Western swing in 1930. Fairly or not, the California State Athletic Commission revoked his license along with those of both boxers and their management teams after the Chevalier affair. Whether a related event or not, it was shortly after that episode that Churchill's heart began to fail.[4]

On April 8 Carnera announced that he was attempting to promote a match between former heavyweight champ Max Schmeling and himself in Rome, sometime after his upcoming bout with Sharkey. In doing so, Primo showed his naiveté, for the political realities of this bout occurring were slimmer than he could have ever known. Far too much money and prestige were at stake for the Madison Square Garden Corporation and Primo's American management not to be involved. Also, the idea of two big-name Europeans fighting it out in a European city frankly did not appeal to many in the American fight game.

* * *

In mid–April, Primo visited Rome. It was during this time that Emilia Tersini took her breach-of-promise case to the High Court of Justice in London. Emilia was well represented in court by her attorney, the famous barrister and King's Counsel Walter T. Monckton. Skillfully guided by Monckton, the now 22-year-old waitress testified that Primo had failed to make good his stated intention to marry her. Emilia spoke of Primo's promises of "a trip with her around the world and a home in Hollywood where she could chum with all the film folk."[5] Emilia shared letters from Primo with frequent mentions of young love such as, "my treasure," "my love," "my Melia for life," "a beautiful little house," "a fine motor car," etc. There was no doubt that he, at one time, felt and openly expressed his love for Emilia.

Primo was again poorly advised by his management and legal advisors, told not to attend the legal proceedings. As usual, Primo listened, and chose not to attend the hearings to argue his case. Instead of appearing, he simply sent a wire to London stating, "Let the case take its course. What can I do?"[6] By not appearing to contest the claims, Primo may well have hurt himself in the eyes of the jury. After listening to the silver-tongued Monckton and Emilia's woeful tales of betrayal, heartbreak and loneliness, Primo's lack of attendance only seemed to support the case against him. The jury found in favor of Emilia and awarded her the then-whopping sum of $14,390 in damages.

On April 15, Primo made a pilgrimage to the Vatican City where he was granted an audience with Pope Pius XI. When his Excellency entered the Throne Room, Primo knelt and took the Pontiff's hand in his huge hand and kissed his ring. Primo's presence and the granting of an audience caused a stir among some in the Vatican due to the Holy See's stated aversion to prizefighting, and the recent death of Ernie Schaaf. *L'Osservatore Romano*, the Vatican's official newspaper since 1861, had written an extremely caustic piece after Schaaf's death. Visiting St. Peter's and meeting the Pope was something that this once poor and unknown son of Sequals could have never dreamed of as a boy.

Primo and Soresi were to sail from Genoa on April 27 on the *Conte di Savoia*, but once again, they were delayed by social events and missed the ship's departure. Soresi booked passage for the next week on the *Rex* and after spending the next three days in Rome and southern Italy, Carnera and his entourage finally sailed for New York in early May, arriving in Manhattan on May 12. While he trained as well as possible during the cruise, Primo was anxious to land and begin serious preparations for the Sharkey rematch. He knew that this was his shot at the heavyweight title and he might not get another.

* * *

Some of the excitement of Primo's return and the Sharkey fight was tarnished when shortly after his arrival in New York, he was served with papers for a suit brought in New York Superior Court by Emilia Tersini in the name of Theodore J. Skratt. The suit was brought to collect the $14,390 judgment awarded to Tersini by the London court for breach of promise.

Primo told the press that it was Emilia who had proposed to him, and that her actions in filing the suit had destroyed any feelings he still had for her. Had he said as much in April

Madison Square Garden boxing promoter Jimmy Johnston, center, holds the hands of Jack Sharkey (l), the world's heavyweight champion, and Primo Carnera (r), the challenger, after the two men had signed up for a title match to take place on June 29, 1933. In the back row (left to right) are Sharkey's manager, Johnny Buckley, Bill Duffy and Louis Soresi. (Bettmann/CORBIS)

to the London jury, he might have limited the financial award to Emilia, but now it was too late and his often difficult finances were in a huge mess.

Financial matters would continue to dog Primo for years. Not having the money to pay the breach of promise judgment, or any of the other bills that had begun piling up, Primo had little choice but to file for bankruptcy. While he was surrounded by the trappings of success, Primo Carnera was in reality broke. The good-natured, trusting, and generous giant had been swindled by most of his managers out of the roughly $1 million he had earned in the ring.

In a bankruptcy petition filed at the United States District Court in New York on June 18, Primo listed assets of $1,182 versus liabilities of $59,829. The petition broke down those assets as $721 in two banks and an automobile. Claimants against Carnera included Leon See who sought $3,779; Jeff Dickson for $1,250; Manhattan's Victoria Hotel who said Primo still owed them $299; and, of course, his former love Emilia Tersini, who was into him for a cool $14,390, simply because Primo had decided that she was not the woman for him. Tersini's legal actions after the breakup surely show that Carnera used sound judgment in breaking off that relationship.

His managers, his former girlfriend, various lawyers, and others all wanted a piece of Carnera. Through his blood, sweat, and hard work, they sought small fortunes. They took advantage of his drawing power, his lack of education, his easy-going personality, and of his kind and generous nature. In his simple and broken English Primo may have summed up the situation best when he stated, "I got no dough. Everybody wants dough, dough, dough. I got no dough."[7]

* * *

In advance of the Sharkey fight, Primo set up his training camp at Dr. Joseph Bier's Health Farm in the northern New Jersey town of Pompton Lakes. Doc Bier's had been the training home to numerous fighters since it opened in 1923. Those who had trained there included Harry Greb, Benny Leonard, and Tony Canzoneri. The quiet, rural setting seemed ideal for Primo as he readied himself for his shot at the heavyweight crown.

Now a booming suburb of Manhattan, Pompton Lakes was then a small country town with just over 3,000 inhabitants. Purchased from its Native American occupiers in 1695, Pompton Lakes became the home of the Pompton Furnace that supplied iron materials to the early American colonies. Notably, the iron works supplied ball and shot to troops during the French and Indian, Revolutionary, and 1812 wars. It was a beautiful and quaint village to which Primo would return a year later, while training for his title defense against Max Baer.

In 1935, Joe Louis adopted the town. The Brown Bomber set up his training camp at Doc Bier's as he readied for his fight with Primo. During his time there, Louis developed a strong bond with its citizenry. Town lore records that Louis fought an exhibition in 1935 to help raise money for the purchase of the Borough's first ambulance. That May, while Louis was in town training for the Carnera fight, Roger Vreeland, a local citizen, died while waiting for medical help to arrive from a neighboring town, after being struck by an automobile. Louis, learning of the local drive to purchase the vehicle, was only too glad to help out by offering to raise money doing what he knew best—boxing. The exhibition was a success. Louis donated $2,935 from the bout, and the town got an ambulance. Louis continued to train in the town for much of his career and several years later he donated $2,000 for a police communication tower. Even in retirement, Louis was known to return to visit old friends and in 1999 the Borough dedicated the Joe Louis Memorial Park in honor of their friend and former champion.

* * *

On June 8 Max Baer and Max Schmeling met in their heavyweight elimination bout in front of nearly 60,000 enthusiastic fans at the Yankee Stadium. A strong, six-fight card and a beautiful, cool, late spring evening helped assure a strong turnout. Both Sharkey and Carnera were in attendance that night, taking time away from their own training to see the featured fight between two of the heaviest punchers in ring history. The winner of this fight would almost assuredly meet the winner of the late June bout between Sharkey and Carnera.

In addition to the fact that two great fighters with tremendous punching power were about to mix it up, the fight took on additional significance as promoter Jack Dempsey and the press played up the fact that Baer, while not a practicing Jew, did have a Jewish grandfather. Schmeling, fairly or not, was seen as representing the new Nazi regime in Germany and their anti–Semitic policies.

Schmeling entered the fight as a 3-to-1 favorite, but that fact did not deter Baer in the least. The Californian came out in the first round full of purpose. Max Baer, with the Star of David prominently displayed on his trunks, was out to whip the Black Uhlan of the Rhine. He put aside the clowning for once, and fought the way his mentor Jack Dempsey had hoped he would — with seriousness and determination. He fought fiercely and was constantly on the attack, with blows landing solidly and wildly. Several times referee Arthur Donovan warned Baer for illegal blows. Schmeling, however, was not cowed by his rival. Relying on his superior ring generalship and equally devastating punching power, he gave back as good as he got for nine intense rounds.

At the tail end of the ninth stave, Baer caught Schmeling with a sudden right hook that rocked the German. Baer, seeing his chance, immediately pounced on Schmeling, raining destructive blows on his opponent. As the bell sounded ending the round, Donovan had to step in and pull the trance-like Baer off his withered opponent. In the tenth round, Baer sensed victory and took up where he left off, pounding the Black Uhlan with savage punches until Schmeling dropped to the canvas, where he took an eight-count before rising. Baer continued to stay after Schmeling, pummeling the still groggy German with savage shots until at 1:51 of the round, Donovan had seen enough. The fight was over and he stepped in to stop the fight, and spare Schmeling from any further punishment.

The fight was chosen by *The Ring* magazine as their 1933 Fight of the Year. It was also a tremendous financial success, with receipts of $239, 676.07, assuring a generous profit for promoter Jack Dempsey and sizable purses for both fighters. Schmeling reportedly received $78,000 and Baer $26,000 for their respective nights' work.

* * *

On Thursday June 29, 1933, the world readied itself for the world heavyweight title fight between the champion, Jack Sharkey, and his challenger, the Italian behemoth Primo Carnera.

Cloudy conditions during the day threatened rain showers into the evening, but the weather gods cooperated, bringing clearing skies as the first preliminaries started at 7:00 P.M. The threatening skies earlier in the afternoon may have played a part in keeping the crowd below the expected gate of 60,000. Still, a respectable crowd of 40,000 headed to

Long Island City for an evening of boxing. A portion of the night's proceeds would go to The Free Milk Fund for Babies, Inc., which was chaired by Mrs. Millicent Hearst, the estranged wife of newspaper magnate William Randolph Hearst.

Going into the fight, odds makers put the bout at virtually even money. It was estimated by betting commissioners that more money had been wagered on the Sharkey–Carnera contest through the day of the fight, than on any since the second Dempsey–Tunney bout in Chicago, in 1927. On the morning of the fight, Sharkey was an 11–1 favorite on the street, but by fight time, according to the Associated Press, Carnera had risen to a 6–5 favorite.

Sharkey was a model of inconsistency. He was a strong, skilled, and powerful fighter who could look like a world-beater one night and a journeyman the next. His biggest liability lay in his moodiness in the ring. If he disagreed with the referee's call or felt as if an opponent's foul had been overlooked, he became distracted and made mistakes. Though controlling the fight, Sharkey almost lost to Carnera in their previous bout by trying to leave the ring after referee Gunboat Smith refused to count Primo out for taking a knee without being hit. Only quick thinking by Sharkey's manager Johnny Buckley kept Sharkey from climbing through the ropes and into a withdrawal.

Associated Press sportswriter Hugh Fullerton wrote on the eve of the contest, "The disparity in the sizes of the contestants; Carnera's undoubtedly great improvement since the Boston Gob handed him an artistic lacing at Ebbets Field two years ago; Sharkey's temperament which betrayed him into costly mistakes in previous bouts; gave the meeting a flock of 'angles' which still had the faithful jittering around in search of a favorite today."[8] "Despite his great bulk and his 6 feet 7 inches of height, the 'Vast Venetian' is fast and a clever boxer lacking only a real knockout punch. He has a quick and accurate left jab and moves with surprising lightness on his oversized feet. He is however shy on ring generalship and unable to cope with sudden shifts in attacking style."[9] "Sharkey, in perfect condition, has displayed everything he needs to defend the crown in his workouts, speed, snap, confidence and a venomous punching power that has worked havoc among his sparring partners. In addition, there is the tragic angle of Ernie Schaaf's death a few days after he was knocked out by Carnera last winter. Although the medical evidence revealed that Carnera's jab had little or nothing to do with Schaaf's death, it gave him a reputation as a 'killer' and it gave Sharkey, Schaaf's stablemate, an incentive to do his best tonight."[10]

Well-wishers had called, sent telegrams, and dropped by. Just prior to the fight a telegram had come from Sequals that read, "Primo, this evening we are praying for you. Mamma and Pappa." Another, somewhat dubious in nature, had arrived from London and read, "Despite everything, I hope you win. Emilia."[11]

A six-fight undercard entertained the crowd at the Garden Bowl. The throng milled about as a series of heavyweights pounded their way through their bouts. The first bout was a welterweight contest and the pro debut for Leonard Del Genio, who won by way of technical knockout over Phil Bruno in three rounds. After a first-round knockout in the second fight, the remainder of the bouts went the distance.

Sharkey climbed into the ring at 9:30 P.M. accompanied by his manager Johnny Buckley, his trainer Al Lacri and seconds Tony Polozzolo and Gus Wilson. The champion received polite applause from the fans. A few minutes later Primo arrived with Billy Duffy and Billy Defoe, wearing a green satin robe and waving to the crowd. The challenger received a thunderous ovation from the crowd.

As the fighters got ready in their corners, former champions Dempsey, Tunney, and

Loughran were introduced from the ring. The referee for the fight was veteran Arthur Donovan and the judges at ringside were Jim Buckley and Charles Lynch. After Donavan gave them instructions, the fighters touched gloves and the bout began.

Sharkey pressed the issue from the start, full of confidence from his previous thrashing of Carnera, in Brooklyn in 1931. Throughout the fight, Sharkey moved forward with his hands tight into his body. The champion was able to avoid Carnera's normally effective left jab, bobbing and feinting until he was able to rock Carnera with a flurry of body shots and right crosses to the head. Fighting in close had its dangers, however — one slip of his defense and Sharkey would leave himself open to a flash of Primo's tremendous power.

While the champion was busy, Primo, by most accounts, took the first round with an edge on jabs in close fighting. After that, Sharkey made a show for the next four rounds. As the second round opened Sharkey took charge, landing at least three shots to the chin that obviously hurt Carnera. The third round was close as the two fighters exchanged shots and frequently fell into the clinches. Throughout the chapter, Carnera used his great strength and shoved Sharkey around the ring. In the fourth, the action moved along slowly as the fighters would exchange a few more punches and then slip back into the clinches. Referee Arthur Donovan had to keep the fighters under control as he warned Carnera against holding and hitting, and later for backhanding.

In rounds two through six, Sharkey really dictated the terms of the fight. The Associated Press reported, "Right up to the last punch tonight he was fighting one of the greatest battles of his career. Bobbing, feinting, his lips in a thin snarl, eyes flashing between narrowed lids, the Boston Sailor ripped into battle in flashes. He moved the Giant Italian around, found his openings, then lashed his punches—long rights to the head—left hooks to the body, straight to the mark."[12]

In the fifth, Sharkey swarmed into Carnera and broke through the Italian's defense. Sharkey pummeled the challenger with a series of rapid and relentless left hooks to the body and powerful rights to the head. The crowd sensed that Sharkey was moving in for the kill. With Primo already shaky, the champ landed another powerful right to the head, and it looked like the challenger was going down. But as Sharkey readied for the coup de grace, Primo steadied himself, raised his massive arms and blocked the champ's savage blows. Primo held on as the bell tolled the end of the round.

Into the sixth round, Sharkey continued to fight Primo in close and land jarring shots to the challenger. The two fighters grappled along the ropes on one side of the ring and then the other. During the round, however, Primo seemed to be strengthening. At one point, Carnera staggered the champion with a left to the head that sent Sharkey to his knees and halfway through the ropes. He got up quickly and without waiting for a count, tore back into Primo, landing a quick and powerful right to the challenger's head.

Late in the round, Sharkey again moved in close. With the two fighters wrestling against the ropes, Sharkey caught Carnera in the temple with a long, crashing right. Primo pulled back in reaction to right himself. With a grimace on his face Carnera unloaded a short, inside right uppercut that caught the champion square on the jaw. Associated Press Sports Editor Plan Gould described the action as follows: "An inside right uppercut brought up swiftly as the giant came to grips along the ropes with his foe, felled Sharkey as though he had been a tree hit by the woodman's final blow."[13] According to *Time* magazine, the power of Carnera's punch raised Sharkey's feet off the ground.[14] The Associated Press reported about the finishing shot, "With one sweep of a paw that must have felt like a cobblestone wrapped in a leather sack,"[15] Carnera wrested the heavyweight crown from the champion.

7. "A Right Uppercut": The Championship, 1933   117

"...Nine, Ten, and Out!" Referee Arthur Donovan waves Jack Sharkey out in the sixth round of his heavyweight title defense on June 29, 1933. Primo Carnera, who had landed a powerful right uppercut on Sharkey's chin just seconds before, reacts with jubilation as he realizes that he is the new heavyweight champion of the world. (Bettmann/CORBIS)

Immediately, Sharkey crumpled to the mat near the ropes. He lay face down and nearly motionless, as the crowd shot to its feet and filled the summer night sky with a deafening roar. Referee Arthur Donovan picked up the official count from timekeeper Eddie Forbes. As Donovan neared the count of ten, Sharkey stirred his head briefly, but then settled his face back into the canvas. At 2:27 of the sixth round, it was over — both the fight and his reign as world heavyweight champion. As Donovan reached ten, Sharkey's corner men jumped into the ring and helped the still dazed Gob back to his corner.

Sharkey had to be lifted bodily from the ring. As a scene of wild excitement ensued at the crowning of a new champion, Bill Duffy, Carnera's chief adviser, had to contend with Johnny Buckley, Sharkey's manager, and his demands that Carnera's gloves be examined. Duffy told the joyful Carnera to remain in the ring until his gloves were removed and examined. "Duffy even invited Bill Brown, recently appointed State Athletic Commission member, into the ring to remove and examine Carnera's huge gloves. But the excitement passed and the ring soon was cleared."[16] The gloves were examined and no irregularities were found.

Scorecards generally gave Sharkey three or four of the six rounds, with the third round scored a draw, but by all accounts Sharkey had outfought Carnera for the bulk of the evening. In its post-fight review, the Associated Press summed up by saying, "Sharkey, at 201 pounds, conceded Carnera almost 60 pounds in weight and the strain was obvious. A far better boxer over the last time they met, improved in his hitting, Carnera still was no match for Sharkey in ring generalship and clean punching. But one hefty belt with all weight behind it, offset all that in the final exchange."[17] In the end, after outboxing, outsmarting, and out punching Carnera by a wide margin throughout the fight, Sharkey fell victim to the power and quickness of the big man.

The Associated Press continued its summation by stating:

> There was no question about the power behind Carnera's final thrust, the climax of a spectacular closing flurry that saw the champion flounder suddenly, lost almost complete control of his defense and crumple under the ponderous punches of the biggest man who ever scaled the world heavyweight heights. It was an uppercut that had everything Carnera could muster in his huge frame behind it and Sharkey looked "cold" if ever a fighter did as he went down. It was his "secret punch" Carnera exclaimed exultantly after the fight, and perhaps he was right, for Sharkey didn't see it coming and may not know yet what hit him.[18]

The *New York Times* ran the story of the fight on its front page on June 29. Writing for the *Times*, James P. Dawson recalled the punch as "a terrific right hand uppercut to the chin which almost decapitated Sharkey and brought Carnera the title."[19]

In his dressing room after the fight the jubilant Primo, speaking in even more Italian-laced English than usual, had nothing but praise for Sharkey. "He fought much better than he did in his last fight," said the Italian, "and he hurt me much more than he did then. But he didn't reach me as often, and when I discovered that, early in the fight, I knew I could win."[20] "Jack never hurt me. I feel better all the time, stronger, and I know I was going to win after the third round. Jack's knees wobble when I hit him in the stomach. I say, 'Oh, oh, it won't be long now.' Then Mr. Duffy tell me to go get him."[21] Carnera might have been fibbing a bit when he claimed that Sharkey never hurt him during the fight, but with just over a half a minute to go in the sixth round, Primo Carnera indeed got him.

Years later Sharkey said, "Carnera was a much better fighter than I gave him credit for. Of course, there's a lot of controversy relative to his bouts, but be that as it may, the fellow's a better fighter than given credit for."[22] Sharkey continued, "Carnera's style and reach, you've got to find a way to get to him. Well I did that the first time. The second time I realized I'd do the same thing again, but I didn't give the guy the credit that he might improve. He handled me with ease."[23]

Even Walter "Good Time Charley" Friedman, who claimed that a number of Primo's early fights were "mischievous," asserted that the Sharkey fight was on the level. "Every once in a while Carnera could complete a perfect punch," Friedman said. "That's what happened when he caught Sharkey with that right uppercut in the sixth round."[24]

In Sequals, Giovanna and Sante Carnera sat up with their friends and listened to news of the fight. Upon learning that her son was the new heavyweight champion of the world, Giovanna burst into tears of joy.

While the NYSAC and the rest of the world were giving Carnera his well-won recognition, Stanley Isaacs' National Boxing Association, in a shallow, sour-grapes move, refused to recognize Carnera as the World Heavyweight Champion, instead claiming that the title was simply vacated when Primo leveled Sharkey.

John D. McCallum, writing in *The World Heavyweight Boxing Championship*, told the story of Rocky Marciano's memories of the Carnera–Sharkey fight. Marciano was just eight years old when Carnera defeated Sharkey for the title. In 1952, when Rocky was champion, he shared his memories of celebrations, singing and large bonfires in the Italian section of his hometown of Brockton, Massachusetts, on the night that Primo knocked out Sharkey. "Rocky said he could still see those bonfires in the James Edgar playground right across the street from his house, and at the time he thought to himself: Gee, if he could win the title, he'd go back to Brockton and he'd throw a big party for the whole town and every kid would be invited and receive an expensive gift."[25]

Shortly after Carnera defeated Sharkey, the new champion went to Brockton to referee at the old arena that was across Centre Street from the Brockton Hospital. Marciano's uncle, John Piccento, took him to see Primo that night. On the way out of the arena, the newly crowned heavyweight champion walked right by the pair, and Rocky reached out and touched his arm. Later that evening, a beaming Rocky shared his excitement with his father, Perrino Marchegiano. "'I saw Carnera and I touched him,' I told my Pop when I got home. 'I really did.' 'How big is he?' my Pop asked me. 'Bigger than this ceiling,' I said, 'and you should see how big his hands are!'"[26]

Walter "Good Time Charley" Friedman was a member of Primo's shady management team. (Chicago History Museum)

* * *

Even the world heavyweight championship did not alleviate Primo's financial woes. Carnera owed almost $60,000 against assets of barely $1,000. Carnera's stated creditors included managers—past and present—promoters, hotels, retailers, and attorneys. He owed his New York tailor $125; the Hotel Victoria, where the champion always stayed while in Manhattan, claimed bills totaling $300; $2,750 had accrued in legal fees; there were over $5,000 in disputed claims from Leon See and Jeff Dickson, as well as over $6,000 in loans from Louis Soresi. By far the biggest and most active claimant was Emilia Tersini with her $14,390 breach of promise judgment.

Various estimates at Carnera's ring earnings suggest that by June 1933 he had won well over $900,000. Most of this he never saw. His multiple layers of "managers" made sure that fees, taxes, and commissions were paid out of Primo's portion, and that they each then took their ample cuts. An example of this fleecing of the fighter took place after the purse was paid on the Sharkey fight. "What evaporated along with the conspiracy theories was the bulk of Carnera's $17,000 purse. After his handlers made their deductions, together with training and other expenses, the new champion of the world was left with a few hundred dollars."[27] From the minimal shares of his purses that Primo saw, he regularly sent money home to his parents. All of this typically left Primo with little more than a fair amount of pocket cash. All the Italian giant knew was that he had cash in his money clip and that his management assured him that they were taking care of the rest of his earnings. Having several hundred dollars in pocket during the 1930s made Carnera feel and appear rich, but his "investments" were virtually non-existent. In 1932 Primo reportedly told his brother Severino that he could afford to splurge and be generous: "There's nothing to worry about, this is only spending money." He then added naively, "Luigi, my banker, is looking after the rest."[28] Soresi was indeed looking after the rest, but it was not usually in Carnera's best interest.

On July 6, Carnera's attorney Max Roxmore, represented his client at a meeting of creditors at the Manhattan offices of court-appointed bankruptcy referee Peter B. Olney, Jr. During the proceedings, Roxmore showed that Primo's stated assets totaled $631 in deposits in two separate bank accounts, his house in Sequals, and a Chrysler Imperial automobile. After reporting on Carnera's poor financial condition Roxmore explained that Primo's purse for the Sharkey fight was currently tied up in litigation surrounding the champion's managerial difficulties. At the meeting, the Irving Trust Company of New Jersey was appointed bankruptcy trustee and another hearing was scheduled for August 15.

On July 21, New York State Supreme Court Justice Peter Schmuck denied an application for an appointed receiver for Primo's nearly $17,000 share of the championship fight purse. The application was made by Theodore Skratt, the assignee for Emilia Tersini's $14,616 breach of promise judgment.

Carnera had testified at the earlier bankruptcy hearing that he transferred his portion of the Sharkey purse to Louis Soresi, as partial payment on $99,000 worth of property in Atlantic Beach, and an estate in Italy that Primo had reportedly purchased from his financial manager. In denying the receivership, the 60-year-old Schmuck commented that good reason existed to question the integrity of Carnera's transfer of his percentage to Soresi's account, but the action was perfectly legal. Schmuck stated, "Reluctantly does the court deny this application; for good reason exists to suspect the honesty and sincerity of the transfer.... Unfortunately for the plaintiff, astute advice has kept the defendant, Carnera, and his mentor, Soresi, within the law."[29] Justice Schmuck added that it was highly probable that the farm was either made up or not being transferred to Carnera, but that no clear proof of its non-existence had been produced.

8

Title Defenses, 1933–1934

Most people tend to forget that Primo held the heavyweight title for a full year and successfully defended his title twice against creditable opponents. With those two bouts and his June 1934 title defense loss to Max Baer, he was the busiest heavyweight champion to hold the crown in years.

In addition to the usual series of exhibition bouts fought by most heavyweight champions in his era, Primo fought a non-title bout versus Harold Mays on August 11 at the Arena in Syracuse in front of a capacity crowd of 5,000 spectators. Mays, a 210-pounder out of Bayonne, New Jersey, began fighting professionally after winning the 175-pound New Jersey amateur title in 1924, and he now owned a 38–15–1 professional record. During his career, he fought a number of big names in the heavyweight division and registered wins against such well-known fighters as Jimmy Braddock, Ted Sandwina, Jack Renault, K.O. Christner, Con O'Kelly, and he split a pair with both Tony Galento and Ernie Schaaf. He was also a regular sparring partner for Carnera, Gene Tunney, and Joe Louis.

In his previous bout, Mays had fought and lost a five-round decision to Bob Moody on the undercard at the Garden Bowl, the night Primo defeated Sharkey for the title. Four months before that, Mays dropped a close ten-round decision to Tony Galento at Laurel Garden in Newark, New Jersey. Harold's career was winding down, but he still had enough gas in the tank for this tour with Primo and to help him prepare for his title defenses.

This was the first stop on an exhibition journey that was originally and loosely scheduled to run through Syracuse; Bangor and Portland, Maine; Erie, Pennsylvania; Troy, New York; Wilkes-Barre and Johnstown, Pennsylvania; Youngstown, Ohio and then to Buffalo to wrap up the Eastern swing of his tour on August 24. Upon completion of his Buffalo engagement, Carnera was to leave for California for more exhibition bouts and an appointment in Hollywood to co-star with Myrna Loy, Max Baer, and Jack Dempsey in the motion picture *The Prizefighter and the Lady*. Predictably, the tour's schedule would change due to promoters' conflicts, promises of bigger gates, and Carnera's required attendance at a bankruptcy hearing in New York, but it would still prove an entertaining and profitable barnstorming tour.

On August 9 the New York State Athletic Commission met at 1:00 P.M. in the Commission offices at 155 Worth Street in Manhattan. During the meeting, the commissioners approved the application of the Disabled Veterans Athletic Club of Syracuse, "to engage the services of heavyweight champion Primo Carnera in an exhibition bout"[1] on August 11.

Syracuse was excited to host the world champion and the thriving Italian-American community turned out to honor Carnera as a hero. But in a case of poor planning and terrible public relations, Primo's handlers failed to take advantage of the good feelings and increased gate receipts that a warm reception would bring. Primo and his entourage arrived in Syracuse by train on the Empire State Express, but due to his late arrival, the large crowd that had awaited him had mostly dispersed. He was expected at mid-day, but by 1:00 P.M. the enthusiastic crowd began to thin, and when Carnera's train finally arrived at mid-afternoon, just a few remained. Primo was then swept away by car and was barely visible to the public until just before the fight at 9:00 P.M.

A five-fight undercard yielded two second-round knockouts, two points decisions, and a no-contest ruling. The 5,000 assembled were now anxious to see the new world champion at work.

In addition to Harold Mays, Carnera wanted to meet Canadian Jack Renault that same night, but the New York State Athletic Commission representative Dan Skilling refused to sanction the second fight, so Primo met only Mays. To allow the fight at all, Skilling declared that it must be at least four rounds. When Mays declared that he couldn't go four rounds with Carnera, the bout was shortened to four, two-minute rounds. During the fight, Primo pushed and pawed his way to an easy four-round decision over Mays. The fight was considered a success by the fans who enjoyed watching Primo as he clowned a bit with the timekeeper and even pretended to hit referee Jack Michaels on the chin.

The *Syracuse Herald* stated after the bout that Primo had improved notably in the ring. "He stands six feet seven inches in height, towering over all other men in the ring. He weighs 270 pounds but he is a lithe athlete, built in splendid proportions. The slowness and, the awkwardness that were his when he reached America a few years ago have vanished."[2] The newspaper went on to state, "He has developed into a remarkably clever individual, a far better fighter today than was Jess Willard, the only man of his size who ever wore the championship crown."[3]

The evening's card was set to raise money for Syracuse's Christopher Columbus Monument Fund, a project enthusiastically supported by the local Italian community. As an Italian, this was near to Primo's heart and he was active in arranging his appearance in the Salt City. Syracuse had seen a steady inflow of Italian immigrants since the 1870s. They had mostly come as day laborers to work on the canals, and to build railroads, streets, and waterworks. They had settled and opened shops and restaurants near the rail yards along the north side of town. The light turnout, however, left little money for the fund after expenses were paid.

In Mays' final ring appearance, he was matched against Italian fighter Raul Bianchi (15–9–0) on October 22 at the Piazza de Siena in Rome, as a preliminary on the Carnera–Uzcudan card. Mays won by way of knockout, in the first round.

* * *

While Carnera was running about Upstate New York and Western Pennsylvania on his exhibition tour, he was frustrating his court-appointed bankruptcy referee back in New York City. Primo failed to show up for a scheduled August 15th hearing on his petition to be relieved of $59,829 of debt. Bankruptcy referee Peter B. Olney, Jr., was furious at Primo's lack of attendance. Carnera's attorney Max Roxmore did attend on his client's behalf and explained that Primo was out of town, touring, but Olney was not impressed and stated that the fighter must understand that he had an obligation to attend or have his petition dismissed.

Olney set a new appointment for August 29 at 11:30 A.M. When Roxmore asked for another date because Carnera's movie contract required his presence in Hollywood that day, Olney's anger bubbled over. "I don't give a damn if he has," exclaimed Olney, "he'll have to be here."[4]

Subsequent information from the petition claimed that Primo's share of the purse from the Sharkey fight went to Louis Soresi to pay off debts owed to his manager.

* * *

In Erie, Pennsylvania, on August 18, Primo got to fight both Renault and Mays, but only in exhibition matches that drew just over 4,000 fans to Erie Stadium. During the undercard, Chicago welterweight Harry Dublinsky scored a TKO over Erie native Frank Bojarski, by opening a cut over Bojarski's eye that stopped him from answering the bell for the eighth round. The two had met at Motor Square Garden in Pittsburgh eight months earlier, with Dublinsky also taking that fight on an eighth-round TKO. The crowd then watched Primo go two rounds each with Renault and Mays.

* * *

Primo and his crew moved on to Youngstown, Ohio, for an August 23 exhibition with Mays and a respectable young fighter out of Cheyenne, Wyoming, named Frankie Edgren. After watching Jackie Davis outpoint Tug Phillips in 10 and Eddie Simms do the same to Joe Doctor, Primo delighted the crowd by going two rounds each with Mays and Edgren.

* * *

On August 25 local promoters in Pittsburgh put together a five-fight program scheduled for Allegheny Stadium. The event featured mostly local talent, the most notable of which was Billy Holt. Holt was a good middleweight from the Homewood section of Pittsburgh. He began fighting professionally in 1929, but after five years in the ring, the 160-pound Holt had to retire from boxing because of failing vision. His diminishing eyesight left him virtually blind by 1938. Coming to the aid of the popular Holt, the local boxing fraternity decided to hold a series of benefits to raise money and establish a trust for him. He finished his professional fight career with a 31–19–3 record.

Tonight, in the final preliminary, Holt would defeat Phil Ross on points in an exciting six-rounder. The previous four fights produced two TKOs and two decisions. In the culmination of the evening, Carnera boxed two, 2-round exhibitions, one each with Mays and Edgren.

* * *

Primo headed back to New York City the day after the Pittsburgh event to keep his appointment at the Rector Street offices of bankruptcy referee Olney on August 29.

On the evening before the hearing, Primo was the guest of honor at a dinner given by the publishers of the *Police Gazette*. Established in 1845, the *National Police Gazette* was known for its sensational and explicit stories about, among other things, crime, the Wild West, burlesque, and sports. The magazine, in addition to engravings of heroes, outlaws, and scantily clad women, often featured stories about boxing, and handed out awards to champions. One-time publisher Richard Kyle Fox had campaigned hard to get boxing legalized in several states in the late 19th century. Fox was a blatant racist, narrow-minded, shameless, and self-serving, but he set the trend for newspapers, magazines, and other media that followed, "for he invented the sports page and the gossip column, and he was the first to use copious illustrations to dramatize the stories in his paper. Before Fox, these things really did not exist. Because of him prize-fighters were suddenly fascinating public figures, and so were actresses and chorus girls."[5] The magazine had been on the decline for years and new owners were now trying their hand at reviving it. Resuming the tradition of feting the heavyweight champion of the world was a good way to start. At the dinner, Carnera was presented with a heavyweight championship belt.

At 11:30 the next morning, Primo was at 19 Rector Street and sitting in referee Olney's office, where he spent much of the day attempting to answer questions about the state of his finances. As usual, Primo could shed little knowledge as to where his earnings had gone. He knew little about his finances and his naive trust and almost complete lack of caring absolutely flummoxed Olney.

The day after the hearing, Carnera and his team headed West. In mid–September, Primo was scheduled to begin his work on the full-length motion picture, *The Prizefighter and the Lady*, an MGM crime-romance-comedy starring Primo, Myrna Loy, Max Baer, Jack Dempsey, and Walter Huston.

* * *

Primo and his mates made it to California by early September and readied for an evening of boxing in San Francisco on Friday the eighth. Four sanctioned fights preceded a four-round exhibition between Primo and old foe Jose Santa.

Highlighting the card along with Carnera and Santa were local welterweights Claude "Kid" Capley and Paul Negri, both of whom won by decision. Those who attended that evening were fortunate to see Negri's win over Spaniard Paolino Egus, for the bout was to be Negri's last professional fight. He finished with a record of 21–5–8. Paul was one-fourth of a quartet of fighting Negri brothers— Frankie Thomas (Frank Negri), Rocco Negri, and Dummy Thomas (Thomas Negri), who was deaf. Paul began boxing professionally in 1929 with a second-round TKO of "Indian" Phil Nance at San Francisco's Dreamland Auditorium. Although retired from the ring, Paul Negri remained active in the sport, becoming a member of the Northern California Boxing Association. He regularly attended fights, shows, and dinners, until he died just short of his 85th birthday in 1993.[6]

Apparently, Primo had a busy time in and out of the ring, while in the city by the bay. On September 9, the Associated Press carried a report that Primo played the role of a human crane, when he came upon the scene of an automobile accident, on the evening of September 7. According to the report, Primo, while barely breaking a sweat, single-handedly righted an overturned sedan, helping to release a pinned motorist.[7] While the level of Carnera's ring skills has long been debated by fight professionals, fans, and in the press, no one to my knowledge has ever begun to question Primo's legendary strength and power.

* * *

Shortly after the Santa event in San Francisco, Primo headed to Los Angeles to make a movie. After Carnera won the title from Sharkey, MGM executives approached his managers with the idea of having Primo co-star in *The Prizefighter and the Lady*, a movie about an ex-sailor turned prizefighter who falls in love with and marries the girlfriend of a mobster. As his pugilistic career takes off, he eventually gets a shot at the heavyweight title. Max Baer played the fighting gob, while Primo appropriately played the imposing foreign heavyweight champion, from whom Baer's character, "Steve Morgan," tries to take the crown.

The film was an interesting event for several reasons. Baer was all but certain to face

8. Title Defenses, 1933–1934

Carnera sometime in the next year, in a championship fight, and the idea of getting them in the ring in advance, and on celluloid, was a dream come true for the movie executives. Getting Primo and his handlers to agree to film the movie at all, however, was tricky. The script originally called for Baer's character to defeat Primo's character. This was unacceptable to Carnera and his handlers. Negotiations continued for several weeks, until MGM agreed to a script change and raised their offer to Primo to $25,000, for just a few days of filming. In the rewrite, "Steve Morgan," against all odds and spurred on by his lady love, would fight the enormous champion to a draw. This made the ending acceptable to Carnera; and for the MGM brass, it conveniently opened up the possibility of a sequel.

The studio was anxious to make the fight scenes very realistic, and Baer was all for that. Max saw the filming of the scenes as a way to be in the ring with the champion for extended periods of time and to have a tremendous chance to test out various game plans, without risking anything. During the course of shooting the scenes, Max gained the equivalent of several dozen rounds of sparring time with the champion. He studied Carnera's style and tested his punching ability and his defense, and saw to which punches Primo was most susceptible. While Max made less money than Primo for their roles in the movie, Baer's payoff was infinitely more profitable to him in the long run.

The film was a box office hit. It was nominated for an Oscar, and the attention to detail during the filming of the boxing scenes helped MGM produce some of the most realistic fight sequences ever filmed. That attention to detail also helped Max win the heavyweight crown from Carnera the following June. The film's success helped Primo's managers increase their holdings by $25,000. Once again, it seemed as if Primo was the only one who walked away with the least to show for his work.

With filming done, it was now time to head back East to New York, where the champion would board a ship for his triumphant return to Italy where he would, with the Garden's permission, keep his 3-year-old promise to Achille Starace and defend his title for the first time in Rome. The bout was scheduled for October 22nd against Paolino Uzcudun.

* * *

Carnera and Soresi arrived at New York's Pier 90 on September 30, to begin their journey back to Italy for Primo's first title defense. The pair was to meet the rest of their contingent, including Severino, Mays, and Renault on board, by sailing time. Taking care of some last-minute business in the city, Carnera and Soresi arrived at the pier late. The *Conte de Savoia* had just pulled away from the pier and the majestic liner was heading down the Hudson River, into New York Bay. Thinking quickly, Soresi engaged a steamboat captain and his crew. Radioing ahead, the steamboat caught up to the liner before it got into the Atlantic.

The *Conte de Savoia* was Primo's ship of choice, because he was always treated like royalty when he sailed. The ship had a berth with a specially constructed bed measuring 7'8" long, as well as training facilities that included a full-size ring for sparring.

On October 7 Primo's ship landed in the Italian port city of Naples where more than 5,000 jubilant admirers were on hand to meet him. After being cheered wildly as he walked down the gangplank, Carnera addressed throngs of fans. Some of what he said that afternoon would be brought back to haunt him in the years to come, by those who attempted to paint him with a Fascist brush. After commenting that he was pleased to make his first title defense in his home country, Primo went on to say, "I will do the utmost I can to honor the Black Shirt organization."[8]

This comment was ironic, because Mussolini's Fascist government had paid scant attention to the young fighter, until it became evident that he was a genuine contender for the world heavyweight crown. With his win over Sharkey, Primo suddenly mattered to them. The Fascists saw a gold mine of propaganda in Carnera. The seed that Achille Starace had planted in 1930 had bloomed and was now ready to bear fruit. In truth, Primo was once again the tool of those who would take advantage of him now and throw him to the gutter when they had squeezed out the very last drop of usefulness they possibly could. Primo was young, naive, and almost totally apolitical. The words he uttered were given to him by Starace, but they were clumsy and ill advised nonetheless, and he would regret them. For now, however, Primo may have felt that he had little choice but to express support for the Fascists in control of his country. Many Italians who had failed to show loyalty to Il Duce and his government were now in prison or harassed and prohibited from plying their trades.

After the welcoming celebrations, Primo headed for Sequals where he would continue to train for the next week and a half.

During his time at home, Primo would rise early and get in several miles of roadwork before breakfast. After a large breakfast, made under the supervision of his trainer Billy Defoe and Primo's mother, he would rest before hitting the gym. In the gymnasium at the Villa Carnera, Primo would work out on the bags, and engage in calisthenics, before getting in some sparring in the ring that his father Sante had built. His sparring partners prior to the Uzcudun title defense were Mays, Renault, and Arthur Huttick, each of whom he would box several rounds daily. Primo then put in some more time doing bag work and finish up the day with some rope jumping. After a homemade dinner, Primo would often relax with cards or take the short walk down through the town square and on to his favorite bar, the Cantina al Bottegon, for an evening with friends.

While Primo and Defoe spent their days in the gym at the Villa Carnera, Luigi Soresi often spent long hours at the Sequals Post Office huddled with the telegraph operator and sending and receiving missives between Sequals, Rome, and New York.

On October 19, Primo was enjoying a break from his routine by driving his American sports car back from the nearby town of Udine. En route, Primo, never the most cautious of drivers, managed to hit a cart, just outside of the village. No one was hurt, but Primo came close to running off the road. The next day he flew from Udine to Rome with his father Sante, his brothers Secondo and Severino, Defoe, and Soresi. They checked into the Plaza Hotel, and readied themselves for the fight.

Uzcudun went to Rome the week before the fight and kept up a similarly tough workout regimen. Two days before the fight Paolino took a lengthy run, sparred six rounds with his partners, Raul Bianchi and Armando De Carolis, and hit the speed and heavy bags. On Friday, he simply jumped rope for about 30 minutes, showered and was pronounced ready. By all accounts he looked to be in fine condition.

* * *

Four months after defeating Sharkey, Primo was ready to put his title on the line against the ever-formidable Spaniard. Going into the fight, Uzcudun held a 50–14–2 record. At a reported 230 pounds, the muscular Uzcudun was much larger than most of Carnera's opponents. He was listed in the *Ring* magazine's top 10 heavyweights each year from 1925 to 1928, ranking as high as 3rd in 1928, but admittedly, at 35 years of age, the Basque woodchopper was past his prime. During the fighters' previous encounter in 1930, Primo won a split but still clear-cut decision in front of 70,000 fans in Barcelona.

8. Title Defenses, 1933–1934

The rematch was set for October 22, 1933, in the Piazza de Siena, in Rome. The piazza was an open, park-like area, most often used for musical shows and equestrian events. Its central location made it ideal for handling traffic and crowd control. Seating was installed for 55,000, but more room was available for those willing and able to stand. By fight time, a sea of 70,000 people surrounded the ring in the tree-encircled piazza, to witness the first-ever heavyweight title fight held in Italy.[9] In the crowd that evening was Italian Premier Benito Mussolini and James Roosevelt, the eldest son of the American president. Also introduced at ringside was former heavyweight champion Max Schmeling.

On the undercard, Primo's two American sparring partners, Mays (38–16–1) of Bayonne, New Jersey, and Huttick of New York, fought their way to heavyweight victories over Uzcudun's sparring partners. In the first fight, Mays scored a two-punch knockout over Argentine Raul Bianchi (15–9–0) just seconds into the first round. Mays rushed toward Bianchi at the bell and almost immediately landed a blistering right, followed by a powerful left, and down Bianchi went for the count. In the second fight, Huttick (25–5–0) cruised to a four-round decision over Armando De Carolis of Rome. De Carolis had an unimpressive record of 6–14–0, and had lost his last seven fights including bouts with Carnera, Tony Galento, and Steve Hamas. According to Associated Press reports, "Huttick led throughout, cutting De Carolis' face and wearing the Roman down with a steady stream of hard rights and a cutting left."[10] It was a night of endings— these would be Mays' and De Carolis' last professional fights, Huttick's last victory, and Bianchi would fight only twice more, both first-round losses in 1934. The remaining three fights on the undercard went 6, 15, and 15 rounds, each of their respective distances

As the crowd readied for the main event, they cheered wildly as Carnera entered the ring. Referee Maurice Nicod, who was chosen to be the third man in the ring for tonight's championship tilt, joined the fighters at center ring.

From the opening bell, Primo took the fight to Uzcudun, and the outcome was never really in doubt. In the opening seconds, the champion rushed toward the challenger, driving him back to the ropes, where he unleashed a flurry of lefts and rights. It became clear very early that Primo meant business.

The first eight rounds went easily to the champion. In the fifth round, Primo tagged Uzcudun with a sharp left that opened a cut above Paolino's eye. The battering Uzcudun took during the first eight rounds severely weakened him. In the ninth, Primo knocked the challenger woozy, but somehow Uzcudun kept his feet and lasted until the bell. From that point on, Carnera pressed for a knockout. He kept up a steady barrage of punches, but Uzcudun, refusing to go down, fought back with shots to the champion's mid-section.

In the 13th round, the fans began to boo Carnera for his inability to put the Spaniard away. This demonstration angered Primo, who was himself already frustrated at Uzcudun's ability to take his best shots.

Uzcudun gamely fought back, wading time and again into the midst of the Carnera onslaught, but Primo was able to thwart Uzcudun with short, crisp uppercuts and his tremendously long reach. When fighting in close, Primo used his massive strength and 30-pound weight advantage to slug it out with Uzcudun for 15 rounds, finally winning a unanimous decision.

Seventy thousand spectators watched as their countryman dominated the Spaniard from start to finish, winning almost every round. Landing steady and strong lefts and rights, the Italian handed the Spaniard what the Associated Press termed "an unmerciful beating."[11] The challenger, who was noted for his great stamina, was still able to last the full 15 rounds.

Carnera won every round, winning the decision by a wide margin, but he couldn't finish the challenger. The crowd was pleased with Primo's efforts until the final two rounds, when they began to weary of his inability to put Uzcudun away. Scattered boos began to ring out at Carnera's lack of a knockout and alternately, cheers were heard in tribute to the challenger's toughness. While saluting Paolino's sturdiness was fully appropriate, the critics fail to consider two important points.

First, failing to knock down Uzcudun was no shame. He had an amazing ability to absorb the punishment dished out by his opponents. Baer, Schmeling, Schaaf, Mickey Walker, King Levinsky and many others had also failed to level the Basque Woodchopper. Only Joe Louis would succeed at knocking out Uzcudun, during their fight on December 13, 1935, when the ever-present Arthur Donovan stopped the bout at 2:32 of the fourth round.

Second, Primo's right hand was badly damaged in the ninth round, the result of a right to Uzcudun's hard head. It was initially reported that Primo had broken the hand, but after further examination doctors revealed that the hand was sprained and the knuckles badly bruised, but there was no fracture. The pain, however, did relegate his right hand to the status of being only a defensive tool for blocking during the remainder of the fight. Primo's doctor bandaged the hand and ordered complete rest for it, for two months.

The receipts of the fight totaled a respectable $117,500. Of this total, Uzcudun received 10 percent, but Primo's cut went to fund relief work by Mussolini's Italian Fascist government. All Primo came away with was a decisive, yet frustrating victory, the ceremonial rank of commander in the Order of the Crown of Italy, and a badly damaged right hand.

After the fight, Carnera and his entourage remained in Rome for several days. During his time there, he was welcomed by Mussolini for lunch and a photo session at the Palazzo Venezia. After lunch with the soldiers at the CXII Legione dell'Urbe, he was photographed with Il Duce doing the Fascist salute. These pictures and others, including wartime photos taken with Max Schmeling in Venice, would come back to haunt the apolitical Carnera in the years to come. Primo had no interest in politics, but this young and minimally educated man, who had risen from the grip of poverty to the pinnacle of the boxing world, simply did not have the wherewithal to know how others might perceive these actions down the road. He simply would never have given it a thought. Carnera had no known feelings for the Fascist Party. He did not care a whit about politics. His supreme naiveté was, however, certainly exploited by the Fascists. They saw an opportunity to use Carnera for their own propaganda purposes. Had Primo chosen to object or simply not play ball, he would have been accused of anti–Fascism, tried and quite possibly jailed. At a minimum, he would certainly have been barred from leaving the country and not allowed to fight.

After a time being wined and dined in Rome, the entourage traveled to Paris for a series of ring exhibitions, in what must have been a gratifying return for Primo, to the city in which he began his journey from the poverty of the streets to the top of the boxing world.

* * *

In November, after touring cities in France and Italy with Soresi and Severino, Primo returned to Sequals to rest and spend time with his family and friends. While there, however, he received word from New York that Emilia Tersini's representatives were stepping up pressure to have Primo's gates garnished for payment of the judgment. The New York courts were still debating the jurisdiction of the British court decision in the United States, against a citizen of a third nation holding legal residency status in the United States. The need became pressing for Carnera to go back to New York to take care of business relating to the breach of promise garnishment proceeding, his bankruptcy proceedings, the upcoming Loughran fight, and to simply enter the United States to help protect his increasingly important status as a legal resident.

On December 6, Primo unexpectedly sailed for New York City on the *Conte di Savoia*. He had stated earlier that his plans were to spend Christmas with his family in Sequals and head back to America in early January to prepare for the Loughran fight. Primo, who was unaccompanied, told reporters that sudden business had come up in New York and that he would only spend a day or two in the city before heading back to Italy. His primary reason for the trip was to attend another hearing on his bankruptcy at Olney's office at 19 Rector Street in Manhattan. While in New York, however, he would also meet with Tommy Loughran and officials of Madison Square Garden to discuss arrangements for their proposed February bout, and have his personal doctor examine the progress of the break in his right hand.

On December 14, Primo walked down the gangplank in New York and immediately into the Italian line's travel office to book passage back to Genoa when the *Conte di Savoia* sailed the next day.

Waiting for Carnera in Jimmy Johnston's Garden offices were Primo's manager Billy Duffy, Loughran and his team, Johnston, and a host of reporters. And wait they did. Primo called Duffy periodically to update him on his whereabouts. After the final call, Duffy told those present that Primo was visiting relatives in Brooklyn and would not appear at the Garden until the next morning. Duffy then apologized to those present and assured them that the champion would be there before he sailed the next afternoon. Primo was in fact still in Olney's office. The bankruptcy hearings had taken longer than anticipated, but Duffy did not want to bring attention to that.

Gathered at Olney's Rector Street offices were Carnera and his counsel, the referee and his staff, and attorneys for Theodore Skratt, the assignee for the breach of promise judgment, and the Irving Trust Company, the bankruptcy trustee.

At the hearings, it was reported that Carnera netted exactly $360 from the Sharkey fight, and he could not recall what he was paid for his part in filming *The Prizefighter and the Lady*. During over two hours of testimony, Primo repeatedly disavowed any knowledge of his financial affairs. He commented that he simply left everything to his financial manager Louis Soresi. When asked why he did not question Soresi on where the money was, Primo answered simply, "Because I trust him."[12] He was also asked why he never attempted to collect on a $63,000 court judgment against his former manager Leon See. To this, Primo explained that it was obvious to everybody that See did not have that kind of money.

Olney set the next hearing for February 1 and gained Primo's promise that he would attend and bring with him all available records of his financial transactions. Olney warned Carnera and his counsel that failing to attend and failure to produce the records would severely damage his chances for the debts being discharged.

On the morning of December 15, Primo and Duffy met with the Garden officials and Loughran's team, to agree to the terms of a February fight. It was agreed that Carnera would risk his crown against Loughran at the Garden's winter bowl in Miami on February 22. Loughran's manager Joe Smith and Duffy agreed to a 12½ percent cut for the challenger and Primo would get the champion's customary 37½ percent. All that remained now was the approval of Louis Soresi, who was in Italy, but who Duffy assured would also put his approval on the fight.

With the fight arrangements made, it was off to lunch and then to the pier. Before boarding, Primo gave an impromptu press conference in which he stated that he wanted to fight Max Baer, after he defeated Loughran. After he defeated Baer, Primo said that he would fight anyone except Max Schmeling, because Schmeling had failed to give him a shot in 1931, when he held the title.

By 3:30 P.M., Primo was back on the *Conte di Savoia* as she was escorted by tug boats into Upper New York Bay on her way back to Italy. The New York papers commented whimsically that Primo may have set a new record for trans–Atlantic travel.

It is interesting to note the extraordinary steps that Carnera took to avoid paying off the breach of promise judgment. The cost and the time invested in the extensive legal and financial maneuvering, and trans–Atlantic travel in 1933, perhaps give an insight to the bitterness he felt towards Emilia for her actions—bitterness that he felt so keenly that he refused to pay her without a fight, but feelings that he would never vocalize.

* * *

On January 10, 1934, Primo sailed once again, from the port of Genoa for New York to prepare for the second defense of his title against Tommy Loughran, in late February in Miami. In New York, Jack Dempsey was busy claiming that in the event of a Carnera–Baer matchup, his fighter should get a share of the gate equal to that of the champion because Baer was just as big a drawing card as Carnera. Dempsey had finally given up any pretense that he would make a ring comeback and was now actively involved in promoting Max Baer. To Dempsey's claims, Bill Duffy simply laughed.

The *Conte di Savoia* docked in New York on January 17, and a smiling and hatless Primo disembarked, commenting to reporters that he would defeat both Loughran and Baer. His brother Severino and his sparring partners Harold Mays and Arthur Huttick accompanied Carnera. Soresi, who was still in Italy attending to personal matters, was to join up with the group later. Waiting for Primo at the pier were his attorney Albert Yuzzolino and Jimmy Johnston and Porter Moore from the Garden.

Primo's arrival was marred by one embarrassing incident in which he got his sedan stuck as he attempted to drive it off the ship, instead of having it rolled off. It took 20 longshoremen to help get the car unstuck and off the ship.

After a few days in New York, Primo and company took a train to Miami to begin preparations for the Loughran fight, but on February 6, Primo left Miami by plane bound for New York, in order to attend the rescheduled bankruptcy hearing at Olney's offices. Accompanying him were Garden president John Reed Kilpatrick and boxing director Jimmy Johnston. The trio was met in New York by Louis Soresi, who had recently arrived from Italy, in time for the meeting with Olney.

At the hearing on February 7, Soresi testified that the world champion boxer was possibly the world's most incompetent financial pupil. "It's no use discussing money with Carnera," Soresi told Olney. "He simply will not listen. He does not understand financial problems, and, what is worse, cares less."[13]

Next, Jacob Schoeler, an attorney for the Irving Trust Company, interrogated Primo at length. Primo simply smiled and confirmed what Soresi had testified: "I don't pay any attention to money and such things. I do the boxing. I'm crazy about boxing. The rest I don't give a damn about."[14] With the mystery about Carnera's finances still unsolved, Olney scheduled yet another hearing for March 12. After the hearing was finished, Primo, Soresi, and Yuzzolino boarded the plane and headed back to Miami Beach, to continue training for the Loughran fight.

8. Title Defenses, 1933–1934

* * *

Primo's second title defense, against long-time light heavyweight king Tommy Loughran (102–21–7), was scheduled for February 28, 1934, in the Madison Square Garden Arena in Miami, Florida. The fight was looked at by many as a terrible mismatch due to the 86-pound difference in weight between the two fighters.

Loughran set up his training camp in West Palm Beach and during preparations for the fight made no bones about the fact that he would beat Carnera. Citing his experience and unquestionably superior ring generalship, he ridiculed the Italian behemoth as an untalented fighter who was lucky to wear the belt. Loughran was wrong about Primo's ring skills and was ignoring Primo's enormous size, strength, and flawless conditioning. While Loughran was absolutely the better ring general, Primo held the cards in size, power, and strength.

Gusty blasts of wind and rain forced a one-day postponement of the fight to March 1st. Weather reports for the 1st offered little encouragement, as they continued to forecast rain and wind into the weekend.

The postponement came early enough in the afternoon that neither fighter left his hotel for the arena and instead both went back to the gym for workouts to keep sharp and burn nervous energy. The Associated Press reported, "Primo promptly hustled into a gymnasium and did enough shadow boxing, bag punching and calisthenics to keep him on physical edge, while Loughran did the same at his camp."[15]

Loughran is a Boxing Hall-of-Famer and considered one of the greatest boxers of all time. Tommy had a terrific left that, while not overly powerful, was known for its accuracy and speed. During his career, Loughran faced 14 different men who held titles in an era when there were only eight divisions and one recognized champion for each.

Having thoroughly dominated the light heavyweight world for 10 years, Loughran moved up to the heavyweight division in 1929. He had been Jack Dempsey's sparring partner when Jack was training for Gene Tunney. By the time of the Carnera fight, Loughran had defeated a number of heavyweights including Max Baer, Paolino Uzcudun, King Levinsky, Steve Hamas, and Jack Sharkey. He had more than proven his ability to stand against the best in the heavyweight class.

Around 12,000 people braved the rain and huddled into Biscayne Arena to watch the fight. It was a small crowd by championship fight standards, reportedly the smallest since Bob Fitzsimmons knocked out Gentleman Jim Corbett in Carson City, Nevada, in 1897. A light rain fell during the preliminaries and a couple of downpours drenched the patrons, just before the main event. A light rain also fell briefly during the tenth and twelfth rounds of the main event. The wind blowing in off Biscayne Bay added to the crowd's discomfort. This, plus the previous day's washout, and the weathermen's predictions of certain rain, no doubt helped keep the crowd down.

Loughran, 32 and already a 15-year veteran of professional boxing, had a terrific left jab, known more for its speed and accuracy than its power. He loved to drop it on his opponents when they were charging, or in a clinch when he could sneak it in. The clinch, however, was a bad strategy against the much larger Carnera, who could use his weight to lean on and exhaust the much smaller challenger. Primo could also knockout an opponent in close, but never could extend his punches as effectively. As a result, Tommy planned to stay out of range, avoid the clinches, and pepper Carnera with his dangerous left jabs.

Despite Loughran's unquestioned ring skills, Carnera entered the fight as the favorite, with odds anywhere from 2–1 to 3–1 on virtually every card. Many pointed to the fact that while Carnera possessed nowhere near the boxing prowess of Loughran, he had improved tremendously and had become a good fighter. Also on many minds was the fact that the bout held the greatest weight disparity in title fight history — an amazing 84 pounds.

The referee for the fight was Leo Shea and the ringside judges were C. S. "Red" McLaghlan and Roy Latham.

Tommy fought valiantly for the first 10 rounds, when he used his speed, superior boxing skills, left jabs, and sudden right crosses to Carnera's head to hold the champion at bay. In the sixth round, Loughran landed a sweeping left hook that caught the champion on the chin and rocked him. Undoubtedly, it was his best punch of the night. For the first half dozen rounds, it looked like he had a chance to pull an amazing upset, but his best simply wasn't enough. He won anything from one to four rounds on various fight cards, but the sheer size and power of the champion wore him down. Quentin Reynolds, writing for the International News Service, reported, "Tommy threw a million left jabs at Carnera, but it was like throwing cream puffs at a battleship. They landed all right, but it came under the heading of, 'what of it?'"[16]

The United Press reported, "Carnera forged ahead in the seventh and started a clubbing, battering attack that kept the challenger in retreat during the rest of the brawl. Loughran's footwork gradually became loggier, his left jab lost its snap and blows to the body brought grimaces to his face."[17]

From about the 10th round on, Loughran took a brutal beating. For the last three rounds, he fought mainly, and admirably, to stay on his feet. Carnera kept forcing Loughran into the ropes and the corners, where he would maul his opponent with combinations. While the 26-year-old Primo was still fresh, the 32-year-old Loughran was almost ready to collapse. As if Tommy weren't miserable enough, a cold, light rain began to fall in the twelfth round.

Shea warned Carnera for hitting while holding and for roughness several times as he pushed the challenger into the corner and smashed him about unmercifully. He also stepped on Loughran's left foot in the first and tenth rounds, and was called for elbowing Tommy in the twelfth. Carnera was anxious to finish off the challenger and was getting sloppy.

Observed United Press Sports Editor Stuart Cameron, "Had Carnera more of the killer instinct and more authority in his punches he could not have failed to win by a knockout." Cameron continued, "A glancing right to the temple staggered Loughran in the fourteenth. Then a bombardment of rights and lefts to head and body kept him bouncing off the ropes. He was so dazed at the bell that he lurched over to Carnera's corner. Bill Duffy, Carnera's chief second, escorted him to his own."[18]

While Primo ultimately commanded the fight, Loughran still gutted out the full 15 rounds and never went down. "Several times in the fifteenth it seemed that Loughran's wobbly knees must buckle beneath him."[19] According to Associated Press reports, "Once in the fifteenth round, when bravery alone was holding the challenger up, the gigantic Carnera, a throwback in size and appearance to some pre-historic man" (another less than generous and less than accurate putdown!), "smashed his ponderous right full on Tommy's jaw. The Philadelphian reeled back drunkenly and would certainly have crashed to the canvas had the ropes not held him up."[20] For a moment, Primo's good-hearted nature kicked in, as he looked almost pityingly at Loughran, before resuming his battering assault. With the aid of the ropes and his sheer courage and willpower, Tommy held on. His legs were rubbery and his head foggy, but with the help of a compassionate opponent, Loughran made it to the end of the round. Within a minute, the final bell rang and Primo lost his only solid chance at downing and possibly finishing off Loughran with a knockout.

The decision was unanimous. Referee Leo Shea and Judges Red McLaughlin and Roy Latham turned in scorecards in Carnera's favor. The United Press tally agreed with that of the officials, giving Loughran four rounds and Carnera eleven. Some in the press gave Primo 10 rounds, Loughran one, and scored four rounds even. Loughran did his best fighting in the third through sixth rounds. The only blood in the fight came in the sixth round when Carnera landed a hard right that opened a cut on Loughran's scalp.

Loughran was a clever and skillful boxer, the type that generally gave Primo a difficult time, but Primo outlasted him. Even with the unanimous decision, however, there was little glory in it for the champion. He had failed to finish off or even floor a man 86 pounds lighter than him, and the heavily pro–Loughran crowd let him know it throughout the fight.

Loughran later commented, "My manager and I had talked the thing over. He said, 'What's going to be your biggest problem?' I said, 'You know, Joe, it's throwing his weight on me in the clinches. We've got to get something together there to make him get away from me. You think up something.' Well he did and, jeez, it was very clever. After we weighed in, he went out and bought a jar of the most sickeningly sweet-smelling hair grease he could get. After we got our instructions in the center of the ring and went back to the corner, he had taken this stuff out and he put a big slab of it on the crown of my head. As soon as we'd clinch, I'd put my head right up under Carnera's nose, and I still have pictures of Carnera, in sheer disgust, trying to shove me off."[21]

The day after the fight, both Loughran and his manager Joe Smith complained that Primo had roughed up, continually fouled, and stepped on the feet of the Philadelphian. Tommy stated, "I thought I was outpointing him up to the last round."[22] Obviously, Loughran and Smith saw a different fight than most anyone else who saw the bout. Loughran, in his final title fight appearance, made a very good showing of himself, but was outgunned and outmuscled by the champion's massive size. His pride and his desire for a rematch were no doubt the prime movers behind Loughran's comments. As John Kieran of the *New York Times* commented, "The voluminous Venetian is sitting on the heavyweight throne and it will take a force to get him out of there. Cleverness won't do. A man might as well try to out-box a freight car or an oak tree."[23]

Even decades later, Loughran continued to maintain that he should have gotten the decision, but then what fighter doesn't claim they won most every fight? Loughran continued, "So I had to knock him out to win, I had to agree to that. And Carnera had a glass chin. I had him in bad shape in the fourth round and in the tenth round, but then, when I couldn't finish him, I knew the thing was over. I'd hit him with a left hook as we would come in, bang him around, and, of course, he was so awkward that the crowd didn't see what was actually happening. I beat him, no question about it. I had agreed to this thing, I didn't care."[24]

The reality was that while Primo didn't have the boxing skills that Loughran possessed, Tommy couldn't get inside or get a clear shot at the champion's chin. Primo had become a respectable fighter, and his significant left kept Loughran at bay all evening. It was clear that Carnera controlled the fight and it was a credit to Loughran that he lasted the entire 15 rounds. Regardless of Loughran's opinion of the fight and what his pride would let him admit, the referee and the judges saw it differently, awarding Primo a unanimous decision.

Carnera's reaction was as magnanimous as Loughran's was petty. After reaching his dressing room after the fight, Primo, who had not a mark on him, praised his opponent. "Tommy Loughran is the greatest fighter I ever met."[25] After showering and dressing, Carnera even hurried over to Loughran's dressing room to pay his respects to his vanquished foe, before vanishing into the Miami night.

The fight was regarded as a financial flop. Gross receipts for the contest were reported as $44,598.70, but after taxes were taken, less than $40,000 remained to divide among the participants. Of this, Loughran took home 5 percent and Primo 37.5 percent, or about $15,000. This did little to alleviate Primo's difficult financial situation.

Adding to the financial pressures of the Carnera camp, a writ of garnishment was served on Primo before the fight to prevent him from paying any monies to his manager Billy Duffy, until Duffy made good a $2,261.15 debt he allegedly owed to the Chateaulido nightclub in Daytona Beach.

Immediately looking to Primo's next title defense, Carnera's financial manager Louis Soresi flatly declared that no further negotiations with Baer's manager Ancil Hoffman would be conducted. Instead, Primo would undertake a South American swing and set up fights in Buenos Aires, Rio de Janeiro, and Montevideo. According to the Brazilian *A Noite* newspaper, Carnera would fight George Godfrey in Sao Paulo in April.

After the fight, Soresi said in exasperated tones, "We are tired of collecting chicken-feed and then being given the run-around on the one match — with Baer — that will mean real money. Carnera is through dallying with Baer. We will leave the end of March for Buenos Aires and hope to get a match with Victorio Campollo. If the Madison Square Garden promoters can sign Baer, we will be willing, if necessary, to fly back to the United States."[26]

Baer, itching for a shot at the champion, used the old tried-and-true method of ridiculing the man he wanted to get into the ring. Max commented about Carnera: "I've lost all respect for him. It's ridiculous that he couldn't knock little Tommy out in fifteen rounds."[27] Max hoped that the press and public had short memories, for this same "little Tommy" that Primo had clearly outpointed had won an easy and unanimous decision over the Livermore Larruper in 1931.

After resting over the weekend, Primo and his entourage traveled to Macon, Georgia, to attend a memorial service for his old foe Young Stribling, who had died in Macon the previous October, in a motorcycle accident. He also agreed to visit Atlanta and perform an exhibition for inmates at the federal penitentiary, before heading back to New York. While there, Primo saw convicted crime boss Al Capone, but the two only exchanged smiles and nods.[28]

On April 6 Peter Olney closed Primo's bankruptcy hearing after being informed by counsel that the ongoing examination of Carnera's finances, begun almost a year before, had uncovered no further assets than Carnera and his advisors had revealed. With Primo and Louis Soresi in attendance, Olney officially pronounced the hearings and investigation closed.

9

Max Baer, 1934

After reading reviews of the Carnera–Loughran fight, Max Baer, in typical fashion, exuded confidence in stating that he would take the champion's end of the purse when he met Primo. Baer reacted to Loughran's claims that the Italian had continually stepped on his feet to tie him up, by commenting that Primo had better not try that when they met in the ring in June. Baer said he would not put up with it and that he did not fear Carnera. "Why that big mountain-like Carnera pushing his opponent — many pounds lighter than himself — into a corner, instead of fighting, makes me laugh."[1]

The fight was an on-again, off-again event, as both camps put forth demands that were unacceptable to the other. Baer said that Jack Dempsey, who held a 7.5 percent stake in the Californian, probably would promote the battle, which created difficulties due to Carnera's affiliations with Madison Square Garden officials and Baer's manager Ancil Hoffman's refusal to meet the Garden's conditions for a championship bout under their auspices. "Sure," said Max, "Jack Dempsey will promote the fight at Yankee Stadium, and I guarantee it won't be a dancing lesson."[2] After much wrangling and negotiation, the fight was set for June 14, 1934, at the Madison Square Garden Bowl in Long Island City, New York.

Carnera once again set up his training camp in the quiet northern New Jersey Borough of Pompton Lakes, a scenic town about 15 miles south of the New York State line. Primo was to be severely handicapped by the absence of his trainer Big Bill Duffy who found himself in jail for failing to report over $30,000 in income in 1930. Released on bail so he could attend to Carnera's training for the Loughran fight, Duffy was to appear back in New York at his sentencing on March 5, but at the appointed time, he was nowhere to be seen. Judge William Bondy, upon discovering that Duffy was still on a Miami train bound for New York, proclaimed that "Big Bill" had better be present in his courtroom at 10:30 the next morning. This time Duffy was there. Bondy promptly sentenced him to four months in the federal lockup, thus taking him out of Primo's training camp and his corner during the Baer fight.

Early reports out of Primo's camp spoke of his terrific conditioning, but also of his erratic sparring skills. In the week before the bout, the Associated Press reported that the champion showed those present at ringside sessions how he could defeat Baer, how he could settle for a draw, and how he could lose decisively. In describing his sparring sessions with Chester Matan, Yustin Sirutis, and Corn Griffin, the news service reported that Primo "gave all three of these contradictory displays in rapid succession against three sparring partners."[3] After decisively beating up on Matan for two rounds, and holding the bobbing and weaving Sirutis to a frustrating draw for two more, the champion squared off with Griffin for two rounds in which he looked completely beatable. Griffin waited patiently for an opening and when Primo lay out his long left jabs, Corn would duck under them and slam hard left hooks into Carnera's body. When Primo inevitably dropped his fists to protect his midsection, Griffin immediately altered his sights to aim for the champion's chin.

It was not uncommon for Primo to become frustrated in the ring when his plans didn't work or when an opponent began to get to him. In describing the sparring session with Griffin, the Associated Press reported in almost an eerie harbinger of what would happen in the ring against Baer, "Once losing command of the situation, Carnera obviously became flustered. He floundered around the ring, all his carefully acquired book knowledge of boxing tossed overboard, and he was wide open to any kind of a punch Griffin wanted to throw."[4]

The next day, Carnera met the same fighters in two rounds each, and he gave a much better showing. He boxed consistently; he was sharp and his hitting was very impressive. Primo sparred a total of six rounds and exercised on the heavy bag for two more. In general, his work was impressive. As long as his huge left arm was extended and he wasn't being pressed, he was nearly impossible to hit. At short range, he was ferocious and punches bounced off him like a hammer on an anvil.

Bill Brown, professional athletic trainer and member of the New York State Athletic Commission, watched Primo work out in early June and following the session, he raved about Carnera's conditioning.

* * *

Max Baer and his entourage also chose a New Jersey site for a training camp, but it could not have been more different from the rustic cottages Carnera employed in Pompton Lakes. Heading down to the Jersey shore, Max stayed at the Asbury Park home of his friend and noted bridge player P. Hal Sims. The house was, by all accounts, luxurious — complete with sunken marble tubs and Italian paintings and sculpture.

Baer was an interesting character. The Californian was a wildly talented athlete both inside and outside the ring. In his school days he played football, baseball, and track. He was excellent at throwing the discus and javelin, and at putting the shot. He was a strong golfer, consistently shooting in the low 80s on the links. Max's interest in athletics was, however, often overshadowed by his nocturnal roamings. Baer absolutely loved the nightlife. He was never happier than when surrounded by good friends, beautiful women, and fine liquor.

He had a torrid on-off marriage and divorce with actress Dorothy Dunbar. He was linked at other times with platinum-blonde actress Jean Harlow, the famous fan dancer Sally Rand, and others, from society women to chorus girls to cocktail waitresses.

On his way up the heavyweight ladder, it is estimated that Baer earned more than a half-million dollars, and as with Primo, Max's "friends," lady companions, and managers had siphoned off most of it. Dempsey, who took an interest in Baer after refereeing Max's 10-round loss to Tommy Loughran in 1931, stated once that Max had squandered every penny of his earnings in the early days of his career. The Manassa Mauler took Baer under his wing and advised him to invest and save. Baer's father once commented, "He's the wildest boy I've ever known."[5]

Baer, like Primo, had the reputation as a killer in the ring. Baer literally punched Frankie Campbell to death in August 1930, when Referee Toby Irwin failed to stop the fight. Some also linked Baer to the death of Ernie Schaaf, even though their battle came six months before Ernie's death, Schaaf fought four more times before he died, and expert medical opinion clearly proved that the cause of Ernie's death was oedema — or swelling —

of the brain, most probably caused by a recent bout with influenza. It happened to be Carnera who fought Schaaf that night, but in the doctor's opinion, Ernie should have been nowhere near the ring, and even a moderate hit from his accountant could have caused the fatal damage to Ernie that night.

According to the press, Baer's training for the Carnera fight did not go well at all. The Associated Press reported on June 5 that Baer's condition was puzzling to boxing experts. Baer had apparently looked so bad in training against two huge sparring partners, Seal Harris and Dynamite Jackson, that a new trainer, Dolph Thomas, was called in, all the way from San Francisco to Asbury Park, and Jack Dempsey began to take an active role in the fight preparations.

On June 7, unseasonably chilly weather forced Primo indoors for his workouts, but bigger news than the cool weather was about to grab the fight news. One week before the fight, reports out of Asbury Park stated that the Baer camp would ask for a week's postponement to give Baer more time to get into better condition. According to the Associated Press, "Down in Asbury Park, N. J. where the night club nabob has been puffing and hauling through his workouts, Ancil Hoffman, his manager, and Jack Dempsey, his advisor, took a long look today and decided Max couldn't possibly be ready for a fifteen round duel in Madison Square Garden bowl one week from tomorrow night."[6]

Baer, Hoffman, and Dempsey, were to appear before the New York State Athletic Commission on Friday June 8 to make their case for a delay. Dempsey stated that Baer "has seven days left to get in shape and that's not enough. The public is entitled to plenty of action for their money and they should see both men at their best. I think he'll come through all right and be the Baer that knocked off Schmeling, but it will require plenty of hard work. Carnera is ready now. Baer isn't."[7]

In response to the request Primo thundered, "I refuse to consent to any postponement. There will be a fight June 14 or not at all."[8] The Associated Press reported, "The monster man is in such perfect condition right now ... that any delay now would wreck his training."[9]

Some claimed that the requested delay was little more than a stunt by Baer, Hoffman, and Dempsey to toy with Carnera and take his edge off. Primo was reportedly in top shape and looking good in his sparring sessions, but they knew that he could easily be rattled and psyched out. Dempsey had learned a thing or two about gamesmanship from his old manager Tex Rickard, and Hoffman was a master of the art as well.

One of those who agreed was Garden boxing manager Jimmy Johnston, who bellowed that Baer was in good shape and that the attempt at delay was nothing more than a trick and a "larcenous attempt" by the Baer camp to keep the sharp and well-conditioned Carnera working another week and bring him into the ring stale so they'll win the championship. He vowed to fight any such attempt by the challenger at delay.

Bill Brown, one of three New York State Athletic Commissioners, stated that he would support the delay if a physical the next day did not reveal Baer to be in top shape. John J. Phelan and D. Walker Wear, the other two thirds of the Commission, did not support a delay under any conditions.

Edward J. Neil of the Associated Press wrote of the attempted delay on the day of the state commission hearing. He saw the ludicrous nature of the Baer camp's plea. He argued logically that the date had been set for two months. The fighters had had equal amounts of time to train, and in one week they were scheduled to meet for 15 rounds in Madison Square Garden's bowl on Long Island. And now Baer, the challenger, to the absolute consternation of the Garden and the champion, was asking for a week's postponement so that he might get in better condition.

Baer, Hoffman, and Dempsey appeared at the New York State Athletic Commission offices on Friday, to plead for the delay. Carnera and his team of handlers, Garden representatives, and several legal advisors, were also on hand to oppose the Baer camp's arguments and they pleaded just as strenuously for the fight to go on as scheduled.

The next day, Commissioner Phelan announced that both Baer and Carnera had passed exhaustive physicals with flying colors and that the attending physicians, Drs. William Walker, Morris Beyer, and Vincent Nardiello, had pronounced the fighters fit and ready to fight. The delay had been avoided, but one can only speculate that the pre-fight distraction may have done some damage to Carnera's psyche anyway, and thus, the effect desired by the Baer camp was achieved.

Conditioning for a long prizefight is, at best, a difficult thing to judge without actually seeing the fighter in the ring for a number of rounds. Sportswriting legend Damon Runyon pointed out during the delay controversy that 100 of the world's best doctors could examine a man in training and find him apparently physically perfect — heart rate, blood pressure, lungs, eyes, hearing, and everything else all 100 percent perfect. But, Runyon pointed out these physicians cannot state with accuracy that the athlete is truly ready to complete the task at hand.

"If you are a confirmed follower of fistic events," stated Runyon, "you have seen hundreds of fighters so tired at the end of a few rounds of fighting they could scarcely hold their hands up, yet these fighters were necessarily passed by physicians as physically all right. This is no indictment of the physicians. They cannot be expected to determine endurance by mere examination. Yet endurance is the sum total of perfect physical condition for prizefighting, and the only way endurance can be determined is by actual competition."[10]

* * *

In the days before the fight, ticket sales were brisk and predictions were that the gate might prove to be as much as $500,000, which would make this fight the most successful at the box office since the first Sharkey–Schmeling fight grossed $749,000 in 1930.

Betting, too, was brisk. The overnight odds still had Carnera listed as the slight favorite, but the line was evening out, rapidly. Should the bout end in a knockout, the odds favored Maxie to be the man still standing, but if the fight went the distance, Primo was the 2–1 pick to take the decision.

Late in the week before the fight, Primo came down with a sore throat and fever that slowed his pre-fight preparation to a crawl for a couple of days. Dr. Vincent Nardiello of the New York State Athletic Commission examined Carnera and raised concerns that the champion should take it easy for a few days, for fear that the pharyngitis could result in a respiratory infection and cause the well-conditioned Carnera to have difficulty breathing. Since the inability to catch one's breath and boxing are a bad mix, Primo and his trainers agreed that he should take it easy for a few days.

Carnera took a final full workout on Tuesday going two rounds each, with sparring partners Lew Flowers and Chester Matan. By all accounts, the champion looked good in battering his opponents around the ring.

While the fight preparations moved along, the wheels of justice continued to turn as well. That afternoon in Manhattan, New York State Supreme Court Justice Ernest Hammer

9. Max Baer, 1934

Primo Carnera in action with a sparring partner at his training camp in Pompton Lakes, New Jersey, before his June 14, 1934, title defense against Max Baer. (Popperfoto/Getty Images)

agreed to appoint Michael Erceg as receiver for Carnera's share of the purse from Thursday night's fight. The application for a receiver of the funds was initiated by Theodore J. Skratt, himself the appointed receiver for the Emilia Tersini breach of promise judgment against Primo. Skratt also announced that he was initiating proceedings against the Madison Square Garden Corporation, to prevent payment of Carnera's share of the purse.

On Tuesday evening, Primo went into Pompton Lakes after dinner and saw the latest Clark Gable movie *After Office Hours*. It was then back home, where the champion was in bed by 10:00 P.M. He exercised lightly on Wednesday morning and relaxed the rest of the day.

While unconfirmed reports had him in Manhattan already, Baer was still in Asbury Park taking his final workouts. Journalist Hype Igoe, writing for the International News Service, reported that Max ended the long grind of his pre-fight training by taking a final early morning, 5-mile run and sparring three rounds with Dynamite Jackson and two more with Larry Johnson. After a shower and lunch, Max and his new trainer Dolph Thomas took a long walk over the back roads of Asbury Park. The two men headed out alone to plot strategy for the upcoming battle and to discuss what to expect from the Ambling Alp.

Entering the fight, Baer conceded all size advantages to Carnera. Max was, however, unmatched by his opponent in confidence, speed, and punching power — three critical points. That said, his erratic fighting style made him an enigma. Would he come out of his corner as the clown prince of the ring, let his guard down, and enable Primo to put him away with an uppercut like he had Sharkey, or to outlast him over 15 rounds; or would Baer enter the ring as a ferocious demon, possessed with savage, anvil-like fists that could end the fight in mere seconds. With Max, it was difficult to know.

How Carnera would fare was also difficult to gauge. Primo's huge size, tremendous strength, resilience, and conditioning were his acknowledged strong suits, but his weak chin and his lack of a consistent power punch were his weaknesses. Against a powerhouse like Baer, they could well be his undoing.

In the days before the fight, the usual prognostications began about who Thursday night's winner might be. Former heavyweight champion James J. Jeffries picked the Italian, stating, "Carnera, I think, is a better boxer than Baer." Former lightweight champion Benny Leonard was quoted as picking Carnera to defend his title successfully, while praising his development from an awkward novice to a clever boxer. He agreed with promoter Floyd Fitzsimmons that with Primo's 85½" reach, and his left arm extended and jabbing, he would be difficult for Baer to hit. Titleholder Barney Ross stated that he favored the hard-punching Baer and that if Baer would only take his training a bit more seriously, he would have no doubt of the outcome of the fight.

Legendary sportswriter Hype Igoe stated his opinion that Max might win, but should avoid fighting Primo in close. "I doubt that Baer ever will get in there where he knows Carnera is dangerous. Baer isn't a boob," he continued. "If Baer wins this fight, it will be because he will have stood off, veered to the left and shot rights to Carnera's body, ducking under Primo's left jab."[11]

The pre-fight weigh-in and final physical for the fighters was scheduled for 1:00 P.M. on the day of the fight — Thursday. On Thursday morning, Primo and his entourage left Pompton Lakes and drove into Manhattan where they set up their pre-fight headquarters at the Hotel Victoria. Baer stayed at the undisclosed home of a friend.

In another ridiculous display, Baer requested of the State Athletic Commission that he be able to use the same Garden Bowl dressing room as the champion. According to the challenger, he was thinking only of Primo and wanted to keep Carnera's spirits up until the fighters were called to the ring. The commission ignored the request.

The fight was carried internationally at 10:00 P.M. Eastern Time by the Blue Network of the National Broadcasting Corporation, with Graham McNamee calling the action and Ford Bond adding between-round commentary. Giulio Rollini and Julio Garza were at ringside to report the action live, respectively, to Italian and Spanish-speaking fans around the world.

On Thursday night, a thundering crowd of 56,000 filled the Bowl to just over two thirds of capacity. The gathering was typical for a heavyweight championship bout and included notables from all walks of life. Most prominent in this evening's crowd were New York Mayor Fiorello LaGuardia, Postmaster General Jim Farley, National Recovery Administration director General Hugh S. Johnson, and a slew of current and former fighters. Before the main event Jack Dempsey, Gene Tunney, Jimmy McLarnin, Jack Sharkey, Benny Leonard, Ray Impelletiere, Tommy Loughran, Willie Ritchie, and Steve Hamas were introduced from the ring.

The huge crowd was treated to a seven-fight card. Most notably, the crowd saw Jim Braddock score a third-round knockout over heavily favored John "Corn" Griffin. Griffin, Carnera's and Baer's sparring partner, was picked to move up the heavyweight ladder, and the choice of Braddock was seen as a way to pad Griffin's record with a respected, if washed up, former contender. Braddock, who took the fight as a replacement on just two days' notice, soon proved he had other ideas. This fight was the first of "The Cinderella Man's" storied comeback from the relief rolls to the world heavyweight championship.

As the headliners made their way from their dressing rooms, Carnera, wearing his customary dark green robe, was in the ring first, climbing over the middle rope. Baer then made his way in, wearing the same white robe he wore in *The Prizefighter and the Lady*. Across the back of the silk robe was the name "Steve Morgan." The third man in the ring that night was veteran referee Arthur Donovan, and the fight judges were Tommy Shawtell and Charley Lynch.

As the fighters and their corner men milled about the canvas, the contest between the men that *New York Times* columnist John Kieran called "The Iron Horse of Italy" and "The Harlequin of Hollywood," was at long last finally ready to begin.

Ring announcer Joe Humphreys, now fully recovered from a stroke suffered one year and a day earlier, was again holding court at center ring. Waving his straw boater and trying to get the crowd's attention, Humphreys pleaded, "Quiet, please, quiet. Quiet, please! Main event, 15 rounds for the world's heavyweight championship, pitting the present holder of the title, the Goliath of fistiana and a son of sunny Italy — Primo Carnera!" After a brief pause, Humphreys continued: "His opponent, the California Adonis, who we all put our faith in as Americans, to bring back the title to the good old U.S.A — Max Baer!" After a period of cheering for the fighters Humphreys added, "Weight: Carnera 263, Baer 210. Judges: Tommy Shawtell, Charley Lynch; Arthur Donovan: referee."

The fighters met with Donovan in the middle of the ring and reviewed the rules, and with that, all was ready to begin.

Shortly after the opening bell, Baer caught Carnera on the jaw with a thunderous straight right that sent the champion to the canvas. Primo was up immediately, but that punch set the tone for the first two rounds. Carnera was knocked down three times in the first minute of the fight, as Baer unloaded a series of smashing rights and lefts to the champ's head and body. The story was much the same in the second, when the champion went down three more times. In both rounds, Primo was quick to his feet, but too much so. He inexplicably did not take advantage of the full count. Baer ignored Donovan's commands to retreat to a neutral corner, and instead lurked nearby, waiting, watching, and ready to pounce. As soon as Carnera got to his feet, he found himself back in the midst of the Baer meat grinder. Had he taken more time to gather his wits, he might have avoided the second or third knockdown in each round. By the third, Primo was still not fighting well, but his head had cleared, and he was able to defend himself again. There were no more knockdowns until the tenth round.

The Associated Press' sportswriter Edward J. Neil, reporting from ringside, wrote of the champion's amazing ability to take all that Baer had, and keep coming back for more. After being soundly beaten in the first three rounds, Neil stated that Carnera suddenly started to stir. The champion began to come back by calling on the tremendous resources of strength in his gigantic frame and wiping out the effects of this punishment. From the fourth through seventh rounds, Primo looked better and made a bit of a rally, but it was not enough.

Baer seemed to take the fourth round off, apparently tired from his flurries of punches in the first three rounds. Primo made a decent showing, pawing at Baer with his ponderous left jab and wearing Max down in the clinches, but in all, the round was largely uneventful.

Baer hit Carnera with perhaps the most devastating clout of the evening, in the fifth. The challenger loosed a powerful right that started in his legs, and with the full force of his body, he followed through and caught Carnera square in the middle of his face. Neil commented, "As the glove came away, and Primo staggered like a mountain riding an earthquake, blood spurted from his broken nose, his lips jumped to twice their normal size, and in an instant his massive face was painted crimson. He was helpless on the ropes, taking a fearful beating around the head and body as the bell saved him there."[12] But even after that explosion, Carnera was not beaten.

In the sixth round, Primo came out looking sharp, as he made Baer retreat against the ropes, where he hit the challenger with a left and two right uppercuts. After Donovan broke the fighters apart, Carnera was still the aggressor, striking Baer with a series of left jabs to the head. These were followed by a wild exchange in which each fighter landed several shots on the other. The final half of the round saw good action, as the men exchanged blows at a rapid pace. After watching the fight on film, I actually gave this round to the champion.

Despite a Baer flurry before the bell, Carnera won the seventh round, by working Maxie repeatedly with his wearing left jabs.

Carnera took the eighth as well, when Baer, who was back to his pounding ways, dropped one punch below the belt. Under New York State's scoring rules, the round went to Primo. During the round Primo seemed to favor his right leg, keeping his full weight off it at times, and even stumbling once.

By round nine, the champion was looking tired, but still game for the fight. He landed three left jabs to the face that registered with Baer, and followed them up with a strong right uppercut that put Max against the ropes, early in the round. After this, the fighters settled into a slower pace of exchanges.

By this time, Primo had made enough of a comeback to begin using his size and reach against his opponent. Max was tired and Primo had done enough to gain a lead on the some scorecards as the fight entered the tenth round.

In his usual style, Primo answered the bell for the tenth by running to the center of the ring, but he seemed a bit slower this time. While the champion exchanged blows with Baer, they didn't have the pop that Maxie's had. In fairness, Primo's punches probably never had the pop that Baer's had, but he was noticeably wearing down. Baer pursued the champion, taunting him with a consistent torrent of punches and taunts.

Late in the round, Baer hit Carnera with two strong rights to the champion's head, the second of which sent Primo reeling around the ring and into the ropes. As he began to go down, Primo caught the ropes, preventing himself from hitting the canvas. Once Carnera was upright, referee Donovan began to size up his condition. He stepped between the two fighters and thought about bringing the fight to an end, but with the corners on their feet and ready to enter the ring, he stopped himself. Baer stood just beyond Donovan, taunting his opponent and ready to continue the carnage. As soon as the referee began to step away, Baer sweeping Donovan back with his left hand, he pounced on the champion. Max threw a sweeping right that caught Carnera's face and a left that missed its mark, but wrapped his arm around the champion, allowing Baer to sling him down to the canvas. Again Primo got up, but only to get knocked down once more under the crushing blows of the challenger. With only seconds left in the round, a wobbly Primo rose once more, but with Baer landing punches at will, it was only the judgment of Donovan and the bell that saved the champion from a knockout in the tenth round. Primo, clearly disoriented, had to be directed back to his corner by Donovan and his seconds.

9. Max Baer, 1934

As the 11th round commenced, Primo came out swinging, again game for the fight and desperate to save his crown, but it wasn't to be. Less than a minute into the round Baer landed a crushing right that sent Carnera back into the ropes and dropped the champion on his butt, like a rock. Quickly up again, Carnera advanced on Baer and refused to quit. After exchanging blows for the next minute, Baer again decked Primo with a crushing right that caught the champion on the left temple. The champion got up one final time, but his reign atop the heavyweight world was almost over. Donovan started to let them continue to fight, but after 2 or 3 seconds and another right by Baer, he had seen enough. Finally, with 43 seconds left in the round, Donovan stepped in between the fighters and stopped the beating. He directed Baer to his corner, and the fight was over. Ring announcer Joe Humphreys then pronounced Max Baer, the clown prince of boxing, as the new heavyweight champion of the world.

Baer had fought a strong fight. From early in the bout, Max smelled blood and the title — and he responded with savage, relentless attacks. Each time he wounded the champion, he chased Carnera around the ring as Primo tried to find a safe haven to steady himself.

Baer was the clear winner, but Primo had shown some skill, great stamina and resilience and had been noble in his brave but fledgling defense. Eleven times, and twice in the final two rounds, the Alp tumbled, but still refusing to quit, he bravely climbed to his feet.

Referee Arthur Donovan steps in to stop the bout between Carnera and Max Baer at the Madison Square Garden Bowl on June 16, 1934. Baer won the championship on a TKO in the eleventh round of their title fight. (Bettmann/CORBIS)

Former champion Gene Tunney, writing for the Associated Press in an article titled, "First Blow Took Alp's Confidence," stated, "The Italian himself cannot hit and he is bewildered as soon as his defense starts to break down. His confidence was shattered in the first minute of last night's fight and it was simply a question of how long it would last."[13]

Tunney continued with his critique of the fight, but this time granted a measure of praise to the former champion: "I was not surprised Baer failed to finish Carnera in either of the first two rounds. The big fellow has amazing stamina and showed he is really game under fire, although he used very bad judgment in not taking longer counts when he was down three times in the first round. A fighter is entitled to all the count he can get under such circumstances and it was ruinous for Primo to leap up at once and stumble into another succession of hard blows."[14] Tunney was dead-on with that assessment. Primo should have taken a full nine-count before rising any of the times he was dropped. Baer was on him instantly, each time he rose, and without time to shake off a few cobwebs, Carnera remained an easy target for Max. This, of course, contributed to the high number of knockdowns.

Tunney added, "I would say on the whole that Baer fought a perfect fight, showing rare confidence at all times and proving himself a terrific hitter. He did not waste time and energy trying to box Carnera."[15]

Former champion Dempsey agreed with Tunney that his protégé had made a terrific showing. Dempsey claimed that Baer made no mistakes and that he followed the pre-fight plan to a tee.

Baer fought the fight that he and his entourage had planned out. According to Dempsey, the challenger, his manager Ancil Hoffman, his trainer Mike Cantwell, and the former champion talked it over in the taxi on the way out to the Madison Square Garden Bowl. They agreed that the way to fight Carnera was to hit him in the body until his guard dropped, then hit him on the head till his hands came up again, then go back down below, then up again, and so forth until the bout was over.

Commissioner Brown, still unimpressed with Baer, stated, "He's still a bum! The fact that Baer defeated Carnera doesn't change my opinion of him."[16]

During the bout Primo suffered an ankle injury that undoubtedly slowed the champion during the fight. After he went to his dressing room he rested on a table with his injured leg up. He could hear the raucous celebration going on in Baer's adjoining quarters. Associated Press sportswriter Edward J. Neil reported that Primo groaned and, pointing to his right foot, said, "Take off my shoe, quick, I got pain there."[17]

Pain he had indeed. His physician, Dr. Vincent Panoni, examined the badly swollen and discolored ankle and declaring the ankle in terrible shape, ordered X-rays to see if there was a break. Dr. Panoni also ordered Primo to use crutches and stay off it for at least two weeks. After keeping several engagements the next day, it became evident that Primo, who could not move about without assistance, needed to get to the hospital right away.

After undergoing a thorough exam and X-rays at Columbus Hospital, it was revealed that Carnera had indeed broken his right ankle. In addition to the break — a clean chip off the anklebone — Carnera had torn ligaments in the ankle. Primo said that he injured the leg in the first round when he was felled by one of Baer's shots. After the exam, his right leg was put in a cast and Dr. Panoni told the press that it was doubtful that Primo would be able to meet Baer in the proposed September rematch. Panoni estimated that the damage would take at least a month or two to heal and that a proper period of 6–8 weeks of training and rehabilitation would necessarily have to follow.

The Associated Press reported on June 16 that Primo, while lying in bed at Columbus Hospital and nursing his damaged ankle, was calling for a rematch with Baer. Carnera said that he would defeat Baer in a rematch and declared that a return bout was only fair since his ankle had slowed him up considerably.

Asked what happened to him in the first round, Primo responded that he was just a bit nervous and confused and that it always took him a long time to get started.

"I was never hurt by his punches," declared Carnera. "He pushed me over every time. A man can't keep himself from being pushed over when he has only one leg, can he?"[18] Primo was undoubtedly slowed by the injury. It is amazing that he was able to box 11 rounds at all, much less in a heavyweight title fight, and he was certainly pushed down a couple of times by Baer, but he also certainly felt the sting of the challenger's anvil-like fists.

Neil reported that "Dumb Dan" Morgan, Carnera's chief second, saw the fight a bit differently than Primo. Morgan observed that Baer stung Carnera in the first round and that Primo didn't completely recover until the third round. Once his head cleared and he got his bearings again, he was all right and actually won some rounds. But then Morgan noted that Baer would land one or two crushing rights and again Primo was in trouble.

From the first round through the 11th, however, Primo, showing amazing resilience, kept coming back. When Primo went down in the opening round from a hard overhand right to the chin, he may have known then that he was overmatched, but as always, he got up. He was dropped twice more in that round and eight more times in the fight. He simply refused to give up. This was a testament to Primo's drive and bravery. Even Max, who had been openly disdainful of Carnera before the fight, showed grudging admiration for Primo's toughness. When referee Arthur Donovan finally stopped the fight at 2:46 of round 11, the big man, battered and bloody, was still on his feet. Donovan knew that Primo was in trouble and acted promptly, stating after the bout, "Carnera asked me to stop the fight, just at the second when I was going to stop it anyway. He didn't know where he was. He could not have continued, and there was no use letting it go on when he was so helpless."[19]

Baer complimented Primo the day after the fight, praising the former champion as a fine sportsman with a huge heart. He went on to describe Carnera as a strong and clean fighter who could take a great deal of punishment and keep on coming.

The Associated Press' Neil noted that the crowd of 56,000 fight fans "went away singing the courage of Carnera, 263 pounds of manhood who earned the right never to hear the word 'freak' again. They'll never forget the sight of him getting up again and again and again."[20]

In his dressing room after the fight, Primo sat with tears rolling down his battered face and his broken right ankle wrapped in ice and bandaged. He was simply devastated that he had disappointed his family, his friends, his countrymen, his fans, and the thousands of Italian-Americans who had made the trek out to the Long Island Bowl to root him on. Over and over he kept reminding the assembled press that he hadn't quit. Though he lost a one-sided affair, it was a source of pride and consolation that he had not taken the easy way out and lain down. It was tearing him apart that he had lost, but it was important to Primo that the public understood that he did not surrender. Say what you will about Primo, he was strong, tough as nails, and anything but a quitter.

Louis Soresi claimed that the ankle injury had cost Carnera the fight. He commented to the press that Primo could have moved away from Baer's deadly right had he had full mobility, but the pain from the break and the ligament damage was too great and it hampered the big man's movements.

* * *

There was grief for Primo in Sequals as well. Primo's mother Giovanna told reporters that her husband, Sante, had left town to escape the sympathy of his friends. He stole away to the nearby town of Fanna until news of the excruciating loss had subsided.

Throughout the Italian peninsula and in Italian neighborhoods throughout the world, Primo's admirers sat in heartbroken disbelief. Their hero had fallen. In Rome, the leaders of the Fascist regime sat in incredulous anger. Their great Italian champion, their fabulous propaganda tool, had lost his title — to a Jew, no less — and embarrassed them.

* * *

The National Broadcasting Corporation reported that the fight was heard clearly by radio around the globe including via shortwave in "Little America," the base of operations for the Byrd Antarctic Expedition.

* * *

On June 22 Baer visited with Carnera in Columbus Hospital. Primo, still immobile while recovering from the ankle injury, was pleased to see Max. During the half hour visit, the new heavyweight champion tried to buoy Primo's spirits. Baer also made a special point of assuring the press that he bore no ill will towards Carnera, had great respect for Primo's ring skills and toughness, and that any disparaging comments he made to the contrary were not to be taken seriously and were simply meant as pre-fight hype.

* * *

As it turns out, both fighters may ultimately have been fighting for free. The United States Government filed an income tax lien of $32,900 against Carnera. The lien covered all income dating from January 1, 1934, in order to have prior claim on his earnings over any pending civil suits. In addition, there was Emilia Tersini's judgment. "The receipts from the fight amounted to £85,000 ($400,000), but it is not certain how much of it will go to the principals. Carnera was due to receive 37½ percent of the proceeds and Baer 20 percent, but both may have fought for nothing. A receiver had been appointed to take charge of Carnera's winnings because the latter failed to appear before the court for examination as to his ability to pay £3,000 ($14,380.25) judgment made against him in favour of Miss Amelia (sic) Tersini, the former London waitress. Baer, too, is being sued for £10,000 by Miss Shirley Labelle for 'heart balm.'"[21]

Ultimately the legal proceedings were settled in Primo's favor. On June 25, federal judge John M. Woolsey signed an order restraining any monies being paid to Skratt until Carnera's bankruptcy petition was decided. Judge Woolsey wrote, "The claim of the creditor is based on breach of promise of marriage. This is dischargeable in bankruptcy. Property acquired by the bankrupt after the filing of the petition is not part of the estate in bankruptcy nor subject to the claims against such estate."[22]

In addition, *Time* magazine reported:

> To the $14,380.25 breach of promise verdict obtained by Emelia Tersini, London waitress, against colossal Primo Carnera, and to Carnera's ensuing petition in bankruptcy (TIME, April 10; et seq.): denial by the New York Supreme Court of Signorina Tersini's application to have a receiver appointed for the $16,000 earned by Carnera when he won the heavyweight championship from Jack Sharkey (TIME, July 10). Champion Carnera — who last week was picking up change by personal appearances in a Broadway vaudeville house — claimed he had paid his fight receipts to his

manager Louis Soresi for a farm in Italy. Said the Court: "Reluctantly does the court deny this application; for good reason exists to suspect the honesty and sincerity of the transfer.... Unfortunately for; the plaintiff, astute advice has kept the defendant, Carnera, and his mentor, Soresi, within the law."[23]

Miss Tersini had stayed up late into the night in an express office to follow the fight round-by-round by ticker report. In an interview in London after the fight she claimed that Baer had fouled Primo and should have been disqualified. Claiming grief and despair over Primo's loss Tersini said, "It's a shame. I know Primo can beat him. I still believe in Primo." It's hard to tell the cause of her post-fight tears, but one has to wonder if they were truly inspired by her upset for Primo or rather by her own financial concerns. No longer the champion, Carnera would receive smaller gates in future fights, thus further endangering her chances of collecting on her breach of promise judgment.

* * *

In a bizarre and unexplained incident, an unidentified man pulled a gun on Primo as he was walking toward the ring at the narrow entrance to the patron-press section of the Garden Bowl. According to International News Service sports editor Davis J. Walsh, an unidentified gunman "with a flair for the dramatic" was boldly planning to shoot Carnera as he walked to the ring in front of 60,000 witnesses.

The gunman waited quietly and unnoticed at ringside until Primo got near and suddenly he produced a gun. There was apparently very little struggle as the stranger was grabbed and pushed out of the way by Primo's seconds. The incident ended very quickly and few in the crowd noticed anything out of the ordinary, assuming that the disturbance was simply the normal commotion generated when a champion enters the ring. Walsh wrote, "And that, they tell me, was the reason Walter (Good Time Charley) Friedman, the friend of Madden and Duffy and Dutch Schultz, did not enter the ring at any time but sat all night on the steps leading up to Carnera's corner. He was awaiting the stranger's return."[24]

Who the violent stranger was or why he was gunning for Primo was never explained, but rumors were in the air about mob hits and jealous boyfriends. Walsh commented further nobody really knew who the attempted assassin might be, but he indicated that the speculation was that there was a woman at the heart of the matter and that inflamed emotions and unrequited love may have been involved. One also might wonder if someone with an axe to grind with Madden, Duffy, or Schultz might be the instigator.

Whatever the case and whomever the stranger, nothing more ever came of the near tragic event and it has now been relegated to the dustbin of history as one of its lesser known footnotes.

10

After the Title, 1934–1935

Following the Baer debacle, Primo needed to rest his injured ankle and think about his future plans. He and his handlers decided that the best thing to do was get right back up on the horse. Primo felt it would be the best thing for his career, while Soresi and company felt it was the best thing for their pocketbooks. Soresi's and Bill Duffy's pocketbooks were now a bit lighter for having bought out Owney Madden's share of the fighter and they were anxious to squeeze as much juice out of the lemon by keeping Carnera fighting as long as they could.

Madden lost interest in Carnera soon after the loss to Baer. He saw that the big man was either on his way down or would be soon so he cashed in his chips and concentrated on other business enterprises. In time he relocated to Hot Springs, Arkansas, where he married local girl Agnes Demby and, while still involved in underworld activity, he lived a quieter life, only occasionally returning to New York. He died in a Hot Springs hospital on April 24, 1965, when emphysema finally did what the police and so many gangland rivals were unable to.

On July 18 Louis Soresi issued an ultimatum to Jimmy Johnston of the Madison Square Garden Corporation that Primo would accept an offer from Jeff Dickson to fight in London if the Garden did not come up with a suitable opponent for Carnera to fight in the next few days. Meeting with Primo and his management in New York the day before, Dickson said that he would guarantee Primo $30,000 or 32½ percent of the gate in a September 20 match against the winner of the bout between Larry Gains and Jack Peterson.

Johnston announced that day that he would put Primo in an elimination tourney with some combination of Steve Hamas, Art Lasky, Max Schmeling, or Walter Neusel. Neither the Dickson fight nor the Garden elimination tournament ever came off. Instead, Primo took a 6-month layoff, returning to action in South America where he fought several exhibitions as well as three sanctioned bouts.

* * *

The ever-evolving story of Carnera's finances continued on August 14 as New Jersey Circuit Court Judge Thomas Brown released $66,000 of the money Primo had earned in the Baer fight to Louis Soresi. The money had been held in escrow in the Commercial Trust Company in Jersey City. Judge Brown ruled that the remaining $22,000 be held pending liens against it. The liens included the Tersini judgment and an additional $3,113.57 claimed by a Philadelphia attorney for unspecified "legal fees." Judge Brown apparently did not do his homework because not two months earlier, Federal Judge John M. Woolsey had ruled that property acquired by Carnera after the filing of the bankruptcy petition was not part of the estate in bankruptcy nor subject to the claims against such estate.

The funds were released after Soresi testified that he had deposited the $88,000 — Primo's share of the Baer gate — in the bank because it belonged to him as a result of a personal loan he had given to Carnera to enable the fighter to purchase a 1,000-acre estate in Italy.[1]

* * *

Primo's financial woes continued to mount as Internal Revenue Service Collector James J. Hoey filed income tax liens against Carnera totaling $2,948.48. Hoey stated that this was money owed by Carnera from his 1929 earnings plus an additional fee of $673.78 said to be interest on the original $2,264.70 owed. In a bit of good fortune, however, this lien was withdrawn by the IRS in October and Carnera given a subsequent tax credit for an over-assessment. Finally some good financial news had come Primo's way.

* * *

Rumors of Carnera's next opponent continued to circulate. On October 31 while Primo was traveling to Sao Paulo, the Associated Press reported that the former champion would meet Paolino Uzcudun for the third time. The fight was reported to be scheduled for December 16 at the Independiente football stadium in Buenos Aires.

* * *

On December 1 Primo met the equally massive Vittorio Campolo at the Club Atletico Independiente, Avellaneda, in Buenos Aires, Argentina. The two fighters had met once before, in New York in November 1931, when Primo scored an easy second-round knockout.

After his decisive loss to Carnera, Campolo stayed out of the ring for almost two years, concentrating on running his Argentine butcher's shop. When he decided to return in 1933 he signed to meet 6' 4" and 225-pound Argentine Epifanio Islas in Buenos Aires. Islas was now 2–11–2 and had shown no improvement in the five years since Primo had stopped him in Milan. The 24 months Campolo had spent away from the ring had apparently not hurt his fighting; they had, however, added weight to the Argentine pugilist who carried a good 20 pounds more than usual and sported what was described by journalists as a decided paunch. Despite the paunch and some obvious awkwardness, he hammered Islas, knocking him out in just 40 seconds of the first round in what turned out to be Islas' last professional fight. Campolo then proceeded to win three of his next four fights, his only loss coming by way of disqualification to Mauro Galusso in Montevideo, Uruguay, on March 18, 1934. While "El Gigante de Quilmes" was on a roll and now owned a record of 21–7–1, Carnera was an odds-on favorite to defeat Campolo again.

On the undercard, the 30,000 fans who only half-filled the Independiente Football Stadium saw Seal Harris win an eight-round points decision over Argentinean Justo Prieto. In the crowd that night were Tommy Loughran and Paolino Uzcudun, both of whom hoped to meet Carnera again in the near future.

Carnera was in excellent condition and took the fight to his opponent from the opening bell. Constantly on the offensive, Primo drove Campolo around the ring with a steady barrage of solid combinations in the early rounds. Campolo was at times able to use his long arms to his advantage. He held Primo literally at arms' length for much of the third and fourth rounds with his long left jabs. In the fifth round Primo, still fresh and strong, resumed the pressing of the attack against his opponent. Campolo was on the other hand beginning to run out of steam. Exhaustion had taken the snap out of his jabs, forcing him into the clinches to conserve energy and avoid Carnera's punches.

Despite the second-round knockout three years earlier and being clearly in control tonight, Carnera could not put the Argentine fighter down this go-around. While Primo made a much better showing than Campolo and landed the lion's share of the punches, neither fighter showed much physical damage at the closing bell.

In the end, Primo won an easy 12-round decision over the 6'9", 259-pound Campolo. "Carnera, making his first appearance in Buenos Aires, had little trouble earning the decision in 12 rather tame rounds, but Campolo, out of the ring for two years, put up a much better fight than had been expected."[2] The contest was, however, a good, solid return for Primo.

Following the fight, Soresi announced tentative plans to sail for New York on December 15 for the previously announced fight against Paolino Uzcudun in the Garden, now scheduled for December 22. On December 8, however, Soresi declared that negotiations between Uzcudun, Carnera, and the Garden had broken down over the gate split and that Carnera would stay in South America through the holidays. Soresi also reported that he was in the process of arranging several more fights in a number of South American cities.

* * *

On January 4, 1935, Primo rang in the New Year with a pair of exhibitions in Montevideo, Uruguay. That night he fought and outpointed Cecil "Seal" Harris and Julia Pantega each for four rounds.

* * *

On January 13 Carnera met Harris (22–20–5) again at the Arena Bella Floresta in Sao Paulo, Brazil, but this time, it counted. The 6'3½" Harris was at the end of a ten-year career that had shown mixed results but had made him a sought-after opponent. While not great, he was a respectable fighter who typically gave his adversaries a workout. Having faced Harris in the exhibition nine days earlier, Primo was familiar with the 240-pound Harris' style. As a result, Primo took just seven of the scheduled 10 rounds to finish Seal by KO. It was Harris' last official bout.

* * *

For the final fight of his South American swing, Primo was set to meet Estonian heavyweight Erwin Klausner (21–7–4) in Rio de Janeiro, Brazil, on January 20, 1935. Klausner was an Estonian national who lived in Brazil. An examination of his record indicates that the 203-pound Klausner was a very good fighter at the lower ranks, but every time he tried to move up to the talent of his opponents, he got belted back down to the minors. He finished his career in 1938 with a record of 22–9–6. Only 11 of his opponents had winning records and he only defeated two of those.

Several thousand fans greeted Carnera at the railway station when he arrived in Rio on Saturday the 19th of January. He then proceeded to the gym for a light workout and then on to his beachfront hotel. Immediately after checking in, he headed for the beach for a swim in the warm summer sun. A crowd made up of fight fans and the curious gathered and stood in awe at the sheer size and powerful build of the former champion.

On Sunday, a good crowd of 23,000 had assembled at the outdoor Fluminese Stadium

10. After the Title, 1934–1935

to watch the fight. Just as the fighters were ready to make their way from their dressing rooms into the ring, a heavy summer downpour struck and made it impossible to hold the fight that night. It was announced to the crowd that the rain had forced a postponement of the event until Tuesday the 22nd. It was also announced over the loudspeakers that no rain checks would be issued. At this the large crowd became so incensed that many began to leave their seats and tear down the ring. Some also threw sticks and stones. Naval fusiliers were called in to quell the riot and prevent further damage to the stadium.

On Monday and Tuesday crews worked to rebuild the ring and repair damage to the stadium and all was ready by the evening of the 22nd. A crowd estimated at 25,000 gathered to watch the former champion score a sixth-round technical knockout over the Estonian.[3]

Primo held the edge from the opening of the bout. He jarred Klausner in the first round with several hard rights. Twice Carnera received warnings from referee Luiz Souto — once for a rabbit punch in the fourth and again in the fifth for a questionable low blow. Undaunted, Primo re-aimed his punches and steadily battered Klausner into acquiescence.

In the fifth round Primo landed a left to Klausner's jaw that sent the Estonian halfway out of the ring and in the sixth, Primo stalked his battered, bloody and retreating opponent around the ring, landing blow after blow to the head and body in a ferocious two-handed assault. After a couple of minutes of the round, referee Souto stepped in and halted the beating.

* * *

In the weeks before the fight, a rumor started circulating that Primo had taken an Argentine bride. The story was a totally fictitious joke played by local Buenos Aires publication *El Grafico* several weeks earlier. The 28th of December in Argentina is the "Day of Innocents," which is roughly equivalent to April Fool's Day in the United States. On that day, *El Grafico* had for years printed a page of pictures that were never to be taken seriously. Apparently, as part of the joke for this particular year, Primo had been photographed with a woman named "Irene Roncales," who was in reality a husky male gymnast in drag. Primo was understandably a bit sensitive about this. While the photo was intended to be all in good fun, it was not terribly funny for a man still smarting from the harassment given him by his former fiancée Emilia Tersini. The photo ran in *El Grafico* with the caption identifying "Irene Roncales" as Carnera's "beautiful Argentine bride." Though a joke, the rumors persisted until Carnera's manager Lou Soresi and Primo held a press conference to put an end to this story before it migrated north. "The report that Carnera is married is without foundation and originated from Carnera's posing for publicity purposes."[4] That seemed to put an end to the story, as no more was heard about the burly Mrs. Carnera.

* * *

While Primo had done well in the ring and the trip had help to raise his spirits, the South American tour had not been particularly successful financially. Even so, Soresi announced that he was in negotiations for a fight to be held in either Buenos Aires or Rio de Janeiro against Big George Godfrey, who was currently in Europe wrestling. The prospects of such a fight were intriguing — a rematch pitting two well-known behemoths, both of whom were bucking for another shot at the heavyweight title. But as they so often do in the fight game, plans unfortunately fell through. With the Godfrey plans nixed, Carnera and his camp headed back to the United States after the Klausner fight to take the next steps on Primo's journey back to a heavyweight title shot.

After a short visit to Miami, the band flew to New York. Upon their arrival in early February Carnera and his managers stopped by Jimmy Johnston's offices in Madison Square Garden anxious to arrange Primo's next fight. Carnera told reporters that he was young, in great condition and ready to fight anyone. It was determined that a bout would be arranged for the Ides of March and a meeting with the equally mammoth young fighter Ray Impelletiere.

* * *

On February 6 the long established and well-respected Irving Trust Company of New York, acting as trustee in bankruptcy for Carnera, brought suit against Max Schmeling for alleged breach of contract. The suit alleged that Schmeling backed out of a contract to fight Carnera in 1931 and sought $125,000 in damages. Primo watched the day's proceedings as New York Supreme Court Justice Edgar E. Lauer and a jury heard attorneys for both sides present their cases.

The plaintiff's attorney, Alfred E. Herz, stated that Carnera spent $15,000 in training costs and suffered $85,000 in damages from lost fight, radio, and movie contracts. He also indicated that $25,000 was due Carnera as Schmeling's penalty for failing to keep the contract.

On February 7 Primo testified that an agreement was signed between the two parties in January 1931 in Damon Runyon's suite in the Hotel Forrest. No date was set at the time, but in July the two agreed by handshake to a September bout. This occurred in Schmeling's dressing room following his defeat of Young Stribling in Cleveland. Albert M. Yuzzolino, Carnera's attorney at the time, confirmed Carnera's story.

Schmeling was at home in Germany during the proceedings, but was represented by his manager Joe Jacobs. Jacobs claimed that promise or no promise, Schmeling could not have fought Carnera in September 1931 because of injuries.[5]

On February 8 Primo testified for another two and a half hours and Jacobs for an additional half hour. Following the conclusion of the testimony, Schmeling's attorney Louis Stillman called on Justice Lauer to dismiss the suit because no proof of "promise" had been established by the plaintiff. Upon review Lauer agreed and dismissed the suit as without merit.[6]

* * *

In late February, Carnera's management team set up training camp at Barney Williams' facilities in Orangeburg, New York. Orangeburg is a small town located on the west side of the Hudson River, not quite 20 miles northwest of Manhattan and just north of the New Jersey state line. Having worked hard in South America, Primo was already in excellent condition upon arrival and predicted that he would finish off Impelletiere within seven of the scheduled 10 rounds. Odds makers seemed to agree, installing Carnera a 3-to-1 favorite at fight time.

Like most fighters, Primo's daily workouts consisted of several miles of roadwork, calisthenics, work on the speed bag and heavy bag, rope jumping, and multiple rounds of sparring. His sparring partners while training for the Impelletiere fight were New Jerseyan Norman Barnett, old foe Cecil "Seal" Harris, and Lew "Tiger" Flowers.

The 6'0", 200-pound Flowers, unlike his Hall-of-Fame, middleweight namesake, was a classic journeyman heavyweight who fought throughout the 1930s, posting a mediocre overall career record of 13–17–0. Flowers battled in several notable contests, losing on points to the then up-and-coming Arthur Huttick and scoring a seventh-round knockout over Charlie Wepner (father of 1970's fringe contender Chuck Wepner—the infamous "Bayonne Bleeder"), but the Queens, New York, native really made his name as a sparring partner. In addition to working for Carnera, Flowers was a regular in the training camps of Jack Sharkey, Joe Louis, and others.

Flowers started his professional career by winning 12 of his first 16 fights in 1930 and 1931. He was off to a promising beginning, but almost overnight his rising star was extinguished. In boxing, like few other sports, an athlete can lose his skills seemingly overnight. Whether from the accumulated damage received during a career in the ring or a particularly bad beating on a specific night, a notable fighter can look sharp in one bout and then have lost his edge by the next or a fighter can even seem to implode from start to finish of a single fight. When this happens, the skills crafted over years of hard work and training simply vanish, never to return. And so it was with Tiger Flowers. A month after losing a close 10-rounder on points to Chester Matan in May 1932, Flowers met Adolph Heinz for an 8-round bout in Queensboro Stadium in New York. During this fight Flowers took a terrific beating, and the fight was stopped by referee Johnny Marto at 2:35 of the seventh round. He was never the same fighter again. After that night, Flowers left the prizefighting ring and for several years continued in the fight game as a sparring partner. In 1936 Flowers began a moderate comeback to the professional ranks, returning to the ring and scoring a third-round knockout over "Young" George Godfrey in Washington, D.C.'s Turner Arena. He should have stopped there, but he continued to fill out undercards for the next six years, losing his last 11 fights in a row from 1936 to 1942, the last seven by knockout.

In the main, visitors to the facility were impressed with Carnera's work and conditioning, convincing many that he was on the comeback trail and would soon be ready for another shot at the heavyweight title. While sparring, Carnera moved well, showing no signs of any lingering effects from the ankle injury suffered in the Baer fight. He danced around, scoring repeatedly with his traditional jabs, uppercuts and overhand rights, but he also exhibited something new as he showed off a real proficiency in landing hard left hooks to the jaw and body.

* * *

Pre-fight reports said that the winner of the Carnera–Impelletiere fight would meet the winner of the March 22 Jim Braddock–Art Lasky fight and that winner would meet Max Schmeling in the final bracket of the elimination for the chance to meet Max Baer for the championship.

On Tuesday March 12, the fighters were examined by Dr. William Walker of the New York State Athletic Commission and pronounced fit for the fight. The fighters and their entourages then returned to their respective camps—Carnera to Orangeburg and Impelletiere to Grippo's Gym in Beacon, New York.

On March 15, 1935, Primo met the once-touted Impelletiere in Madison Square Garden in Manhattan. Nicknamed "The Skyscraper," Impelletiere stood a towering 6'7½" and weighed 258 pounds, closing Primo's usual gargantuan weight advantage to a mere 10 pounds. While a shade taller than Carnera, Impelletiere was not nearly as powerful as his Friulian opponent. Impelletiere was briefly considered to be a real comer in the heavyweight ranks,[7] but for all of his size and potential, he only fought for five years, winding up with a 9–7–0 record. Ray won his first five fights by knockout, but went 4–7 the rest of the way when the competition got stiffer. Despite his brief and mediocre record, his losses were all to good fighters and he took most fights to their scheduled finish and hung in pretty well. In addition to his loss to Primo, he dropped three ten-round decisions to Tommy Loughran, decisions to Walter Neusel and Marty Gallagher, and in 1936, his final fight by TKO to Bob Pastor.

The fight was generating a frenzied interest. Carnera, who had always drawn well, was now also the former heavyweight champion. He had just come off three wins in South America and was frequently mentioned as a leading contender to challenge Baer in a return bout to regain his lost title. A win for Impelletiere would make him an automatic contender. A solid crowd of 19,000 paid to see Impelletiere try to stop Carnera in his first return to New York since losing the title nine months earlier to Baer. The other two frequently mentioned contenders for Baer's crown were in attendance that night: Jimmy Braddock and Art Lasky were at ringside. The winner of their upcoming fight was tentatively scheduled to meet the winner of this night's bout.

The undercard featured Steve Dudas and Abe Feldman in an eight-round preliminary. Feldman took the fight on points. Each of the five preliminary bouts went the scheduled distance. While that was good for the Garden and the fans, the Carnera and Impelletiere camps were forced to cool their heels and wait.

Impelletiere entered the arena wearing a red, white, and blue robe embroidered across the back with "The American Giant." The referee for the bout was former champion Jack Dempsey, who had his hands full breaking the fighters from frequent clinches.

The fight opened with both men fairly active. Impelletiere, showing good hand speed, was able to land a solid left that slowed Carnera a bit and gained Ray the first round on the judges' cards on aggressiveness. Initially, Carnera had some difficulty in sizing up his large opponent and had trouble connecting with him and was actually outboxed by the comparatively inexperienced fighter in the opening round.

In the second, Primo was back at full strength and caught Impelletiere with two strong right uppercuts that took their toll on Ray. Impelletiere then finished out the round trying to last by leaning on his opponent to avoid further damage.

In the third round Primo set the pace early, but following Dempsey breaking the two fighters from a clinch, Impelletiere connected with a hard left to Carnera's body and then kept up the heat for the remainder of the round. Overall, the session was fairly even with a possible nod to Impelletiere for his work later in the round.

The fourth round started with the two titans holding and mauling each other. In a flash Impelletiere landed a couple of good right-left combinations. Primo answered with the same at the closing bell. They were probably the best shots of the round. A low blow warning against Primo gave Ray the round.

Whether from the shots he took at the end of round four, simple exhaustion or a combination of both, Impelletiere started looking very tired by the fifth. With Primo using his left hook effectively, Impelletiere began wading into Carnera, grabbing and clinching his opponent to avoid the powerful blows. With the crowd and the referee getting impatient with that tactic, Dempsey tried to part the two men. As he did, Ray refused to let go. Primo, with a shrug of his shoulders and a look of frustration on his face, said to Dempsey, "It's not my fault!" "In the sixth, the ex-titleholder succeeded in getting through Impelletiere's defense, when he crashed a resounding left hook off the latter's jaw. Ray shook perceptibly, and from that point on, Carnera was wholly in control."[8] Primo anxiously ran across the ring at the bell, meeting his opponent past mid-ring. He was on his toes and looking sharp while Impelletiere was obviously tired and beginning to get sloppy. Still, he lasted the round.

By the seventh Primo was beginning to unload big lefts and rights to his opponent's head while Impelletiere was doing little more than surviving. The pattern continued into the eighth round. Carnera was giving Ray an absolute pounding and Impelletiere just took it, offering no real defense. His legs were rubbery, and he looked spent, but Primo couldn't finish him. At one point, Dempsey asked Impelletiere if he wanted to continue. Ray nodded yes, but even that simple acknowledgement seemed strained. He was staying up on sheer willpower. As hard as the former champion tried, he could not floor his gritty American foe. Impelletiere was unable to land a punch in either the seventh or eighth rounds, and could offer little in the way of defense. Even so, Primo, putting all his strength behind his punches, still could not bring the big New Yorker down.

As the fight progressed into the ninth round it was just a matter of time. Looking fresh, Carnera picked up where he left off in the eighth by continuing to look for the one big punch that would send everybody home. It never came. While he brutally punished his opponent, Primo simply couldn't drop the equally massive Impelletiere. Just over half a minute into the round Primo landed one hard right that sent Impelletiere reeling into the ropes. With his opponent holding onto the ropes, Carnera, sensing the knockout, waded in and landed a hard left-right combination. Now with Dempsey just about ready to step in, Impelletiere's manager, Harry Lenny, crossed the ring and threw in the towel to stop his now virtually defenseless fighter from receiving any more unnecessary punishment. "Primo Carnera has hit the comeback trail with a technical knockout in nine rounds over fistiana's now exploded 'mystery man,' Ray Impelletiere, taller than Primo but not quite so heavy." Carnera "fought a well-planned battle against Impelletiere, finally cutting down the Cold Springs, New York giant after 38 seconds of fighting in the ninth. Referee Jack Dempsey stepped in to halt the bout just as Harry Lenny, the 'Imp's' manager, rushed into the ring to save his charge from further punishment."[9]

With Carnera knocking Impelletiere out of the picture and Jimmy Braddock taking an upset unanimous decision over Art Lasky, there remained only three recognized contenders to vie for Baer's title — Carnera, Braddock, and Max Schmeling.

* * *

Although initial reports speculated that Primo would meet Braddock sometime in June, the Cinderella Man and his manager Joe Gould saw no benefit in their man squaring off with the Italian man mountain. In late March it was reported that Braddock would not fight Carnera, but would only accept a fight with either Baer or Schmeling. This did not disturb Primo and his team, who were now leaning heavily towards a bout with up-and-coming Detroit heavyweight phenom Joe Louis. Both camps got their wishes.

The *New York Times* reported on March 26 that Braddock had been named top contender and would meet Baer in June.[10]

Just prior to this, the New York State Athletic Commission had determined that Carnera was out of the heavyweight title picture anyway when Louis Soresi, the former champion's manager, made it clear to the commissioners that he was not willing to match Camera in an elimination bout with Braddock unless the management of Madison Square Garden would post a guarantee of $550,000 that the winner of the bout would be matched with Baer for the title.

With the Garden having no intention of posting such a guarantee, Carnera and his managers signed to meet Joe Louis under the auspices of the Twentieth Century Sporting Club. The Commission, with its ties to the Garden, took the position that Primo had eliminated himself from the title competition.

Although Carnera and Braddock would not be squaring off against each other, the table was set for pivotal fights for both men.

* * *

On April 9 Primo was once again in hot water with the courts when a New York City Magistrate issued an arrest warrant in Traffic Court because the former champion failed to appear in court to answer a summons issued to him for making an illegal turn. Primo was never picked up and a legal representative appeared the next day to answer the charge and pay the fine for Carnera. Primo loved his fast cars, but they caused him equal parts enjoyment, aggravation, and headache.[11]

11

The Joe Louis Fight, 1935

Joe Louis Barrow was the son of an Alabama sharecropper, who died when Joe was still a young child. Joe was the seventh of eight children born to Munroe and Lillie Reese Barrow.

Munroe Barrow worked hard to provide for his family, until his physical and mental health began to deteriorate in 1916, when Joe was just two years old. Mun lost his struggle with ill health in 1918. Three years later, Lillie married a local contractor named Patrick Brooks. In the summer of 1926, 12-year-old Joe and his family left Alabama and moved north to Detroit, Michigan, in search of stable work. As a young man, Joe worked odd jobs to help his family make ends meet. One job he held was carrying 50-pound blocks of ice up the stairs of homes, in the days before electric refrigerators. Years later he would comment that this arduous work helped prepare him mentally and physically for the fight game.

Joe apprenticed as a cabinet maker and later began working at the Ford Motor Company's River Rouge Plant. It was during this time that he began boxing occasionally, with his friend Thurston McKinney. Thurston was a good amateur in the Detroit area and when Joe, with virtually no training at all, gave him a run for his money, McKinney encouraged Joe to head to the gym for formal instruction. Louis liked to tell the story of how McKinney talked him into spending his violin lesson money on fight lessons.

Joe was an apt pupil and a natural in the ring. He soon found himself fighting amateur bouts. He dropped his last name of Barrow and fought under the name of "Joe Louis" to keep his mother from knowing that he was boxing. After losing his first amateur bout, Louis became a standout light heavyweight and he won the AAU National title in 1934. He posted an amateur record of 53–3 and determined to turn professional.

Louis made his professional debut at Bacon's arena in Chicago, on July 4, 1934. In a scheduled six-round affair, Louis knocked out his opponent, Jack Kracken, in the first, with an anvil-like left hook that caught Kracken on the jaw. Kracken managed to get to his feet, but as soon as he did, Louis knocked him through the ropes and into the lap of Joe Triner, the official timekeeper for the Illinois State Athletic Commission. A legend had been born. Louis defeated the next 17 in a row, all but four by way of knockout. He then came calling at Mr. Carnera's door.

While he was no longer the world champion, Primo was still a big name, a big draw, and was seen as a formidable force to reckon with, but one Louis' handlers believed their young fighter was ready for. Carnera's post–Baer record of 4–0 and his third-place ranking made him interesting to Joe Louis' promoter Mike Jacobs, who decided to engage Primo as a suitable opponent for the young Brown Bomber. He knew that publicity from the fight would help promote Louis as a rising star; he also knew that the gate would be tremendous. Louis had agreed earlier that year to allow Jacobs to be his promoter and Jacobs did not disappoint. The fight was scheduled for June 25, 1935, in Yankee Stadium in the Bronx, N.Y. Louis, the rising star of the heavyweight class, was 22–0 and looking to make a statement by moving up in his level of competition and fighting the former heavyweight champ.

Noted boxing scribe Bert Sugar points out, "Jacobs' choice of Carnera was a master stroke. It would be a good little man making his lasting reputation beating a bigger man and upsetting the old bromide that holds a good big man will always beat a good little man."[1] Louis was 6 inches and some 60 pounds smaller than Carnera and while Baer had dominated Carnera while taking his title, Primo was still considered one of the top 10 heavyweights in the world and a formidable force in the ring.

The young Louis was always supremely confident in his ring abilities. He was not worried about fighting the former heavyweight champion or being ready for the first 15-round fight of his career. "It isn't going to last more than five rounds," he told a group of reporters gathered in Detroit in late March as he prepared for his bout with Natie Brown.[2]

While Joe was simply looking for a fight against a well-known and ranked heavyweight, geopolitics began intermingling with the sports world. With much of the world falling into the grasp of totalitarian regimes and beginning to spiral toward the reality of a second world war, symbolism took a front seat in athletics. As fight night approached the press heavily played up the fact that Primo was Italian and Louis of African heritage. In 1935, Mussolini's Italy was preparing to invade Haile Selassie's Ethiopia. Playing up the contest against the drama of the world stage helped to hype the fight, but as Louis recalled, "They put a heavy weight on my twenty-year-old shoulders. Now, not only did I have to beat the man, but I had to beat him for a cause."[3]

Primo felt that with his post–Baer record of 4–0, he was no more than one or two victories from another shot at the title. A win over the highly touted Louis would place him once again squarely in the middle of the title hunt.

On March 28 Baer came out in favor of Primo to win the fight. Max told the press at an impromptu gathering after a round of golf in Sacramento that Carnera "would explode the meteoric rush" of the young Louis.[4] He acknowledged that Louis might well knock Carnera down, but recalling his own fight with the tenacious Italian nine months earlier the champion predicted with his usual certainty that Primo would get back on his feet. "I haven't forgotten he was down and up so many times in my fight with him I got dizzy trying to keep track of the knockdowns, and I wasn't fooling when I hit him, either."[5] Max predicted that if Primo were in as good physical condition as he was when they fought, he would wear the young man from Detroit down.

On May 22 Primo, Billy Defoe, and sparring partner Harry Ebbets left Hot Springs, Arkansas, bound for Owasco Lake in Central Upstate New York where his training facility was being prepared near the town of Auburn. Primo would finalize his preparations for Louis there over the next five weeks.

On June 13 the entire heavyweight championship picture turned upside down when Jimmy Braddock "The Cinderella Man" made complete his comeback with a stunning victory over Max Baer to take the world title at the Garden Bowl on Long Island. No longer was Baer the man to beat except perhaps as a stepping stone to Braddock. And how long would Jersey James sit on the title before he was willing to risk it to either Louis or Carnera? No one had the answers, but for now at least both camps had the more immediate need to worry about their upcoming clash.

In the week before the bout, both camps were filled with reporters, fight officials, boxing enthusiasts, and the curious, all of whom would watch the daily sparring sessions with interest. Joining Carnera's camp as he readied himself for the Louis fight were Art Sykes of Elmira, New York; Jack Redman of South Bend, Indiana; Willie McGee of Orlando, Florida; and Louis' most recent victim: Washington, D.C., heavyweight Natie Brown.

Reports out of Primo's camp were mixed. While his commitment and fitness were never in doubt journalists covering the former champion were less enthused about his sparring. One day, news stories would express concern that Carnera was off balance, too easy to hit, and unable to hit his sparring partners regularly. The next day the same reporter would state that Primo looked sharp and handled his opponents like children by swatting away their blows and landing lefts and rights with ease.[6]

Louis boxed about six rounds per day against a stable of large sparring partners that included Bob Frazier, 6'5" Roy "Ace" Clark, Lew "Tiger" Flowers, 6'7" Leonard Dixon, and the equally sizable Seal Harris. These men, who all stood well over six feet, attempted to mimic Carnera's tactics by roughing Louis up, leaning on him and tying up his arms in the clinches. Louis worked hard on picking off left jabs and avoiding uppercuts. Colonel D. Walker Wear and Deputy Commissioner Patrick Callahan visited Louis' camp on the Friday before the fight and reported that Louis was impressive.

Wear and Callahan also visited Carnera's camp and found Primo to be in fabulous condition and ready for the fight. While in camp they also granted Primo an exemption from the State Commission rule that required participants of major bouts to be within 90 miles of the battle venue at least five days before the fight. Lake Owasco was nearly twice that far, but the commission agreed to let Primo stay in his camp until his training was complete on Sunday.

On Sunday, both fighters and their entourages broke camp and headed for Manhattan. The official weigh-in was to be held at noon on Monday at the offices of the New York State Athletic Commission. A crowd of several thousand gathered outside the State Office Building trying to catch a glimpse of the fighters. Policemen — some on horseback — had to clear a walkway for the participants. During the proceedings Louis remained stone faced and silent, not even responding to a greeting uttered by Carnera. Dr. William Walker commented that Louis was the closest thing to a wooden Indian that he had ever seen.[7] Both men registered strong vital signs as Dr. Walker performed the pre-fight physical. At the weigh-in Louis tipped the scales at 196 pounds and Carnera just over 260. After choosing the gloves they would use on Tuesday night, the fighters departed the Commission's offices and with New York City's finest leading the way, walked to their cars and departed.

* * *

A crowd of more than 60,000 showed up at the Yankee Stadium that late June evening. The gates of the great stadium were thrown open at 5:00 P.M. The crowd included more than 1,500 police officers both uniformed and in plain clothes, on foot and mounted on horseback. There were over 400 journalists from around the world, the most to cover a single boxing event in years. Notable personalities in attendance included Mayors Fiorello H. LaGuardia of New York, Meyer C. Ellenstein of Newark, Frank J. Hague of Jersey City, and Edward J. Kelly of Chicago, as well as Postmaster General James A. Farley, and President Roosevelt's sons James and John.

Present that evening at ringside were five heavyweight champions of the world. Each stood as they were announced from the ring: Jack Johnson, Jack Dempsey, Gene Tunney, Max Baer, and present title-holder Jim Braddock. Two other title-holders — welterweight Barney Ross and lightweight Tony Canzoneri — were also on hand.

The fight card was sponsored by Mike Jacobs and his Twentieth Century Sporting Club and as was Jacobs' custom, would benefit Mrs. William Randolph Hearst's Free Milk Fund for Babies.

The preliminaries began at 8:15 P.M. as light heavyweights Red Burman and Joe Kaminski met in a four-rounder, with Burman taking the decision. In the second bout, Eddie Mader gained a four-round decision over Philadelphia heavyweight Eddie Houghton. Fight number three was also scheduled for four rounds, but South American heavyweight Johnny Brescia kayoed Andy Wallace at 1 minute 26 seconds of the second after delivering a couple of clean rights to the jaw. In another light-heavyweight battle Nathan Mann knocked out Al Zappala after 54 seconds of round three. Referee Jack Denning stopped the next fight inside of a round, awarding Abe Simon a quick knockout victory over Chris Karchi.

In the main preliminary bout of the evening Max's brother Buddy Baer scored an easy 53-second knockout over Frank Wotanski of Utica, New York. Wotanski engaged in several lively exchanges before the 239-pound Baer deposited him on the canvas with a sweeping right to the side of his head. Wotanski had only taken the fight the day before after Big Boy Rawson was forced to withdraw after the weigh-in.

The last two fights ended so quickly that two emergency bouts were inserted into the card to fill in the almost 45 minutes before the scheduled main event. In the first emergency bout German heavyweight Hans Kohlhaas scored a second-round knockout over Billy Juliano of New Jersey in both fighters' professional debuts and in the second fight, welterweight Ralph Vona won a four-round decision over Joey Haas. After eight preliminary fights, the fans were ready for what would be a memorable main event.

Louis was fabulous that night. The more than 60,000 in attendance saw a masterful performance. As Bert Sugar said, "Joe Louis turned a crowd of curious into a crowd of believers. For on that night they saw the closest thing to fighting perfection ever unleashed in the ring."[8]

Just before 10:00 P.M. the fighters left their dressing rooms and began to head for the ring. The tension was palpable as those who had assembled began to stir with an anxious pulse. As the fighters and their entourages climbed through the ropes and began to mill about, ring announcer Harry Balogh implored all present to practice good sportsmanship.

At four minutes past the hour, the fight commenced. In the opening round, Carnera jabbed at Louis to some effect with his left. When Carnera landed a solid left to Louis' ribs, Joe countered with a devastating right that landed squarely to the north of Primo's chin, tearing open his lower lip and leaving him a bloody mess.

Carnera had flashes of strength, but Louis quickly countered every time. Poet and novelist Maya Angelou, in her book *I Know Why the Caged Bird Sings*, remembers how important this fight was to the African-American community. How pivotal this fight was to debunking the myths about white superiority. Angelou stated metaphorically, "This might be the end of the world. If Joe lost we were back in slavery and beyond help. It would all be true, the accusations that we were lower types of human beings. Only a little higher than apes. True that we were stupid and ugly and lazy and dirty and, unlucky and worst of all, that God Himself hated us and ordained us to be hewers of wood and drawers of water, forever and ever, world without end."[9] She relays how she and her whole people groaned as the radio announcer said, "[Carnera's] got Louis against the ropes and it looks like Louis

Opposite: Joe Louis was 19–0 going into his June 1935 bout with Carnera — 15 of those wins had come by way of stoppage. (*New York Daily News*)

is going down." He didn't, but Angelou described that moment as one of disappointment and despair, one that brought back the ghostly images of subservience and mistreatment suffered by black Americans. "We didn't breathe; we didn't hope; we waited." When the announcer continued after what seemed like minutes, he pumped life back into the African-American community: "He's off the ropes, Ladies and Gentlemen!" shouted the announcer. "Carnera is on the canvas."[10]

In the second round Primo seemed to come alive a bit landing a good left hook to the body early and following it up with a long right to Louis' jaw. After exchanging punches late in the round Primo landed another long right to his opponent's jaw. Louis countered with a combination to the chin, and Carnera snapped Louis' head back by driving two sharp, straight lefts into Joe's chin. The second round could be arguably awarded to Carnera.

In the third, the fighters exchanged blows evenly with neither fighter gaining a clear points lead. For the only extended period of the fight, Louis was missing with his punches as they landed harmlessly around Primo's massive arms and shoulders.

Round four started with an early exchange in which Louis connected with Carnera's head, but the Italian responded with a hard right that landed squarely on Joe's jaw, backing the young fighter up. As the round progressed Louis again began to find his range and bounce shots off Primo's chin.

In the fifth round Louis battered Carnera with continual high-powered shots to the body. After landing a countering left to Louis' head, Primo began to hold, trying to tire his opponent out. Louis would have none of it and instead of wrestling in a match he couldn't win, Louis stepped away and rocked Primo by landing a hook to Carnera's jaw and another long right to his head. Louis began to sense victory, but Carnera was not quite through. After Louis landed another right to the head he left himself open and walked right into a hard, heavy left to the body. After backing up and gathering himself again, Louis went back on the attack and the two fighters duked it out for the final minute of the round. Primo knew that he was in trouble and that if he stood any chance of winning this fight, he had to make his move quickly.

As the sixth round began Primo drove Louis into the ropes, but could not seem to get through his defense. Louis held Carnera off easily and when Primo swung a wild right at Louis' head, Joe countered with a jarring right to the jaw that dropped Carnera like a rock. From that point on, Louis was in complete control of the fight.

In his typical fashion, Primo hopped up quickly, too quickly. Instead of taking eight or nine seconds to gather himself, Carnera was up at the count of four. Immediately the Brown Bomber was on him. The unsteady giant was still dazed and unable to defend himself against the storm of Louis' blows. After another right to the head, the former champ went down again. Once more Carnera was on his feet at the count of four and, still groggy, he was unable to halt Louis' punches. Once again, under a hailstorm of Louis punches Primo went down, but by the count of three, he stood up on rubbery legs. According to the *New York Times*, Primo was "utterly helpless, clinging to the rope," desperately trying to avoid a fourth knockdown.[11] With 28 seconds remaining in the round and Primo ready to go down again, referee Arthur Donovan stepped in, bringing the one-sided affair to a merciful end.

Louis told reporters after the fight: "I knew in the fifth round that I would get him."[12] He also claimed that Carnera never hurt him, which a quick view of the fight video clearly proves untrue. While the Brown Bomber clearly controlled the fight, it was not as totally one-sided as Louis wanted others to believe. Primo landed several good shots that gave Louis pause.

In defeat, Carnera offered no excuses. After the fight, Primo, bloody from the gash under his lower lip and his left eye terribly swollen, commented that Louis hit harder than Baer. He continued, "He's a very good boy, a very good fighter and will go far. Some day he may be champion. He punches harder than any man I've ever met."[13]

The press praised Louis' performance. Paul Gallico in the *New York Daily News* wrote, "Louis transformed a brawny, courageous man into a bubbling, goggle-eyed jelly."[14] James P. Lawson opined that Louis was a truly great fighter and stated, "He punches like Dempsey. He is a reminder of the one and only Sam Langford."[15]

While Primo's manager Billy Duffy called his fighter's effort "a stupid performance," many praised Primo for his performance, his effort, and his courage. Louis' brother DeLeon Barrow recalled later: "Carnera fought from bell to bell, and he didn't get no credit for it."[16]

The fact that Carnera took a beating that night is less due to Primo's fistic ability than to Louis'. Primo was certainly not the last notable fighter that the Brown Bomber would demolish. Louis soundly defeated a string of quality heavyweights including Max Schmeling, Max Baer, Jimmy Braddock, Jack Sharkey, Paolino Uzcudun, Bob Pastor, John Henry Louis, Buddy Baer, Billy Conn, Lou Nova, Charley Retzlaff, King Levinsky, Al Etorre, and Two Ton Tony Galento.

Former champion Max Schmeling hit the canvas three times in 2:04 of the first round of their second fight. When referee Arthur Donovan looked at the badly beaten Schmeling after the third knockdown, he quickly stopped counting and waved him out. The *New York Times* reported that Donovan "could have counted off a century and Max would not have regained his feet."[17]

Heavyweight champion Jimmy Braddock, after taking a terrific beating from Louis for eight rounds, said, "When he hit me with that left-right combination I could've stayed down on the canvas for three weeks."[18]

Who can forget seeing the powerfully built Paolino Uzcudun lying flat on his back under the ropes, knocked down and out for the first and only time in his 12-year, 70-fight career—the victim of a Louis right hand that struck the Basque Woodchopper's jaw like a sledgehammer.

There was the hard-hitting and seemingly fearless Max Baer, who, after losing by KO in the fourth round, stated that his definition of fear was, "Standing across the ring from Joe Louis and knowing he wants to go home early."[19]

And there was King Levinsky, who by his own admission was frightened enough of Louis that he wilted more from fear than a beating in the first round. The Kingfish, "hopelessly beaten in those exciting two minutes, sat on the bottom rope of the ring in a neutral corner, and appealed to Norman McGarrity to stop the battle. 'Don't let him hit me again. I am through.' Referee McGarrity took the beaten Levinsky by the arm and helped him to his corner and into the arms of his stunned handlers."[20]

No, Primo was not the last victim of the destructive Joe Louis, but rather one of many. Losing to Joe was no shame, nor was it an indication of poor boxing ability any more than giving up a home run to Babe Ruth was an indication of a bad pitcher. Louis in his prime was simply on a different level than almost any fighter in the history of the sport.

The next day while Joe Louis visited Mike Jacobs' Twentieth Century Athletic Club offices looking dapper and vibrant in a brown suit and a light colored fedora, Primo convalesced in his hotel room. Louis and his management team were eager to take advantage of the Brown Bomber's newly elevated status by getting Max Baer to agree to a fight in September. Louis had caught the public's imagination and there was no doubt that his future was bright. But Louis and Carnera were like ships passing in opposite directions. One was a fast rising star on his way to becoming not only the champion, but also to becoming arguably the greatest heavyweight in history. The other was supremely strong and brave, but an aging warhorse, a brawling former champion whose reputation as a boxer is still debated more than 70 years later.

As for Carnera's future plans, no one seemed to be sure what would happen. With this decisive loss, Primo was all but erased from the heavyweight title contention. It would take a miracle to put him back in the hunt, but then so many fighters hang on past their time, trying to catch lightning in a bottle. Louis Soresi said that he did not know what Carnera would do. "He said last night that he wanted to retire and return to Italy to live."[21] But Soresi continued by pointing out that no decision would be made until Carnera had rested both physically and mentally and could make a balanced decision. That same day Primo was offered $10,000 by Los Angeles promoter Lou Daro to wrestle 317-pound Frank (Man Mountain) Dean in the LA Coliseum.[22] While his professional wrestling days were still a decade away, the seeds of change had been planted.

* * *

On July 23 Theodore J. Skratt declared to the New York State Supreme Court that Soresi was involved in a plot to defraud both Carnera and his creditors. Skratt, the court appointed receiver for the judgment awarded to Emilia Tersini for breach of promise, was seeking an extension of his receivership to monies won by Carnera in the Louis fight.

Skratt claimed that Carnera had earned more than $400,000 in the United States since bankruptcy was declared in 1933 and that Soresi had been hiding it through elaborate claims of home and real estate purchases on behalf of his fighter. While Soresi claimed that he had purchased a home in Atlantic Beach and two villas in Italy for Carnera with the money, Primo under questioning in April could not describe the homes, their colors, or remember how many rooms each had. Again, Primo was too disinterested and far too trusting for his own good, letting Soresi handle his money without any accounting for its whereabouts. The court ruled in favor of extending the receivership.

Later that day, Primo and Soresi boarded the *Conte di Savoia* for a trip home to Sequals to visit his family. He would arrive in an Italy full of still-adoring fans, but also full of a suddenly cool Mussolini government. His plans were to spend some time at home resting and then prepare for a bout with Walter Neusel in Amsterdam on September 8. Following the Neusel fight, Carnera would return to New York in search of other opponents. Italian Fascist Party Secretary Achille Starace had other ideas.

The Fascists in Italy, smarting from what they perceived as a public relations headache, determined to do some damage control. Afraid that Italians would see Louis' TKO of a seemingly invincible Italian champion as a sign that the black race was equal to their race, European masters began to take action to control the Italian media. Editors throughout the country were ordered by the Fascist Ministry of Popular Culture that "in no circumstance are you to publish any photograph of Primo Carnera knocked off his feet."[23]

The Italian Boxing Commission made an investigation into a claim that one of Primo's seconds had doped him with a foreign substance on a sponge during the fight. This was of course as ridiculous as many of the claims of a fix in some of Primo's earlier fights, but the Fascists and Primo's camp were happy to have a ray of hope that perhaps their man had an excuse for his somewhat sluggish performance against Louis. The Commission's finding clearly state that no doping or any other funny business had taken place and that Louis had fairly beaten Carnera.

The Fascists now began to distance themselves from Carnera. Like many others, they had used him for their own purposes and squeezed out of him all they possibly could. They now determined that it was time to hide their "embarrassing" pugilist from the press and the boxing world for a time. Achille Starace ordered the suspension of Carnera's passport and it was announced that Primo's fight with German heavyweight Walter Neusel scheduled for Amsterdam in September would not proceed. Another order came from the Fascists that no further mention of the sponge allegations would be allowed.

12

After Louis, 1935–1939

No longer a useful tool for Mussolini, Primo quietly spent the rest of the summer in Italy, his passport revoked and under orders by the Fascist regime to remain in Italy and not to make a stir or to fight. Having their Italian champion lose high-profile fights first to a Jew and then to a Negro was a humiliation that the Fascists would not tolerate. He was now considered a traitor and a non-person by his country's government.

By the fall, however, the Fascists had mostly forgotten about and had lost interest in Primo. Achille Starace and the Italian Boxing Federation lifted the ban on Primo fighting outside of Italy. His passport was returned and he was allowed to leave Italy quietly. On September 13 Primo boarded the Italian liner *Rex* in Genoa and returned to New York, thus paving the way for a November 1 rescheduling of his fight with German heavyweight Walter Neusel at Madison Square Garden. The fight with "The Blonde Tiger" had originally been set for September 1 in Amsterdam, but was cancelled after the loss to Louis.

The brief layoff did not appear to hurt Primo as he looked strong in training and readied himself for the fight that he hoped would return him to heavyweight prominence. Knowing he had to make a good showing if he stood any chance of gaining a shot at either Braddock or a rematch with Louis, Primo trained diligently in the weeks before the fight and was in top condition.

On October 29 the New York State Athletic Commission determined that the fight would be a 10-round affair instead of the 12- or 15-rounder that Louis Soresi was pushing for. Neusel's manager Paul Damski was insistent, however, that the 10 rounds contracted for be upheld and the commissioners agreed with him.

Both fighters completed their hard training on October 30 and headed into Manhattan on Halloween day in time for the pre-fight weigh-in at the offices of the state athletic commission. Carnera weighed in at a solid 268 with Neusel registering 201.

Neusel had never lost a fight in the United States, registering a perfect 6–0 record, but the former champion was an 8-to-5 favorite on the day of the fight.

The 6-round semi-final between Tony Galento and Eddie Mader was gathering as much attention as the main event. Two Ton Tony's left hook was considered by many to be the most powerful in the heavyweight division at that time and perhaps the one punch that could stop Joe Louis. Mader was, however, a shifty and durable fighter capable of causing problems for Galento. Also on the undercard was Max Marek, who to that time was the only fighter to defeat Louis—this in an amateur bout a couple of years earlier when he managed a points decision. Marek was matched against Bob Pastor in another 6-rounder. The preliminaries were rounded out with four other bouts.

12. After Louis, 1935–1939

Twelve thousand fans filled about two thirds of the Garden seats on November 1. Just past 1:00 A.M. on the previous night a mild earthquake had been felt throughout the Northeast United States and Canada. The excitement generated by the quake had nothing on the excitement felt in the Garden that night.

In the preliminaries, the faithful saw two knockouts and four six-round points decisions. In the most notable of these bouts, Galento was upset by Mader; former New York University gridiron star Pastor outpointed former Notre Dame football player Marek in a grueling and close contest; and in a battle of Oklahoma heavyweights, George Turner came back from an unsteady start to outpoint Primo's former opponent James Merriott.

In the main event referee Arthur Donovan took control of the ring and the fighters while judges Bill Healy and Billy Joh kept their scorecards at ringside.

Primo made good use of his long, left jab, keeping it regularly in his opponent's face and racking up points. Even so, "Neusel made his best showing in the first round. He rushed at Carnera with the opening bell and the force of his attack completely surprised the ex-champion."[1] Early in the round Neusel landed a barrage of combination punches to Carnera's head and shook the massive Italian, who pawed futilely and ineffectively at his opponent. As the round wore on, however, Primo regained his composure and began pummeling Neusel with lefts and rights to the head and body in what was to become a rout.

The second round was fairly even for the first minute. Neusel started fast, but soon began missing as Primo ducked and weaved. An unaffected and smiling Carnera then began landing unanswered blows. Two quick rights to the jaw snapped Neusel's head back, staggering the German into the ropes. He spent the rest of the round trying to avoid Carnera's blows by going into the clinch.

Neusel again rushed Carnera as the third stanza began. He landed a quick left and right to Primo's body, but this time Carnera countered with a hard left and right to Neusel's face. For the rest of the round Primo landed punishing combinations with minimal response from his opponent. By the end of the session Neusel, who was now clearly in trouble, staggered around the ring.

In the fourth round Neusel was near exhaustion. Still game, however, he mustered what energy he had left and put it all into a hard right cross that landed high on Carnera's head. The shot rocked Primo, but he quickly steadied himself and continued stalking his worn-out foe. Soon afterward Primo landed a hard left hook to the head that opened a deep gash over the German's right eye and left him clearly stunned. Still lacking the killer instinct and disinclined to hit Neusel again, Primo "looked at Referee Arthur Donovan in the hope that the arbiter would stop the bout."[2] To Primo's dismay, Donovan waved to the men to continue. With his eyesight impaired by the ugly gash and the stream of blood it exuded, Neusel raised his right hand as a sign of surrender and walked to his corner. The wounded and exhausted German was declared the loser by a technical knockout after 2 minutes, 23 seconds of the round.

The Neusel fight was significant in that Walter was 43–3–5 and had been ranked in *The Ring*'s top 10 heavyweights in 1932 and 1933. Primo, after being trounced by Louis, came back and again — showing no fear — mixed it up with a creditable heavyweight and came away with an impressive victory.

In his first 35 fights Neusel won 33 and drew twice. He defeated a number of notable heavyweights including Rudi Wagener, Larry Gains, Gypsey Daniels, Reggie Meen, Ray Impelletiere, Stanley Poreda, King Levinsky, and Tommy Loughran. During the first 11 years of his career The Blonde Tiger lost only eight fights. These came at the hands of Carnera,

Max Schmeling, Tommy Farr, Pierre Charles, Don McCorkindale, and three times in European championship fights to Austrian Heinz Lazek. There was not an easy fighter among them. Due to the second world war, Neusel was forced to take three years off from the ring. When the war ended, he was on the first post-war boxing card held in Germany after the war. On September 23, 1945, Neusel fought Richard Vogt to an 8-round draw in the main event at the HSV Sportplatz Rothenbaum, Hamburg, Germany. Neusel continued to fight until 1950, retiring from the ring with a strong 68–13–9 record.

* * *

On November 25 Primo met Ford Smith at the Arena in Philadelphia for a scheduled 10-round fight. It was Carnera's first fight in the City of Brotherly Love since the George Godfrey fight in 1930. The 7,000 fans saw 23 rounds of preliminary action prior to the main event including a heavyweight contest between Argentine bank clerk Jorge Brescia and Primo's 1932 rival James Merriott. Merriott was pummeled throughout the fight until he was finally knocked out by a right to the jaw in the fifth. In the other preliminary, Alvaro de Silva overcame an early-round cut over his left eye to take a six-round decision over Lew Raymond of Baltimore.

Ford Smith had once shown promise, but his career had never really taken off. The Missoula, Montana, native had staged a bit of a comeback in 1935 with back-to-back wins against Art Lasky and Buddy Baer and close, even controversial points losses to Charley Retzlaff and Ray Impelletiere. In the Lasky fight, Ford opened a cut over his opponent's left eye that caused referee Toby Irwin to call a halt to the contest in the fifth round. He had bested Buddy Baer on the undercard of the Joe Louis vs. Max Baer fight at Yankee Stadium.

The first round went to the 209-pound Smith, who was more active as he danced around the ring landing several quick combinations to Carnera's head. Primo rallied in the second and began pounding Smith with a series of left jabs to his face. As Smith began to go into repeated clinches, Primo was warned several times about using his elbows.

During the entire second half of the fight, Carnera swarmed over Smith. The Montanan, however, was full of fight and Primo had his left eye and nose cut at the finish. "Smith received an ovation from the crowd for his gameness."[3] Primo outweighed his opponent by 58 pounds, but was unable to score a knockout, settling instead for a unanimous decision after 10 rounds. In the scoring Carnera won seven rounds to three for Smith.

After Primo's 10-round unanimous decision, the end was in sight for Smith's boxing future. Although he would fight sporadically until 1941, Smith only won four more times before finally retiring after a fourth-round TKO loss to Connie Norden in Oakland in 1941 with a 32–27–8 record.

* * *

Two weeks later Primo had moved on to Buffalo, New York, where he met George "Big Boy" Brackey in the Broadway Auditorium. The 208-pound Brackey was born George Brajkovich in Buffalo, and began fighting professionally in 1934. Brackey, who won his first six fights by early-round knockouts, was exciting to watch and was a big draw in Western New York. By the time he met Primo, he had put together a good 14–2–2 record, with his biggest bout being a loss to Buddy Baer the previous May. But Brackey had fought mostly local talent from the Buffalo area, and proved to be no match for Carnera.

Brackey was a brawler who was frequently warned by referees about illegal punches and he often liked to wrestle opponents to the mat during clinches. Brackey had a disdain for any training regimen that entailed much exertion. Not without power, he had a hard punch that enabled him to register 68 knockdowns and 24 of his wins had come by way of knockout, but he also had a glass jaw that caused him to be floored 96 times over the course of his 44-fight career. On this December evening the 21-year-old Brackey would visit the canvas eight of those times courtesy of Mr. Carnera.

After five preliminary contests, Brackey and Carnera climbed in to the ring. As he often did, Primo let his opponent set the pace in the first round while he sized Brackey up. In the second, however, Carnera began to stand the Buffalo hopeful straight up with repeated right uppercuts, one of which dropped Brackey for a nine-count. The third continued in the same fashion with Brackey stepping into "a shower of rights and lefts"[4] that sent Big Boy to the canvas five times. In the fourth chapter Primo, in complete control, sent Brackey to the mat for counts of seven and nine before landing a right to the chin that ended the bout. Referee Luke Carr waved Brackey out at 1:06 of the fourth after Primo had completely dominated the affair. Primo was now 3–0 in his comeback.

Brackey continued to fight for several more years, losing again to Buddy Baer in their return bout and once to King Levinsky. When Brackey ended his career in 1940, he owned a professional record of 28–14–2. He was lured out of retirement once in 1946, but after losing by TKO in six rounds, the rusty fighter resumed his retirement.

* * *

On December 14 Primo set sail aboard the liner *Rex* for Italy to spend Christmas back home. He arrived in Naples on December 22 where he was met by a large gathering of fans. Primo then spent a couple of days in Venice before Christmas and while there he participated in two exhibition matches to benefit the Italian Red Cross.

On December 27 after spending Christmas in Sequals, Primo was told to report to his local Army recruiting station. Carnera sent a cable to Soresi explaining that he had been called up to active duty under Italy's compulsory military training law. It was rumored that he and the special mountain artillery unit of which he was a member would be sent to fight in Ethiopia with Mussolini's invading army. Before boarding the *Rex* in December, Primo had been asked by a reporter if he expected to join the Italian army, to which he replied with a smile, "I hope not." By January 14, 1936, it was reported that Carnera was free of further army obligations after having served his two weeks of compulsory service. Apparently, Italian military leaders decided that sending the former world heavyweight champion to the Ethiopian front was not a great idea, or Soresi had pulled enough strings to complete Carnera's service, or both. Either way, Primo gladly hung up his uniform. Wasting little time, Carnera and Soresi boarded the *Conte Di Savoia* and sailed for New York, arriving on January 23.

With no fights scheduled until March, Primo headed to Florida to train in the warmth of the Sunshine State's mid-winter sun. On February 14 while driving back to New York with business manager Eddie Grill, Primo was involved in a minor automobile accident in Savannah, Georgia. No one was injured, but one has to wonder how Carnera managed to hit a parked car.

* * *

After a three-month break, Primo headed back to Madison Square Garden for a March 6th date with Isidoro Gastanaga. The Spaniard, who owned a 35–20–1 professional record, had fought in the United States three years earlier, meeting moderate success. The Argentine fighter, also under Soresi's management, had reappeared on the radar screen when he was tapped by Mike Jacobs to face Joe Louis in Havana the previous December. The fight was officially cancelled due to "political unrest" in the Cuban capital. Some speculation has circulated that this may have worked to Louis' favor in keeping the young fighter from having to face Gastanaga's devastating punching power, in a case of nothing to gain and much to lose. In truth, Louis would more than likely have had no problem dispatching Gastanaga in much the same manner that he had finished off his other ring rivals. Shortly thereafter, Louis decided to meet the aging Paulino Uzcudun at Madison Square Garden in New York instead. It was a relatively easy fight for Louis and when referee Arthur Donovan called a halt to the fight at 2:32 of the fourth round, it brought the curtain down on Paulino's successful 13-year career. The Basque Woodchopper left the ring that December night with his head held high and owning a strong professional record of 50–17–3. And as far as Gastanaga, Louis fight or no Louis fight, Izzy was now again an item of interest in boxing circles.

Primo entered the fight as a 2–1 favorite. He was in terrific condition, looked good in sparring sessions, and had a size advantage of six inches and 55 pounds over his opponent.

Before the bout, the New York State Athletic Commission began to check rumors that Louis Soresi had a stake in the management of Gastanaga as well. NYSAC Chairman John J. Phelan commented that the commission would conduct a proper investigation, but it would not interfere with the scheduled contest.

Five fights filled the undercard at the Garden that night, providing 31 rounds of action to warm up the crowd of 9,500. In the main event, Gastanaga hoped to use his powerful right hand to stop his huge opponent, but Primo, using good boxing technique, wisely steered clear of this for most of the fight. While Gastanaga threw rights constantly, he missed his opponent repeatedly.

The fight opened to a brisk pace. "Carnera sprang from his corner at the start of the bout and sent two lefts and a right to the head before Gastanaga could unwind a punch. Then the Spaniard threw his right, but missed by so great a distance that he almost fell."[5]

Throughout the remainder of the round and in the second, Carnera continually rocked his opponent with right uppercuts and straight lefts. Primo's punches were strong and true on this night, but Gastanaga was able to hold on.

In the third round, Primo "gave the Spaniard all he had and weakened Gastanaga perceptibly."[6] Evidently tiring, Gastanaga went down once during the round in what Referee Arthur Donovan ruled a push, but he was up quickly.

In the fourth, Gastanaga came out quickly and attempted to show some steam. He finally landed a long right that caught Carnera on the jaw, but he was so out of steam by this point that the blow barely registered with Primo, who was largely unfazed. Late in the round, Primo landed a vicious right cross that crashed into Gastanaga's head, opening a gash above the Spaniard's left eye. Donovan inspected the heavily bleeding wound, but decided to allow the fighters to continue.

As the fifth round progressed Primo was again on the attack. As he battered his opponent about the head the cut over Gastanaga's eye became worse and the flow of blood "so copious that Gastanaga spent more time trying to clear his eye than reach Carnera, and Donovan stepped in and ended the hostilities."[7]

Primo was well in control of the fight from start to finish. Gastanaga suffered a terrible beating at the hands of Carnera throughout the battle. While Donovan's intervention halted the fight after 46 seconds of the fifth to prevent any more damage from being inflicted on the Spaniard, it was clear to most observers that a true knockout was not far behind and that Gastanaga stood little chance of defeating Carnera. "From the outset Carnera overwhelmed Gastanaga with all the punches in boxing's category. The Spaniard stood up with boundless courage in the face of these blows, but had little with which to meet them."[8]

This would prove to be the last fight in which Carnera looked like a possible championship contender. Something was wrong with Primo, but only time would reveal the malady. For tonight at least he looked like a world-beater and was still on the comeback trail, eyeing another shot at the title. Any slowing down that appeared evident could easily be dismissed as, "Carnera is now pushing 30 years old. Who doesn't slow down?" Certainly his management was none too anxious to acknowledge any problems with the Primo — at least not as long as there was a nickel to be squeezed out of his hide.

* * *

Things seemed to be going pretty well for Primo since the Louis loss. He was 4–0, winning three by knockout. He was fighting well and was optimistic about his future. A week and a half after the Gastanaga fight, Carnera engaged Leroy Haynes. His fighting career would never be the same.

Primo traveled to Philadelphia to meet Haynes at the Arena on March 16. Haynes, 34–6–1, was considered a rising star in the heavyweight division in 1936, but he was beatable. Strictly a West Coast fighter until 1935, Haynes had come east that year and began fighting out of Philadelphia. His four most recent losses had come at the hands of only two men — Maxie Rosenbloom and Al Etorre, each to whom he'd lost twice. Haynes ended his career in 1941 with a 68-fight record of 44–21–3 with 34 knockouts.

A crowd of 10,000 showed up to see if Carnera could keep his comeback alive. The four-bout undercard featured a young Jersey Joe Walcott fighting in just his 14th professional contest. Walcott defeated the notable Philadelphia heavyweight Willie Reddish on points in eight rounds.

Haynes, weighing in at 198 pounds, came out fighting at the first bell, but Primo held him off with his still formidable left throughout the first round. In the second round, however, Haynes began to duck under those lefts and bob back up inside, scoring repeatedly with powerful shots to Carnera's jaw and body. By the third round, it was over.

Primo could not seem to get on track against Haynes and wound up dropping a third-round TKO. Feeling confident that Primo was simply caught off guard by a good young fighter that he should have beaten, Carnera's handlers quickly saw to it that a rematch was set for May 27 at Ebbets Field in Brooklyn. Over twenty thousand people would show up to see if Carnera could even the score with Haynes or if Haynes was for real.

In between the two Carnera bouts, Haynes, who was on a roll, KO'ed Natie Brown in Philadelphia on April 15. Brown was a decent, but average fighter who had fought many big names including a young Max Baer in 1929. He registered losses to Leon Chevalier and Frankie Campbell in 1930, a 10-round loss to Maxie Rosenbloom in 1932, a two-fight split with Tony Galento in 1932, and had lasted a full 10 rounds with Joe Louis just 17 days before.

* * *

On May 27, 23,000 fans filed into Brooklyn's Ebbets Field to see if Primo could find a measure of redemption in his rematch with Haynes. He claimed that he simply took Haynes too lightly in their first fight and was simply the victim of his own carelessness. The day before the fight, however, the papers reported that Haynes was a 13–5 favorite.

The fight was scheduled for 10 rounds and was part of a six-bout marathon that also included a heavyweight rematch between Steve Dudas and Izzy Gastanaga. Gastanaga had knocked Dudas out in the first round just a month before and Dudas was like Primo, looking for revenge. Unlike Primo, however, Dudas still had some gas left in his tank. In the semifinal, held after the marquee match, Dudas a 190-pound New Jerseyan, won the rematch by TKO when referee Jack O'Sullivan called the fight at the 2:55 mark of the third round after Gastanaga quit the fight and walked abruptly to his corner complaining of a broken rib.

The first round of the main event found Primo, employing a new style of defense, holding his hands higher than usual. It did not work as the slow Carnera was an easy target for Haynes throughout the fight. Primo opened the fight by landing a left to Haynes' face, but he soon found himself in trouble as Haynes, looking to put the big man away early, saw his openings and pounded the former champion's head with sledgehammer-like blows. Primo kept on his feet only by holding on to the ropes and swaying to avoid the punches.

Carnera rallied in the second and third rounds, taking advantage of Haynes' exhaustion from punching himself out in the first. Primo roughed his opponent up and made a decent showing hitting Haynes with a hard right to the jaw and following up with a left that was powerful enough to twist Haynes around. At the end of the round Primo landed two hard rights to the jaw and a left uppercut and a right to the chin that lifted Haynes' head with a snap. At the bell, Primo sent the Philadelphian back with a sharp left to the head. In the third Primo continued to mix lefts and rights, most of which found their targets, and Primo went ahead on the scorecards two rounds to one.

Primo started the fourth round with a rush and began pounding his opponent and snapping his head back with sound punches. By the middle of round four, however, Haynes had recovered enough to resume his fistic onslaught and again, Primo had to hold on to survive.

Replacement of a torn right glove extended the break between the fourth and fifth rounds to the benefit of both fighters, but Primo came out the more determined. Both fighters landed several good shots, but Carnera took the round by landing a massive right to Haynes' head that rocked the Philadelphian.

From the sixth round on, however, it was all Haynes as his corner had deciphered Primo's new hands-before-the-face style. In each round Haynes went on the offensive, bobbing and weaving, feinting high and then slamming hard shots to the body, then feinting low and pounding Carnera's head. By the end of the seventh round, Primo struggled to get back to his corner. By the eighth round Primo was in retreat and clearly in trouble, but still proud, determined, and tough, he stayed on his feet. Carnera landed several good punches in the clinches, but on the whole it was Haynes who was forcing the fight.

Primo looked better in the rematch and the fight was anyone's to be had through the sixth round. He had effectively hammered his opponent with left jabs and the occasional hard right. But over the next three rounds, Primo, who had always been in peak condition, began to tire visibly. He was missing badly with his punches and seemed to have no energy. It was almost as if someone had flipped the power switch off between rounds six and seven. While Carnera lasted into the ninth of a scheduled 10 rounder, Haynes was arguably in control of the exhausted ex-champion from round seven on.

Just seconds into the ninth round it was clear that something was dreadfully wrong with Carnera. Throughout the round, Carnera absorbed a tremendous amount of punishment. Haynes continued to press his attack, landing shot after devastating shot of punishment to Primo's body. Just a half a minute in, Haynes landed a heavy left-right combination to the body that shook Primo. The former champion seemed to deflate on his left side. With his face contorted in pain, Carnera, in obvious distress, turned and weakly grasped the ropes to steady himself. He looked over his left shoulder at referee Arthur Donovan who had officiated so many of Primo's American fights, as if to say "enough." Donovan, a veteran of hundreds of fights, knew something was terribly wrong and immediately stepped between the fighters, calling the bout just 40 seconds into the round. To his lasting credit, veteran referee Donovan sensed that something more than a whipped boxer was the cause of this and that it was time to call a halt to the fight.

The highly respected Donovan became a referee partly at the urging of NYSAC head James A. Farley. He was the third man in the ring for hundreds of professional bouts from 1926 to 1948. During that time he officiated 14 heavyweight championship fights. He was the son of "Professor" Mike Donovan, a former middleweight champion and boxing instructor. Growing up in a boxing family, Donovan knew the sport well. While he was growing up, stars of the fight game like former heavyweight champion "Gentleman" Jim Corbett were common around his home and his father's workplace. Against his father's wishes, Arthur boxed professionally for a time, under the name "Young Mike" Donovan. Like his father, he fought as a middleweight. He finished his 10-year career with a third-round knockout of Ray Cooper in 1922. In 28 professional fights, Donovan ended up with a record of 19–8–0 and one no contest. The no contest ruling came in a scheduled 10-round bout at the Peerless Athletic Club in Wilkes Barre, Pennsylvania. The contest was called on account of darkness when the gas lights went out.[9] Upon his father's retirement as the boxing instructor at the New York Athletic Club, Donovan accepted the job and held it until his death in 1980. He is the father of NFL Hall of Fame tackle Art Donovan, and an elected member of both the World and International Boxing Halls of Fame. Donovan refereed seven of Carnera's fights including his championship win over Sharkey, the Baer and Louis fights and Primo's first and last North American bouts—the Haynes rematch and Primo's first-round knockout of Big Boy Peterson in Madison Square Garden on January 24, 1930.

While Donovan was lifting Haynes' arm in victory at the center of the ring, Primo was being helped to his corner by Duffy and Joe Florio. They were able to get the colossal Italian to his stool, but could get him no farther. This enormous and powerful giant of a man sat in his corner virtually helpless. Primo's left side was numb and suffering a paralysis from waist to foot. Primo was then laid flat on his back by his seconds as the fight doctors examined him for the next 15 minutes. Their high level diagnosis suggested that the paralysis was temporary, but of uncertain cause. While the cause of the paralysis was undetermined, it would soon become apparent that Primo was a physical wreck. Damage to his right kidney and the poison leaking into his body was weakening his normally powerful frame and threatening his health. Upon completion of the examination, fight officials summoned several of the policemen scattered at ringside. Unable to walk, Primo had to be carried to his dressing room by six of New York City's finest.

Haynes was the winner again and he fought well, but his victory over Carnera was as much due to the former champion's deteriorating health as it was to his admittedly strong showing. Haynes finished his career with a very respectable 45–20–4 record, but most of his 20 losses came following his defeats of Carnera. Riding high a month after his second victory over Primo, Haynes was brought back to earth by Al Ettore, to whom he lost his third fight in three attempts. He then lost six of his next 14 bouts and by 1939 he began losing regularly, winning only once in his last 11 contests.

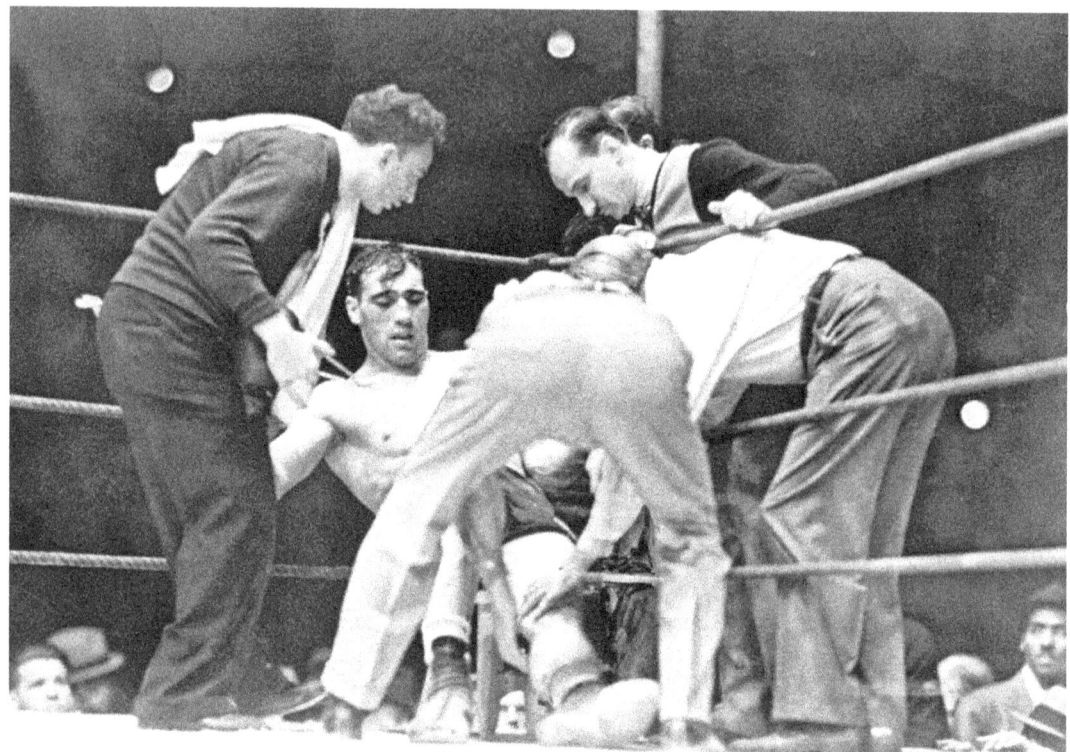

Doctors and his corner men examine Carnera's temporarily paralyzed left leg after referee Arthur Donovan called a halt in the ninth round during Primo's bout against Leroy Haynes on May 27, 1936, at Ebbets Field in Brooklyn. Haynes won by TKO. (*New York Daily News*; photographer: Hank Olen)

* * *

Once in his Ebbets Field dressing room, Primo's personal physician Dr. Vincent Farrini and his trainer Ray Arcel examined Carnera. They ordered him back to his hotel room and declared that with rest, Primo would be as good as new. By the weekend, however, it was obvious that he was in need of a hospital.

Primo was taken to New York's Columbus Hospital where he was admitted and remained for the next three weeks. While tests were being run on the ex-champion, his own doctor tried to play down the seriousness of Primo's condition. Dr. Farrini flatly stated that Primo had only suffered a sprained back, brought about by the strain of the twisting and turning during the fight. Farrini's diagnosis was completely ignored by the medical staff at Columbus as they began running their own unbiased tests on Carnera. The results of their examination revealed that Primo was suffering from a damaged right kidney, and the temporary paralysis in his left leg the result of thrombosis in the central part of the brain artery. As one might suspect, they immediately recommended that he stop fighting.

At this point, the rats began to leave the ship. Lou Soresi and Bill Duffy decided that it was time to take their leave of the fallen giant. They had bled Carnera dry and since their meal ticket would no longer be able to line their pockets, it was pointless to hang on.

12. After Louis, 1935–1939

In July, Primo, alone and supported by a cane, returned to Italy to rest and recover. The Fascist regime, anxious to downplay what they perceived as an embarrassment to the party, ignored him, but the vast majority of Italians to whom the name Carnera was still a source of pride welcomed him with open arms. When Primo reached his home in Sequals he was still treated like a conquering hero. After a few days convalescing at home, Primo left for several weeks of treatment and rest at the Abano thermal baths, just south of Venice. By early September he was feeling well enough to go back to Sequals.

The swindling of his managers and two months of medical bills left Primo in difficult financial straits. Against the advice of doctors, but desperately in need of money, Primo accepted several exhibition bouts with Italian heavyweights during the fall. He returned to Sequals in time to spend Christmas with his family.

* * *

In July 1937, the court-appointed bankruptcy referee in New York recommended to the courts that Primo should not yet be discharged from bankruptcy. Peter B. Olney, Jr., stated that while Primo was "inherently honest and entirely lacking any conscious intent to cheat or deceive," the fighter's total lack of bookkeeping, understanding of his accounts, and his general confusion about financial matters had led to an unsatisfactory explanation of his deficiency of assets. In his report, Olney commented that Carnera "left to others the management of his affairs, devoting his energies to participating in and preparation for pugilistic contests."[10]

Primo's discharge from bankruptcy was actively opposed by Theodore J. Skratt, who was acting on behalf of Emelia Tersini, and the judgment she had obtained in her breach of promise suit against Primo.

Ten days later, broke and unsure of what else to do, Primo announced that he was beginning to train for a return to the ring.

* * *

In September a young British promoter by the name of Benny Huntman determined to bring Primo back to England for a series of fights against British heavyweights. The plan was for Primo to fight his way back into shape and ultimately meet Tommy Farr in October. The British Boxing Board, however, showing more sense, ruled that Primo was unfit to fight and refused to sanction him in England. Huntman tried in vain to have the Board change its mind, but to no avail.

With England out for now, Jeff Dickson decided to get involved. He spoke to Huntman and arranged for Carnera and his new manager to fly to Paris to set up a fight in the City of Lights.

On November 18, 1937, Primo squared off against Albert DiMeglio at a comfortable old haunt, the Salle Wagram in Paris. Looking terribly rusty after not stepping into the ring in 18 months, and with his weight down to 256 pounds, Primo was looking for a way to jumpstart his sputtering career. He would not find it tonight. In what should have been a tune-up against a novice, Primo was, quite frankly, embarrassed. DiMeglio owned a record of 0–2–1 and hadn't fought in two and a half years when he entered the ring that night. After defeating Carnera, he would never win another bout.

The 199-pound DiMeglio had a good showing against the former champ as he belted him around the ring for much of the fight. For most of the late rounds, Primo found himself against the ropes where he fought to keep DiMeglio away. He was slow and ineffective.

After decisioning Primo, he dropped three straight including a first-round knockout to Larry Gains, and retired. DiMeglio wound up his career in 1938 with a seven-fight record of 1–5–1— his only win coming by decision over the former champ.

The *New York Times* reported, "Primo Carnera came back tonight, but only to Salle Wagram, the arena where he fought his first battle for a $20 purse. He lost on points to a second-rater. Those among the 3,000 spectators who had seen Carnera's debut seemed to agree either he had not learned much boxing in the meantime or else he had forgotten what he had ever known about it. The only damage done in the ring was a pair of black eyes, one for Carnera and the other for the referee who received one of the giant's wild swings."[11]

The several thousand spectators roundly booed the former champ for his very poor and disappointing showing. It easily had to be the lowest point of his fighting career. Officials of both the French and Italian Boxing Federations were on hand and seriously questioned Primo's fitness for a new boxing license. They had reason to. Primo was obviously in serious physical straits. It was now even more obvious than ever that he was very ill. The big man's heart was still filled with the willingness to force the battle, but his body was without the ability. He couldn't even defeat a third-rater like DiMeglio. This was clearly not the Carnera of even six months before.

Jeff Dickson could now see that Primo was finished as a fighter and, therefore, as a draw. He quickly cancelled a December 6 card in which Primo was to fight an as yet unnamed opponent. In short order, Dickson forgot about Carnera and moved on to other more profitable events. Dickson remained in Paris until just before the Nazi occupation of the city in June 1940. He then returned to New York and joined the U.S. Army Air Corp at the outset of America's entry into World War II. As in World War I, Dickson was assigned work as a photographer in the Intelligence Corp. In 1943 Captain Dickson was reported as missing in action and presumed dead when his plane went down during a mission over Germany.

* * *

In an effort to get back on the horse quickly, Benny Huntman scheduled another fight, to be held against 243-pound Englishman Bob Adams in Budapest. Adams had lost his only professional bout, to Jim Wilde in Wales in August. The bout was scheduled for December 4 at the Budapest Zirkus as the main attraction of a three-fight card. Shortly after the fight was announced, Adams was out and retired French heavyweight Maurice Forgeon was in. But on December 1, Forgeon, too, pulled out with no apparent explanation. Scrambling for a last-minute replacement, Huntman settled on Josef Zupan.

Zupan, a professional wrestler, had only fought once before that, a points loss in six rounds to unknown Karel Nejtek the previous November. Nejtek fought professionally only three times, finishing up with a 2–1–0 record. It's safe to say that this was another attempted tune-up for Primo, but it's equally obvious that Primo was a sick man who had no business climbing into the ring.

The three-fight card included preliminaries in which Karl Putz outpointed Bela Gardos in eight and Sandor Korosi kayoed Laszlo Pozsonyi also in the eighth round.

According to *Box-Sport*, December 14, 1937 (page 9), *The Gazzetta dello Sport,* and *Sport Tagblatt* of Vienna, Primo knocked out Zupan in the second round of a scheduled ten. It was reported to be an easy win for Carnera, but for some unknown reason the fight is often listed incorrectly as a knockout loss for Primo.[12] One of the major proponents of the Zupan victory line is noted boxing historian Nat Fleischer. In his book *The Heavyweight Championship* Fleischer, whose opinions I normally have a great amount of respect for, asserts with no credible evidence I can see that the local papers were in error and that it was Zupan who won in two rounds. Fleischer did not attend the fight and has no more evidence with which to question the news reports than anyone else, yet he unilaterally decided that Carnera must have lost, contrary to what several local newspapers stated. Apparently the win for Carnera was reported as part of an orchestrated conspiracy by the Italian Fascists to protect their image. In light of no further evidence than Fleischer's conjecture, it appears evident from the local press reports that Primo indeed defeated his novice opponent in two rounds, but still he looked slow and sluggish. Regardless, a win was a win and Huntman planned for a return bout with Albert DiMeglio to be fought on December 15. The bout never came off.

On December 13, while passing through the lobby of his hotel, Primo collapsed and was rushed to the hospital. He was admitted to Budapest's Park Sanatorium where his condition was listed as serious but not critical.

Although Primo lay in desperate straits in the hospital, Benny Huntman would still not be deterred. He headed off to London to "raise money" for Primo's hotel and medical costs. The funds never arrived, but he was able to announce that he was pursuing a series of bouts for Carnera in Egypt in January. He told the press and anyone else who would listen that Primo's kidney problems were merely the result of a punch taken while training for the DiMeglio rematch and that a little rest was all Carnera required to again be in fighting shape. The fact that the Italian Boxing Federation had now also refused to sanction further bouts only told Huntman to book outside of Italy and England, not that it might be unsafe for Primo to continue to fight.

The doctors in Budapest were of a very different and medically sound opinion. Carnera, now a diabetic, was diagnosed as suffering from a hemorrhage of his right kidney. The doctors reported that they believed he would make a full recovery, but that he must retire from boxing or risk further and potentially deadly consequences. The condition finally forced him to quit the ring. After defeating Zupan, Primo retired with a heavyweight title, a career record of 87–14–0, and a heavily stamped passport, but very little money.

Time Magazine reported on Carnera's illness and retirement in the January 3, 1938, edition:

> Giant Retires— Primo Carnera, onetime side-show freak and carnival wrestler, beat Jack Sharkey in six rounds and became heavyweight champion of the world in 1933. ... Carnera, a bewildered, grinning hulk, probably earned a million dollars. His managers got most of it. ... One of his few prudent acts while in the money will save him from the fuddled penury of most prizefighters' declining years. He had given his mother a little hotel in Venice. The injured and obsolete giant plans to go there and retire. He is 31.[13]

Accompanying the article is a picture of Primo with his mother.

Time was mostly accurate in its story. After dropping the two fights to Haynes, a clearly washed up Primo did leave the United States, but he fought the DiMeglio and Zupan fights before the kidney hemorrhage finished him for good. He also did not completely squander his earnings. While I've found no evidence of a hotel in Venice, Primo had built his beautiful villa in Sequals to which he planned to retire.

* * *

With Carnera in the hospital, Benny Huntman wasted little time in scrambling back to London to consider his next moves. With total disregard for Primo's health, Huntman announced that Carnera's condition had been exaggerated. He stated that with a short rest, Primo would be back in fighting trim. With that, Huntman set about arranging several bouts to be held in Egypt in early 1938.

Anyone anywhere near to the situation knew this was complete tripe. Primo was a dangerously sick man who had no business ever getting into the ring again. He was, however, willing to listen to all offers as he was broke both physically and financially and was wondering how he would ever meet his current medical obligations. The doctors who were treating Carnera in the sanatorium feared that another hemorrhage was very possible, and they were unanimous in the judgment that he should never be allowed to fight again.

Whether for medical, humanitarian, or propaganda reasons, the Italian Pugilistic Federation seemed to agree with the medical professionals. On December 14, the day after Primo collapsed in his Budapest hotel, they suspended Primo and declared that he was not to fight internationally. One spokesman may have given an insight to the Federation's thinking when he declared that Primo had fallen so far from his championship form that Italian national prestige demanded that he retire.

The Associated Press reported on December 19 that Primo, pale, ill, lonesome, broke, and washed up in the ring, would be taken home to Italy on December 21. The Associated Press also commented that Primo was homesick and anxious to get home and the Italian legation had arranged the travel. Carnera commented, "My mother didn't know I was sick. Otherwise, she would have spent all she had to come to see me. I was desperately lonesome in this hospital. I hope I recover my health in Venice."[14]

In one of the few generous acts Carnera ever saw from any of his managers, the almost broke ex-champ's medical bills for his Budapest hospital stay were seen to by Luigi Soresi. Soresi, via whatever form of motivation, acted on Primo's behalf in getting Carnera's impounded bank account unfrozen by the bankruptcy court. Soresi made certain that Emilia Tersini was paid in full, the lawyers' fees were settled, and — because even when performing magnanimous acts, a louse is still a louse — he repaid himself for "loans" made to Primo. After this, Soresi cabled Carnera a sum equal to roughly $9,000 (3,200 UK Pounds), which was enough to pay off the medical bills in Budapest, secure travel home to Sequals in time for Christmas and still have some money in his pocket.

Christmas was as always a time of family and friends, but the lavish meals and plentiful gifts of recent holidays were tempered this year. Primo was washed up as a fighter and his monetary and propaganda usefulness finished, so the holiday greetings from Mussolini, Starace, local Black Shirt leaders, as well as those from promoters and the boxing elite never came. Primo's physical condition was still grave and not improving and his energy level was low. All through the holidays, the future weighed heavily on Primo's mind. Without a boxing career Primo was uncertain as to how he would provide for himself and his family.

The citizens of Sequals were still his biggest fans and Primo was greeted by their warm smiles and handshakes as he traveled through town on errands or on his way to the Bottegon for an evening with friends or a game of cards. He was not, however, himself. The once indomitable tower of strength was in bad straits. He was a sick and injured man. His appetite was small and he did his best to heed his doctors' advice and avoid alcohol. He suffered from regular spasms that caused him to wince in pain. The holidays came and went, but still there was no improvement in Carnera's health. The pounding he had taken in the ring was finally catching up with him.

12. After Louis, 1935–1939

A second collapse, this time in the Villa Carnera in mid–January, prompted further medical treatment. On January 29 Primo was taken by ambulance to a hospital in Padua. Here after further examination it was determined that there was no hope to save the damaged right kidney. A surgeon named Dr. Fosiani removed the organ on February 2, 1938.[15]

* * *

The long period of convalescence further depleted Primo's already meager bank account and he knew that with boxing finished, he would have to find some other way to provide for his family.

The first answer came in the form of a visit by a traveling variety show leader named Renato Rascel. Rascel offered the still extremely popular former champion 50 percent of the show's gate receipts to perform on tour with his troupe. He would jump rope, ham it up on stage, and occasionally spar a round with a volunteer from the audience. He had been on stage in London, Rome, Atlantic City and Hollywood and had been in the ring in front of thousands of fans the world over, so this to Primo was easy money and he jumped at the opportunity.[16]

On July 22 the Associated Press reported that Primo debuted with a company of dancers in a vaudeville program. While female dancers pranced around him, Primo simply jumped rope. For the remainder of the year, desperate to make money to support his family, Carnera "danced" on stage in variety shows visiting the principal cities of Italy.[17]

It appeared too that Carnera's film acting career was going to be resurrected. News out of Rome on October 24, 1938, reported that Primo would appear in the Italian movie *Dark Crossing* as a "besotted dumb waiter."[18] Primo began to find some financial peace and his anxiety abated somewhat as work outside of the boxing ring began to appear. With active participation in the fight game behind him, some avenues were opening up for Primo in a different area of the entertainment field.

In November, Carnera would make a trip to a small town on the Italian-Yugoslavian border that would forever change his life. While visiting Gorizia, Primo met an attractive young woman by the name of Giuseppina Kovacic. Giuseppina, or "Pina" as she became known, was a clerk at the central post office in Gorizia and lived in the nearby village of Santa Lucia d'Isonzo, where her father Giuseppe Kovacic was the mayor. Primo was immediately smitten by the tall, 24-year-old brunette.

Even with Primo's earnest feelings, the relationship seemed doomed from the start. To begin with, Pina was already engaged to another. She also was well educated and had no interest in boxing. To Pina, Primo seemed like a nice, but simple man in whom she had no interest beyond sharing some mutual acquaintances. Still, the smitten Primo persisted and inside her heart a love for this enormous and powerful man with the scarred face and crooked nose was blooming.

While he had grown up poor, he had, despite being swindled out of his fortune, built a beautiful villa and was continuing to put bread on the table for his family. He had a limited formal education, but he was curious and eager to learn. He had been a poor boy from Sequals who had risen from poverty and odd jobs to the top of his profession. He had dined with British monarchs, and rubbed elbows with politicians and entertainers. He had starred in Hollywood films and performed on stages around the world. He had left Sequals in 1920 in ill-fitting, hand-me-down clothes and borrowed sandals, and returned with a wardrobe of tailored suits from London and New York. He was worldly in a curious way. He had made his living in a violent and brutal sport, but he was kind and gentle. He had been bilked out of a fortune by unscrupulous management and promoters, but throughout all of this, he had never lost his kind heart or his giving nature. He never became full of himself or braggadocios. As Primo continued to pursue her, Pina's interest began to grow.

Adding to the difficulty of the relationship was Pina's father, who was less than happy about his daughter spending time with a man who he felt was not worthy of his daughter's attention. By many accounts, Giuseppe Kovacic, a former colonel in the Serbian army, was a stern man. When Primo continued to call on Pina and to send her letters and flowers, Giuseppe became enraged and berated his daughter. In time, despite her father's ardent opposition, Pina determined she would marry Primo. The couple was married in Sequals on March 13, 1939. The newlyweds then hit the road as they honeymooned in Capri, the Cote d'Azur, Spain, and Paris.[19]

The first months of their marriage were at times difficult as the couple sought common ground and attempted to adjust to a full-time life together. As in any relationship, time reveals blemishes. The well-educated and refined Pina grew apprehensive about the poorly educated and sometimes unrefined Primo. While Leon See had helped to refine Carnera a good deal, Primo had, as Frederic Mullally states, spent many years "in the company of fairground barkers, an uncouth prize-fight fraternity and American hoodlums."[20] In addition, the couple was living at the villa in Sequals surrounded by Primo's family and friends. For the first time in her life Pina was separated from her hometown and her friends and was now alienated from her father.

As time went by, the couple's relationship grew closer and Pina worked to share her education and her knowledge of the arts and culture with her husband. The couple grew to be extremely devoted to each other and the marriage would flourish for a lifetime.

13

The War Years, 1939–1945

The years leading up to and encompassing World War II found Primo being used as a propaganda tool by numerous groups. Not only was he taken advantage of by his boxing managers, but the Fascists in Italy and Germany saw an opportunity for positive gain in using Carnera's fame to their advantage.

Throughout his rise to fame and the championship, seemingly everyone wanted to be associated with the fighter. Some wanted to bask in the aura of a man on his way up, some in the championship, some to take advantage of his wealth, and others to milk the publicity value of a noted prizefighter. Most, however, had ulterior motives in their association with the big man.

While in Italy for the Christmas holidays in 1935, Carnera was called up to active duty in the Italian Army. After a brief holiday in Sequals, Primo was told to report to his local Army recruiting station to start a two-week stint in the Italian Army. It was rumored that the two weeks of training would be lengthened and that he would be sent to fight in Ethiopia, with Mussolini's invading army. By January 14, 1936, however, it was reported that he was free of his Army obligations, having served his two weeks of compulsory service. Soresi decided that it would be better for his fighter to leave Italy before the Army changed its mind. Wasting little time, Carnera and Soresi boarded the *Conte di Savoia* and sailed for New York, arriving on January 23.

After a failed attempt by the French Army to get Primo to serve in 1930, they tried once again in 1940, desperate for manpower. Both attempts were made on a weak claim of his French citizenship given the document he reportedly signed during his years in France in the 1920s. He ignored the first summons without consequence. On April 23, 1940, Carnera was again called for duty and told to report to a Paris recruiting station. He had never considered himself a French citizen and had no more intention of reporting in 1940 than he had 10 years earlier. On April 27 he was declared a deserter and an order was issued for his arrest.[1]

During the war, Primo found himself at the head of an extended household. He was the only one of the three Carnera sons in Italy and it fell to him to care for the family. Severino was now married and living with his wife Mary and working as a mosaicist in New Jersey and Secondo was an interned guest of the Crown on Britain's Isle of Man with other "unfriendly aliens." His wife Marianna and young sons Elvio and Giovanni had returned to Italy to avoid detainment. In addition to Secondo's family there was of course Pina, and his mother and father, and in 1940 Pina gave birth to the couple's first child. Umberto was born in Rome.

During the war Primo was employed in the Italian film industry and split his time between Sequals and Rome. Primo's father Sante passed away in 1941 at the age of 65 from a stroke.

After some immediate military conquests, Italy would find limited success in the war. Mussolini's initial triumphs in Africa, Greece and Yugoslavia were tempered by poor showings in southeastern France in 1940 and against the strained British forces in North Africa. The British gained major naval victories over the Italians at Taranto and Cape Matapan, severely damaging Il Duce's navy. Major land defeats at Tobruk, Benghazi, in Eritrea, and at Amba Alagi eliminated the Italian presence in Egypt and the Sinai Peninsula, as well as in Ethiopia, Somalia, and Eritrea. By early 1941, the damaged British forces "had knocked out ten Italian divisions, taken 113,000 prisoners, captured 1,300 guns and hundreds of tanks, and eliminated the threat to Suez."[2] With the major Italian defeats, Hitler was forced to send in General Erwin Rommel to North Africa to avoid ceding it back to the Allies completely.

The British had also been a thorn in Mussolini's side in Greece. After invading Greece from across the Albanian border in late October 1940, things went precipitously downhill for the Italians. The British immediately offered aide to the Greeks and sent in troops from North Africa. Strengthened and emboldened by the British support, the Greeks chased the Italians back into the Albanian mountains where Il Duce's troops would hold up for the winter. Only a spring offensive by the Germans down the Balkan Peninsula would rescue the humiliated Italian army. "The attack on Greece was an act of rash folly. Mussolini's armies, as their record in France and North Africa had already shown, were far from ready for combat; their equipment was inferior, their morale was low."[3]

Periodically throughout the war, Carnera fought in some "catch matches" which are more akin to street fight, where anything is legal, than they are to a boxing match. This was yet another way to make money and feed his family. Mario Minini, an acquaintance of Carnera's, described one such event in Milan in 1942, "That night, he had earned 500 Italian lira."[4]

In a moment of joy amidst the chaos of war and occupation, Pina gave birth to the couple's second child, a daughter named Giovanna Maria, on June 5, 1943.

With their losses mounting due to poor leadership in the military, and lack of fuel to power their forces, Italy was losing the war. On July 10, 1943, the Allies began their assault on Italy with the invasion of Sicily. The presence of Allied armies on the Italian mainland was now only a matter of time. Later in July, at the urging of a combination of monarchist conservatives and Fascist dissidents, Italian King Vittorio Emmanualle III dismissed Mussolini and replaced him as Prime Minister with Field Marshal Pietro Badoglio, who had led the successful Ethiopian invasion, but who was now an ardent anti–Fascist who hoped to get Italy out of the war relatively unscathed. As Mussolini left the palace, he was arrested and interned. Later that year, German paratroopers stormed the mountaintop villa in which Mussolini was imprisoned and liberated him in the daring Gran Sasso raid. The Nazis then installed the former leader as the head of the Italian Socialist Republic in German-held northern Italy.

Allied forces landed in Calabria on the toe of the Italian peninsula and in Salerno just south of Naples in early September. The Germans responded by pouring into the northern and central parts of the country and occupying Rome. The King, Prime Minister Badoglio, and the government fled south as the Nazis declared martial law.[5] For the next year and a half, the Italian peninsula would be divided between the Germans and their puppet leader

13. The War Years, 1939–1945

Mussolini in the north and the King and Badoglio, who were supported by the Allies, in the south. "Between the two hovered the uncertain mass of Italians—half-starved, half-frozen, and miserable in the damp Mediterranean winter."[6]

On November 22, 1943, the United Press reported that Primo had been wounded and taken prisoner by Axis forces while fighting for the Italian resistance. Primo had reportedly been shot in the leg during a skirmish with a German patrol near the northern Italian town of Cremona. His leg injury was said not to be serious, but his predicament was. The Nazi authorities were said to be considering executing Carnera and his companions for anti–Fascist activity. Primo was said to have joined the Italian anti–Fascist movement when Italy broke with the Axis.[7] The following day the Associated Press reported that Primo had not been shot or captured and that he was alive and well in Como.[8]

During the Nazi occupation of Northern Italy, German officers in Sequals were often known to visit and even drink with Carnera. Primo thought nothing of it as he suffered their visits, posed for photographs, and signed autographs. It was routine for people of all stripes to want to meet and be seen with the former world champion. Once again, Carnera's naiveté would get him into trouble—this time with Italian anti–Fascist partisans who saw these acts, so simple and natural for Primo, as an act of comfort to the enemy.

In explaining that a steady stream of soldiers came by the villa during the war, Giovanna and Umberto Carnera mentioned that Primo welcomed them all. First the Italians, both Fascists and anti–Fascist partisans, then the German occupiers, and finally, the American liberators, all came by to meet the man mountain. "It is true that Daddy had worn the black shirt—as had many people in that period—and had met Mussolini, but that does not mean he was a Fascist. He was only a sport champion and a patriot." Primo's children expressed that their father "had no ideologies, he was neutral."[9] In an example of his openness and generosity, the story is told of how Primo induced the owner of the Bottegon to cook a 44-pound turkey in the kitchen's industrial-sized oven and then deliver it to the Villa Carnera, where Primo then fed a large number of American troops dinner on Thanksgiving Day in 1945.

During the war Max Schmeling sent word to Primo that he would like to visit with Primo while visiting Venice. The Nazis orchestrated the event as a piece of pure propaganda to display Italian-German unity to the Italian people. Primo, initially not smelling the set-up, agreed to meet his old comrade, whom he believed simply wanted to relive their glory days. During the visit photographs were taken showing the two former heavyweight champions laughing, drinking, and even sharing a gondola tour of the canals. As the visit progressed, Primo began to feel a bit uneasy about the real intent of the meeting. Belatedly realizing that this was not really such a good idea, Carnera excused himself early claiming ill health. The photographs taken that day were to haunt Primo in the years to come. Rumors started that he was a Fascist sympathizer and the local partisan group even arrested Primo and questioned him upon his return to Sequals. Leo Picco, also called "Commander Tom," was the leader of the anti–Fascist forces in the Sequals area. He spoke at length with Primo and after the interrogation, fully believed his story of being duped by the Nazis. The commander's trust cleared Primo's name.[10]

Carnera was soon to repay that trust. One winter evening in early 1945, Primo was walking near his villa when he came upon a young partisan who was being questioned by German soldiers. The young man had been shot in the leg during fighting in the mountains and had come down to find refuge and medical attention at a safe house in Sequals. The young man was weak from the loss of blood and was leaning upon a young woman who was assisting him to the house. Suspicious of the bandaged leg, the German patrol had stopped him and things looked bad for the young couple. Coming upon the scene and seeing the anguished look on the young woman's face, Primo immediately knew what was happening and went into action. He walked up to the group and placing his massive hand on the boy's shoulder he said, "My friend, you should not be out in this cold. Get along to your house at once." The German soldiers recognized Primo and were clearly in awe of this giant Friulian fighter about whom they had heard so much. Primo shook their hands, signed autographs, and continued to chat with the soldiers while the young couple slipped away to safety.[11]

In March 1945, Carnera was arrested by the Gestapo following a barroom free-for-all in Rome during which Primo is said to have added several persons to his knockout total. The brawl reportedly started after Pina insulted the Nazi regime and several German soldiers took exception to her comments. After a few more invective-laced words were spoken, the fists began to fly. By the end of the affair, Primo had been incarcerated and an unspecified number of Germans lay about the floor nursing wounds. Primo was freed shortly thereafter, but was to remain under Gestapo surveillance for the brief remainder of the war.[12]

On April 28, 1945, with the Germans in retreat, Italian partisans near Lake Como once again arrested Mussolini and his mistress Clara Petacci, who were attempting to make good an escape over the Swiss border.[13] Shortly after their arrest, the couple was shot to death and their bodies were beaten and strung upside down at a gas station in the town square for all to see.[14] Freed from the oppression of the Italian Fascists and the occupying Nazis, many citizens were ready to exact a measure of revenge against those whom they saw as collaborators. Soon after Mussolini's death angry mobs began to form throughout Italy roaming through towns and villages and taking justice into their own hands.

One such crowd gathered outside the Villa Carnera. Some in the crowd were questioning Primo's allegiances and pointed to pictures of a Black Shirted Carnera shaking hands with Il Duce, with other party officials, and in Venice during the war with Max Schmeling. Manlio Cancogni, the editor of the Italian publication *La Fiera Letteraria*, wrote this about the event: "The day when Mussolini was hanging in Piazzale Loreto (in the presence of a very ignited public), Carnera — with his 6'7" and his 265 pounds — was standing in front of a group of Friuli partisans with rifles ready to shoot those who wanted to kill him as a hated symbol. He was saved by a sheer miracle which was just since his faults and responsibilities were only imaginary."[15] The pictures were a ridiculously thin prosecution of Carnera given the fact that everybody — from politicians to bell boys to chorus girls on both sides of the Atlantic — wanted their picture taken with the fighter in his heyday.

Following the war Primo, like so many in the ruins of Europe, needed work to support his family. Desperate and against his doctor's advice, the big man returned for a short while to the only thing he really knew — the ring.

14

The Comeback/Wrestling, 1945–1965

After the war ended, Primo, the sole breadwinner of his clan, needed to find a job to support his extended family. Jobs were scarce and the Italian film industry was not yet again in full swing. After looking at his somewhat limited options, he decided to return to what he knew best — to enter the ring again and fight. Primo had not fought a round since knocking out Josef Zupan in Budapest in December 1937. While he had stayed in good shape by working out daily in his personal gym at the Villa Carnera, sparring partners were hard to come by during the war. He was also pushing 40 and was short one kidney, but none of that mattered to Primo, for this time he was not looking to scale the ladder to the top of the sport. Boxing was strictly utilitarian. It was a way to generate some quick cash until something else opened up. If he had some success, so be it, but trading on his name and his boxing skills and knowledge were the thing at present.

In early 1946, American promoter Harold Harris wrote to Carnera in Italy, asking him to consider participating in professional, all-in wrestling contests. Harris told Carnera that he believed that the former heavyweight boxer had all of the tools to be a success in the professional wrestling arena. He was well known throughout the world and would, therefore, need no introduction. While he had never been formally coached, he had wrestled as a young man for a number of years in fairs throughout France. His enormous strength and size were already the stuff of legend and the fact that he was nudging 40 years of age and short one kidney would not affect him adversely. Also, Primo's considerable acting experiences would be beneficial in the highly scripted and choreographed sport.

Primo was quite interested in what Harris had to say. Professional wrestling was becoming a huge attraction in North America and a good wrestler with a big name could make substantial amounts of money. All-in wrestling was an event that took the leading styles of wrestling and combined them with timed rounds to make a more exciting sport for the casual fan. The shorter, more defined matches and the theatrics of the fighters, both in and out of the ring, were more to the general public's liking than traditional Greco-Roman matches.

It was not the first time that Carnera had been approached about professional wrestling. On June 26, 1935, Primo was offered $10,000 by Los Angeles promoter Lou Daro to wrestle 317-pound Frank (Man Mountain) Dean in the Los Angeles Coliseum.[1] While his professional wrestling days were still more than a decade away, the seeds of change had been planted. On August 29, 1941, Primo announced that he would indeed return to his roots and become a pro wrestler. In many ways it was a return to the sport that had enabled his rise from poverty-stricken laborer to boxing's heavyweight champion of the world. But this time the war put an end to his plans for another five years.

Primo's doctors were against his returning to the boxing ring. They feared that he would further damage his body and specifically, worsen the damage caused by the temporary paralysis in his left leg. The paralysis had become manifest during the second Leroy Haynes bout in 1936, the result of thrombosis in the central part of the brain artery. His body showed continued signs of wear and weakness through the Zupan fight in December 1937. The doctors also feared the risk to his one remaining kidney. But Carnera knew he had to make a better life for his family, so, ignoring the doctors' reservations, Primo signed to fight Michel Blevens at the Moretti Stadium in Udine, Italy, on July 23, 1945. It was Blevens' first professional fight and he spent most of it trying to keep his distance from the Italian giant. Even against this elusive opponent, a slow and rusty Carnera was able to score a knockout in the third round. He was happy for the victory and it felt good to be in the ring again, but this time it wasn't for the glory of the victory and it wasn't a championship that Primo was gunning for; it was all about the gate. Primo needed money to take back home to his family and he needed money to head back to the United States where, according to Harold Harris, there was a lucrative future in professional wrestling awaiting him.

On September 25, Primo was in Trieste at San Sabba Stadium where he met Sam Gardner, an American soldier who, like Blevens, had experienced some amateur ring success and thought that he could take on Carnera. Also like Blevens, he was very wrong. With a little of his rust worked out, Primo dropped Gardner for the count in the first round. The crowd of 12,000 provided for another big gate and a good cut for Carnera. Gardner would fight professionally just one more time. On March 7, 1946, he met heavyweight Doc Bee at the Metropolitan Opera House in Philadelphia. The 2–2–0 Bee also finished Gardner off inside a round.

In an October bout listed as an exhibition, Primo looked fluid as he toyed with Joe Biro for three rounds in the Tuscan town of Livorno. Upon returning to Youngstown, Ohio, Biro had a brief professional ring career in 1946 defeating Art Boykins twice and losing a four round decision to Grady Welch. Now 2–0 in his comeback and feeling more confident, Carnera felt he was ready to step up the competition, but more importantly, to step up the gate, in his next fight. Enter Luigi Mussina.

It was not just a step, but a full-blown leap for Primo. The 31-year-old Mussina was the former European heavyweight champion and held a 29–4–0 record. Mussina was a respectable fighter, who turned professional after winning the Amateur Light Heavyweight Championship of Europe in 1937 and 1939. He met immediate success as a professional winning the European and Italian heavyweight championships. He retired in 1947 with a record of 38–9–5, but his career was without note except for his three victories over Carnera.

The bout was set for Milan's National Theatre on November 21. The fight itself didn't go so well for Carnera, who was decked three times before the referee stopped the fight in the seventh round awarding Mussina the TKO. An estimated 20,000 persons arrived at the National Theatre in hopes of gaining admission to the 6,000-seat venue. The fights were delayed by almost two hours as authorities tried to accommodate as many people as they could. People were desperately trying to see the former world champion try to reestablish himself against the European champion. Primo, though he took a beating for it, carried a good paycheck home to Sequals.

Italian fight fans wanted more and Mussina and Carnera were more than happy to oblige. A return bout was scheduled for Trieste on March 19, 1946. While Mussina won again, the fight was actually close with a split points decision after the scheduled eight rounds. The competitiveness and the financial success of their second fight made a third all but inevitable. Primo knew that this would very probably be his last-ever prizefight. With one more big gate, he would have enough of a nest egg to leave his family financially secure in Sequals while he traveled back to the United States to establish himself in his new career in professional wrestling.

The final fight was scheduled on May 12 in Gorizia. Another large crowd assured a big gate and the ability for Primo, at 39, to put boxing forever in his past. He answered the bell for the first round and took the fight to Mussina, giving it everything he had. Again, the fight was competitive and went the scheduled eight rounds. But again, despite Primo's best efforts, Mussina won the decision on points. As the decision was announced, Primo knew this was it, his prizefighting days were at an end. With mixed emotions, he climbed between the ropes and out of the boxing ring for the last time as a combatant.

Two months later, Primo was off to America to begin a new and very happy chapter in his life. On July 26, 1946, Primo arrived once again in New York to pursue a ring career. This time, however, he arrived by plane at LaGuardia Airport and the sport was professional wrestling. Harris paid Carnera's expenses for the first month while the big man trained for his professional wrestling debut. While Primo prepared, Harris began setting up appearances for the former champion. They would start on the West Coast with a series of engagements in which Carnera would wrestle and occasionally act as a guest referee at boxing matches.

By mid–August he was ready and Harris set up Carnera's first match. On August 16th Primo was granted a California wrestling license and four days later he met and defeated Jules Strongbow in Wilmington, California. He would meet the Oklahoman at least 10 more times in the next several years. Two days later, Carnera defeated long-time wrestling legend Tommy O'Toole in front of 10,000 fans at Los Angeles' Olympic Auditorium and his career was off and running.

For the rest of the year Primo wrestled at a furious pace — as many as four times in a week — from coast to coast. As he had as a fighter, Primo had his detractors when he became a professional wrestler. But soon he became a fan favorite drawing large crowds and pleasing the crowds, the promoters, and his managers. Unlike his days as a boxer, he was surrounded by scrupulous managers who took only their agreed upon shares of the gates. Men like Harris — a former middleweight wrestling champion — promoter Toots Mondt, and Milo Steinborn, another retired wrestler, treated Carnera fairly. Primo also had another ace in the hole that he never had while boxing. Pina, acting as Primo's business manager, scrutinized all contracts and accounted for the last dime of every gate. After wrestling for two months up and down the West Coast, Carnera headed east for Atlanta engagements with Chief Saunooke and the first of many return engagements with Jules Strongbow. He then continued north to New York City.

The crowds loved Primo as they poured into arenas from coast to coast to watch the Man Mountain steamroll all comers throughout the rest of 1946 and 1947, defeating all opponents. On November 22, almost 8,000 fans filed into Chicago Stadium and watched as Carnera defeated Fred Von Schacht. The gate for the evening was $17,525 — a terrific amount in 1946.

By the end of 1946, Primo's fortunes had turned dramatically. His brief pugilistic comeback, while not artistically beautiful, had provided financial relief for his family and given him the seed money to begin his wrestling career. Wrestling had been very good to him and he was proud of his success. He had left the United States in 1937 physically and financially broke. He was now back and on top of the world. He was wildly successful, the fans loved him, and due to honest management, his bank account was growing exponentially.

On November 6, 1948, Carnera met another former heavyweight boxer, "Two Ton" Tony Galento, at the Laurel Garden in Newark, New Jersey. Newark's Laurel Garden was a popular venue located on Springfield Avenue and South 7th Street in the middle of the West Side Park neighborhood. The arcade entrance was across the street from Nussbaum's Drug Store and soda fountain and a local bakery. Descriptions of Laurel Gardens from Newark residents of the era describe it lovingly as old, worn out, and dilapidated, but also intimate. The balcony, which ringed the arena, was steep, giving every seat the feel of being close and right on top of the action. Galento and Carnera wrestled for over an hour before the match was declared a draw.[2]

In December he took a southern swing to Miami, where he met and defeated legendary ring star Ed "Strangler" Lewis twice. Over the next year Primo's popularity continued to grow as he traveled throughout North America meeting well-known opponents such as Jules Strongbow, Sandor Szabo, and Mike Mazurki.

On April 20, 1949, Primo Carnera's winning streak came to an end when he finally lost in his 322nd match to Antonino Rocca in New York City.

In 1950 the legendary Jim Londos came out of a four-year retirement for a match against Primo. The much-ballyhooed event was refereed by Max Baer and ended in a draw. Another noteworthy opponent was former gridiron great Bronko Nagurski, to whom Primo lost a bout in Minneapolis in July 1951. In October of that year he squared off once again against old prizefighting foe Larry Gains in two bouts in London.

In April 1956, Carnera's managers sent a challenge to former boxing champion Joe Louis to meet in the wrestling ring in Los Angeles that summer. "Carnera's wire was sent through his agent, Guido Orlando. Carnera agreed to turn his share of the purse over to the Olympic Games Fund."[3] The match never occurred as Louis chose not to continue his flirtation with all-in wrestling. Primo did meet another former opponent and heavyweight champion when he grappled with Max Baer in an exhibition draw in 1957. Earlier that year Primo had won the world heavyweight crown of wrestling by defeating "King Kong" in Melbourne, Australia, thus becoming the first man to ever win the heavyweight titles in both boxing and wrestling.

Primo's second ring career kept him constantly on the road traveling from city to city throughout the United States and Canada and across the seas to England, Germany, South Africa, Latin America and Australia. He wrestled in venues large and small from old haunts like Madison Square Garden, Chicago Stadium, and Yankee Stadium to unfamiliar local spots such as the Mississippi Valley Sports Club; Charleston, West Virginia's, American Legion Armory; and the Ron De Voo Ballroom in Milwaukee. He compiled a record of 152 wins, 14 losses, 19 draws and 2 no contests in 187 wrestling matches.[4]

On October 25, 1962, Primo was a competitor in the ring for the last time. He wrestled and defeated "The Destroyer" at Strelich Stadium in Bakersfield, California. After 16 years of wrestling, Primo finally retired from the ring at the age of 56. In 1990, Primo was inducted into the World Boxing Hall of Fame. His wrestling career helped Primo to amass a small fortune and made for a comfortable life for his family.

15

The Films

In 1933, Primo was asked to play a role in a Hollywood film that was very familiar to him, that of the heavyweight champion of the world. He launched his film career in *The Prizefighter and the Lady*. The movie stars Myrna Loy as a socialite, Max Baer plays "Steve Morgan" as an ex-sailor turned prizefighter, and Primo is the reigning heavyweight champion, whom Baer's character is gunning for. Morgan falls in love with and marries the girlfriend of a mobster (Loy). As his pugilistic career takes off, he eventually gets a shot at the heavyweight title. Walter Huston also starred in the picture along with Jack Dempsey. The film was released on November 10, 1933.

He also appeared in the 1933 Ed Sullivan comedy *Mr. Broadway*, which was shot in May and released in September. In the film Primo plays himself in a brief cameo. Sullivan introduces the film, calling it "a Broadway travelogue" of nightclubs where celebrities congregate. Primo also played himself in the opening of *Bombshell*, but since former champions do not possess the drawing power of current titleholders it was to be his last appearance on the silver screen for six years.

News out of Rome on October 24, 1938, reported that Primo would appear in the new Italian movie *Dark Crossing* as a "besotted dumb waiter."[1] In 1939, Primo made his return to the movies, a place he had not been since 1933, when he had appeared in three films. The newly married Primo was offered a series of parts in films to be shot in Rome. The stage appearances he had been making since his fighting days had ended in December 1938 had helped Primo provide for his family, but the series of motion pictures would bring steady work and a more steady and comfortable living for the Carneras. From 1939 through 1943 Primo had roles in 10 films. None of the roles were major, but they paid a steady wage at a time when Primo was the sole provider for his parents, his brother's wife and two children, and his own wife and growing family.

After filming *Due cuori fra le belve* in 1943, Primo went into a period of forced retirement as the political and military climate continued to depress an increasingly war-torn Italy. After Mussolini was deposed in 1943 and Italy's Nazi "friends" had occupied the peninsula declaring martial law, Primo returned to Sequals where he stayed for much of the remainder of the war.

In 1949, Primo played the role of a strong man in the Hollywood film *Mighty Joe Young*. It marked his first film appearance in six years and his first Hollywood appearance since 1933. Over the next 10 years Primo would make eight more film appearances with a variety of roles on the silver screen and television.

In 1952 he returned to the Italian film industry and 1954 was a busy year as he juggled wrestling, his restaurant and liquor store and two films. The first was an uncredited role as Sligon in *Prince Valiant*. This was followed by a larger role in the Bob Hope film *Casanova's*

Big Night. He had a good-sized role in 1955 in a British film called *A Kid for Two Farthings*. His last film appearance was, fittingly, as Antaeus, the Giant in the 1960 release *Hercules Unchained*.

One movie in which Primo did not appear may have had as much of a lasting impact on his reputation as anything in his life. In 1956, *The Harder They Fall* was released to theatres. Advertised by Columbia Pictures as a film that told the naked truth about professional boxing, the film, based on Budd Schulberg's novel, unquestionably concerned the criminal exploitation of Primo Carnera. The movie starred Humphrey Bogart as a former sportswriter who is hired by a shady fight promoter to help sell his newest fighter, a towering giant of a man from Argentina named Toro Moreno. Despite his size and power, Toro is ill equipped as a boxer. Despite this fact the fight promoter is building Toro's reputation up through a series of fixed fights. The movie obviously plays off the alleged fixed fights from Primo's career. The movie even stars Max Baer as the reigning heavyweight champion who vows to punish the Argentine Man-Mountain in the ring.

During one scene in the film, Max makes the claim that his character killed another boxer — obviously Ernie Schaaf — in the ring when he says, "You know, I'm the guy who nailed Gus, murdered him for 15 rounds. Don't know what held him up, but when Gus left the ring that night he was a dead man. All your joker did was tap him. I did all the work and they gave your guy all the glory." In this dark and thinly disguised telling of Primo's story, Baer basically plays himself, "Gus" is obviously Ernie Schaaf, and "your joker/your guy" is undeniably Primo Carnera. The movie was so far off on any number of points, but many forgot that it was just a Hollywood movie and heard what they wanted to hear.[2]

In April 30, 1956, the Associated Press ran an article that screamed the headline: "Primo Carnera Files Big Lawsuit — Santa Monica, California. — Former heavyweight boxing champion Primo Carnera, today sued Columbia Pictures for $1.5 million, charging invasion of privacy in the film *The Harder They Fall*. The big athlete contends the picture has caused him to be subjected to scorn and ridicule and that as a result of it he has lost the respect and admiration of many friends."[3]

Journalist Ken Jones, writing for Britain's *Independent* newspaper in 2003, wrote, "What is true is that Carnera suffered a great deal from the release of *The Harder They Fall*. 'That's not true, that's not true. That is not my story,' Primo said. 'I haven't done any harm to anybody, why do they want punish me? I have retired from boxing [a career as an all-in wrestler proved lucrative and kept Carnera employed all around the world until his retirement], why do they want to treat me so badly?'"[4]

Primo would sue Columbia Pictures for $1.5 million for damages. It would seem to be an open-and-shut case, but not in a Santa Monica courtroom. Judge Stanley Mosk threw out the claim, stating, "One who becomes a celebrity waives the right to privacy and does not regain it by changing his profession from boxer to wrestler."[5]

The Harder They Fall would haunt Carnera even in the short time that was left when, seriously ill, he returned from California to his birthplace of Sequals. Giancarlo Governi, an RAI (TV) director, who produced a documentary of Carnera's life, said: "Carnera was one of our 'fathers.' He gave an important contribution to Italy's fame. Shortly after he came home to die, *The Harder They Fall* was due to go out on our network. I said that I felt it was better not to broadcast it, but they went ahead." Carnera was deeply hurt. "I come home to die and my ungrateful country pays me back like that."[6] Films were good and bad for Carnera. Acting helped him provide for his family and he enjoyed the work, but *The Harder They Fall* wounded his enormous pride greatly.

15. The Films

Much of Primo's work in the movies was gratifying and fun for him. He was able to make some money and had additional exposure that helped his career in boxing and wrestling. While his roles were never large, they were numerous and at times fairly consistent. From 1933 to 1960 Primo made 21 appearances in movies and on television. Carnera's film credits include[7]:

Hercules Unchained (1959)
Sheriff of Cochise
—*Maniac* (1957) TV episode
—*Human Bomb* (1956) TV episode
A Kid for Two Farthings (1955)
Casanova's Big Night (1954)
Prince Valiant (1954)
Il Tallone di Achille (1952)
Mighty Joe Young (1949)
Due cuori fra le belve (1943)
Harlem (1943) aka: *Knockout* (1942)
Sette anni di felicità (1943)
I Cavalieri del deserto (1942)—Unfinished
La Corona di ferro (1941)
La Figlia del corsaro verde (1940)
Senza cielo (1940)
La Nascita di Salomè (1940)
Vento di milioni (1939)
Traversata nera (1939)
The Prizefighter and the Lady (1933)
Bombshell (1933)
Mr. Broadway (1933)

16

Boxing Ability

What kind of fighter was Primo Carnera? That is a question that has been bandied around by the press and the fight crowd for more than 80 years now. So often the answer comes back that he was a stumblebum who did not belong in the ring, the stooge of unscrupulous managers who exploited his size to line their pockets, a bum who couldn't put his fists through a piece of balsa wood on a good day. A thorough look at the existing evidence—films, newspapers and magazines, and other eyewitness accounts—shows these views to be tainted and overblown.

For all of the negative that has been written about Primo's boxing ability, there is a preponderance of positive that can be found in the press reports of his era. The day after his first bout in the United States, a first-round KO over Clayton "Big Boy" Peterson, the United Press reported, "As far as Carnera's fighting ability is concerned, he proved in his first American match that he is big, strong and a hard hitter."[1]

Of Primo's performance, it was said, "It can not be denied Carnera has some promise as a fighter. Not alone does his tremendous size recommend him, but he was remarkably fast last night and fought with a reckless abandon, which foreshadows an advance beyond the average when and if Carnera gets some more schooling. This he needs of course. Until the Venetian shows against a more formidable foe, however, it is wise to withhold judgment."[2]

International News Service Editor Davis J. Walsh, commenting on the same fight, said, "He proved to be remarkably fast on his feet."[3]

John Kieran of the *New York Times* described his fleetness of foot this way: "He has 'viability' and plenty of it. He bounds hither and yon in a way that is astonishing, considering his height, girth, and total tonnage."[4]

Writing for *The Ring* magazine, Ed Sullivan relayed that, despite his size, Carnera was "as fast in his movements as a huge cat." Sullivan continued: "Carnera is a straight puncher, avoiding the round-house swing of the novice for the deadly short, straight blow."[5] He commented that Primo was especially tough in the clinches where his terrific strength and sheer power could easily wear down most opponents and he described Carnera's "clubbing uppercut that sprawled Peterson on the floor as though he had been ejected from a cannon."[6]

Lynn Wagner, sports editor of the *Akron Times-Press*, said of Primo's June 5, 1930, knockout in Detroit of K.O. Christner: "Don't let anyone tell you that Carnera can't fight. The knockout he registered under the glare of a flock of powerful lights here last night was the real McCoy. It was genuine and clean-cut, it was not an act."[7]

Anthony Marenghi of the *Newark Star-Eagle* wrote of Primo's third-round TKO over Roberto Roberti at Newark's Dreamland Park in 1931: "Carnera last night exhibited a great punch, a genuine right hand uppercut in the third that drove the giant Roberti into the ropes and almost through them."

While George Barton of the *Minneapolis Tribune* did not believe that Primo would ever become the heavyweight champion due to his lack of a powerful knockout punch, he did concede in 1932 that Carnera had become a good fighter by the time of the Lasky fight. Two days after that bout he wrote that "the giant Italian has improved fully 50 per cent since he knocked out Sully Montgomery in Minneapolis two years ago. He has mastered ringcraft in an astonishing manner, and disports himself like a fellow who knows what it's all about." Barton continued: "Primo moves around the ring with astonishing speed and grace for a man of his bulk, seldom gets off balance, and always is in position to hit. He has become a veritable sharpshooter with his left, the most valuable weapon in boxing."[8] While Barton stated his belief that Carnera would never be the champion, he also commented that Primo would provide Jack Sharkey, Max Schmeling, and Max Baer with stubborn battles.

There is a terrific amount of mixed views about Primo's ring skills. Frankly, more of it is positive than negative, but there is a wide range. Former heavyweight champion James J. Corbett had this to say about those conflicting views: "Some experts tell me that the Venetian has tremendous possibilities. Others say he is a pusher and is so muscled that he never will be anything but that. Some say he is fast, others decry his ungainliness. I don't remember when there was so much conflicting opinion on an outstanding heavyweight, that is, outstanding in so far as public attention is concerned." Corbett continued: "But there may be possibilities in Carnera, after all. You must admit that he is comparatively inexperienced, and that considering his background, he has done pretty well. It seems impossible to hurt the giant, and a man of that type may be the answer to the 1931 prayer among heavyweights."[9]

Bill Wathey of the *Newark Star-Eagle* often spoke disparagingly of Carnera, but gave him his due on the eve of his fight with Pat McCarthy at the Newark Velodrome in 1930. He recognized the improvements in Carnera's ring skills when he wrote, "Carnera has learned to place his hands properly. For a big man, he has developed surprising footwork. He has acquired a dangerous one-two punch that straightens up a rival and then upends him mercilessly. Carnera has learned to use his huge bulk and great strength and really become a threat to the big men of the profession."[10] After the fight, Wathey expressed frustration that Primo's management would not let him consistently meet better fighters. "There is something tremendous about Carnera which should make him formidable in the ring and which should erase the fears of his handlers and allow Carnera to fight himself out of difficulties."[11]

He absolutely had his weaknesses in the ring. He was never a technically good boxer. For a man of his massive size, however, he was quick and light on his feet. He moved fluidly and he did learn, never hesitating to apply that knowledge. Sportswriter Jack Kofoed noted in the fall of 1933: "The Italian's rise to the heavyweight championship of the world was due not to size alone, but to his vast improvement in boxing and hitting."[12]

He became easily flustered and frustrated in the ring when his plans didn't work or when an opponent began to get to him. This frustration probably led to Carnera's 1929 disqualification in his second bout with Young Stribling. A sparring session with Corn Griffin during Primo's preparations for the Max Baer fight in 1934 illustrates this tendency. The Associated Press reported, in an eerie harbinger of what would happen in the ring against Baer, "Once losing command of the situation, Carnera obviously became flustered. He

Primo doing some roadwork on a snowy street in Chicago in 1930. (Chicago History Museum)

floundered around the ring, all his carefully acquired book knowledge of boxing tossed overboard, and he was wide open to any kind of a punch Griffin wanted to throw."[13]

For his size, his punch was never as powerful or savage as it might have been, but at 6'7" and averaging 265 lbs. of solid muscle, the man could hit. And it was more than just Carnera's size that won him the championship. If size was all that mattered, 7'2" South African Ewart Potgeiter, who tipped the scales at a whopping 326 pounds, would have dominated the heavyweight division in the 1950s. Instead, he boxed professionally for less than three years. Fighting strictly unknown opponents, Potgeiter finished his career in 1957 with an 11–2–1 record.[14]

Primo was a tall, powerful man who fought like a tall, powerful man. I'm often reminded of his style while watching Vitali Klitschko. Vitali and his brother Vladimir also have their share of detractors. Some critics would prefer that they mix it up more, with less standing back and jabbing. Some claim that they don't hit hard enough, some that they are simply not all that good, and the list goes on, but like Primo, they both hold the title of heavyweight champion. That, and their records, speak for themselves.

While Primo had a "glass chin" that made him susceptible to the powerful blows of many top heavyweights, he had the heart of a lion, always rising before the count of ten.

Although he went down regularly, he only stayed on the canvas once — this in 1945, in his first fight against Luigi Musina, during his ill-advised and ill-fated comeback attempt.

He was undeniably tough and he never quit. Dropped 11 times by Max Baer's devastating rights, Da Preem kept getting up. He was taking a terrible beating, but he simply refused to give up, somehow willing his massive body off the canvas again and again when most people would just say, "No mas." He forced himself to his feet three times to walk back into the Joe Louis maelstrom. Most men would have stayed down, and many did, but not Carnera. He fought with broken ribs against Jim Maloney in 1931, and against the advice of his doctors, who genuinely feared for the big man's life, Primo made a post-war comeback in 1945 and 1946 to provide for his family. Even O.F. Snelling, who wrote a sympathetic if not flattering piece on Carnera in 1971, gave Primo his due when he wrote that, while the sixth round of the Louis–Carnera fight distinguished the Brown Bomber as a world-class heavyweight, it also "stamped Carnera, with all his faults and deficiencies, as a man of the highest courage."[15]

His amazing 86-inch reach helped him land his effective left jabs, and often to keep the opposition at bay. While preparing for his title defense against Max Baer, Primo's arduous training was noted by the press. In referring to his sparring sessions, his reach and the fortress-like arms were noted. "In all Carnera boxed five rounds and exercised two more and in general, his work was impressive. As long as his tree-trunk left hand was extended and he wasn't being pressed, he was all but impossible to hit. He was vicious at short range and punches bounced off him like hammer raps on an anvil."[16]

Could he hit? Absolutely. Were his punches powerful? Just ask any of the 72 men he knocked out. Carnera may never have had the power that one might expect from a man of his size and strength, but his punch was still powerful. There is ample print, video, and photographic evidence to support these assertions.

There is a terrific photo of Primo walking coolly away from 207-pound Chuck Wiggins who, having just landed on his back, with his legs straight up and arms spread, was the victim of a second-round knockout in 1930. There is another one of Primo in Ebbets Field in Brooklyn, having just tagged Jack Gross in the head with a right-hand howitzer that surely contributed to Carnera's seventh-round TKO.

Renowned boxing reporter Hype Igoe of the International News Service once wrote, "I'll say that the Preem's port poke is a demoralizing dew-drop, as Jack Sharkey will attest. It was Jack who thought he could stand up and fire lefts with Carnera in their first fight. The bout didn't go far, say five rounds, before Sharkey decided that if his head was bashed back much more it might be torn loose from its moorings." Igoe continued, "It was these right hand up-see-doosies that started Jack Sharkey on his visit to the floor in the championship fight. The one that put Jack down didn't hold a candle to the two he got over on the other side of the ring, two blasting blows that were cruel in their power."[17] The legendary New York sportswriter continued with his review of Carnera's abilities, "My contention is that Carnera is somewhat muscle bound. That accounts for his inability to snap a hard punch. With the uppercut, it is different. He isn't afraid to step in close and when he's in the position, he brings his right up like an elevator in a new, snappy tower building."[18]

After Carnera defeated Reggie Meen in December 1930, the *New York Times* reported, "Carnera soon convinced critics that no boxer less skillful than Peter Jackson, or lacking the demon-like qualities of Jack Dempsey at his best, or who is unable to cope with Carnera's arms in clinches by tying them up in a manner disapproved by British referees, is likely to beat a man as exceptionally powerful as the Italian."[19]

Italian boxing legend and former world middleweight champ Nino Benvenuti became a friend of Carnera's towards the end of Primo's life. Benvenuti, one of Italy's most popular living athletes and *The Ring* magazine's 1968 Fighter of the Year, spoke with reporters for *Italy* magazine in 2008 and reminisced about Primo, whom he met at the 1960 Olympics. "When I was a kid Primo was a legend for me. I saw him as the unbeatable giant in the fairy tales." Benvenuti still tries to change the myth that Carnera had little or no boxing ability. "They used to say he wasn't skillful. That's false. He had one of the best jabs I've ever seen in a boxer of that size."[20]

In February 1930, International News Service Sports Editor Davis J. Walsh quoted British writer Trevor Wignall, author of the 1924 book *The Story of Boxing* and 1926's *The Sweet Science,* as saying of Carnera, "He's unbeatable and being that he is only 23 and improving all the time, I believe he will stay that way." Wignall continued prophetically: "His strength, his speed, his punch, his size combine to make him a man apart from all others. He's going to win the heavyweight championship and all the Sharkeys, Schmelings, and Scotts in the world can't alter that."[21]

On the eve of his heavyweight championship contest with Jack Sharkey, Associated Press sportswriter Hugh Fullerton wrote about Primo's ring prowess: "Despite his great bulk and his 6 feet 7 inches of height, the 'Vast Venetian' is fast and a clever boxer lacking only a real knockout punch. He has a quick and accurate left jab and moves with surprising lightness on his oversized feet. He is, however, shy on ring generalship and unable to cope with sudden shifts in attacking style."[22]

Even in fictitious accounts, Primo's size, strength, and power were legendary. In a short story in *The Saturday Evening Post,* Eddie Orcutt wrote about a fictitious fighter named "Brooklyn Mick." Mick was a journeyman, who like many fighters padded his bankroll between fights by picking up work as a sparring partner for big-name fighters who were preparing for headline fights. Orcutt has Mick say, "I will never forget the first time I seen this Carnera. He was out on the lawn at Doc Bier's place, playin' wit a little brown dog. He sure was very big. He looked like a sea-sperrint playin' wit a goldfish." The story: "'Sparrin' wit a guy,' the Mick said, 'you learn him like a book. Carnera couldn't let go his right, bein' muscle-bound, see, but if you run into his left, it would knock your teeth out. He was always holdin' it out, stickin' wit it, an' stickin' and stickin.' He could stick good wit' it. You had to watch out for that left, you had to ride him in the clinches, not try to rassle wit' him.' If you watched those things, the Mick said, you could give Primo a good workout without getting hurt."[23]

The caliber of men he fought ran the gamut from very good to very bad, but that's true of most boxers and especially so of those whose careers are handled by managers who see the chance of their man as a potential contender. They schedule some easy fights early in a career to help build their fighter's confidence with a solid number of victories. Leon See and Billy Duffy undeniably did that for Primo, but it is easily or conveniently forgotten that Carnera also fought a high percentage of quality fighters, many of whom were listed in *The Ring* magazine's annual top 10 heavyweights for periods of time. He was a very busy fighter, entering the ring an average of almost once a month for his entire career — an enormous burden for a heavyweight. Furthermore, when did it become uncommon for promoters and trainers to pad their fighter's records with some easier opponents?

* * *

Primo got his first taste of the ring when he was 17, but did not start boxing seriously until the somewhat advanced age of 21 years old. While he was virtually a novice when he started to concentrate on the ring in 1928, he was blessed with massive size and strength, terrific conditioning, and an iron will that simply would not let him quit. From a belated and humble fistic beginning, he came a tremendous way.

Primo's improvement was notable, especially during late 1929 and 1930. Long-time British referee Moss Deyong commented after the Carnera–Uzcudun fight in November 1930: "Uzcudun put up a good fight, but he was meeting the future world's champion in my opinion. Carnera's improvement was surprising."[24]

It took a heavy hitter to bring down Primo. John Kieran of The *New York Times* often took journalistic pokes at Primo, but after the Carnera–Louis fight in 1935, he reminded readers, "It's custom to laugh at Carnera's crude efforts to punch, or even to pity poor Primo when he is torn apart by a terrific puncher like Shufflin' Joe Louis, but it might be remembered that the fellows who upset Primo in recent years were only three in all—Joe Louis, Max Baer, and Jack Sharkey. Two were heavyweight champions for a sour spell and the other is the best fighter who has come along in years."[25] Kieran went on to point out that with size and weight on his side, it took a hard puncher to defeat Carnera and that those of lesser power held less chance of emerging victoriously.

BBC sports commentator Harry Carpenter may have said it best: "Primo Carnera, the Ambling Alp, a circus strongman fashioned into a fighter, has been derided as a freak foisted on the public purely on his size. His boxing was not as crude as all that and probably a good deal better than Jess Willard's, the other six-and-a-half-foot champion. The tragedy of Carnera lies not in his lack of craft but his exploitation by unscrupulous managers, who left him without a cent and forced him into wrestling, where at length he made a good living."[26]

I thoroughly enjoy boxing historian Don Stradley's work, but in his 2008 article "Let's Go to the History Books," he took a misinformed and unnecessary shot at Primo Carnera. Stradley implies that all of Primo's fights were fixed, that he couldn't hit, and that he took the crown from Jack Sharkey with "a powder puff punch."[27]

While he rarely hit with the power that a man his size might have, his solid left jabs and powerful right uppercut were consistent. He could throw a notable left hook. These were joined at times by a good straight right. There is ample video and photographic evidence to support this. Watch the film of the coup de grace in the Reggie Meen fight from December 1930. Primo landed a crushing overhand right that rocked Meen. Were his punches powerful? Again, just ask any of the 72 men he knocked out.

His punches were described by various sportswriters as ones "which would have shaken the Statue of Liberty," "which would have tunneled the Eighth Avenue subway," and "that must have felt like a cobblestone wrapped in a leather sack." Again, noted boxing journalist Hype Igoe described Primo's right this way: "He brings his right up like an elevator in a new, snappy tower building," and James P. Dawson, who witnessed the second Carnera–Sharkey fight, recalled "a terrific right hand uppercut to the chin which almost decapitated Sharkey and brought Carnera the title." Former world middleweight champ Nino Benvenuti says, "He had one of the best jabs I've ever seen in a boxer of that size."

And by the way, United Press Sports Editor Stuart Cameron, who witnessed the Loughran fight that Stradley refers to in the aforementioned article, stated, "Carnera forged ahead in the seventh and started a clubbing, battering attack that kept the challenger in retreat during the rest of the brawl." Cameron added, "A bombardment of rights and lefts to head and body kept him bouncing off the ropes. He was so dazed at the bell that he lurched over to Carnera's corner. Bill Duffy, Carnera's chief second, escorted him to his own."[28] Funny, but that doesn't sound like the work of a man who "punched like an old lady" and had to resort to stepping on his opponent's feet to win.

Aaron Tallent, writing for *TheSweetScience.com* in 2007, made a strong case for Primo's election to the International Boxing Hall of Fame:

> At first glance, this incites laughter. The Italian heavyweight is referenced by writers more as a plodding oaf than as a heavyweight champion. However, Carnera is the only linear heavyweight

Primo Carnera was an imposing figure in the ring. Here he is in January 1930. (Chicago History Museum)

titleholder from John L. Sullivan to Muhammad Ali's second championship run who is not in the IBHoF. Carnera won the title in 1933 with a sixth-round knockout of Jack Sharkey and successfully defended the belt twice. Included in those wins is a 15-round decision over Tommy Loughran. Those two defenses are more than Max Schmeling, Jack Sharkey, Max Baer, and James J. Braddock—all the heavyweight champions between Gene Tunney and Joe Louis—accumulated COMBINED during their title runs. And not to diminish these fighters accomplishments, but if the voters consider Baer and Braddock to be hall-of-famers, then Carnera deserves induction as well.[29]

Every fighter has his detractors and each detractor is entitled to hold their opinion, but those opinions are open to questioning. Even undefeated heavyweight champion Rocky Marciano was not completely above the fray. On May 16, 1955, Marciano met British heavyweight Don Cockell for his fifth title defense, in Kezar Stadium in San Francisco. Cockell was a respectable fighter who entered the ring with a 66–11–1 record. He was 10–0 since October 1952 and held a 16-pound weight advantage over the champ. That night, Rocky had a difficult time with Cockell, who finally succumbed when referee Frankie Brown stopped the fight with just under a minute to go in the ninth. Rocky knew it had been a tough fight for him and said after the bout, "That was a very bad fight. I wasn't sharp, and I knew it.... He's better than rated. But I had trouble with him. Shortest man I ever fought. Couldn't use my overhands that I like." Some in the press were harsh in rating Rocky's performance. Even after five successful title defenses and an unblemished professional record, the *New York Times* called Marciano "as clumsy as any champion since Carnera," and longtime scribe Arthur Daley, typically a Marciano fan, wrote, "Marciano is the best amateur ever to win the world professional championship."[30] It's safe to say that many would disagree with Daley's assessment.

If one reviews the evidence from the day, it is clear that Primo Carnera was an adequate fighter—no Joe Louis, but an adequate fighter—who used his size, strength, conditioning, and toughness to reach the pinnacle of the boxing world. He was trained by men who knew how to box—Paul Journee, Maurice Eudeline, Abe Attell, and Billy Defoe, to name a few. He learned his craft and was eager to apply the lessons. His managers and promoters, although many had shady connections, knew how to get their man publicity and build his resume. Unfortunately, they also knew how to use Carnera and bilk their fighter out of his prizefighting fortune.

17

The Fix Question

Carnera's career was managed by numerous men of questionable character. Some had gangland connections, some not, but all were schemers looking to make a buck at Primo's expense. As noted sportswriter Paul Gallico stated, "Poor Primo! A giant in stature and strength, a terrible figure of a man, with the might of ten men, he was a helpless lamb among wolves who used him until there was nothing more left to use, until the last possible penny had been squeezed from his big carcass, and then abandoned him. His last days in the United States were spent alone in a hospital. One leg was paralyzed, the result of beatings taken around the head. None of the carrion birds who had picked him clean ever came back to see him or to help him."[1]

Primo Carnera was a much better fighter than many have given him credit for. His record was quite good (89–14–0) and it is simply ludicrous to claim that a hack — no matter what his connections — could win and twice successfully defend the world heavyweight crown. His defenses came against Paolino Uzcudun and Tommy Loughran, two very notable fighters of the era. A simple viewing of his fight videos clearly shows his skills, without the mist and cobwebs of years of editorial speculation.

The fight films show that Primo was a brawler. He was not particularly strong in the technical skills of boxing or in ring generalship, but he was not afraid to mix it up. He was susceptible to being knocked down, but only once in 103 fights did he stay down and that not until his first fight against Luigi Musina, during an ill-advised, but financially necessary, comeback after World War II. Primo had a good left jab, a strong right uppercut, and a respectable overhand right with which he dispatched 72 opponents by knockout. He is simply not the foolish and clumsy circus freak that many have painted him as.

* * *

Pundits and fans, too, are only human. Everyone has an opinion, but people's opinions can change and their assessments can be wrong. Sometimes writers make claims that simply have no merit. Recently, in *The Greatest Fight of Our Generation,* a terrific look at the Joe Louis and Max Schmeling story, author Lewis Erenberg blatantly claims that the Carnera–Sharkey fight was fixed. He bases his assessment on two pages from Jeffery T. Sammons' 1988 book *Beyond the Ring,* and from where else, I cannot tell. Sammons' book is an interesting, but negatively biased, look at boxing and its role in American society. Sammons' views are clear from the start; Chapter 1 is titled "Crime or Sport?: The Development of Modern Prizefighting." It gets no better from there with other chapters titled "Chaos Reigns: The Exit of Champions" and "The Unholy Trinity: Television, Monopoly & Crime." Boxing's loose structure, inexact scoring system, and admittedly shady connections, have long left it open to attacks of this nature, and Erenberg's study fairly points out many of the sport's blemishes, but his assertions have a blatantly negative spin. Erenberg's opinion is his right, but it needs to be based on more than a 75-year-old rumor and speculations based on someone else's speculation.

Baseball had the 1919 Black Sox gambling scandal but dealt with its disgrace by creating a powerful commissioner's post that has worked long and hard to keep the taint of gambling away from the game. Professional football has had brushes with gambling, most notably the 1946 NFL championship game, but they, too, through the strong central power of the commissioner's office, doggedly police the sport. Professional and college basketball have had point shaving and most recently officiating scandals, but on the whole, most major sports have avoided much controversy. On the other hand, the fight game and its participants have long been subject to claims of the fix being in.

* * *

Carnera's managers, beginning with Leon See and Billy Duffy, and continuing through Luigi Soresi, stole much of Primo's money and left him all but broke financially, but their actions and shady connections have harmed Primo as much as or more than all of their unconscionable money grabbing. See's 1934 book, *Le Mystere Carnera*, and Duffy's and Soresi's underworld connections to Owney Madden, Walter Friedman and others have continued to fuel the fix speculations. But Primo was not unique. Ties to the underworld in boxing were quite common in the early and mid–20th century. According to former middleweight champion Mickey Walker, Madden secretly managed many top boxers including Carnera, Bob Olin, Ace Hudkins, Pancho Villa, Maxie Rosenbloom, Jimmy Braddock, and Leo Lomski, as well as top managers Joe Jacobs and Joe Gould.[2] When you mention Joe Jacobs, obviously the name Max Schmeling can't be far behind. And Joe Gould, Jimmy Braddock's close friend and manager, was arguably a close associate of Madden's—so close, in fact, they were photographed walking out of Sing Sing prison together when Madden was released in July 1933.

Madden also reportedly pulled the strings behind the career of Gene Tunney, and Tunney even flew to Hot Springs, Arkansas, to golf with Madden after the New York police had run Madden out of the city. This was, however, nothing out of the ordinary for the time. Madden and Duffy were two of the men to see when aspiring fighters were trying to make a name for themselves in the 1920s and 1930s. "To jump right over the heads of perspiring and able others in the search of good money in Madison Square Garden, a foreign entry must see Mr. Duffy, Mr. Johnston, Mr. Flynn, Mr. Jussel Jacobs or some other frock-coated Broadwayite."[3] The word "see" in this case was a euphemism for "grease the palm of."

The mere mention of an Abe Attell connection by the United Press International was enough to raise some eyebrows. Attell, a known associate of notorious gambling kingpin Arnold Rothstein, and a named conspirator in the 1919 World Series fix, had a long history of questionable dealings and trouble with the law. Within weeks of his first New York arrival, newspapers carried the stated plans for the Italian pugilist. "Primo Carnera will be built up into the biggest fistic attraction since Jack Dempsey's hay-day by touring the country and fighting more or less easy opponents, the United Press learned from the giant Italian's crafty board of managers." The news agency went on to report, "Under no circumstances will Carnera be allowed in the ring with ... any formidable heavyweight until he gains experience and is taught to box by Abe Attell, former featherweight champion."[4] How much time Attell actually spent tutoring Carnera is not well chronicled, but the mere mention of association was enough to keep pundits guessing on the legitimacy of the big man's record.

* * *

It has become almost sport to take shots at Carnera. In the book *East Side, West Side: Tales of New York Sporting Life 1910–1960*, author Lawrence Ritter bluntly stated that "Most of the Italian giant's opponents were pushovers, paid to take a dive or too frightened to stand up for three minutes in a row."[5] Ritter, a very reputable author who has written some terrific works, indicts Carnera as a bum, but shows no evidence to support his allegations. But this is not entirely unique to Primo. Heavyweight champion Jack Sharkey was dogged for the rest of his life by questions about fight fixes and him taking a dive in his title defense against Carnera. He swore until the day he died that he had not. Still, the rumors persisted. They persisted for Sharkey, but they also have persisted for other champions who have long been the targets of fix rumors. Such noteworthy heavyweight champions as Jack Dempsey, Gene Tunney, Max Baer, Jess Willard, Jack Johnson and others were all accused, at one time or another, of being involved in fixed fights.

* * *

Some of Primo's detractors and accusers can be dismissed as nothing more than racists who had a difficult time watching an Italian Catholic hold the crown. While it is difficult to imagine today, racism ran rampant in the sports pages of the 1920s and 1930s. Many racially insensitive journalists of the time commonly used terms like ebony and dusky to describe black athletes. Joe Louis was routinely referred to with such monikers as "the fat-faced, cafe-au-lait colored, sloe-eyed" boxer. It is common to read reports from the time referring to black fighters as animals, sub-human, and as possessing jungle-like skills. Were these references used to describe white fighters as well, they might be considered somewhat complimentary, but a simple reading of the articles about black fighters makes the meaning of the dehumanizing phrases clear.

A glaring example of racism targeted at Primo can be found in sports journalist Blinkey Horn's "From Bunker to Bleacher" article from the day of the Carnera–Loughran fight in 1934. In playing loose with the facts, Horn claims that the heavy wind and rain that had delayed the fight the previous evening were a ruse to buy time to sell more tickets to an uninterested public. Owney Madden was indeed well connected, but it is safe to say that he had no ability to control the weather. Horn's flights of fancy are amazing as he claims that Miami is a dry and dusty place in which rain is as rare as it is in Southern California. He also claims that Primo faked an injured thumb to delay the fight.

Horn states, "The boys do not appear to be eager to pay much to watch the massive Mr. Carnera. If he was in a circus tent they'd probably surge in to see a freak." He goes on to insult Primo further by dropping allegations of early fixes. "Most all the boys remember that several boys consented for so much per night to kiss the canvas in behalf of the '*Eyetalian*' [italics mine] — when he first came to this land. Mr. Carnera is a clown. Clowns belong in a circus. Not in a ring."[6]

Later in the same article, Horn takes up the issue of black and white fighters competing. To his credit, he defends the fact that they should compete against one another, but instead of stopping there, he goes on to make such statements as, "Some of the boys have been around suggesting that there ought to be some sort of color line in this Golden Gloves so that Caucasians wouldn't get smut on themselves when they find a Senegambian in the other corner." He compliments the ring skills of Joe Gans, but then says, "His color was black yet his behavior in the ring was whiter than that of many an Anglo-Saxon. Like those who took a dive for Mons. Primo Carnera when the Venetian Carpenter was being 'built up.'"[7]

He continues by stating, "A negro (Jack Johnson) whipped Jim Jefferies and he was a white man's negro, a stevedore from Galveston. So was Tiger Flowers meek and humble with his 'Yassah Cap'n and 'Sho boss.'"[8]

His final comment on the subject is all telling: "Fighting a negro is merely encountering another dark spot in life."[9] While Horn was a well-respected journalist in his day, it is fair to say that he was also a blatant racist who, at least in some cases, played loose with the facts. This type of journalism was of course not entirely the source of the fix theories and the image of Carnera as a clown, but they certainly added to the myth.

* * *

While there is evidence to suggest that some of Carnera's opponents may have been less than eager to remain in the ring for whatever reason, it stretches the level of credulity to argue that all or even most of his opponents took dives for money or survival.

In his book *Ring of Hate*, Patrick Ayler argues convincingly that some of Primo's opponents may have been personally anxious or encouraged by outsiders to take an early exit. It is, however, not believable that this was a widespread pattern. It is simply not feasible to argue that See's agents, and later underworld henchmen, traveled around Europe and North America prearranging the fight outcomes, and given the frequency with which Carnera fought, with many bouts just days apart, it seems a foolish and impractical endeavor and highly unlikely. "The sheer logistics of such an enterprise would seem to rule that out."[10]

One also has to think of the fact that if, as See claims in *Le Mystere Carnera*, many of Primo's fights in Europe were fixed, who did the fixing? By all accounts, Owney Madden and his boys didn't get involved with Carnera until after his arrival in the United States in 1930. From 1928 until he arrived in America in late 1929, Primo had built up a noteworthy 16–2 record, having dropped only two fights, both by disqualification.

Ayler also rightfully points out that pride would play a factor, as would the difficulty in convincing a fighter that a loss would help their career and gate attraction.

Also in the mix is the fact that those fixing Carnera's fights would have had a terrific amount of overhead if they truly fixed all of his fights that were rumored to be prearranged. Logistics, money, and hoping that no one talked — someone always talks — would have made this a wildly unattractive venture to embark upon. Why pay off so many fighters and their management for so long a period of time? Many of these fighters were mediocre, so why pay them off at all?

If these fights were indeed fixed to build up Carnera's record and confidence, how did Primo's managers think that he would ever learn enough to stand up to the higher-level opponents that he would ultimately face when finally in contention for the heavyweight crown? A phony paper record would not last a round against a strong opponent who couldn't be bought.

It's an interesting paradox that while some claimed that Primo couldn't hit hard enough to harm a flea, others were convinced that he shouldn't be allowed to fight anyone under 6'2" and 220 pounds. New York State Athletic commissioner William Muldoon originally introduced the idea of a "dreadnought" weight division in 1931 as a reaction to Carnera's significant size advantage over most of his opponents. After the tragic death of Ernie Schaaf in 1933, critics claimed that he was too big and powerful to be allowed in the ring with smaller fighters. Muldoon and fellow commissioner General John J. Phelan announced they would again attempt to establish the "super-dreadnought" class for over-sized heavyweights like Carnera. If successful, Muldoon and Phelan's action would force Carnera to choose opponents from only within this super-sized weight class. The move would limit Primo to fewer than 10 known opponents, all but one of whom he had already defeated. Muldoon was quoted as saying, "Carnera is a great athlete from the feet up. He has the speed and agility of a middleweight and as far as punching is concerned he needs no snap to his blows. His weight is enough. He is the greatest physical specimen I have ever seen."[11] For a variety of financial, philosophical, and other reasons, Muldoon and Phelan were shouted down by Jimmy Johnston of the Garden, National Boxing Association President James M. "Bingo" Brown, and other state commissions.

* * *

The cries of fix and tainted fight came once again from some corners when Primo knocked out Jack Sharkey for the championship in 1933. How critics missed the simple reality of how Carnera did it, is the question to be asked. A simple viewing of the fight film clearly shows a short, tight, and powerful right uppercut that catches the champion on the chin. His head jerks up violently with the punch and down Sharkey crumples to the canvas with a thud.

Sharkey's manager, Johnny Buckley, saw the punch. He had no doubt that it landed. His concern was whether Carnera had a horseshoe in his glove or not. He immediately called for officials to examine the Italian's gloves. With nothing to hide, Billy Duffy told Carnera to leave the gloves on until they could be examined. No sleep aid was found other than Primo's right fist.

I have great respect for Bert Sugar's opinion on boxing matters, but he got this one completely wrong. In referring to the blow that transferred the championship belt, Sugar states, "People are still looking for that punch to land. It even surprised Carnera."[12] Again, a viewing of the fight video clearly shows that the right uppercut was a legitimate shot. News reports from the time generally ran along the lines of the *New York Times,* which on Page One called the punch "a terrific right hand uppercut to the chin which almost decapitated Sharkey and brought Carnera the title."[13]

* * *

Primo's children, who themselves are not certain about the legitimacy of some of their father's fights, have been quoted as saying about the set-up claims, "Daddy told us that he never knew that. He told us that he never knew and that the decision only depended on the boxing ability of the opponents. He was too naive. We are sorry to say so, but it is like that. His relation to arranged bouts is to be found in his naivete, which came from the goodness of his heart. We do not want to sanctify him, however the importance of what he did and his honesty helped him to survive everything and everybody." They did, however, quote their father as being certain of one thing: "The world title match was not fixed." According to him, "It was too important and could not be fixed."[14]

* * *

It's fair to say that Tommy Loughran did not take a dive, yet Primo decisively beat this unquestionably deserving Hall of Famer. Over 15 rounds, Carnera systematically wore down his formidably seasoned opponent.

During his career, Loughran had beaten such light heavyweight notables as Mickey

Walker, Jimmy Slattery, Georges Carpentier, Harry Greb, and Mike McTigue. He proved that he belonged in the ring with such heavyweight talent as Jack Sharkey, Ernie Schaaf, Max Baer, Steve Hamas, Jim Braddock, Paolino Uzcudun, and Young Stribling. Loughran's defeat can't be explained away as simply a size issue. Twice, including just three months before meeting Primo, the Philadelphia Phantom outpointed the Carnera-sized Ray Impelletiere.

Loughran blamed his loss on a series of issues including Carnera stepping on his feet, the fact that Carnera wasn't repelled by the foul-smelling grease Tommy had applied to his hair before the fight to keep the big man off of him, and to Primo wearing him down by leaning on him with all his weight, but ultimately, Primo's size was only one factor in Loughran's loss. His protests were certainly more his pride talking than fact.

* * *

Primo's managers ran the gamut from the mostly decent to the beneath contempt. Leon See, the diminutive Frenchman who helped Carnera get his start in the prizefighting ring, was one of the mostly decent crowd, but even he was not above bitterness when he was muscled out of Carnera's corner by Owney Madden and his thugs.

See claimed in his 1934 book *Le Mystere Carnera* that most of Primo's fights between 1928 and 1931 were fixed. Remembering that See had recently been edged out of his management role for the man who now wore the crown of heavyweight champion of the world, could this be simply a severe case of sour grapes? See had long dreamed of managing a heavyweight to the title. He had given up on that hope when, out of nowhere, Paul Journee dropped Primo in his lap. See had seen something in Carnera that made him decide to take one more dip into the pond of professional boxing. See had been instrumental in training and helping to mature Primo both inside and outside of the ring, but now he, Journee, and Maurice Eudeline had been elbowed out of the picture by Primo's new and undoubtedly shady American management team. He was by all accounts bitter, and understandably so. He chose to fight back with the deadliest weapon in his arsenal—the pen. Whether See reported the facts accurately, embellished them, or outright made them up is impossible to say, but it is fair to say that he was resentful, had an axe to grind, and employed a scorched earth policy when he released the book.

The Frenchman claims that 31 of Carnera's 48 fights were "Combat arrange," or arranged combat, during that time. See's claims were widely ignored by sportswriters and others in the boxing world, but the stench of "fix" still lingered.

See claimed that he and Pa Stribling arranged the outcome of both Carnera–Stribling bouts in 1929, to make money and to give each fighter a boost in publicity. Stribling dropped his decision to Primo on a low blow, but it should be noted that Stribling's style often tended to low blows as he began to chop down an opponent with ferocious attacks to the body. Just five months earlier referee Dave Barry had disqualified Stribling in Tulsa, Oklahoma, when a powerful right hand landed south of Babe Hunt's belt line, disabling Hunt. In the second Stribling–Carnera affair, Primo was disqualified when he continued to hit "Strib" well after the bell, but Primo was known to show periodic flashes of anger, particularly when provoked or frustrated. He was reportedly very frustrated at the end of the seventh round, the result of receiving a final hard body blow from Stribling at the bell. Young Stribling's voice had been silenced when "The King of the Canebrakes" died in a motorcycle accident in October 1933, but Pa Stribling refused to respond to See's allegations, stating that he was simply not interested in commenting on the scurrilous accusations.

Hurt and bitter at losing control of his dream of managing a fighter to the world heavyweight title, Leon See went to his grave in 1963 never recanting his claims. The question, however, remains, had Carnera truly been such a poor and talentless fighter, why would See have taken him on when Paul Journee introduced them? See himself claims that the only reason that he agreed to manage Primo was that he saw the real possibility of finally fulfilling his dream of managing a world heavyweight champion.

* * *

As discussed, Jack Sharkey had to deny rumors that he had taken a dive in the championship fight with Carnera. To the day he died, he swore that the fight was legitimate. But rumors have a way of living on, with or without merit. Carnera and Sharkey were, however, not the only fighters of the era implicated by rumors of shady dealings. Notables such as Jack Dempsey, Gene Tunney, Jack Johnson, Kid Chocolate, Young Stribling, Max Baer, Jess Willard and Gene Tunney all were at one time or another, accused of being involved in set-ups.

During Carnera's career, it was not uncommon for the various boxing and athletic commissions to investigate fights and withhold fighters' purses. Primo and his opponents had this happen several times, but they were not alone. The reasons varied from allegations of corruption to officials simply feeling that a fighter had not put forth his all during a bout.

In April 1930, the Ontario Athletic Boxing Commission withheld the purse of well-known Cuban fighter Kid Chocolate after his defeat of Johnny Erickson in a 10-round decision in Toronto. Despite the fact that the Cuban had given Erickson "a thorough trouncing and almost knocked him out in the last round," fight officials were "dissatisfied" with Chocolate's overall performance.[15] According to both the *Toronto Star* and the *Toronto Globe & Mail*, fight referee Lou Marsh had warned both fighters several times to "fight or get out"[16] and for Chocolate to "put a bit more vim and vigor"[17] into his punches. The fans in attendance seemed satisfied with the fight and its outcome, and Chocolate's manager, Luis Guitierrez, testified both during the contest to Marsh, and later at the inquiry, that his fighter had injured both of his hands during the fight and was disinclined to open himself up to a fluke punch in a bout that he knew he had well in hand and would win on points, without a knockout. This is a basic pugilistic instinct. It's taught in the early lessons in Boxing 101, but the Commission still took what seems to be rather arbitrary action. After an examination, the Ontario Commission's official physician reported that Chocolate's left hand was undoubtedly injured.

The New York State Athletic Commission investigated the sixth Billy Petrolle–King Tut fight of February 27, 1931, after Petrolle knocked Tut, whose real name was Harry Tuttle, out in the fourth round. Petrolle and Tut had pretty evenly split their head to head record since their first meeting in 1927, with Petrolle taking the first two bouts and Tut the next three. Just three and a half weeks earlier, Tut had knocked "the Fargo Express" out in the first round in St. Paul. Going into this fight, Tut was favored to win, but a late surge of pro–Petrolle money abruptly changed the odds before the bout from 8 to 5 in favor of Tut, to 2 to 1 in Petrolle's favor. Tut battered Petrolle in the first round, staggering him with rights and lefts to the jaw, but Petrolle refused to go down. Regaining his legs, Petrolle took over and decked Tut once in each the second and third rounds and twice in the fourth, finishing Tut and ending their four-year-long series.

The rapid and unexplained change in the pre-fight odds caused the NYSAC to look into allegations of fraud following the contest. The investigation proved nothing and the charges against the fighters were dropped. The Associated Press pointed out, "Most of the ringside critics refused to view the proceedings with any great alarm and the faithful who turned out to the number of 14,000 and rooted wildly were pleased with the battle."[18] They also quoted New York City Mayor and enthusiastic fight fan Jimmy Walker, who witnessed the battle, as saying, "If that fight was a fake let's have more of them."[19]

* * *

Suggestions of fixed fights have tainted boxing for most of its history. Shady characters have long been associated with the fight game and, frankly, of all the major sports, fixing a prizefight, where only the fighter taking the dive and maybe his manager have to agree to the fix, is easier than fixing a team sport, where more people need to be involved to adversely affect a game's outcome.

As far back as May 18, 1771, it is reported, Colonel Dennis O'Kelly, a noted horseman and gambler, paid off Bill Darts to take a dive against Peter Corcoran.

On August 30, 1900, Kid McCoy reportedly took a dive in the fifth round against James J. Corbett in their heavyweight bout at Madison Square Garden. McCoy was said to need the quick cash to pay off his mounting gambling debts.

Later that year, Terry McGovern knocked out Joe Gans in the second round of a lightweight fight at Tattersall's horse market and exhibition space in Chicago. Strong and persistent rumors of a fix in that bout helped end the sport in the states of Illinois and New York for years.

Did Jack Johnson take a dive against Jess Willard in their title fight in Havana, Cuba, in 1915? It's doubtful, but it is a common assertion. On January 2, 1916, Johnson "confessed" to having thrown this fight. Most boxing historians don't think so, but *The Ring* magazine has visited the subject twice and Johnson's recent biography *Unforgivable Blackness* considers the possibility.

Gene Tunney has long been linked with a number of shady characters. In May 1923, when Tunney lost to Harry Greb, Abe Attell was reportedly in Tunney's corner. In 1925, bookmaker, bootlegger, and Rothstein associate Max "Boo Boo" Hoff lent $20,000 to Billy Gibson and Gene Tunney in return for a 20 percent share of the up-and-coming fighter. While Tunney clearly had the better of Jack Dempsey in their September 23, 1926, bout in Philadelphia, in what *The Ring* magazine proclaimed the "Upset of the Decade," their rematch in 1927 still draws questions. How many articles have been written about the Dempsey–Tunney "Long Count" fight? It's said that Arnold Rothstein made over a half million dollars on Tunney that night as well. Why was he willing to bet more than $100,000? What did he know that others did not? Was the fight fixed? Who can say, but it certainly has been suggested a multitude of times and, as stated earlier, Tunney was very closely connected to Owney Madden.

Dempsey, too, had some shady types in his camp from time to time. At Tex Rickard's insistence, Bill Duffy joined Dempsey's team as he prepared for the Sharkey fight in 1927. Rickard was anxious to put some boxing gravitas back into Dempsey's corner and Duffy's experience and knowledge were of greater concern to Rickard than Duffy's sordid side.[20]

It has long been alleged that great 1920s and 30s welterweight Ruby Goldstein's contract was at least partially owned by gangster Waxey Gordon. Gordon was an associate of Arnold Rothstein and heavily involved in bootlegging and gambling. He reportedly got his nickname "Waxey" because he was so good at picking pockets that his victims' pockets were seemingly waxed.[21]

As noted earlier, Joe Gould, Jim Braddock's long-time manager and friend, was a close enough associate of Owney Madden's that he was photographed escorting Madden out of the prison doors when the notorious mobster was released from incarceration in July 1933, following his yearlong stay at Sing Sing for violating his parole on a manslaughter conviction.

Rumors have long circulated around the Benny Leonard–Jack Britton fight in 1922, the Willie Pep–Lulu Perez fight in 1954, Clay–Liston in 1964, and the 1999 draw between Lennox Lewis and Evander Holyfield brought a wave of allegations and official investigations, but for the most part nothing has come of any of the charges over the years. As recently as September 2003 the FBI and New York City Police Department opened an investigation after that month's Shane Mosley–Oscar De La Hoya fight. Bob Arum's Top Rank offices were raided, with federal agents seizing computers, files and fight tapes. Nikolay Valuev's decision over Evander Holyfield in 2008 prompted an investigation as well. Once again, the charges were dropped and nothing was found.

"Bill Cayton, former manager for Mike Tyson, says fixed fights are more grist for pulp fiction and cinema verite. 'In all the time I was involved in boxing, from 1948 for the next 30 years, there was only one fixed fight that I knew of. And I'm not going to tell you which one.' Cayton said. 'All that talk about the days of the fixed fights is total B.S. It's total perception. If you owned a fighter, you took pride in the fact that he is a winner.'"[22]

In the 1960s the United States Congress investigated fixed fights and organized crime influence on the sport. During this investigation, it was alleged, and fairly well substantiated, that the November 14, 1947, fight between Jake LaMotta and Billy Fox was fixed. After the fight, the New York State Athletic Commission withheld both fighters' purses and investigated the claims. LaMotta was fined $1,000 and suspended for 6–7 months, but the purses were later paid. LaMotta would admit much later that he threw this fight to get a shot at the middleweight title. Of all of these fix allegations, only those associated with the LaMotta–Fox fight have been openly admitted, but the list goes on.

It was not simply Carnera who has been accused of participating in or benefitting in fixed fights. If you point fingers at Primo, you must point fingers at hundreds of other members of the fight fraternity about whom rumors have circulated and many of whom had the same connections as Carnera.

The point here is that, yes, Primo Carnera was surrounded by underworld types throughout his American career, and tales of fixed fights and shady dealings have long been rumored, but boxing is littered with other fighters, notable and unknown, who have been on the edge of the underworld and involved in other questionable activities. The rumors simply don't prove or disprove that Primo Carnera or any of these men were involved in throwing fights.

Are fights fixed from time to time? Undoubtedly. There are fighters who are occasionally paid to lose. Were some of Carnera's fights fixed? Possibly so, but there was no title fight by fight orchestration that has been alleged by his detractors for so long. It simply doesn't make sense. Too many factors work against it — logistics; cost; the tremendous risk of it being revealed; the fact that in over 80 years no one has credibly shown it to be true — and frankly, because while not an elite boxer, Carnera could fight. The man simply did not need that much help in the ring.

18

Primo Carnera: The Man

Size

Primo Carnera was a remarkable individual in size and personality. He was an extremely well built and powerful man. Carnera stood 6' 7" and weighed between 260 and 275 solid lbs. during his prime. He was well coordinated and very mobile for his size. Many of his 48 KOs and 24 TKOs were the direct result of his considerable strength and power. His long arms (86-inch reach) gave him a sizable advantage in reach over most opponents. Most heavyweights of Carnera's day weighed 50 to 60 pounds less and stood a good half foot shorter. His enormous size earned him the nickname The Ambling Alp. Primo's daughter Jean recalls, "Everything was bigger for daddy."[1]

Until December 17, 2005, when the 7 ft. 1 in., 325-pound Nikolay Valuev won the WBA title, Carnera and Jess Willard, who stood 6' 6½" but weighed about 30 pounds less, were the biggest heavyweight champions in boxing history. While Primo had a "glass chin" that made him susceptible to the powerful blows of many top heavyweights, he had the heart of a lion, always rising before the count of ten. Although he went down regularly, he only stayed on the canvas once — this in 1945 in his first fight against Luigi Mussina during his ill-fated comeback attempt.

Carnera's suits reportedly had enough material in them for two full suits for an ordinary man. Primo's suits required 3 yards for the coat, 4 yards for the pants and 1¼ yards for the vest. His chest measured 52 inches and the coat length 38 inches. The average suit for a man today typically requires 3 to 3½ yards.[2]

According to a *New York Times* article from 1930, Primo wore a size 21 shoe. "The largest pair of shoes ever manufactured in this city (Brockton, Massachusetts) were sent tonight by air mail to Primo Carnera, giant Italian boxer. They were boxing shoes and measured 9 inches across the sole and 18½ inches from heel to toetip."[3] The massive amount of leather required to resole his shoes apparently cost Primo a whopping Depression-era sum of $7.50.

While Primo was in Omaha, Nebraska, for his second fight with K.O. Christner, the *Omaha World-Herald* ran a picture of local cobbler John Pistone holding an enormous pair of new shoes that Primo had ordered. The photograph was titled "Carnera Boosts Leather Trade" and the caption related that the leather industry had reached that corner. And all because Primo Carnera decided to buy a new pair of shoes, thereby reviving the industry in one fell swoop.[4] The shoes measured 13 inches in length.

Here Primo is being measured for a suit by his New York tailor Billy Taub. Looking on is Primo's friend and trainer Maurice Eudeline. (Underwood & Underwood/CORBIS)

Appetite

His appetite was said to be legendary. It was reported that for breakfast, Primo could consume a quart of orange juice, two quarts of milk, 19 pieces of toast, 14 eggs, a loaf of bread and half a pound of Virginia ham. Of his dinner menu before a fight, Primo com-

By all accounts, Primo Carnera had a voracious appetite. (Chicago History Museum)

mented, "I'll have spinach and some other vegetable, couple of lamb chops, a little salad and a glass of Italian table wine. Then a pear or an apple and that's all." When asked about spaghetti, Primo responded, "No it's too heavy. When I train I don't eat it. But after the fight I'll eat some. Most of the time, I eat only two meals a day, even when I don't train."[5]

Following his first U.S. fight on January 25, 1930, the United Press reported, "He is jovial, carefree and good-natured. He shakes hands with all and smiles happily even though he doesn't know half the time what's being said, as he speaks no English. Carnera smokes innumerable cigarettes and has no respect for training rules."[6] All of this is no doubt true with the exception of the training discipline. Primo would come to be known as a diligent and disciplined trainer who possessed legendary strength and stamina every time he entered the ring.

Family

Family was always important to Primo. In addition to his devotion to his mother, father, and brothers, Primo had a large extended family with whom he was close. And then there was Pina. Primo met Guiseppina Kovacic (Pina) in the extreme eastern Italian town of Gorizia in 1938. He was just beginning to fully recover from the loss of a kidney. Primo and the Yugoslavian girl met at a cafe owned by mutual friends. Pina was a local girl who worked at the central post office in Gorizia. She was excited to meet the former world heavyweight champion. According to their children, Primo fell in love at first sight. Primo told Pina that he saw in her eyes the same goodness and kindness that he saw in his mother's eyes. Soon he asked her to marry him, but Pina was uncertain that they were ready. Though her father was against the relationship, Primo went to visit her regularly and started a daily correspondence with Pina that lasted until they were married on March 13, 1939.

Pina and Primo have two children, Umberto and Giovanna Maria (Jean). *Time* magazine reported on January 15, 1940: "Born. To Primo ("Old Satchelfoot") Carnera, 33, hulking, gullible Italian roustabout, who became world heavyweight champion prize fighter in 1933, later a cinema actor, and Giuseppina Cavazzi Carnera, 27; their first child, a son; in Sequals, Italy. Weight: 11 lbs. Name: Umberto."[7] Primo and Pina's daughter, Giovanna Maria, was born in Italy in 1943.

Carnera arrived in New York City on July 29, 1946, to pursue a wrestling career. He quickly decided to relocate to the West Coast, thinking that he would be closer to the film industry and that New York City was no place to raise a young family. He continued to wrestle and put money away so that his family could join him in the United States as soon as possible.

April 6, 1948, Pina arrived in New York from Italy with their two children, son Umberto E., 9 years, and daughter, Giovanna Maria, 6 years. Primo didn't want to raise the children in New York City. He decided to take the family to California. He bought a new home on Genesee Avenue in Los Angeles for $30,000. Once settled into life in Southern California, Pina became Primo's business manager. She had a shrewd business mind and made a great deal of money investing in real estate in the San Fernando Valley. In addition to his burgeoning wrestling career, Primo opened a restaurant and liquor store in Los Angeles. According to some reports, Primo made between $50,000 to $100,000 per annum in the years from 1946 to 1962. He became a U.S. citizen in 1953.

Carnera was insistent that his children apply themselves in school and receive the solid education that he had never received. Umberto served a hitch in the United States Navy and became a doctor. Giovanna Maria graduated from Immaculate Heart High School in Los Angeles in 1961 and majored in psychology at UCLA. On February 8, 1964, she was married.

An interesting story illustrating the value that Primo placed on family came out in a United Press report out of Rome in March 1930. The article stated that Primo had forwarded to a female cousin $1,000 to repay a one thousand lire ($52.63) loan granted him by the cousin so he could travel to Paris years before. Primo said the interest paid was a show of gratitude for her generosity.[8]

Primo's generosity was also legendary. Jean tells of Christmases in Sequals when Primo and Pina would buy small gifts for all of the children in the town to make sure that they all had something for the holiday. Pina would organize a party in the town square and small gifts of candy, fruit, and nuts would be given to each child. She also tells the heartwarming story of another Christmas in California when her father came to the aid of a needy family.

> I was a little girl and I was with him. We were in Los Angeles and had gone out together to buy some Christmas presents. It was late and we were coming out of a shop. He saw a mother with a little girl — she must have been five years old — who was looking at a shop window with some

toys. She had fallen in love with a doll, but her mother was telling her that that year Santa Claus was poor and could not satisfy all the children of the world. Daddy began talking with the woman and soon came to know that her husband had died the previous year and that she had three other children at home. So, he took the woman and the little girl into the shop, bought the doll and other toys for the other children, and then gave her fifty dollars for their Christmas dinner. Daddy often behaved like that.[9]

During the late 1940s, while touring Eastern cities, a chance meeting with one of his old managers provided a moment of poetic justice. "One of these men who had held the giant in bondage for so many years, one of the elite of the once high-riding mob, approached Primo Carnera after a wrestling match and, in our own graceless, work-a-day language, he put the bite on him. 'He looked very bad,' Primo said, 'but I could not find it in myself to give him money. Instead, I bought him a meal.'"[10] The fact that Primo even uttered a civil word to the man, much less bought him a meal, speaks volumes about his character.

Wrestling legend Bruno Sammartino told this story about his experiences with Primo:

> Carnera was also a tag-team partner in my rookie years. He was getting up there in age. He wasn't in really the best of health anymore. But he was a name and I was not in those years. I was honored to be his tag-team partner. The idea was he was the attraction and I was his tag-team partner and it was expected of me to spend more time in the ring. But by the same token, I had heard so much about Carnera and I spent a lot of time with him. We stayed in the same hotel, we would go to the restaurant and eat and talk to him. To give you a quick little story about Carnera, to tell you what kind of a heart the man had: He and I were going to go to dinner at Mama Leone's. When we approached it, there was a man sitting on the sidewalk with his hand out selling pencils—a beggar. He had two missing legs; very obvious. To show you the man Carnera was, he dropped some money in there. We both did. When we went to eat and [the restaurant people] saw us, and at the time all Italians were working in the place, they took care of us. I saw [Primo] with some tears in his eyes. I asked him, we spoke in Italian, "Primo, what's wrong? What's the matter?" He said, "All this food and there's a guy out there with no legs begging, hoping that people will take a pencil and drop a buck. He probably can't raise enough money to eat. Life is cruel sometimes." He had tears in his eyes. This was the kind of guy he was and the kind of heart he had. If you ask people who knew him, they'd say people took advantage of his good heart financially. He was hurt many times because of his good heart.[11]

Primo once told the readers of the Italian newspaper *La Domenica del Corriere* that he left carpentry for the circus for two reasons. First the long hours, minimal pay, and drudgery of the job and second, he never had enough to eat. Boxing seemed to offer a better future than the strongman role in the circus so he moved up again and while the long hours continued, drudgery and having enough to eat never again were an issue for him. According to Primo's son Umberto, "For him boxing was first a job to earn a living, then a means to have a discipline in his life, and in the end, a great love."[12]

Caught in the Politics of the Era

Italian Dictator Benito Mussolini used Carnera's success to the Fascist cause's benefit. Posing as Primo's friend and supporter, he saw to it that good crowds attended his Italian fights. He made sure that Primo was photographed in the Fascist uniform he had ordered for the champion. After Primo defeated Sharkey, Il Duce sent Carnera a telegram that stated, "My congratulations. Fascist Italy and its sports-loving people are proud that a Blackshirt has become boxing champion of the world."[13] But in reality Mussolini, like the underworld thugs in America, played Carnera for all he could.

After the war, many saw Primo as a pawn of Mussolini's who had no choice but to play along or suffer consequences. Many Italians refused to accept this argument and immediately after Mussolini's death, an angry crowd gathered in front of the Villa Carnera in Sequals. Fearing for his family and his own life, Primo, who had faced some of the toughest and most dangerous heavyweights of the previous 20 years, met this crowd head on. With the crowd threatening to kill Primo for his Fascist ties, Carnera emerged on the front porch armed with a shotgun and a steely nerve. He let the crowd know that he would not go down without a fight and that he would take as many of them with him as he could. The specter of the enormous and still powerfully built ex-heavyweight champion brandishing a shotgun and threatening to use it had a calming effect on the crowd and they dispersed without further incident.

In truth, Carnera was virtually apolitical. Like most people would, he responded to the lure of the famous and powerful. When the leader of your nation asks you to dine with him or her, you are flattered and you do so. Regardless of ideology, you enjoy the uniqueness and the grandeur of the event, and you probably have a splendid time. It matters not whether that leader is Benito Mussolini or the Prince of Wales. Primo was simply a naive young man caught up in the politics of an explosive era.

The Final Round

In the fall of 1966, Primo was taken to a Los Angeles-area hospital in a state of near collapse. After a battery of tests it was determined that he had suffered a series of internal hemorrhages. Pina told the press that the doctors had brought Primo back from the dead, but the sickness left him weak and gaunt, and more ill health lay just ahead. By March of 1967, doctors reported that he was suffering both from diabetes and an advanced case of cirrhosis of the liver.[14]

Jean Carnera recalled an evening in early May when her parents and Umberto gathered at her house for dinner. Although he was already seriously ill, Primo did his best to set a happy tone, telling jokes and remembering good times. He spoke of his parents and Sequals and how he would soon go there to rest and recover.

Pina sold the liquor store in Glendale to family friend Vincente Garofano and prepared for her husband's illness and its inevitable outcome. The children were grown. Umberto, having completed his Naval service, was now enrolled in medical school, and Jean had graduated from UCLA and was married to an engineer. After the family's arrival in 1948, Pina and the children had quickly adapted to American styles and customs. They were fully involved with their lives and happy to be American citizens. This was not entirely the case for Primo. However much he loved America, Primo still pined for Italy and for his villa in Sequals. He wanted to go home.

Life was losing its appeal to this once vibrant man. He could no longer drink wine and his once enormous appetite was all but gone, so he was rapidly losing weight. Though just 60 years old, Primo was now having difficulty walking and was forced to use a cane. He believed or at least hoped that a return to his villa would do him some good. It would cheer him up and possibly even restore a measure of good health to his now ravaged body.

In mid–May, Primo Carnera began his final journey home. Umberto and Jean drove their parents to Los Angeles International Airport. Not knowing when or if he would see his children again, he left them with these words before boarding the flight: "Be always

Primo continued to follow boxing for the rest of his life. Here he is in New York City attending the weigh-in for the Joe Louis and Ezzard Charles fight on September 27, 1950. (Bettmann/CORBIS)

together, love each other and take care of your mother when I am no longer here with her. Always live your life with honesty and dignity. See you soon."[15]

With Pina by his side, the former champion arrived by plane at Rome's Fiumicino Airport on May 20, 1967. A large crowd of friends, fans, and reporters greeted him. As the once great man appeared through the airliner's door, a hush fell over the crowd. Those who expected to see the strong and rugged man who towered over all others were shocked to their cores to see a stooped and gaunt old man aided by a cane and others as he descended that stairwell. Journalist Mario Salvetti described the sad moment for *Il Messaggero* this way: "Many years ago, he was said to be the strongest man in the world. Now, when you look at him, you wonder what is the separation between friendship and pity.... You look at him and you feel moved. This man—held up with love and almost in trepidation by his wife Pina—smiles bitterly, as if here in his country he wanted to hide the poverty of his body. He smiles and lifts a hand in the air—a huge hand that had terrified many big men in the past. It is a tired gesture, almost a due thank you."[16]

Another journalist, Nantas Salvalaggio, noted that Primo was emaciated and no longer dominated the crowd like he used to.

With the aid of a wheelchair Primo was taken to the VIP Lounge where he answered questions for journalists. Before leaving Rome he attended a luncheon hosted by local sportsmen, but he really could not eat much and he was growing tired. That afternoon, Primo and Pina boarded a train for Udine and the final leg of the journey home to Sequals.

Once he arrived at the villa, Carnera was examined by a team of physicians who confirmed that the American doctors had been correct in their diagnosis—Primo's illnesses were in the final stages and were terminal.

He seemed to rally a bit in early June and was strong enough to attend the Rose Festival activities in Sequals. On June 4 he attended a ceremony given to honor Primo and Italian fighter Nino Benvenuti, who had won the world middleweight title on April 17. The two fighters were given gold medals in honor of their fistic accomplishments. Primo had a wonderful time, but this would be his last public appearance. He could only stand for short periods of time, could not eat, and drank only solutions of sugar and water to keep himself hydrated and maintain some level of energy. His ready smile, his sense of humor, and his good nature still shined through, but his body was wearing down as his liver grew weaker. After raising a final toast with Benvenuti, he appeared on the balcony to the assembled crowd, waved, turned and returned to the Villa Carnera.

By mid–June he rarely left the house. Each day he rested, but each day he seemed to grow weaker. Eventually he became too weak to stay long out of bed. He began to take fewer visitors. Jean arrived from California on June 27, but Umberto was busy with final exams and could not make it to his father's side. The great man was slipping in and out of a coma. When he was lucid, Primo spoke with Pina and Jean. He understood that Umberto could not be there. He commented, "Now my son can have his own business card with the doctor title. The blows I got during my career had been useful for something serious."[17]

On June 28 Monsignor Giuseppe Dalla Pozza, the priest who had married Primo and Pina in 1939, gave Primo the last rites of the Catholic Church.

Pina later remembered Primo's final days. "In those moments, he kept on caressing my hand and then he held it tight as a child. It was the only way to keep him quiet. As soon as I went away, he started to call me, desperate and in his harsh voice: 'Pina ... Pina....'"[18]

On the morning of June 29 Primo, still lucid, told his wife, "I hope I'll recover; however, if God wants me to die, then I accept his will."[19] At 10:47 A.M., after whispering Pina's name one last time, the bell rang to close the final round of the life of Primo Carnera. It was 34 years to the day since he had defeated Jack Sharkey for the heavyweight crown.

Thousands of people converged on Sequals in the days following Primo's death. People both famous and unknown paid their respects to the man through personal visitation, notes, and flowers.

The open, dark wood casket lay in the Villa for two days as mourners paid their last respects to the Italian giant. Journalists reported that Carnera again looked huge as he lay there in his black suit. His hands were resting together on his chest holding a rosary and his championship belt was draped across his waist.

Tributes came from all over the world. In Primo's adopted hometown of Los Angeles the city council passed a resolution extending sympathy to the family and called for members to stand for a moment of silence as the June 29 meeting concluded.

On the day of the funeral, hundreds gathered at the Villa Carnera. A large, black hearse carried Primo's casket through the village and to the funeral mass. Preceding the hearse, middleweight champion Nino Benvenuti carried Primo's world championship belt. After the service, Primo was interred in a large white mausoleum with his parents and brothers. Pina would join her husband upon her passing in 1980. A bust now sits upon a pedestal in front of the structure. The pedestal bears the inscription "— Primo Carnera, 1906–1967, boxing champion of the world."

Legacy

Jean Carnera recalls her father as an idol who gave her strength and courage. "A man who always gave his best, without asking for anything in exchange for it. I saw his extraordinary pity towards people in need, especially children. I saw him forgive those who hurt him. I saw him get up with honor every time he fell down. I saw a husband loving only his 'Pina'"[20]

Primo is the only linear heavyweight champion not elected to the International Boxing Hall of Fame. A number of fighters who Primo defeated, including Jack Sharkey, Tommy Loughran, Young Stribling, and George Godfrey, have been inducted at the Hall in Canastota, New York. Primo was, however, inducted into the World Boxing Hall of Fame in 1990. The World Boxing Hall of Fame is located in Riverside, California.

The Primo Carnera Foundation was established in 1998 when his children, Umberto, now a medical doctor, and Jean, recognized their personal obligation to preserve and honor their father's profound commitment to encouraging children pursue their dreams. The foundation is committed to offering neglected children from abusive environments the financial support and motivation to stay in school and fulfill their dreams. Affiliated with St. Thomas University in Miami, Florida, and the National Italian American Foundation (NIAF), the foundation is an international not-for-profit organization dedicated to providing financial assistance and emotional support for children in need from all cultures and backgrounds. In addition to financial support, the foundation provides an educational/athletic program in the summer, college scholarships, and motivational outreach programs.

Interest in Carnera continues. In April 2008 a movie about Primo's life was released. The film is titled *Carnera: The Walking Mountain*.

Appendix I: Ring Record

Note: Information that is unknown or unclear is indicated by a question mark.

Legend

DQ: Disqualification; the losing fighter was disqualified by the referee
KO: Knockout
L: Loss
NWS: Newspaper Decision; a win on points awarded by the press
PTS: Win by Points
TKO: Technical Knockout
UD: Win by Points with a Unanimous Decision
W: Win

220 Appendix I

Date	Carnera's Weight	Opponent	Record	Weight	Location	Result	Referee	Attendance
9/12/1928	266½	Leon Sebilo	1-8-0	196	Salle Wagram, Paris, France	W TKO 2/4	?	?
9/25/1928	275½	Joe Thomas (1)	0-0-0	189½	Cirque de Paris, Paris, France	W KO 3/4	?	?
10/30/1928	270	Salvatore Ruggirello	7-7-0	217	Cirque de Paris, Paris, France	W TKO 4/10	?	?
11/25/1928	?	Epifanio Islas	0-1-0	225	Pallazzo dello Sport, Milan, Lombardia, Italy	W UD 10/10	Carlo Lomazzi	?
12/1/1928	282¼	Constant Barrick	1-13-3	195	Velodrome d'Hiver, Paris, France	W KO 3/?	?	?
1/18/1929	?	Ernst Rosemann	15-11-4	210	Sportpalast, Berlin, Germany	W TKO 5/8	?	?
4/28/1929	284½	Franz Diener (1)	19-7-3	203	Leipzig, Sachsen, Germany	L DQ 1/10	?	?
5/22/1929	?	Moise Bouquillon (1)	25-5-0	195	Salle Wagram, Paris, France	W PTS 10/10	?	?
5/30/1929	265	Marcel Nilles	13-24-2	189	Cirque de Paris, Paris, France	W TKO 3/?	?	?
6/26/1929	265	Jack Humbeeck	36-31-12	220	Paris, France	W TKO 6/10	?	?
8/14/1929	275¼	Jose Lete	3-0-1	205¼	San Sebastian, Pais Vasco, Spain	W UD 10/10	?	?
8/25/1929	?	Joe Thomas (2)	1-2-0	189½	Prado, Marseilles, Bouches-du-Rhône, France	W TKO 4/10	?	?
8/30/1929	?	Feodor Nikolaeff	0-1-0	191	Dieppe, Seine-Maritime, France	W KO 1/?	?	?
9/18/1929	265	Hermann Jaspers	0-1-0	185	Salle Wagram, Paris, France	W KO 3/10	?	?
10/17/1929	?	Jack Stanley	10-17-3	200	Royal Albert Hall, Kensington, London, U.K Stanley down 3 times	W TKO 1/8; Time: 1:45	?	?
11/18/1929	263	Young Stribling (1)	227-12-15	188	Royal Albert Hall, Kensington, London, U.K.	W DQ 4/15	?	10,000
12/7/1929	273	Young Stribling (2)	227-13-15	184	Velodrome d'Hiver, Paris, France	L DQ 7/10	?	?
12/17/1929	284½	Franz Diener (2)	20-8-3	203	Royal Albert Hall, Kensington, London, U.K.	W TKO 6/15	?	?
1/24/1930	269	Clayton (Big Boy) Peterson (1)	49-27-8	209	Madison Square Garden, New York, U.S.A.	W KO 1/10	Arthur Donovan	18,500
1/31/1930	269	Elzear Rioux	29-14-4	210	Chicago Stadium, Chicago, Illinois, U.S.A. Judges: Lee Cook; W.A. Battyle	W KO 1/10; Time: 0:47	Dave Barry	17,500
2/6/1930	276	Cowboy Billy Owens	18-10-2	220	113th Infantry Regiment Armory, Newark, New Jersey, U.S.A.	W KO 2/10; Time: 2:22	Gene Roman	8,000
2/11/1930	270	Buster Martin	0-4-1	209	Arena, Saint Louis, Missouri, U.S.A.	W KO 2/10; Time: 0:56	Harry S. Sharpe	12,000
2/14/1930	267	Jim Sigmund	6-16-1	235	Memphis, Tennessee, U.S.A.	W KO 1/8; Time: 1:35	?	7,000
2/17/1930	284	Johnny Erickson	11-3-0	227	Coliseum, Oklahoma City, Oklahoma, U.S.A.	W KO 2/10; Time: 1:45	?	6,000
2/24/1930	275	Farmer Lodge	12-20-2	235	Heinemann Park, New Orleans, Louisiana, U.S.A.	W KO 2/10; Time: 1:22	?	?
3/3/1930	272	Roy (Ace) Clark	4-9-1	234½	Arena, Philadelphia, Pennsylvania, U.S.A.	W KO 6/10; Time: 2:38	Tommy Reilly	11,000

Ring Record

Date	Carnera's Weight	Opponent	Record	Weight	Location	Result	Referee	Attendance
3/11/1930	275	Sully Montgomery	38–31–1	220	Minneapolis, Minnesota, U.S.A.	W KO 2/10; Time: 1:15	?	14,000
3/17/1930	271	Chuck Wiggins	87–45–19	207	Arena, Saint Louis, Missouri, U.S.A.	W KO 2/10; Time: 1:00	Walter Heisner	25,000
3/20/1930	275	Frank Zaveta	1–7–0	235	Jacksonville, Florida, U.S.A.	W KO 1/10; Time: 1:51	?	"a few thousand"
3/26/1930	271½	George Trafton	4–0–0	229	Kansas City, Missouri, U.S.A.	W KO 1/10; Time: 0:54	?	8,000
3/28/1930	273	Jack McAuliffe	18–13–6	207½	Stockyards Stadium, Denver, Colorado, U.S.A.	W KO 1/10; Time: 2:18	Dan Darnell	6,500
4/8/1930	273	Neil Clisby	38–18–11	198½	Olympic Auditorium, Los Angeles, California, U.S.A.	W KO 2/10	Larry McGrath	12,000
4/14/1930	276	Leon Chevalier	18–9–4	216	Oaks Ballpark, Emeryville, California, U.S.A.	W TKO 6/10	Toby Irwin	10,000
4/22/1930	273	Sam Baker	9–9–1	246	Ice Coliseum, Portland, Oregon, U.S.A.	W KO 1/10	?	?
6/5/1930	265	K O Christner (1)	23–9–0	201	Fairgrounds Arena, Detroit, Michigan, U.S.A.	W KO 4/10; Time: 1:26	Slim McClelland	18,000
6/23/1930	262	George Godfrey	67–15–1	250	Baker Bowl, Philadelphia, Pennsylvania, U.S.A.	W DQ 5/10; Time: 1:13	Tommy Reilly	40,000
7/17/1930	263	Bearcat Wright	54–13–11	218	Omaha, Nebraska, U.S.A.	W KO 4/10	Miller of Chicago	?
7/29/1930	270	George Cook (1)	33–37–12	200½	Taylor Bowl, Cleveland, Ohio, U.S.A.	W KO 2/10	?	10,000
8/30/1930	263	Riccardo Bertazzolo	16–7–2	212	Atlantic City Auditorium, Atlantic City, New Jersey, U.S.A.	W TKO 3/15	Harry Ertle	10,500
9/8/1930	265	Pat McCarthy	45–27–6	214	Velodrome, Newark, New Jersey, U.S.A.	W KO 2/10; Time: 1:16	Hank Lewis	13,000
9/17/1930	267	Jack Gross (1)	42–3–1	200	Chicago Stadium, Chicago, Illinois, U.S.A.	W KO 4/10	?	10,000
10/7/1930	260	Jim Maloney (1)	44–10–2	195	Boston Garden, Boston, Massachusetts, U.S.A.	L PTS 10/10	?	12,000
11/30/1930	271¼	Paolino Uzcudun (1)	41–9–2	207	Montjuiche Stadium, Barcelona, Cataluña, Spain	W PTS 10/10	Moss Deyong	90,000
					Judges Juan Casanovas; Maggia			
12/18/1930	268	Reggie Meen	26–12–2	203	Royal Albert Hall, Kensington, London, U.K.	W TKO 2/15	Moss Deyong	10,000
3/5/1931	273	Jim Maloney (2)	45–11–2	199½	Madison Square Garden Stadium, Miami, Florida, U.S.A.	W PTS 10/10	Elmer (Slim) McClelland	20,000
6/15/1931	271¼	Pat Redmond	25–6–0	246	Ebbets Field, Brooklyn, New York, U.S.A.	W KO 1/10; Time: 2:24	Billy "The Kid" McPartland	25,000
6/26/1931	273	Umberto Torriani	1–11–2	215	Broadway Auditorium, Buffalo, New York, U.S.A.	W KO 2/10; Time: 0:43	?	?

Appendix I

Date	Carnera's Weight	Opponent	Record	Weight	Location	Result	Referee	Attendance
6/30/1931	273	Bud Gorman	46–17–11	223½	Arena Gardens, Toronto, Ontario, Canada	W KO 2/10; Time: 2:35	Lou Marsh	5,000
7/24/1931	274	Knute Hansen	18–10–1	205	Edgerton Park Arena, Rochester, New York, U.S.A. Hansen down 4 times Fight Judges: Joe Oca and Lew Smith	W KO 1/10; Time: 2:10	King Mahoney	5,000
8/4/1931	274	Roberto Roberti	32–12–7	228	Dreamland Park, Newark, New Jersey, U.S.A.	W TKO 3/10; Time: 2:25	Gene Roman	12,000
8/6/1931	272¼	Armando De Carolis	5–9–0	187	Shellpot Park, Wilmington, Delaware, U.S.A.	W KO 2/10; Time: 1:08	Joe Denny	?
10/12/1931	261	Jack Sharkey (1)	34–9–2	202	Ebbets Field, Brooklyn, New York, U.S.A. Judges: George Kelly and Charles Mathison	L PTS 15/15	Ed "Gunboat" Smith	30,000
11/19/1931	272½	King Levinsky (1)	39–14–4	194	Chicago Stadium, Chicago, Illinois, U.S.A.	W PTS 10/10	Ed Purdy	20,000
11/27/1931	266½	Victorio Campolo	17–5–1	224½	Madison Square Garden, New York, U.S.A.	W KO 2/15; Time: 1:27	Ed "Gunboat" Smith	12,000
1/25/1932	?	Moise Bouquillon (2)	32–11–0	195	Palais des Sports, Paris, France	W TKO 2/10	Rene Schemann	?
2/5/1932	?	Ernst Gühring	29–2–9	205	Sportpalast, Berlin, Germany	W TKO 5/10	?	"a large crowd"
2/29/1932	280	Pierre Charles	52–19–8	215	Palais des Sports, Paris, France	W PTS 10/10	Mr. Chavanne	?
3/23/1932	244 (?)	George Cook (2)	37–43–12	187	Royal Albert Hall, Kensington, London, U.K.	W KO 4/10	C.H. Douglas	?
4/7/1932	266	Don McCorkindale	14–5–3	182	Royal Albert Hall, Kensington, London, U.K.	W PTS 10/10	?	?
4/29/1932	266	Maurice Griselle	16–13–1	211	Palais des Sports, Paris, France	W TKO 10/10	?	?
5/15/1932	?	Hans Schonrath	15–10–4	206	San Siro Stadium, Milan, Lombardia, Italy	W TKO 3/10	?	20,000
5/30/1932	268	Larry Gains	72–12–4	200	White City Stadium, London, U.K.	L UD 10/10	Jack Hart	70,000
7/20/1932	268	Jack Gross (2)	46–7–1	206½	Ebbets Field, Brooklyn, New York, U.S.A.	W TKO 7/10; Time: 2:50	Arthur Donovan	5,000
7/28/1932	265	Jerry Pavelec	2–8–0	216	Playground Arena, West New York, New Jersey, U.S.A.	W TKO 5/10; Time: 0:51	Jim Manley	18,500
8/2/1932	264	Hans Birkie	21–15–2	202	Queensboro Arena, Long Island City, New York, U.S.A. Judges: Jim Buckley; Bob Cunningham	W PTS 10/10	Eddie Forbes	?
8/16/1932	264	Stanley Poreda	25–5–0	201½	Dreamland Park, Newark, New Jersey, U.S.A.	L PTS 10/10	Joe Mangold	15,000
8/19/1932	264	Jack Gagnon	32–26–1	219	Tiverton, Rhode Island, U.S.A.	W KO 1/10; Time: 1:35	?	5,000
9/1/1932	266	Art Lasky	14–1–0	188¾	Auditorium, Saint Paul, Minnesota, U.S.A.	W NWS 10/10	Mike Gibbons	4,000
10/7/1932	255	Ted Sandwina	48–24–6	207	Tampa, Florida, U.S.A.	W KO 4/10	?	2,500
10/13/1932	266	Gene Stanton	11–17–1	209	114th Reg. Armory, Camden, New Jersey, U.S.A.	W KO 6/10	?	?

Ring Record

Date	Carnera's Weight	Opponent	Record	Weight	Location	Result	Referee	Attendance
10/17/1932	262	Jack Taylor	20–29–9	212	Jefferson County Amory, Louisville, Kentucky, U.S.A.	W KO 2/10	Tommy Yum	1,433
11/4/1932	260	Les Kennedy	33–13–0	205	Arena, Boston, Massachusetts, U.S.A.	W KO 3/10	?	?
11/18/1932	270	Jose Santa	37–11–4	247	Madison Square Garden, New York, U.S.A.	W TKO 6/10	Jed Gahan	6,000
12/2/1932	262	John Schwake	12–3–2	231	St. Louis Coliseum, St. Louis, Missouri, U.S.A.	W KO 7/10	?	?
12/9/1932	261	King Levinsky (2)	43–19–4	197	Chicago Stadium, Chicago, Illinois, U.S.A.	W PTS 10/10	Ed Purdy	14,333
12/13/1932	262	Clayton (Big Boy) Peterson (2)	52–40–9	205	Grand Rapids, Michigan, U.S.A.	W TKO 2/10	?	?
12/15/1932	261	K O Christner (2)	45–31–3	203	Omaha, Nebraska, U.S.A.	W KO 4/10	Johnny Lee	1,500
12/19/1932	261	Joe Rice	4–2–0	195	North Side Coliseum, Fort Worth, Texas, U.S.A.	W KO 2/10	?	?
12/20/1932	262	James Merriott	3–1–0	213	City Auditorium, Galveston, Texas, U.S.A. Merriott reportedly 23–2 going into this bout	W KO 1/10	?	?
12/30/1932	261	Young Spence	11–8–1	190	Fair Park Auditorium, Dallas, Texas, U.S.A.	W KO 1/10	?	?
2/10/1933	250	Ernie Schaaf	59–13–2	207	Madison Square Garden, New York, U.S.A.	W KO 13/15	Billy Cavanaugh	20,000
6/29/1933	260½	Jack Sharkey (2)	36–9–2	201	Madison Square Garden Bowl, Long Island City, New York, U.S.A. NYSAC/National Boxing Association/World Heavyweight Title Judges: James Buckley; Charley Lynch	W KO 6/15; Time: 2:27	Arthur Donovan	40,000
8/11/1933	260	Harold Mays	38–15–1	210	The Arena, Syracuse, New York, U.S.A. Non-title fight	W UD 4/4	Jack Michaels	5,000
10/22/1933	259½	Paolino Uzcudun (2)	50–14–2	229¼	Piazza de Siena, Roma, Lazio, Italy World Heavyweight Title Judges: Juan Casanovas; Mazzia	W SD 15/15	Maurice Nicod	70,000
3/1/1934	270	Tommy Loughran	102–21–7	186	Madison Square Garden Stadium, Miami, Florida, U.S.A. NYSAC/National Boxing Association/World Heavyweight Title Judges: Colin S. "Red" McLaghlan; Roy Latham	W UD 15/15	Leo Shea	12,000
6/14/1934	263¼	Max Baer	39–7–0	209½	Madison Square Garden Bowl, Long Island City, New York, U.S.A. NYSAC/National Boxing Association/World Heavyweight Title Judges: Tommy Shawtell; Charley Lynch	L TKO 11/15; Time: 2:16	Arthur Donovan	56,000
12/1/1934	281	Victorio Campolo	21–7–1	259	Club Atletico Independiente, Avellaneda, Buenos Aires, Argentina	W PTS 12/12	?	30,000

224 Appendix I

Date	Carnera's Weight	Opponent	Record	Weight	Location	Result	Referee	Attendance
1/13/1935	?	Seal Harris	22–20–5	240	Arena Bella Floresta, Sao Paulo, Brazil	W KO 7/10	?	?
1/22/1935	264	Erwin Klausner	21–7–4	202	Fluminese Stadium, Rio de Janeiro, Brazil	W TKO 6/10	Luiz Souto	25,000
3/15/1935	268	Ray Impelletiere	6–3–0	258	Madison Square Garden, New York, U.S.A.	W TKO 9/10; Time: 0:38	Jack Dempsey	19,000
6/25/1935	260½	Joe Louis	22–0–0	196	Yankee Stadium, Bronx, New York, U.S.A. Judges: Charley Lynch; Tommy Shortell	L TKO 6/15; Time: 2:32	Arthur Donovan	60,000
11/1/1935	268	Walter Neusel	43–3–5	201	Madison Square Garden, New York, U.S.A. Judges: Bill Healy; Billy Joh	W TKO 4/10; Time: 2:23	Arthur Donovan	12,000
11/25/1935	267½	Ford Smith	27–13–7	209	Arena, Philadelphia, Pennsylvania, U.S.A.	W PTS 10/10	Toby Irwin	7,000
12/9/1935	269½	Big Boy Brackey	14–2–2	208	Broadway Auditorium, Buffalo, New York, U.S.A.	W TKO 4/10; Time: 1:06	Luke Carr	?
3/6/1936	268¼	Isidoro Gastanaga	35–20–1	208¼	Madison Square Garden, New York, U.S.A.	W KO 5/10	Arthur Donovan	9,500
3/16/1936	265	Leroy Haynes (1)	32–7–1	197½	Arena, Philadelphia, Pennsylvania, U.S.A.	L TKO 3/10	?	10,000
5/27/1936	265	Leroy Haynes (2)	34–7–1	200½	Ebbets Field, Brooklyn, New York, U.S.A.	L TKO 9/10; Time: 0:40	Arthur Donovan	23,000
11/18/1937	255¾	Albert DiMeglio	0–1–1	199	Salle Wagram, Paris, France	L PTS 10/10	?	3,000
12/4/1937	?	Joseph Zupan	0–1–0		Budapest Zirkus, Budapest, Hungary Zupan was a wrestler. Carnera knocked him out easily according to both *Box-Sport*, 14 December 1937, page 9, and *Sport Tagblatt* of Vienna. For some unknown reason the fight has sometimes been listed incorrectly in Carnera's record as a knockout loss.	W KO 2/10	?	?
7/22/1945	?	Michel Blevens	0–0–0		Moretti Stadium, Udine, Friuli-Venezia Giulia, Italy	W KO 3/4	?	?
9/25/1945	?	Sam Gardner	0–1–0		San Sabba Stadium, Trieste, Friuli-Venezia Giulia, Italy	W KO 1/4	?	12,000
11/21/1945	264	Luigi Musina (1)	29–4–4	184½	National Theatre, Milan, Lombardia, Italy Primo floored three times before the referee stopped the bout.	L KO 7/8	?	7,000
3/19/1946	?	Luigi Musina (2)	32–5–4	184½	Trieste, Friuli-Venezia Giulia, Italy	L PTS 8/8	?	"another large crowd"
5/12/1946	?	Luigi Musina (3)	34–5–4	184½	Gorizia, Friuli-Venezia Giulia, Italy	L UD 8/8	?	?

Appendix II: Undercards

Legend

DQ: Disqualification; the losing fighter was disqualified by the referee
Draw: Fight judged a draw, no winner
KO: Knockout
NC: Fight stopped by referee and ruled no contest
NWS: Newspaper Decision; a win on points awarded by the press
PTS: Win by Points
PTS UD: Win by Points with a Unanimous Decision
RTD: Fighter retired from the fight
TKO: Technical Knockout

Date	*Location*	*Winner*	*Opponent*	*Result*	*Round/ Scheduled*	*Attendance*
9/12/1928	Salle Wagram, Paris, France	**Primo Carnera**	Leon Sebilo	TKO	2 of 4	?
		Felix Sportiello	Arthur Vermaut	PTS	?	
9/25/1928	Cirque de Paris, Paris, France	Eugene Huat	Pierre Dussol	RTD	2 of 10	?
		Johnny Cuthbert	Antoine Ascencio	DQ	10 of 10	
		Primo Carnera	Joe Thomas (1)	KO	3 of 4	
		Aime Raphael	Paul Fritsch	PTS	?	
10/30/1928	Cirque de Paris, Paris, France	Andre Regis	Jean Gregoire	PTS	15 of 15	?
		Primo Carnera	Salvatore Ruggirello	TKO	4 of 10	
		Ted Sandwina	Luigi Buffi	KO	1 of 10	
11/25/1928	Pallazzo dello Sport, Milan, Lombardia, Italy	**Primo Carnera**	Epifanio Islas	PTS UD	10 of 10	?
		Cleto Locatelli	Paul Fritsch	PTS	10 of 10	
12/1/1928	Velodrome d'Hiver, Paris, France	Emile Pladner	Corporal Izzy Schwartz	PTS	12 of 12	?
		Ted Sandwina	Carl Carter	TKO	6 of 10	
		Primo Carnera	Constant Barrick	KO	3 of ?	
1/18/1929	Sportpalast, Berlin, Germany	Paul Noack	Robert Tassin	Draw	10 of 10	?
		Hein Domgorgen	Poldi Steinbach	Draw	8 of 8	
		Emil Scholz	Helmut Hartkopp	Draw	8 of 8	
		Primo Carnera	Ernst Rosemann	TKO	5 of 8	
		Jakob Domgoergen	Hans Schumacher	KO	4 of 8	
4/28/1929	Leipzig, Sachsen, Germany	Franz Diener (1)	Primo Carnera	DQ	1 of 10	?
		Hein Müller	Eddie Riches	KO	2 of 10	
		Hans Schonrath	Karl Walter	PTS	6 of 6	
		Moise Bouquillon	Ludwig Bach	KO	2 of ?	
5/22/1929	Salle Wagram, Paris, France	**Primo Carnera**	Moise Bouquillon (1)	PTS	10 of 10	?
5/30/1929	Cirque de Paris, Paris, France	Maurice Griselle	Knute Hansen	TKO	5 of 10	?
		Primo Carnera	Marcel Nilles	TKO	3 of ?	
6/26/1929	Paris, France	**Primo Carnera**	Jack Humbeeck	TKO	6 of 10	?
		Singer Thomas	Georges Brisset	KO	5 of ?	

Appendix II

Date	Location	Winner	Opponent	Round/Result	Scheduled	Attendance
8/14/1929	Atocha, San Sebastian, País Vasco, Spain	**Primo Carnera**	Jose Lete	PTS UD	10 of 10	?
		Ignacio Ara	Louis Vauclard	PTS	10 of 10	
		Fillo Julian Echevarria	Adorni	PTS	4 of 4	
		Ricardo Alis	Georges Brisset	KO	1 of ?	
		Antonio Horas	Juan Berasategui	PTS	?	
8/25/1929	Prado, Marseilles, Bouches-du-Rhône, France	**Primo Carnera**	Joe Thomas (2)	TKO	4 of 10	?
8/30/1929	Dieppe, Seine-Maritime, France	**Primo Carnera**	Feodor Nikolaeff	KO	1 of ?	?
9/18/1929	Salle Wagram, Paris, France	**Primo Carnera**	Hermann Jaspers	KO	3 of 10	?
10/17/1929	Royal Albert Hall, Kensington, London, U.K.	Frankie Genaro	Ernie Jarvis	PTS	15 of 15	?
		Johnny Cuthbert	Edouard Mascart	PTS	12 of 12	
		Primo Carnera	Jack Stanley	TKO	1 of 8	
		Jack Griffiths	Fred Green	PTS	6 of 6	
		Johnny Peters	Evan Lane	PTS	4 of 4	
11/18/1929	Royal Albert Hall, Kensington, London, U.K.	Primo Carnera	Young Stribling (1)	DQ	4 of 15	10,000
		Alf Mancini	Yvon Laffineur	Draw	12 of 12	
12/7/1929	Velodrome d'Hiver, Paris, France	Young Stribling (2)	Primo Carnera	DQ	7 of 10	?
		Bob Carvill	Joe Thomas	KO	2 of 10	
		Jose Santa	Robert Villard	KO	?	
12/17/1929	Royal Albert Hall, Kensington, London, U.K.	Primo Carnera	Franz Diener (2)	TKO	6 of 15	?
		Maurice Griselle	Bob Carvill	TKO	3 of 10	
		Dick Power	Marine Bill Trinder	Draw	6 of 6	
		Jose Santa	Jack Stanley	Draw	10 of 10	
		Bobby Shields	Jack Maurer	PTS	6 of 6	
1/24/1930	Madison Square Garden, New York, U.S.A.	Larry Johnson	Fred Lenhart	KO	7 of 10	18,500
		Add Warren	Buck Weaver	PTS	10 of 10	
		Primo Carnera	Clayton 'Big Boy' Peterson (1)	KO	1 of 10	
		Dick Gibbons	Bill Duggan	TKO	6 of 6	
		Tom DeStefano	Abe Lipschitz	DQ	3 of 4	
1/31/1930	Chicago Stadium, Chicago, Illinois, U.S.A.	Primo Carnera	Elzear Rioux	KO	1 of 10	17,500
		King Tut	Bruce Flowers	PTS	10 of 10	
		Ray McIntyre	Mickey Gill	PTS	6 of 6	
		King Levinsky	Jack Barry	PTS	6 of 6	
2/6/1930	113th Infantry Regiment Armory, Newark, New Jersey, U.S.A.	Primo Carnera	Cowboy Billy Owens	KO	2 of 10	8,000
		Buck Weaver	Jack Shaw	TKO	4 of 8	
		Charlie Rosen	Yvan Laffineur	TKO	8 of ?	
		Jean Boireau	Jack Pelecos	TKO	3 of ?	
2/11/1930	Arena, Saint Louis, Missouri, U.S.A.	Primo Carnera	Buster Martin	KO	2 of 10	12,000
		King Tut	Russie LeRoy	KO	1 of 10	
		Al Stillman	King Levinsky	NWS	5 of 5	
		John Schwake	Buck Weaver	KO	4 of 5	
		Chuck Heffner	Patsy Pollock	NWS	5 of 5	
		Lou Terry	Jean Boireau	NWS	5 of 5	
2/14/1930	Memphis, Tennessee, U.S.A.	Primo Carnera	Jim Sigmund	KO	1 of 8	7,000
		Jack League	Paul Cannon	KO	2 of ?	
2/17/1930	Coliseum, Oklahoma City, Oklahoma, U.S.A.	Primo Carnera	Johnny Erickson	KO	2 of 10	6,000
		Buck Weaver	Telden Stulz	Draw	8 of 8	
		Ralph Abel	Wild Bill Cox	PTS	6 of 6	
		Dickey Dillman	Lester Allen	PTS	4 of 4	
		Jean Bordeux	Buck Stewart	KO	2 of ?	
2/24/1930	Heinemann Park, New Orleans, Louisiana, U.S.A.	Primo Carnera	Farmer Lodge	KO	2 of 10	?
		Matt Brock	Vic McCormick	PTS	6 of 6	
		Jean Boireau	Joe Roman	PTS	6 of 6	
		Pomp Romero	Roy Calamari	PTS	6 of 6	
		Erwin Berlier	Ray Cullotta	PTS	6 of 6	

Undercards

Date	Location	Winner	Opponent	Round/Result	Scheduled	Attendance
		Dummy Martin	Eddie Walters	PTS	4 of 4	
		Patsy Flanagan	Baby Manila	PTS	4 of 4	
3/3/1930	Arena, Philadelphia, Pennsylvania, U.S.A.	Primo Carnera	Roy (Ace) Clark	KO	6 of 10	11,000
		Yvan Laffineur	Eddie Dempsey	PTS	6 of 6	
		Leon Lucas	Peggy Sullivan	KO	2 of 6	
		Leonard Dixon	Buck Weaver	PTS	6 of 6	
		Jean Boireau	Calvin Reed	PTS	6 of 6	
		Willie Henry	Johnny Alberts	KO	3 of 6	
3/11/1930	Minneapolis, Minnesota, U.S.A.	Primo Carnera	Sully Montgomery	KO	2 of 10	14,000
		Paul Wangley	Bobby Laurent	KO	1 of 6	
		Jackie Sharkey	Glen Kid Lehr	NWS	6 of 6	
		Andy Shanks	Tim Derry	KO	4 of ?	
3/17/1930	Arena, Saint Louis, Missouri, U.S.A.	Primo Carnera	Chuck Wiggins	KO	2 of 10	25,000
		Chuck Heffner	Tiger Johnny Cline	NWS	10 of 10	
		Barney Ross	Jackie Davis	NWS	5 of 5	
		Jackie Horner	Yvan Laffineur	Draw	5 of 5	
		Jackie Purvis	Hershie Wilson	Draw	5 of 5	
		Dave Knost	John Schwake	Draw	5 of 5	
		Walter Madey	Sgt Jack Adams	KO	1 of 5	
3/20/1930	Jacksonville, Florida, U.S.A.	Primo Carnera	Frank Zaveta	KO	1 of 10	"a few thousand"
		Jean Borreau	Billy Temmes	KO	2 of ?	
		Frank Montagna	Joe Smith	KO	1 of ?	
3/26/1930	Kansas City, Missouri, U.S.A.	Primo Carnera	George Trafton	KO	1 of 10	8,000
		Young Jack Dillon	Sammy DiSalvo	NWS	10 of 10	
		Meyer Grace	Yvan Laffineur	TKO	6 of ?	
3/28/1930	Stockyards Stadium, Denver, Colorado, U.S.A.	Primo Carnera	Jack McAuliffe	KO	1 of 10	6,500
4/8/1930	Olympic Auditorium, Los Angeles, California, U.S.A.	Primo Carnera	Neil Clisby	KO	2 of 10	12,000
		Oscar Rankin	Guy Salerno	PTS	6 of 6	
		Jimmy Hanna	Wally Fraser	PTS	6 of 6	
		Steve Hayden	Tony Randolph	TKO	5 of 6	
		Henry Rollins	Ora Smith	PTS	4 of 4	
4/14/1930	Oaks Ballpark, Emeryville, California, U.S.A.	Primo Carnera	Leon Chevalier	TKO	6 of 10	10,000
		Wesley "Red" Millett	Revelle Barnes	PTS	?	
		Red Williams	Johnny Morris	PTS	?	
		Joe 'Doc' Limas	Jean Borreau	PTS	?	
		Paul Drake	Bob Jenkins	PTS	?	
		Racehorse Roberts	Tony Clawson	PTS	?	
4/22/1930	Ice Coliseum, Portland, Oregon, U.S.A.	Primo Carnera	Sam Baker	KO	1 of 10	?
		Mickey Dolan	Frankie Monroe	PTS	6 of 6	
		Battling Slim Ryan	Tom Moore	PTS	6 of 6	
		Al Straub	Pat Davenport	PTS	4 of 4	
		Jimmy Dolan	Brownie Buskirk	TKO	3 of ?	
		Indian Jack Crim	Ray McQuillan	DQ	2 of ?	
6/5/1930	Fairgrounds Arena, Detroit, Michigan, U.S.A.	Primo Carnera	K O Christner (1)	KO	4 of 10	18,000
		Frankie Simms	Bennie Touchstone	Draw	8 of 8	
		Jack Silvers	George Wilson	PTS	6 of 6	
		Tony Powell	Jack Lewis	KO	2 of 4	
		Jack Redman	Larry Creighton	KO	2 of 6	
		Dan Gasparo	Al Cohen	KO	1 of 4	
		Charley Retzlaff	Tom Sayers	KO	1 of 4	
6/23/1930	Baker Bowl, Philadelphia, Pennsylvania, U.S.A.	Primo Carnera	George Godfrey	DQ	5 of 10	40,000
		Jack Gross	Mike Sankovitch	PTS	6 of 6	
		Billy Angelo	Shuffle Callahan	TKO	1 of 6	
		Billy Jones	Jack Silver	KO	4 of 6	
		Gene Moretti	Tony Tedesco	PTS	6 of 6	
		Al Walker	Leonard Dixon	PTS	6 of 6	
7/17/1930	Omaha, Nebraska, U.S.A.	Primo Carnera	Bearcat Wright	KO	4 of 10	?
7/29/1930	Taylor Bowl, Cleveland, Ohio, U.S.A.	Primo Carnera	George Cook (1)	KO	2 of 10	10,000
		Joe Zeeman	Lou Nickolette	PTS	4 of 4	
8/30/1930	Atlantic City Auditorium,	Primo Carnera	Riccardo Bertazzolo	TKO	3 of 15	10,500

Appendix II

Date	Location	Winner	Opponent	Round/Result	Scheduled	Attendance
	Atlantic City, New Jersey, U.S.A.	Gene Moretti	Billy Murphy	KO	3 of 6	
9/8/1930	Velodrome, Newark, New Jersey, U.S.A.	Primo Carnera	Pat McCarthy	KO	2 of 10	13,000
		Cowboy Frank Willis	Borack Czirolnik	TKO	5 of 8	
		Al Walker	George Smith	KO	5 of 8	
		George Rosselli	Johnny Petrullo	KO	1 of 6	
		Jack Marion	Gene McCue	KO	1 of 6	
9/17/1930	Chicago Stadium, Chicago, Illinois, U.S.A.	Dick Daniels	Al Fay	PTS	10 of 10	10,000
		Primo Carnera	Jack Gross (1)	KO	4 of 10	
		Johnny Indrisano	Tommy Rios	PTS	8 of 8	
		Paul Pantaleo	Pete Wistort	PTS	5 of 5	
10/7/1930	Boston Garden, Boston, Massachusetts, U.S.A.	Jim Maloney (1)	Primo Carnera	PTS	10 of 10	12,000
		Jack Dorval	George Cook	TKO	7 of 10	
		Jimmy Mendes	Roy Moore	TKO	5 of 10	
		Tommy Rawson Jr.	Baby Jack Renault	PTS	6 of 6	
		Joey Mack	Johnny Delano	PTS	6 of 6	
11/30/1930	Montjuiche Stadium, Barcelona, Cataluña, Spain	Primo Carnera	Paolino Uzcudun (1)	PTS	10 of 10	90,000
		Carlos Flix	Kid Socks	PTS	10 of 10	
		Jose Girones	Jack Kirby	KO	4 of 10	
12/18/1930	Royal Albert Hall, Kensington, London, U.K.	Primo Carnera	Reggie Meen	TKO	2 of 15	10,000
		Jack Pettifer	Dick Power	PTS	12 of 12	
3/5/1931	Madison Square Garden Stadium, Miami, Florida, U.S.A.	Jim Braddock	Jack Roper	KO	1 of 6	20,000
		Primo Carnera	Jim Maloney (2)	PTS	10 of 10	
		Maxie Rosenbloom	Marty Gallagher	PTS	8 of 8	
		Jack Dorval	Prince Salah el Din	PTS	6 of 6	
		Walter Cobb	Ralph Ficucello	PTS	6 of 6	
		Joe O'Donnell	Harry Paul	PTS	4 of 4	
6/15/1931	Ebbets Field, Brooklyn, New York, U.S.A.	Primo Carnera	Pat Redmond	KO	1 of 10	25,000
		Harold Mays	Jack Renault	PTS	6 0f 10	
		Ted Sandwina	Tom Kirby	PTS	8 0f 10	
		Ernie Schaaf	Jack Gagnon	KO	1 of 10	
6/26/1931	Broadway Auditorium, Buffalo, New York, U.S.A.	Primo Carnera	Umberto Torriani	KO	2 of 10	?
		Eddie Ran	Meyer Lichtenstein	KO	5 of 6	
		Joe Doctor	Tom Kirby	PTS	6 of 6	
		Frankie Linhardt	George Parker	PTS	6 of 6	
		Perry Lacey	Johnny Doolin	PTS	4 of 4	
		Pietro Georgi	Al Jaderberg	TKO	3 of ?	
6/30/1931	Arena Gardens, Toronto, Ontario, Canada	Primo Carnera	Bud Gorman	KO	2 of 10	5,000
		Jackie Johnston	Raymond Lirzin	PTS	6 of 6	
		Jimmy Darcy	Maxie Brown	PTS	6 of 6	
		Eddie Judge	Knute Christner	PTS	6 of 6	
		Paul Hansen	Elmer Hebner	PTS	4 of 4	
7/24/1931	Edgerton Park Arena, Rochester, New York, U.S.A.	Primo Carnera	Knute Hansen	KO	1 of 10	5,000
		Mickey Gelb	Joe Marciente	TKO	6 of 8	
		Jimmy Darcy	Joe Lillich	KO	4 of 6	
		George Parker	Frank Polito	TKO	4	
		Johnny Doolin	Bobby Cleary	PTS	1	
8/4/1931	Dreamland Park, Newark, New Jersey, U.S.A.	Primo Carnera	Roberto Roberti	TKO	3 of 10	12,000
		Al Rossi	Lou Halper	PTS	8 of 8	
		Salvatore Red Affinito	Johnny Carlo	KO	2 of 6	
		Bobby Mess	Stanley Siernos	KO	3 of 6	
		Joey Woods	Eddie Dries	KO	4 of 4	
		Joe Ross	Al Kronick	KO	1 of 4	
8/6/1931	Shellpot Park, Wilmington, Delaware, U.S.A.	Primo Carnera	Armando De Carolis	KO	2 of 10	?
		Morris Gross	Spike Hemlock	PTS	4 of 4	
		Paulie Brown	Martin Lechwar	TKO	? Of 4	
		Blackie Marks	Georgie Roberts	PTS	4 of 4	

Undercards

Date	Location	Winner	Opponent	Round/Result	Scheduled	Attendance
		Harry Serody	Johnny Maher	DQ	1 of 4	
10/12/1931	Ebbets Field, Brooklyn, New York, U.S.A.	Jack Sharkey (1)	Primo Carnera	PTS	15 of 15	30,000
		Pete Suskey	Sergeant Sammy Baker	PTS	5 of 5	
10/12/1931	Ebbets Field, Brooklyn, New York, U.S.A.	Walter Cobb	Jack Rose	KO	1 of 5	
		Yale Okun	Don Petrin	PTS	5 of 5	
		Jack Poliseo	Presidio Pavesi	PTS	5 of 5	
		Jack McCarthy	Pietro Corri	Draw	5 of 5	
11/19/1931	Chicago Stadium, Chicago, Illinois, U.S.A.	Primo Carnera	King Levinsky (1)	PTS	10 of 10	?
		Battling Battalino	Bushy Graham	KO	1 of 10	
		Paulie Walker	Tommy Rios	PTS	8 of 8	
		Frank Battaglia	Young Johnny Burns	KO	1 of 8	
		Mickey O'Neill	Kelly Kulac	PTS	4 of 4	
11/27/1931	Madison Square Garden, New York, U.S.A.	Primo Carnera	Victorio Campolo	KO	2 of 15	12,000
		Stanley Poreda	Ralph Ficucello	TKO	7 of 8	
		Walter Cobb	Ted Sandwina	KO	2 of 8	
		Steve Hamas	Hans Birkie	PTS	8 of 8	
1/25/1932	Palais des Sports, Paris, France	Primo Carnera	Moise Bouquillon (2)	TKO	2 of 10	?
		Georges Gardebois	Ernesto Baggiani	KO	7 of ?	
		Maurice Griselle	Johannes van Vliet	KO	4 of ?	
2/5/1932	Sportpalast, Schoeneberg, Berlin, Germany	Primo Carnera	Ernst Güehring	TKO	5 of 10	"a large crowd"
		Helmut Hartkopp	Josef Hampacher	PTS	10 of 10	
		Franz Duebbers	Alex Sandor	PTS	8 of 8	
		Clemente Meroni	? Anckmann	PTS	8 of 8	
		Vincenz Hower	? Stoertebecker	KO	2 of ?	
2/29/1932	Palais des Sports, Paris, France	Primo Carnera	Pierre Charles	PTS	10 of 10	?
		Walter Neusel	Soren Petersen	KO	5 of 10	
		Innocente Baiguera	Marcel Moret	KO	4 of ?	
		Hans Baumann	Raymond Lepage	KO	1 of ?	
		Arthur Meurant	Salvatore Zaetta	PTS	?	
		Luigi Sciutto	Marcot	Draw	?	
		Italo Colonello	Luigi Tiramini	KO	1 of ?	
3/23/1932	Royal Albert Hall, Kensington, London, U.K.	Walter Neusel	Bobby Shields	KO	3 of 12	?
		Primo Carnera	George Cook (2)	KO	4 of 10	
		Ivor Malcolm	Jim Wilde	TKO	7 0f 8	
		Wally Hutchins	Ted Kendall	PTS	6 of 6	
		Eddie Robinson	Edwin John	PTS	6 of 6	
		Fred Chandler	Peter Price	TKO	4 of 6	
4/7/1932	Royal Albert Hall, Kensington, London, U.K.	Walter Neusel	Gunner Mick Bennett	KO	1 of 12	?
		Primo Carnera	Don McCorkindale	PTS	10 of 10	
		Jack O'Malley	Jack Mansfield	PTS	8 of 8	
		Jack Pettifer	Jack Murphy	TKO	3 of 8	
		George Daly	Tommy Kirkland	PTS	6 of 6	
		Ivor Malcolm	Jeff Wilson	PTS	6 of 6	
4/29/1932	Palais des Sports, Paris, France	Primo Carnera	Maurice Griselle	TKO	10 of 10	?
		Cleto Locatelli	Gustave Humery	KO	2 of ?	
		Italo Colonello	? Vander	KO	1 of ?	
		Karl Beneck	Peter Kusak	Draw	?	
5/15/1932	San Siro Stadium, Milan, Lombardia, Italy	Primo Carnera	Hans Schonrath	TKO	3 of 10	20,000
5/30/1932	White City Stadium, London, U.K.	Don McCorkindale	Maurice Griselle	TKO	3 of 12	70,000
		Larry Gains	Primo Carnera	PTS UD	10 of 10	
		Walter Neusel	Willie Snowy Unwin	PTS	6 of 6	
		Billy Bird	Arthur Unwin	KO	1 of ?	
		Kid Farlo	Peter Nolan	KO	4 of ?	
7/20/1932	Ebbets Field, Brooklyn,	Primo Carnera	Jack Gross (2)	TKO	7 of 10	5,000

Date	Location	Winner	Opponent	Round/Result	Scheduled	Attendance
	New York, U.S.A.	Bob Olin	Muggs Kerr	PTS	8 of 8	
		Jack Redman	Eddie Benson	TKO	7 of 8	
		Jerry Pavelec	Artie Suess	KO	2 of 8	
		Marco Appicello	Billy Tosk	PTS	4 of 4	
7/28/1932	Playground Arena, West New York, New Jersey, U.S.A	Primo Carnera	Jerry Pavelec	TKO	5 of 10	18,500
		Tony Galento	Charley Boyette	TKO	4 of 10	
		Jack Redman	Pietro Corri	PTS	10 of 10	
		Walter Cobb	Gene Stanton	NC	2 of 10	
8/2/1932	Queensboro Arena, Long Island City, New York, U.S.A.	Primo Carnera	Hans Birkie	PTS	10 of 10	?
		Andy Mitchell	Jimmy Tarante	PTS	10 of 10	
		Yustin Sirutis	Eddie Malcolm	PTS	6 of 6	
		Eddie Mader	Charley Massera	PTS	6 of 6	
		Tony Brescia	Joe Valenti	KO	2 of 6	
8/16/1932	Dreamland Park, Newark, New Jersey, U.S.A.	Stanley Poreda	Primo Carnera *	PTS	10 of 10	15,000
		Maxie Fisher	Skeets Dundee	PTS	6 of 6	
		Joe Longo	Al Reid	PTS	4 of 4	
		Joe Ardito	Jake Giordano	PTS	4 of 4	
		Steve Cheloc	Lester Miller	PTS	4 of 4	
		Walter Cobb	Chester Matan	KO	5 of 6	
8/19/1932	Tiverton, Rhode Island, U.S.A.	Primo Carnera	Jack Gagnon	KO	1 of 10	5,000
9/1/1932	Auditorium, Saint Paul, Minnesota, U.S.A.	Primo Carnera	Art Lasky	NWS	10 of 10	4,000
		Buck Everett	Larry Udell	PTS	8 of 8	
10/7/1932	Tampa, Florida, U.S.A.	Primo Carnera	Ted Sandwina	KO	4 of 10	?
10/13/1932	114th Reg. Armory, Camden, New Jersey, U.S.A.	Primo Carnera	Gene Stanton	KO	6 of 10	?
		Jack Kilbourne	Jack Mackaway	PTS	8 of 8	
		Billy Hendrie	Buddy Pierce	KO	4 of 6	
		Costas Vassis	Joe O'Neill	PTS	6 of 6	
		Elmer Bezenah	Patsy Carlo	TKO	2 of 6	
10/17/1932	Jefferson County Armory, Louisville, Kentucky, U.S.A.	Primo Carnera	Jack Taylor	KO	2 of 10	1,433
		Tim Charles	Pat Kenney	PTS	8 of 8	
		Art Schultz	Al Hamilton	PTS	8 of 8	
		Bill Shirley	Donald Fagg	Draw	8 of 8	
		Zeke Lucas	Harley Costner	PTS	6 of 6	
11/4/1932	Arena, Boston, Massachusetts, U.S.A.	Primo Carnera	Les Kennedy	KO	3 of 10	?
		Walter Cobb	Tiger Henderson	PTS	10 of 10	
		Bud Mignault	Elmer Chase	TKO	6 of 6	
		Obie Walker	Frankie Simms	PTS	6 of 6	
		Steve Carr	Eddie Mandell	PTS	4 of 4	
11/18/1932	Madison Square Garden, New York, U.S.A.	Primo Carnera	Jose Santa	TKO	6 of 10	6,000
		Walter Cobb	Jack Dorval	PTS	6 of 6	
		Tony Shucco	Arthur Huttick	PTS	6 of 6	
		Bob Olin	Tommy Walsh	PTS	6 of 6	
		Charley Massera	Juanito Olaquibel	PTS	6 of 6	
		Andy Mitchell	Yale Okun	TKO	4 of ?	
12/2/1932	St. Louis Coliseum, St. Louis, Missouri, U.S.A.	Primo Carnera	John Schwake	KO	7 of 10	?
		Allen Matthews	Indian Benny Deathpaine	PTS	6 of 6	
		Les Schulte	Sgt Jack Adams	KO	4 of 6	
		Buster Newberry	Frank Stolsek	PTS	6 of 6	
		Nick Broglio	Joe Huff	Draw	6 of 6	
		Eddie Edson	George Daw	PTS	6 of 6	
12/9/1932	Chicago Stadium, Chicago, Illinois, U.S.A.	Primo Carnera	King Levinsky (2)	PTS	10 of 10	14,333
		Young Terry	Young Stuhley	PTS	8 of 8	
		Martin Levandowski	Harold Scarney	TKO	3 of 8	
		Tony Cancela	Les Marriner	PTS	6 of 6	
		Texas Moore	Tommy Davenport	PTS	6 of 6	
		Jack Moran	Ray Tramblie	PTS	4 of 4	
12/13/1932	Grand Rapids, Michigan, U.S.A.	Primo Carnera	Clayton (Big Boy) Peterson (2)	TKO	2 of 10	?
12/15/1932	Omaha, Nebraska, U.S.A.	Primo Carnera	K O Christner (2)	KO	4 of 10	1,500
		Sonny Sofio	Buzz Smith	PTS	8 of 8	

Undercards

Date	Location	Winner	Opponent	Round/Result	Scheduled	Attendance
		Happy Jack Spurgin	Big Boy Sullivan	KO	1 of 6	
		Jimmy Wooten	Canada Lee	PTS	6 of 6	
		Ray McMillan	Kid McCaffrey	PTS	6 of 6	
12/19/1932	North Side Coliseum, Fort Worth, Texas, U.S.A.	Primo Carnera	Joe Rice	KO	2 of 10	?
12/20/1932	City Auditorium, Galveston, Texas, U.S.A.	Primo Carnera	James Merriott	KO	1 of 10	?
		Bobby Pitts	Del Hawkins	PTS	8 of 8	
12/20/1932	City Auditorium, Galveston, Texas, U.S.A.	Paul Gritta	Young Sessoms	PTS	8 of 8	
		Chuck Oliver	James Smith	KO	3 of 8	
12/30/1932	Fair Park Auditorium, Dallas, Texas, U.S.A.	Primo Carnera	Young Spence	KO	1 of 10	?
		Kid Granite	Bobby Fernandez	PTS	6 of 6	
		Frenchy LeFevre	Frankie Burke	KO	2 of 6	
		Bobby O'Dowd	Joe Montana	Draw	6 of 6	
2/10/1933	Madison Square Garden, New York, U.S.A.	Primo Carnera	Ernie Schaaf	KO	13 of 15	20,000
		Adolf Heuser	Harry Ebbets	PTS	10 of 10	
		Lou Barba	Marty Fox	KO	2 of 5	
		Bob Moody	Pietro Corri	PTS	5 of 5	
		Eddie Malcolm	Lou Poster	Draw	4 of 4	
6/29/1933	Madison Square Garden Bowl, Long Island City, New York, U.S.A.	Primo Carnera	Jack Sharkey (2)	KO	6 of 15	40,000
		Tony Shucco	Al Stillman	PTS	6 of 6	
		Chester Matan	Innocente Baiguera	PTS UD	5 of 5	
		Bob Moody	Harold Mays	PTS	5 of 5	
		Frankie Edgren	Hans Birkie	PTS	5 of 5	
		Arthur Huttick	Vic Bernard	KO	1 of 5	
		Leonard Del Genio	Phil Bruno	TKO	3 of 4	
8/11/1933	The Arena, Syracuse, New York, U.S.A.	Primo Carnera	Harold Mays	PTS UD	4 of 4	5,000
		Joey Brown	My Boy Lathron	KO	2 of 6	
		Matty Mathewson	Willie Dorenzo	PTS	6 of 6	
		Mickey Serrian	Mickey Coogan	KO	2 of 4	
10/22/1933	Piazza de Siena, Roma, Lazio, Italy	Vittorio Venturi	Michele Palermo	PTS	15 of 15	70,000
		Primo Carnera	Paolino Uzcudun (2)	PTS	15 of 15	
		Cleto Locatelli	Francois Sybille	PTS	15 of 15	
		Vittorio Tamagnini	Tommy Rogers	PTS	6 of 6	
		Arthur Huttick	Armando De Carolis	PTS	4 of 4	
		Harold Mays	Raul Bianchi	KO	1 of 4	
3/1/1934	Madison Square Garden Stadium, Miami, Florida, U.S.A.	Primo Carnera	Tommy Loughran	PTS UD	15 of 15	12,000
		Eddie Hogan	Jack Pettifer	PTS	4 of 4	
		Tony Cancela	Merrill 'Red' Tonn	TKO	4 of 4	
		Johnny Miler	Al White	PTS	4 of 4	
		Chester Matan	George Neron	PTS	4 of 4	
		Jackie Reid	Joe King	PTS	4 of 4	
		Buck Everett	Eddie Houghton	PTS	4 of 4	
6/14/1934	Madison Square Garden Bowl, Long Island City, New York, U.S.A.	Max Baer	Primo Carnera	TKO	11 of 15	56,000
		Charley Massera	Al Ettore	PTS	6 of 6	
		Eddie Hogan	Chester Matan	PTS	5 of 5	
		Lou Poster	Al White	PTS	5 of 5	
		Dynamite Jackson	Willie McGee	PTS	5 of 5	
		Jim Braddock	Corn Griffin	TKO	3 of 5	
		Don Petrin	Eddie Karolak	PTS	4 of 4	
12/1/1934	Club Atletico Independiente, Avellaneda, Buenos Aires, Argentina	Primo Carnera	Victorio Campolo	PTS	12 of 12	30,000
		Seal Harris	Justo Prieto	PTS	8 of 8	
1/13/1935	Arena Bella Floresta, Sao Paulo, Brazil	Primo Carnera	Seal Harris	KO	7 of 10	?
1/22/1935	Fluminese Stadium, Rio de Janeiro, Brazil	Primo Carnera	Erwin Klausner	TKO	6 of 10	25,000
3/15/1935	Madison Square Garden, New York, U.S.A.	Primo Carnera	Ray Impelletiere	TKO	9 of 10	19,000
		Abe Feldman	Steve Dudas	PTS	8 of 8	

Appendix II

Date	Location	Winner	Opponent	Round/Result	Scheduled	Attendance
		Eddie Hogan	Joe Uzdavinis	PTS	6 of 6	
		Melio Bettina	Jimmy Varrelli	PTS	6 of 6	
		Ralph Ficucello	Al Boros	PTS	6 of 6	
		Eddie Mader	Norman Barnett	PTS	4 of 4	
6/25/1935	Yankee Stadium, Bronx, New York, U.S.A.	Joe Louis	Primo Carnera	TKO	6 of 15	60,000
		Buddy Baer	Frank Wotanski	KO	1 of 6	
		Abe Simon	Chris Karchi	TKO	1 of 4	
		Red Burman	Joe Kaminski	PTS	4 of 4	
		Eddie Mader	Eddie Houghton	PTS	4 of 4	
6/25/1935	Yankee Stadium, Bronx, New York, U.S.A.	Jorge Brescia	Andy Wallace	KO	2 of 4	
		Nathan Mann	Al Zappala	KO	3 of 4	
		Ralph Vona	Joey Haas	PTS	4 of 4	
		Hans Kohlhaas	Billy Juliano	KO	2 of 4	
11/1/1935	Madison Square Garden, New York, U.S.A.	Primo Carnera	Walter Neusel	TKO	4 of 10	12,000
		George Turner	James Merriott	PTS	6 of 6	
		Eddie Mader	Tony Galento	PTS	6 of 6	
		Jorge Brescia	Hans Kohlhaas	PTS	6 of 6	
		Bob Pastor	Max Marek	PTS	6 of 6	
		Frank Connolly	Jerry Pavelec	TKO	3 of 6	
		Joe Lipps	Jack Corrigan	KO	1 of 4	
11/25/1935	Arena, Philadelphia, Pennsylvania, U.S.A.	Primo Carnera	Ford Smith	PTS UD	10 of 10	7,000
		Jorge Brescia	James Merriott	KO	5 of 6	
		Lew Raymond	Alvaro de Silva	PTS	6 of 6	
		Johnny Hutchinson	Norman Rahn	PTS	6 of 6	
		Wicky Harkins	Vincent Reed	PTS	6 of 6	
12/9/1935	Broadway Auditorium, Buffalo, New York, U.S.A.	Primo Carnera	Big Boy Brackey	TKO	4 of 10	?
		Mickey Devine	Tommy Howells	PTS	10 of 10	
		Frankie Eagan	Eddie Dempsey	PTS	6 of 6	
		Carl Menza	Joe Napoleon	PTS	4 of 4	
		Tony Paul	Norman Cordaro	TKO	3 of ?	
		Tommy O'Brien	Evans Smith	TKO	4 of ?	
3/6/1936	Madison Square Garden, New York, U.S.A.	Primo Carnera	Isidoro Gastanaga	KO	5 of 10	9,500
		Rafael Hurtado	Leonard Del Genio	PTS	10 of 10	
		Freddie Fiducia	Al White	PTS	6 of 6	
		Chester Palutis	Humberto Curi	PTS	6 of 6	
		Pete DeRuzza	Willie Pal	Draw	6 of 6	
		Lou Nova	Jerry Johnsen	TKO	3 of 4	
3/16/1936	Arena, Philadelphia, Pennsylvania, U.S.A.	Leroy Haynes (1)	Primo Carnera	TKO	3 of 10	10,000
		Jersey Joe Walcott	Willie Reddish	PTS	8 of 8	
		Tom Henry	Humberto Curi	PTS	6 of 6	
		Paul Hoft	Vic Smith	KO	2 of 6	
		Lou Berg	Ed Pinsky	KO	2 of 6	
5/27/1936	Ebbets Field, Brooklyn, New York, U.S.A.	Leroy Haynes (2)	Primo Carnera	TKO	9 of 10	23,000
		Abe Feldman	Ralph Barbara	TKO	5 of 8	
		Steve Dudas	Isidoro Gastanaga	TKO	3 of 6	
		Abe Simon	Lou Berg	KO	3 of 6	
		Sandy McDonald	Al Demedowitz	KO	6 of 6	
		Sol Flaum	Frank Gregor	KO	1 of 4	
11/18/1937	Salle Wagram, Paris, France	Albert DiMeglio	Primo Carnera	PTS	10 of 10	3,000
12/4/1937	Budapest Zirkus, Budapest, Hungary	Primo Carnera	Joseph Zupan	KO	2 of 10	?
		Karl Putz	Bela Gardos	PTS	8 of 8	
		Sandor Korosi	Laszlo Pozsonyi	KO	8 of 8	
7/22/1945	Moretti Stadium, Udine, Friuli-Venezia Giulia, Italy	Primo Carnera	Michel Blevens	KO	3 of 4	?
9/25/1945	San Sabba Stadium, Trieste, Friuli-Venezia Giulia, Italy	Primo Carnera	Sam Gardner	KO	1 of 4	12,000
11/21/1945	National Theatre, Milan, Lombardia, Italy	Luigi Musina (1)	Primo Carnera	KO	7 of 8	7,000
3/19/1946	Trieste, Friuli-Venezia Giulia, Italy	Luigi Musina (2)	Primo Carnera	PTS	8 of 8	"another large crowd"

Undercards

Date Attendance	Location	Winner	Opponent	Round/ Result	Scheduled	
5/12/1946	Gorizia, Friuli-Venezia Giulia, Italy	Luigi Musina (3) Gino Bondavalli	Primo Carnera Ulderico Sergo	PTS UD Draw	8 of 8 8 of 8	?

Chapter Notes

Introduction

1. Joseph de Beauchamp, "Number One Primo Carnera," *Boxing News* SaddoBoxing.com, December 27, 2004.

Chapter 1

1. Barnett, *The Great War*, p. 57.
2. www.worldwar1.com/itafront/carso.htm.
3. Fantuz, *My Father, Primo Carnera*, p. 16.

Chapter 2

1. *New York Times*, June 19, 1921.
2. *New York Times*, June 21, 1921.
3. *The Ring* magazine, April 1930, p. 56.
4. Fantuz, *My Father, Primo Carnera*, p. 30.
5. Fantuz, *My Father, Primo Carnera*, p. 32.
6. "Europe's Rickard," *Time* magazine, Monday, Apr. 20, 1936.
7. Fantuz, *My Father, Primo Carnera*, p. 34.
8. Mullally, *Primo*, p. 22.
9. Fantuz, *My Father, Primo Carnera*, p. 42 (*Gazetto dello Sport*).
10. Fantuz, *My Father, Primo Carnera*, pp. 52–54
11. Phillip Ramati, Macon.com, October 1, 2008.
12. Phillip Ramati, Macon.com, October 1, 2008.
13. Phillip Ramati, Macon.com, October 1, 2008.
14. *Nashville Tennessean*, December 29, 1929.
15. *Nashville Tennessean*, November 19, 1929 (AP).
16. *New York Times*, November 19, 1929.
17. *New York Times*, November 19, 1929.
18. *Nashville Tennessean*, November 19, 1929 (AP).
19. *New York Times*, November 20, 1929.
20. *New York Times*, December 8, 1929.
21. *Nashville Tennessean*, December 9, 1929 (UPI).
22. *Nashville Tennessean*, December 29, 1929 (UPI).
23. *New York Times*, December 8, 1929 (AP).
24. *New York Times*, December 11, 1929.
25. Willie Ratner, *Newark Evening News*, December 31, 1929.
26. Karl Baedecker, *London and its Environs*, p. 14.
27. "People," *Time* magazine, May 3, 1954.
28. Fantuz, *My Father, Primo Carnera*, p. 49.
29. Mullally, *Primo*, pp. 37–38.

Chapter 3

1. *Time* magazine, December 28, 1929.
2. *New York Times*, January 24, 1930.
3. According to the Mayo Clinic, "Acromegaly is a hormonal disorder that develops when your pituitary gland produces too much growth hormone during adulthood. When this happens, your bones increase in size, including those of your hands, feet and face." Primo did not suffer from this disorder (mayoclinic.com).
4. John Kieran, "Sports of the Times," *New York Times*, January 24, 1930.
5. *New York Times*, January 1, 1930.
6. *New York Times*, January 1, 1930.
7. *Nashville Banner*, January 26, 1930 (UPI).
8. Bill Wathey, *Newark Star Eagle*, January 27, 1930.
9. James, Rian. *Dining in New York*. pp. 176–177.
10. *Time* magazine, October 2, 1939.
11. *Nashville Banner*, January 26, 1930 (UPI).
12. Bert R. Sugar, *Boxing's Greatest Fighters*, pg 136.
13. Barbara H. Soloman, *Ain't We Got Fun?*, Introduction.
14. *The Wall Street Journal*, October 1989.
15. *The Wall Street Journal*, October 1989 .
16. *The Wall Street Journal*, October 1989.
17. Weinstein and Wilson, *Freedom and Crisis (vol. 2)*, p. 705.
18. Weinstein and Wilson, *Freedom and Crisis (vol. 2)*, p. 705.
19. Dundee and Sugar, *My View from the Corner*, p. 29.
20. Lawrence Ritter, *Eastside, Westside*, p. 183.
21. *Newark Star-Eagle*, January 24, 1930.
22. *Nashville Banner*, January 25, 1930 (INS).
23. *Nashville Tennessean*, January 25, 1930 (AP).
24. *Nashville Tennessean*, January 25, 1930 (UPI).
25. Anthony Marenghi, *Newark Star-Eagle*, January 25, 1930.
26. James P. Dawson, *New York Times*, January 25, 1930.
27. James P. Dawson, *New York Times*, January 25, 1930.
28. *Nashville Tennessean*, January 25, 1930 (UPI).

29. *Newark Evening News*, January 25, 1930.
30. Ed Sullivan, "Along the Great Fite Way," *The Ring* magazine, March 1930.
31. Ed Sullivan, "Along the Great Fite Way," *The Ring* magazine, March 1930.
32. *Nashville Banner*, January 31, 1930 (INS).
33. *New York Times*, February 1, 1930.
34. *Nashville Banner*, February 5, 1930 (AP).
35. *Nashville Banner*, February 5, 1930 (AP).
36. *Nashville Banner*, February 5, 1930 (AP).
37. Doctor, a Buffalo area pugilist who generally rounded out the cards for local headliners, had in reality two careers in the ring. The first came from January 1930 to early 1931 when he defeated 21of his first 22 opponents, losing only on points in his debut against Joe Juhasz. The second came when Doctor, heady from his success against local competition, stepped up and determined to test his skills outside of his home region and against better fighters. After some mixed success early on, the "test" proved to be a failure. From February 1932 to 1936, Doctor became fodder for other fighters as he lost 26 of his final 30 fights.
38. *Newark Star-Eagle*, February 5, 1930 (AP).
39. *Nashville Tennessean*, February 7, 1930 (UP).
40. *Nashville Banner*, February 7, 1930 (INS).
41. *Nashville Banner*, February 12, 1930 (AP).
42. *Nashville Banner*, February 14, 1930 (AP).
43. *Nashville Tennessean*, February 18, 1930 (UPI).
44. *New York Times*, February 18, 1930 (AP).
45. *Nashville Banner*, February 20, 1930 (AP).
46. *Nashville Tennessean*, March 15, 1930 (AP).
47. *New Orleans Times-Picayune*, February 25, 1930 (AP).
48. *New York Times*, March 4, 1930.
49. *The Ring* magazine, April 1950.
50. *Nashville Tennessean*, March 2, 1930 (The Bell Syndicate, Inc.).
51. Carl Thompson, "The Bum Of The Month Club," *Eastside Boxing*, September 9, 2007.
52. *Nashville Banner*, March 14, 1930 (INS).
53. John Kieran, "Sports of the Times," *New York Times*, July 13, 1930.
54. *Nashville Banner*, March 12, 1930 (AP).
55. Boxrec.com.
56. Boxrec.com.
57. *New York Times*, March 18, 1930 (AP).
58. *New York Times*, March 18, 1930 (AP).
59. *Nashville Banner*, March 18, 1930 (AP).
60. Boxrec.com.
61. *Nashville Tennessean*, March 28, 1930 (AP).
62. *Nashville Tennessean*, March 28, 1930 (AP).
63. *New York Times*, April 9, 1930 (AP).
64. *Nashville Banner*, April 15, 1930 (AP).
65. *Nashville Banner*, April 15, 1930 (AP).
66. *Nashville Banner*, April 22, 1930 (AP).
67. *Nashville Banner*, April 22, 1930 (AP).
68. Grantland Rice, "The Sportlight," *Nashville Banner*, April 25, 1930.
69. *New York Times*, April 23, 1930 (AP).
70. *Nashville Tennessean*, May 15, 1930 (UPI).
71. James Schlemmer, *Akron Beacon Journal*, June 5, 1930.
72. Lynn F. Wagner, *Akron Times-Press*, June 4, 1930.
73. Lynn F. Wagner, *Akron Times-Press*, June 6, 1930.
74. Lynn F. Wagner, *Akron Times-Press*, June 6, 1930.
75. *Nashville Tennessean*, June 6, 1930 (UPI).
76. "Brobdingnagians," *Time* magazine, June 16, 1930.
77. *Omaha World Herald*, December 15, 1932.
78. James Schlemmer, *Akron Beacon Journal*, June 6, 1930.
79. Lynn F. Wagner, *Akron Times-Press*, June 6, 1930.
80. Lynn F. Wagner, *Akron Times-Press*, June 6, 1930.
81. Michael DeLisa, *Cinderella Man*, p. 69.
82. *Nashville Banner*, March 14, 1930 (INS).
83. *Nashville Tennessean*, June 22, 1930 (UPI).
84. "Brobdingnagians," *Time* magazine, June 16, 1930.
85. *New York Times*, June 23, 1930.
86. *Nashville Banner*, June 24, 1930 (INS).
87. *Nashville Tennessean*, June 24, 1930 (UPI).
88. *Nashville Tennessean*, June 24, 1930 (UPI).
89. "Fights," *Time* magazine, June 30, 1930.
90. *New York Times*, June 24, 1930.
91. *Toronto Globe*, August 16, 1928.
92. *Nashville Tennessean*, June 25, 1930 (AP).
93. *Nashville Tennessean*, June 25, 1930 (AP).
94. *New York Times*, June 25, 1930.
95. *Nashville Banner*, June 24, 1930 (INS).
96. *New York Times*, July 18, 1930 (AP).
97. *New York Times*, July 18, 1930 (AP).
98. *Nashville Banner*, July 18, 1930 (AP).
99. *New York Times*, July 22, 1930 (AP).
100. *New York Times*, July 23, 1930 (AP).
101. *New York Times*, July 24, 1930.
102. *Nashville Banner*, July 31, 1930 (AP).
103. *New York Times*, July 30, 1930.
104. *Nashville Tennessean*, August 14, 1930 (AP).
105. *Nashville Tennessean*, August 30, 1930 (UPI).
106. *New York Times*, August 31, 1930.
107. Thomas Myler, *The Sweet Science Goes Sour*.
108. Boxrec.com, Borack Czirolnik.
109. Willie Ratner, *Newark Evening News*, September 9, 1930.
110. *Nashville Tennessean*, September 9, 1930 (UPI).
111. James P. Dawson, *New York Times*, September 9, 1930.
112. *New York Times*, September 18, 1930 (AP).
113. *Nashville Tennessean*, September 17, 1930 (AP).
114. *Nashville Tennessean*, October 8, 1930 (AP).
115. *Nashville Tennessean*, October 8, 1930 (AP).
116. *Nashville Banner*, October 9, 1930 (AP).
117. *New York Times*, January 7, 1931.
118. Craig, *Europe Since 1815*, p. 680; Hughes, *Contemporary Europe*, p. 303.
119. *New York Times*, December 1, 1930.
120. *New York Times*, December 1, 1930.
121. *Nashville Tennessean*, December 1, 1930 (AP).

122. *New York Times*, December 1, 1930.
123. *New York Times*, December 1, 1930.
124. *Nashville Banner*, December 1, 1930 (AP).
125. *New York Times*, December 1, 1930.
126. Boxrec.com, (UPI).
127. *New York Times*, December 19, 1930.
128. *New York Times*, December 19, 1930.
129. *Nashville Tennessean*, December 19, 1930.
130. *Nashville Banner*, December 19, 1930 (AP).
131. *Nashville Banner*, December 19, 1930 (AP).

Chapter 4

1. *New York Times*, February 1, 1931 (AP).
2. John Kieran, "Sports of the Times," *New York Times*, June 5, 1931.
3. "Sport: Carnera v. Maloney," *Time* magazine, March 16, 1931.
4. John Kieran, "Sports of the Times," *New York Times*, June 5, 1931.
5. *New York Times*, March 6, 1931.
6. "Sport: Carnera v. Maloney," *Time* magazine, March 16, 1931.
7. *New York Times*, March 6, 1931.
8. *Nashville Banner*, March 6, 1931 (AP).
9. *Nashville Banner*, March 6, 1931 (AP).
10. John Kieran, *New York Times*, March 6, 1931.
11. *Nashville Banner*, March 6, 1931 (AP).
12. James P. Dawson, *New York Times*, April 28, 1931.
13. Paddy Heaney, Offaly Historical & Archaeological Society.
14. James P. Dawson, *New York Times*, June 16, 1931.
15. James P. Dawson, *New York Times*, June 16, 1931.
16. *New York Herald Tribune*, June 16, 1931.
17. *Nashville Tennessean*; June 27, 1931 (AP).
18. *New York Times*; July 1, 1931 (AP).
19. *New York Times*, July 25, 1931 (AP).
20. Boxrec.com.
21. *New York Times*, August 4, 1931.
22. *Newark Star-Eagle*, August 5, 1931.
23. *New York Times*, August 5, 1931.
24. Anthony Marenghi, *Newark Star-Eagle*, August 5, 1931.
25. *New York Times*, August 27, 1931 (AP).
26. Heller, *In This Corner*, p. 154.
27. *Nashville Tennessean*, October 13, 1931.
28. *Nashville Banner*, October 23, 1927.
29. Evans, *Kings of the Ring*, p. 88.
30. Frank Getty, *Baltimore Post*, June 13, 1930 (UPI).
31. John Kieran, "Sports of the Times," *New York Times*, October 14, 1931.
32. "Misfortunes of a Monster," *Time* magazine, October 5, 1931.
33. Herbert W. Barker, *Nashville Banner*, October 13, 1931 (AP).
34. *New York Times*, October 13, 1931.
35. Herbert W. Barker, *Nashville Banner*, October 13, 1931 (AP).
36. John Kieran, "Sports of the Times," *New York Times*, October 14, 1931.
37. John Kieran, "Sports of the Times," *New York Times*, October 14, 1931.
38. Herbert W. Barker, *Nashville Banner*, October 13, 1931 (AP).
39. Primo Carnera, *Nashville Banner*, October 13, 1931 (INS).
40. "Sport: Levinsky v. Walker," *Time* magazine, May 9, 1932.
41. *Nashville Banner*, November 22, 1931.
42. *Nashville Banner*, November 27, 1931 (AP).
43. *Nashville Banner*, November 28, 1931 (AP).

Chapter 5

1. *Nashville Tennessean*, January 26, 1932 (UPI).
2. *Dallas Morning News*, January 4, 1932 (UPI).
3. *Nashville Tennessean*, February 5, 1932.
4. *Dallas Morning News*, March 25, 1932 (UPI).
5. *New York Times*, March 1, 1932.
6. *New York Times*, March 24, 1932 (AP).
7. *New York Times*, May 1, 1932 (AP).
8. *Dallas Morning News*, May 16, 1932 (AP).
9. *New York Times*, May 31, 1932 (AP).
10. *Nashville Banner*, Tuesday May 31, 1932 (INS).
11. *New York Times*, May 31, 1932 (AP).
12. *Newark Star-Eagle*, July 20, 1932.
13. *Newark Star-Eagle*, July 21, 1932.
14. Joseph C. Nichols, *New York Times*, July 21, 1932.
15. Joseph C. Nichols, *New York Times*, July 21, 1932.
16. Allen Weinstein and Jackson R. Wilson, *Freedom and Crisis: An American History*; Vol. 2, pg 684.
17. "The Bonus Army," EyeWitness to History, www.eyewitnesstohistory.com (2000).
18. Michael E. Parrish, *Anxious Decades*, pp. 260–261.
19. Michael E. Parrish, *Anxious Decades*, p. 261.
20. *Newark Star-Eagle*, July 29, 1932.
21. *Newark Star-Eagle*, July 29, 1932.
22. Murray Robinson, *Newark Star-Eagle*, August 16, 1932.
23. James P. Dawson, *New York Times*, August 17, 1932.
24. *Nashville Banner*, August 17, 1932 (INS).
25. James P. Dawson, *New York Times*, August 17, 1932.
26. James P. Dawson, *New York Times*, August 17, 1932.
27. Murray Robinson, *Newark Star-Eagle*, August 17, 1932.
28. Murray Robinson, *Newark Star-Eagle*, August 17, 1932.
29. *Newark Star-Eagle*, August 18, 1932 (AP).
30. Willie Ratner, *Newark Evening News*, August 17, 1932.
31. *Newark Evening News*, August 20, 1932.
32. *St. Paul Dispatch,* September 1, 1932.
33. *St. Paul Dispatch*, September 1, 1932; *St. Paul Pioneer Press*, September 2, 1932.

34. Lou McKenna, *St. Paul Pioneer Press*, September 2, 1932.
35. Mike Gibbons, Boxrec.com.
36. *Minneapolis Tribune*, September 2, 1932.
37. *Minneapolis Tribune*, September 2, 1932.
38. *Minneapolis Tribune*, September 2, 1932.
39. James P. Dawson, *New York Times*, November 19, 1932.
40. *Nashville Banner*, November 19, 1932 (AP).
41. *Nashville Banner*, December 10, 1932 (AP).
42. *New York Times*, December 14, 1932.
43. Lynn F. Wagner, *Akron Times-Press*, June 6, 1930.
44. *Akron Times-Press*, December 15, 1932.
45. *Omaha World-Herald*, December 15, 1932.
46. *Omaha World-Herald*, December 16, 1932.
47. *Akron Beacon Journal*, December 16, 1932.
48. *Omaha World-Herald*, December 16, 1932.
49. *Akron Times-Press*, December 16, 1932.
50. Boxrec.com.
51. *Dallas Morning News*, December 31, 1932.
52. *Dallas Morning News*, December 31, 1932.
53. *Dallas Morning News*, December 31, 1932.

Chapter 6

1. Nashville Banner; February 18, 1933 — Tom Anderson.
2. The Harder They Fall (1956). Dir. Mark Robson; Starring Humphrey Bogart, Rod Steiger. USA.
3. *Los Angeles Times*, "Mad Max," J R. Moehringer, January 7, 2007.
4. *Los Angeles Times*, "Mad Max," J R. Moehringer, January 7, 2007.
5. *Contra Costa Times*, "Movie's Portrayal of Baer Unfair, Incorrect," Ann Tatko-Peterson, March 20, 2006.
6. *Los Angeles Times*, "Mad Max," J. R. Moehringer, January 7, 2007.
7. *New York Times*, February 25, 1933.
8. *New York Times*, January 7, 1933.
9. *New York Times*, January 7, 1933.
10. The *New York Times*, January 7, 1933.
11. E.C. Wallenfeldt, *The Six Minute Fraternity*, p. 12.
12. *New York Times*, February 11, 1933 — James P. Dawson.
13. International Boxing Research Organization, Michael Hunnicutt, April 5, 2005.
14. Attending physicians during the surgery included Dr. Byron Stookey, Dr. Harold Meeker, Dr. William V. Healy, and Dr. Phillip Goodhart, who was also a professor of Neurology at Columbia University.
15. *Nashville Banner*, February 14, 1933, Eddie Neil (AP).
16. *Nashville Banner*, February 14, 1933 Eddie Neil (AP).
17. *Nashville Banner*, February 14, 1933 (AP).
18. *New York Times*, February 17, 1933.
19. *Nashville Banner*, February 15, 1933 (AP).
20. *Nashville Banner*, February 18, 1933 (INS).
21. *Nashville Tennessean*, February 17, 1933 (AP).
22. *Nashville Tennessean*, February 18, 1933 (AP).
23. International Boxing Research Organization, Michael Hunnicutt, April 5, 2005.
24. *Brazos Living*, June 9, 2005, Alan Tays (Cox News Service).
25. *Brazos Living*, June 9, 2005, Alan Tays (Cox News Service).
26. *The Ring* magazine, April 1972.
27. The Florida Department of Corrections Website — Centuries of Progress, 1933–35.
28. Fantuz and Malfatto, *My Father, Primo Carnera*, p. 72.

Chapter 7

1. *New York Times*, March 15, 1933.
2. *New York Times*, March 15, 1933.
3. *New York Times*, March 15, 1933(AP).
4. *New York Times*, March 31, 1933.
5. *Newsweek*, April 15, 1933, p. 20.
6. *Newsweek*, April 15, 1933, p. 20.
7. Mullally, *Primo*, p. 114.
8. Hugh S. Fullerton, Jr., *Nashville Banner*, June 29, 1933 (AP).
9. Hugh S. Fullerton, Jr., *Nashville Banner*, June 29, 1933 (AP).
10. Hugh S. Fullerton, Jr., *Nashville Banner*, June 29, 1933 (AP).
11. Mullally, *Primo*, p. 119.
12. *Nashville Tennessean*, June 30, 1933 (AP).
13. Plan Gould, *Nashville Banner*, June 30, 1933 (AP).
14. "Carnera v. Sharkey," *Time* magazine, Monday, Jul. 10, 1933.
15. *Nashville Tennessean*, June 30, 1933 (AP).
16. James P. Dawson, *New York Times*, June 30, 1933.
17. *Nashville Tennessean*, June 30, 1933 (AP).
18. Plan Gould, *Nashville Banner*, June 30, 1933 (AP).
19. James P. Dawson, *New York Times*, June 30, 1933.
20. *New York Times*, June 30, 1933.
21. Gayle Talbot, *Nashville Banner*, June 30, 1933 (AP).
22. Peter Heller, *In This Corner*, p. 158.
23. Peter Heller, *In This Corner*, p. 159.
24. *St. Petersburg Times*, June 30, 1967.
25. Russell Sullivan, *Rocky Marciano: The Rock of His Times*, p. 73.
26. W.C. Heinz, The Book of Boxing, p. 219.
27. Patrick Ayler, *Ring of Hate*, p. 39.
28. Mullally, *Primo*, p. 104.
29. "Breach of Promise Verdict," *Time* magazine, Monday, July 31, 1933.

Chapter 8

1. New York State Athletic Commission Minutes, August 9, 1933.
2. *The Syracuse Herald*, August 12, 1933.

3. *The Syracuse Herald*, August 12, 1933.
4. *New York Times*, August 16, 1933.
5. Gene Smith, *American Heritage Magazine*, October 1972.
6. Boxrec.com.
7. *New York Times*, September 9, 1933 (AP).
8. *New York Times*, October 8, 1933 (AP).
9. Mullally, *Primo*, p. 135.
10. *Nashville Tennessean*, October 23, 1933 (AP).
11. *Nashville Tennessean*, October 23, 1933 (AP).
12. *New York Times*, December 15, 1933.
13. *New York Times*, February 8, 1934.
14. *Newsweek*, February 17, 1934.
15. *Nashville Tennessean*, March 1, 1934 (AP).
16. Quentin Reynolds, *Nashville Banner*, March 2, 1934 (INS).
17. Stuart Cameron, *Nashville Banner*, March 2, 1934 (UPI).
18. Stuart Cameron, *Nashville Banner*, March 2, 1934 (UPI).
19. Stuart Cameron, *Nashville Banner*, March 2, 1934 (UPI).
20. *Nashville Tennessean*, March 2, 1934 (AP).
21. Heller, *In This Corner*, p. 125.
22. *New York Times*, March 2, 1934.
23. *New York Times*, March 9, 1934.
24. Heller, *In This Corner*, pp. 125–126.
25. *New York Times*, March 2, 1934.
26. *Nashville Tennessean*, March 3, 1934 (AP).
27. *Newsweek*; March 10, 1934; p. 22.
28. *Newsweek*, March 17, 1934, p. 24.

Chapter 9

1. *Nashville Banner*, March 2, 1934 (INS).
2. *Nashville Banner*, March 2, 1934 (INS).
3. *Nashville Tennessean*, June 6, 1934 (AP).
4. *Nashville Tennessean*, June 6, 1934.
5. *Newsweek*, June 23, 1934, p. 17.
6. *Nashville Tennessean*, June 6, 1934.
7. *Nashville Tennessean*, June 6, 1934.
8. *Nashville Tennessean*, June 7, 1934 (AP).
9. *Nashville Banner*, June 7, 1934 (AP).
10. Damon Runyon, *Nashville Banner*, June 14, 1934 (INS).
11. Hype Igoe, *Nashville Banner*, June 5, 1934 (INS).
12. Edward J. Neil, *Nashville Tennessean*, June 15, 1934 (AP).
13. *Nashville Banner*, June 15, 1934 (AP).
14. *Nashville Banner*, June 15, 1934 (AP).
15. *Nashville Banner*, June 15, 1934 (AP).
16. *Nashville Banner*, June 15, 1934 (INS).
17. Edward J. Neil, *Nashville Tennessean*, June 15, 1934 (AP).
18. *Nashville Tennessean*, June 16, 1934 (AP).
19. James P. Dawson, *New York Times*, June 15, 1934.
20. *Nashville Tennessean*, June 16, 1934 (AP).
21. *Mid-Day Standard of London* (UK), Friday, June 15, 1934.
22. *New York Times*, June 26, 1934.
23. "Champion Carnera," *Time* magazine, Monday, July 31, 1933.
24. Davis J. Walsh, *East St. Louis Journal*, June 22, 1934 (INS).

Chapter 10

1. *New York Times*, August 15, 1934.
2. *New York Times*, December 2, 1934.
3. *New York Times*, January 23, 1935.
4. *Nashville Tennessean*, January 23, 1935 (AP).
5. *New York Times*, February 8, 1935.
6. *New York Times*, February 9, 1935.
7. *The Ring* magazine Top Ten Heavyweight Rankings lists Impelletiere as 8th in 1935 and 6th in 1936.
8. *The New York Times*, March 16, 1935.
9. *Barre (VT) Daily Times,* March 16, 1935, p. 2.
10. *New York Times*, March 26, 1935.
11. *New York Times*, April 10, 1935.

Chapter 11

1. Bert Sugar, *Bert Sugar On Boxing*, p. 111.
2. *New York Times*, March 26, 1935.
3. Joe Louis with Edna Rust and Art Rust, Jr., *Joe Louis: My Life*, p. 134.
4. *New York Times*, March 28, 1935.
5. *New York Times*, March 28, 1935.
6. *New York Times*, June 20 and 21, 1935 — Joseph C. Nichols.
7. *New York Times*, June 26, 1935.
8. Sugar, *Bert Sugar On Boxing*, p. 111.
9. Angelou, *I Know Why the Caged Bird Sings*, pp. 132–133.
10. Angelou, *I Know Why the Caged Bird Sings*, pp. 132–133.
11. *New York Times*, June 26, 1935.
12. *New York Times*, June 26, 1935.
13. *Nashville Tennessean*, June 26, 1933 (AP).
14. Paul Gallico, *New York Daily News*, June 26, 1935.
15. James P. Dawson, *New York Times*, June 26, 1933.
16. Mullally, *Primo*, pp. 156–157.
17. *New York Times*, June 23, 1938.
18. Heller, *In This Corner*, p. 177.
19. Max Baer quote.
20. *Burlington (VT) Free Press*, August 8, 1935, p. 15.
21. *Nashville Tennessean*, June 27, 1935 (AP).
22. *Nashville Banner*; June 27, 1935 (UP).
23. Mullally, *Primo*, p. 157.

Chapter 12

1. *New York Times*, November 2, 1935.
2. *New York Times*, November 2, 1935.
3. *New York Times*, November 26, 1935.
4. *New York Times*, December 10, 1935.
5. *New York Times*, March 7, 1936.

6. *New York Times*, March 7, 1936.
7. *New York Times*, March 7, 1936.
8. *New York Times*, March 7, 1936.
9. Boxrec.com.
10. *New York Times*, July 18, 1937.
11. *New York Times*, November 19, 1937.
12. Boxrec.com.
13. "Giant Retires," *Time* magazine, January 3, 1938.
14. *New York Times*, December 20, 1937.
15. Fantuz, *My Father, Primo Carnera*, p. 154.
16. Mullally, *Primo*, p. 176.
17. *New York Times*, July 23, 1938 (AP).
18. *Nashville Tennessean*, October 24, 1938.
19. Mullally, *Primo*, p. 177.
20. Mullally, *Primo*, p. 177.

Chapter 13

1. *New York Times*, April 28, 1940.
2. Craig, *Europe Since 1815*, p. 729.
3. Hughes, *Contemporary Europe*, p. 336.
4. Fantuz, *My Father, Primo Carnera*, p. 114.
5. Hughes, *Contemporary Europe*, p. 360.
6. Hughes, *Contemporary Europe*, p. 360.
7. *New York Times*, November 23, 1943 (UP).
8. *New York Times*, November 24, 1943 (AP).
9. Fantuz, *My Father, Primo Carnera*, p. 119.
10. Fantuz, *My Father, Primo Carnera*, p. 119.
11. Mullally, *Primo*, p. 181.
12. *New York Times*, March 29, 1945.
13. Hughes, *Contemporary Europe*, p. 376.
14. Hughes, *Contemporary Europe*, p. 376.
15. Fantuz, *My Father, Primo Carnera*, p. 117.

Chapter 14

1. *Nashville Banner*, June 27, 1935 (UP).
2. Interviews with former Newark, NJ, residents Len and Jean Lepore, and Rose Werner.
3. *Los Angeles Times*, April 28, 1956.
4. WrestlingClassics.com.

Chapter 15

1. *Nashville Banner*, October 24, 1938 (AP).
2. The Harder They Fall (1956). Dir. Mark Robson; Starring Humphrey Bogart, Rod Steiger. USA.
3. *Los Angeles Times*, April 30, 1956.
4. Ken Jones, "Carnera's Family Sheds New Light on Tale of Sad Exploitation," *The Independent Newspaper, UK*, March 20, 2003.
5. Mullally, *Primo*, p. 127.
6. Fantuz, *My Father, Primo Carnera*, p. 135.
7. IMBD.com.

Chapter 16

1. *Nashville Banner*, January 26, 1930 (UP).
2. *New York Times*, January 25, 1930.
3. *Nashville Banner*, January 25, 1930 (INS).
4. John Kieran, "Sports of the Times," *New York Times*, August 20, 1932.
5. Ed Sullivan, "Along the Great Fite Way," *The Ring* magazine, March 1930.
6. Ed Sullivan, "Along the Great Fite Way," *The Ring* magazine, March 1930.
7. Lynn F. Wagner, *Akron Times-Press*, June 6, 1930.
8. *Minneapolis Tribune*, September 3, 1932.
9. Daniel M. Daniel, "Corbett Still Visions Sharkey as Champion," *The Ring* magazine, May 1931.
10. Bill Wathey, *Newark Star-Eagle*, September 8, 1930.
11. Bill Wathey, *Newark Star-Eagle*, September 10, 1930.
12. Jack Kofoed, "Giants Not So Hot!," *The Ring* magazine, November 1933.
13. *Nashville Tennessean*, June 6, 1934 (AP).
14. Boxrec.com, "Ewart Potgeiter."
15. O.F. Snelling, *A Bedside Book of Boxing*, page 146.
16. *Nashville Tennessean*, June 6, 1934 (AP).
17. Hype Igoe, *Nashville Banner*, June 5, 1934 (INS).
18. Hype Igoe, *Nashville Banner*, June 5, 1934 (INS).
19. *New York Times*, December 19, 1930.
20. "Carnera Stars Again," *Italy* magazine, April 21, 2008.
21. Davis J. Walsh, *Nashville Banner*, February 12, 1930 (INS).
22. Hugh S. Fullerton, Jr., *Nashville Banner*, June 29, 1933 (AP).
23. Eddie Orcutt, "Brooklyn Mick," *The Saturday Evening Post*, February 26, 1938.
24. *New York Times*, December 1, 1930.
25. John Kieran, "Sports of the Times," *New York Times*, November 1, 1935.
26. Mullally, *Primo: The Story of "Man Mountain" Carnera*, Introduction.
27. Don Stradley, "Let's Go to the History Books," *The Ring* magazine, December 2008.
28. Stuart Cameron, *Nashville Banner*, March 2, 1934 (UPI).
29. Aaron Tallent, "A Case for Primo Carnera, Ray Mancini, and a Few Observers," TheSweetScience.com.
30. Russell Sullivan, *Rocky Marciano: The Rock of His Times*, p. 237.

Chapter 17

1. W.C. Heinz and Nathan Ward, *The Book of Boxing*, p. 109 (Paul Gallico).
2. Peter Benson, *Battling Siki*, p. 58.
3. Bill Wathey, *Newark Star-Eagle*, January 27, 1930.
4. *The Nashville Banner*, January 26, 1930 (UPI).
5. Lawrence S. Ritter, *East Side, West Side: Tales of New York Sporting Life 1910–1960*, p. 110.
6. Blinkey Horn, *Nashville Tennessean*, March 1, 1934.
7. Blinkey Horn, *Nashville Tennessean*, March 1, 1934.

8. Blinkey Horn, *Nashville Tennessean*, March 1, 1934.
9. Blinkey Horn, *Nashville Tennessean*, March 1, 1934.
10. Patrick Ayler, *Ring of Hate*, p. 37.
11. *Nashville Banner*, February 15, 1933 (AP).
12. Bert Sugar, HBO Interview, 2007.
13. James P. Dawson, *New York Times*, June 30, 1933.
14. Fantuz, *My Father, Primo Carnera*, p. 128.
15. *Nashville Banner*, April 29, 1930 (AP).
16. *Toronto Globe & Mail*, April 29, 1930.
17. *Toronto Star*, April 29, 1930.
18. *Nashville Tennessean*, March 1, 1931 (AP).
19. *Nashville Tennessean*, March 1, 1931 (AP).
20. Jack Cavanaugh, *Tunney*, p. 329.
21. Allen Bodner, *When Boxing was a Jewish Sport*, p. 130.
22. Tim Smith, *New York Daily News*, September 24, 2003.

Chapter 18

1. Fantuz, *My Father, Primo Carnera*, p. 69.
2. Per David Levy, owner/proprietor, and Loretta Thompson, master tailor, Levy's Clothiers, Nashville, TN.
3. *New York Times*, January 31,1930 (AP).
4. *Omaha World-Herald*, December 16, 1932.
5. *Nashville Banner*, January 14, 1930.
6. *Nashville Banner*, January 28, 1930 (UP).
7. *Time* magazine, January 15, 1940.
8. *Nashville Tennessean*, March 21, 1930 (UP).
9. Fantuz, *My Father, Primo Carnera*, p. 43.
10. Jack Sher, "The Strange Case of Carnera," *Sport* magazine, February 1948;.
11. David Skolnick, "Interview with Bruno Sammartino," *Wrestling Perspective*, 1998;.
12. Fantuz, *My Father, Primo Carnera*, p. 31.
13. Mullally, *Primo*, p. 143.
14. Mullally, *Primo*, p. 190.
15. Fantuz, *My Father, Primo Carnera*, p. 135.
16. Fantuz, *My Father, Primo Carnera*, p. 129.
17. Fantuz, *My Father, Primo Carnera*, p. 131.
18. Fantuz, *My Father, Primo Carnera*, p. 131.
19. Fantuz, *My Father, Primo Carnera*, p. 131.
20. Fantuz, *My Father, Primo Carnera*, p. 135.

Bibliography

Books

Allen, Frederick Lewis. *Only Yesterday*. New York: Harper Perennial, 1931, 1959, 1964, 1992.

Andre, Sam, and Nat Fleischer (Nat Loubet). *A Pictorial History of Boxing*. Secaucus, NJ: Citadel Press, 1959 (1987 Edition).

Angelou, Maya. *I Know Why the Caged Bird Sings*. New York: Random House, 1969, (1997 Edition).

Baedecker, Karl. *London and Its Environs*. Leipzig, Germany: Karl Baedecker, 1911.

Barnett, Correlli. *The Great War*. New York: G.P. Putnam's Sons, 1979.

Benson, Peter. *Battling Siki: A Tale of Ring Fixes, Race, and Murder in the 1920s*. Fayetteville: The University of Arkansas Press, 2006.

Blady, Ken. *The Jewish Boxers Hall of Fame*. New York: Shapolsky, 1988.

Bodner, Allen. *When Boxing was a Jewish Sport*. Westport, CT: Praeger, 1997.

Cavanaugh, Jack. *Tunney*. New York: Ballantine Books/Random House, 2006.

Collins, Nigel. *Boxing Babylon: Behind the Shadowy World of the Prize Ring*. New York: Citadel Press, 1990.

Craig, Gordon A. *Europe Since 1815*. New York: Holt, Rinehart, & Winston, 1961.

Daniels, Jonathan. *The Time Between the Wars*. Garden City, NY: Doubleday & Co., 1966.

Daniels, Roger. *The Bonus March: An Episode of the Great Depression*. Westport, CT: Greenwood Publishing, 1971.

DeLisa, Michael C. *Cinderella Man: The James J. Braddock Story*. Wrea Green, UK: Milo Brooks, Ltd., 2005.

Dundee, Angelo, and Bert Randolph Sugar. *My View from the Corner: A Life in Boxing*. New York: McGraw-Hill, 2008.

Erenberg, Lewis. *The Greatest Fight of Our Generation*. New York: Oxford University Press, 2006.

Evans, Gavin. *Kings of the Ring*. London: Orion Publishing Group, 2007.

Fantuz, Giuliana V., Ivan Malfatto, and Gino Argentin. *My Father, Primo Carnera*. Milan, Italy: SEP Editrice Srl., 2002.

Fleischer, Nat. *The Heavyweight Championship: an Informal History of Heavyweight Boxing*. New York: Fleet Publishing, 1958.

Fleischer, Nat. *The Ring Record Book and Boxing Encyclopedia*. Norwalk, CT: O'Brien Suburban Press, Annual.

Hague, Jim. *Braddock: The Rise of the Cinderella Man*. New York: Chamberlain Bros./Penguin, 2005.

Heinz, H.C., and Nathan Ward. *The Book of Boxing*. New York: Bishop Books, 1999.

Heller, Peter. *"In This Corner...!" 42 World Champions Tell Their Stories*. New York,: De Capo Press, 1973, 1994.

Hughes, H. Stuart. *Contemporary Europe: A History*. Englewood Cliffs, NJ: Prentice Hall, 1961 (Fifth Edition 1981).

Humber, William. *A Sporting Chance: Achievements of African-Canadian Athletes*. Toronto, ON: Natural Heritage Books, 2004.

James, Rian. *Dining in New York*. New York The John Day, Co., 1930.

Kahn, Roger. *A Flame of Pure Fire: Jack Dempsey and the Roaring '20s*. San Diego and New York: Harcourt, 1999.

Louis, Joe, with Edna Rust, and Art Rust, Jr. *Joe Louis: My Life*. New York: Harcourt, Brace, Jovanovich, 1978.

Margolick, David. *Beyond Glory: Joe Louis vs. Max Schmeling, and a World on the Brink*. New York: Vintage Books/Random House, 2005.

McCoy, Donald R. *Coming of Age*. Baltimore: Penguin Books, 1973.

Mitgang, Herbert. *Once Upon a Time in New York*. New York: The Free Press, 2000.

Mullally, Frederic. *Primo: The Story of "Man Mountain" Carnera*. London, UK: Robson Books, 1991.

Myler, Patrick. *Ring of Hate: Joe Louis vs. Max Schmeling: the Fight of the Century*. New York: Arcade Publishing, 2005.

Myler, Thomas. *The Sweet Science Goes Sour: How Scandal Brought Boxing to its Knees*. Greystone Books, 2007.

Parrish, Michael E. *Anxious Decades: America in Prosperity and Depression, 1920–1941*. New York: W.W. Norton & Co., 1992.

Ritter, Lawrence S. *East Side, West Side: Tales of New York Sporting Life 1910–1960*. New York: Total Sports Publishing, 1998.

Schaap, Jeremy. *Cinderella Man: James J. Braddock, Max Baer, and the Greatest Upset in Boxing History*. New York: Houghton Mifflin, 2005.

Schulberg, Budd. *The Harder They Fall*. New York, NY: Random House, 1947.
See, Leon. *Le Mystere Carnera*. Paris, France: Gallimard, 1934.
Snelling, O.F. *A Bedside Book of Boxing*. London, UK: Pelham Books, 1972.
Solomon, Barbara H. *Ain't We Got Fun*. New York: The New American Library, 1980.
Sugar, Bert Randolph. *Bert Sugar on Boxing*. Guilford, CT: The Lyons Press, 2003.
Sugar, Bert Randolph. *Boxing's Greatest Fighters*. Guilford, CT: The Lyons Press, 2006.
Sullivan, Russell. *Rocky Marciano: The Rock of His Times*. Urbana and Chicago: University of Illinois Press, 2002.
Wallenfeldt, E.C. *The Six Minute Fraternity: The Rise and Fall of NCAA Tournament Boxing, 1932–1960*. Westport, CT: Praeger, 1994.
Weinstein, Allen, and R. Jackson Wilson. *Freedom and Crisis: An American History*. New York: Random House, 1974, 1978 (2nd Edition).
Weston, Stanley. *Heavyweight Champions*. New York: Ace Books, 1970, 1976.

Newspapers and Magazines

Akron Beacon Journal
Akron Times Press
American Heritage Magazine
The Baltimore Sun
Brazos Living
Collier's magazine
Contra Costa Times
Dallas Morning News
East St. Louis Journal
The Independent Newspaper (UK)
International Boxing Research Organization
Italy magazine
Literary Digest
Los Angeles Times
Macon.com (*The Telegraph*—Macon, Georgia)
Mid-Day Standard (London)
Minneapolis Tribune
Nashville Banner
Nashville Tennessean
The National Police Gazette
Newark Evening News
Newark Star-Eagle
Newark Star-Ledger
New Orleans Times-Picayune
New York Daily News
New York Herald
New York Times
Newsweek
Omaha World-Herald
The Ring magazine
St. Louis Post-Dispatch
St. Paul Dispatch
St. Paul Pioneer Press
St. Petersburg Times
San Francisco Chronicle
San Francisco Examiner
The Saturday Evening Post
Sport magazine
Syracuse Herald
Time magazine
Toronto Globe and Mail
Toronto Star
Vermont Boxing History & International Pugilist Review
The Wall Street Journal

Web Sites

"The Bonus Army," EyeWitness to History, 2000, www.eyewitnesstohistory.com.
BoxRec, www.boxrec.com.
The Cyber Boxing Zone, www.cyberboxingzone.com/boxing/gaines-1.htm.
East Side Boxing, www.eastsideboxing.com.
The Florida Department of Corrections, "Centuries of Progress, 1933–1935," www.dc.state.fl.us/oth/timeline/1933–1935.html.
International Boxing Research Organization, www.ibroresearch.com.
The Mayo Clinic, www.mayoclinic.com.
The New York Stock Exchange (NYSE Euronext), http://www.nyse.com/.
Offaly Historical & Archaeological Society, by Paddy Heaney; (1997) www.offalyhistory.com/articles/254/1/Dick-McRedmond/Page1.html.
Winkler, Robert. Fistic Descriptions by Date, *Vermont Boxing History & International Pugilist Review*, copyright 1997–2000, http://esf.uvm.edu/vtbox/Rounds.html.
World War I—Trenches on the Web, www.worldwar1.com/itafront/carso.html.
WrestlingClassics.com, www.wrestlingclassics.com.
Wrestling Perspective: The Thinking Fan's Newsletter, www.wrestlingperspective.com.

Films

The Harder They Fall. Dir. Mark Robson. Based on the book by Budd Schulberg. Perf. Humphrey Bogart, Rod Steiger. Columbia Pictures, 1956.

Index

Adams, Bob 176
Ali, Muhammad (Cassius Clay) 2, 199, 208
Anderson, Tom 100
Angelo, Billy 51
Angelou, Maya 161, 162
Arcel, Ray 174
Arum, Bob 208
Attell, Abe 28, 29, 32, 199, 201, 207
Attell, Monte 28
Ayler, Patrick 203

Badoglio, Pietro 182, 183
Baer, Buddy 161, 163, 168, 169
Baer, Max 2, 53, 91, 93, 95, 100, 101, 103, 107–109, 110, 113, 114, 121, 124, 125, 128, 130, 131, 134–149, 153–155, 157–159, 163, 164, 168, 171, 173, 188, 189, 190, 193, 195, 197, 199, 202, 205, 206
Baer, Max, Jr. 101
Baiguera, Innocente 80
Baker, Sam 45, 46
Ballerino, Mike 27
Balogh, Harry 161
Barker, Herbert W. 73
Barnett, Norman 152
Baronnet 8
Barrick, Constant 13, 14, 82
Barrow, DeLeon 163
Barrow, Lillie Reese 157
Barrow, Munroe 157
Barry, Dave 34, 35, 205
Barry, Jack 33
Barton, George 193
Baruch, Bernard 30
Battalino, Battling 76
Battey, W.A. 34, 35
Bee, Doc 186
Benson, Eddie 68, 83
Benvenuti, Nino 196, 197, 216, 217
Berings, Louis 25
Berlenbach, Paul 18
Bertazzolo, Riccardo 15, 55, 56
Beyer, Morris 138
Bianchi, Raul 122, 126, 127
Biener, George A. 64, 76
Bier, Joseph "Doc" 113, 196
Birkie, Hans 77, 86, 91, 93
Biro, Joe 186
Blake, George 18
Blevens, Michel 186

Bogart, Humphrey 190
Boireau, Jean 25, 36, 42
Bojarski, Frank 123
Bolitho, William 32
Bondy, William 135
Borrell, Joe 39
Bouquillon, Moise 14, 15, 79
Boyette, Charley 86
Boykins, Art 186
Bozic, Fred 97
Brackey, George "Big Boy" 168, 169
Braddock, Jim 2, 3, 65, 66, 91, 101, 121, 140, 141, 153–156, 158, 159, 163, 166, 199, 201, 205, 208
Bray, Henry 43
Brescia, Jorge "Johhny" 161, 168
Brescia, Tony 86
Britton, Jack 208
Brooks, Patrick 157
Brown, Bill 117, 136, 137, 144
Brown, Frankie 199
Brown, James M. "Bingo" 107, 204
Brown, Natie 158, 159, 171
Brown, Thomas 148
Brown, Warren 35
Bruen, Frank J. 64, 66
Bruno, Frank 115
Buckley, Jim 86, 116
Buckley, Johnny 55, 74, 104, 105, 106, 112, 115, 117, 204
Burks, Francis 98, 99
Burman, Red 159
Buzzoni, Frankie 57
Byrd, Richard E. 146
Byrne, Jimmy 46

Callahan, Patrick 159
Cameron, Stuart 132, 197
Campbell, Frankie 100, 101, 109, 136, 171
Campolo, Victorio 55, 75–78, 107, 134, 149, 150
Cancogni, Manlio 184
Cannon, Paul 98
Cantwell, Mike 144
Canzoneri, Tony 113, 159
Capley, Claude "Kid" 124
Capone, Al 134
Cappelletti, Nino 13
Carey, William 71
Carnera, Elvio 181

Carnera, Giovanna Maria "Jean" 182, 183, 204, 209, 212, 214, 216, 217
Carnera, Giovanna Mazziol 5, 6, 7, 13, 59, 115, 118, 126, 146
Carnera, Giovanni 181
Carnera, Giuseppina Kovacic "Pina" 7, 179–181, 184, 187, 211, 212, 214, 215, 216, 217
Carnera, Marianna 181
Carnera, Mary 181
Carnera, Sante 5, 6, 7, 115, 118, 126, 146, 182
Carnera, Secondo 5, 126, 181
Carnera, Severino 5, 119, 125, 126, 128, 130, 181
Carnera, Umberto 181, 183, 204, 212–214, 216, 217
Carpegna, Giuseppe 12, 13
Carpenter, Harry 197
Carpentier, Georges 9, 26 31, 205
Carr, Luke 169
Carroll, Dan 65
Carter, Carl 31
Carvill, Bob 20, 22
Cavanaugh, Billy 104, 106
Cayton, Bill 208
Cecconi, Anselmo 6
Cermak, Anton J. 108
Charles, Ezzard 215
Charles, Francois 79
Charles, Pierre 17, 22, 56, 80, 82, 168
Chavez, Caesar Julio 39
Chevalier, Leon 44, 45, 52, 55, 66, 98, 111, 171
Chevalier, Maurice 33
Chocolate, Kid (Eligio Sardinas Montalvo) 48, 206
Christner, Meyer "K.O." 18, 46–50, 56, 69, 79, 93, 94, 95, 96, 97, 121, 192, 209
Churchill, Frank 26, 27, 45, 46, 111
Clark, Roy "Ace" 38, 39, 159
Clawson, Tony 46
Clinnin, John V. 46, 64
Clisby, Neil 44
Cobb, Walter 77, 86, 87
Cockell, Don 199
Coll, Vincent "Mad Dog" 27
Collett, Charlie 17

Collins, Mike 97
Conn, Billy 163
Connelly, Francis 53
Cook, E.L. 34, 35
Cook, George 55, 80, 81
Cooper, Ray 173
Corbett, James J. "Gentleman Jim" 131, 173, 193, 207
Corcoran, Peter 207
Corri, Pietro 86
Creighton, Larry 47, 50
Cunningham, Bob 86
Czirolnik, Borack 56, 57

Daley, Arthur 199
Dalla Pozza, Giuseppe 216
Daly, James P. 106
Daly, May Schaaf 105, 106
Damski, Paul 166
Daniels, Billy "Gypsey" 167
Daniels, Dick 88
Darcy, Les 41
Darnell, Dan 44
Daro, Lou 164, 85
Darts, Bill 207
Davis, Harry 43
Davis, Jackie 123
Dawson, Al 46
Dawson, James P. 87, 118, 197
Dean, Frank "Man Mountain" 164, 185
Deathpaine, "Indian" Benny (Bennetto Payne) 47
Deaver, Vaughan 51
De Carolis, Armando 71, 126, 127
Defoe, Billy 83, 104, 109, 115, 126, 158, 199
De La Hoya, Oscar 208
Delerole, Fr. 109
Del Genio, Leonard 115
DeLisa, Michael 49
Delleau, Lucien 69
de Mange, George "Big Frenchy" 26, 27
Demby, Agnes 148
Dempsey, Jack 9, 27, 28, 33, 38, 39, 40, 47, 51, 55, 56, 72, 75, 79, 80, 88, 92, 97, 110, 114, 115, 121, 124, 130, 131, 135–138, 140, 144, 154, 155, 159, 163, 189, 195, 201, 202, 206, 207
Denning, Jack 161
Denny, Joe 71
de Silva, Alvaro 168
Deyong, Moss 61–63, 127, 197
Diamond, Jack "Legs" 26
Dickson, Jeff 10, 11, 13, 14, 16, 22, 28, 60, 62, 79, 113, 119, 148, 175, 176
Diener, Franz 14, 15, 22–24, 25, 31, 82
DiMeglio, Albert 175–177
Dixon, Leonard 159
Doctor, Joe 35, 123
Donovan, Art 173
Donovan, Arthur 32, 83, 102, 103, 114, 116, 117, 128, 140–143, 145, 162, 163, 167, 170, 173, 174
Donovan, "Professor" Mike 173

Dougherty, Jimmy 52, 71
Douglas, Buster 2, 3
Dublinsky, Harry 123
Dudas, Steve 93, 154, 172
Duffy, Bill 2, 25–27, 31, 33, 45, 46, 49, 53, 54, 64, 66, 71, 83, 104, 112, 115, 117, 118, 129, 130, 132, 134, 135, 147, 148, 163, 173, 174, 196, 197, 201, 204, 207
Dunbar, Dorothy 136
Dundee, Angelo 31, 40
Dundee, Johnny 33

Ebbets, Harry 158
Edgren, Frankie 123
Edgren, Robert 19, 21, 39, 66
Edward, Prince of Wales 19, 20, 24, 214
Egus, Paolino 124
Eisenhower, Dwight D. 85
Ellenstein, Meyer C. 159
Emanuel, Armand 58
Engel, Gene 39
Erceg, Michael 139
Erenberg, Lewis 200
Erickson, Johnny 37, 38, 206
Ertle, Harry 18, 56
Etorre, Al 163, 171, 173
Eudeline, Maurice 10, 12, 14, 24, 25, 83, 199, 205, 210
Everett, Buck 89, 90

Falegano, Henry 96
Farley, James A. 31, 66, 107, 140, 159, 173
Farr, Tommy 168, 175
Farrini, Vincent 174
Feldman, Abe 154
Fernandez, Bobby 98
Ficuello, Ralph 77
Finnegan, Gene 33
Firpo, Luis Angel 56
Fisher, Irving 30
Fitzsimmons, Bob 131
Fitzsimmons, Floyd 46, 47, 48, 140
Fleischer, Nat 176, 177
Flint, Otto 57
Flix, Carlos 60
Flood, John 86, 88
Florio, Joe 173
Flowers, Bruce 33
Flowers, Lew "Tiger" 138, 152, 153, 159
Flowers, Theodore "Tiger" 41, 203
Flynn, Edward 71
Flynn, Leo P. 33, 201
Forbes, Eddie 86, 117
Foreman, George 50
Forgeon, Maurice 176
Fosiani, Dr. 179
Fox, Billy 208
Fox, Richard Kyle 123, 124
Fox, "Tiger" Jack 45, 95
Fraser, Billy 69
Frazier, Bob 159
Frederick Wilhelm, Crown Prince of Germany 80

Freeman, Johnny 94
Freeman, Tommy 59
Friedman, Walter 25, 26, 27, 28, 31, 34, 45, 46, 97, 118, 119, 147, 201
Fugazy, Humbert J. 66, 83, 91
Fullerton, Hugh 115, 196

Gable, Clark 139
Gadbois, J.P. 34
Gagnon, Jack 68, 88
Gahan, Jed 94
Gains, Larry 15, 23, 52, 82–84, 148, 167, 176, 188
Galento, Tony 1, 44, 86, 88, 108, 121, 127, 163, 166, 167, 171, 188
Gallagher, Marty 65, 154
Gallico, Paul 163, 200
Galusso, Mauro 149
Gans, Joe 202, 207
Garafano, Vincente 214
Gardner, Frederick 34
Gardner, Sam 186
Gardos, Bela 176
Garner, John Nance 93
Garza, Julio 140
Gastanaga, Isidoro 169, 170, 171, 172
Getz, George 34
Gibbons, Floyd 68
Gibbons, Mike 41, 90, 91
Gibbons, Tommy 41, 90
Gibson, Billy 207
Gill, Mickey 33
Girones, Jose 60
Glassford, Pelham D. 84, 85
Glover, Kid 96
Godfrey, George 40, 44, 46, 50–53, 57, 58, 71, 83, 134, 151, 168, 217
Godfrey, "Young" George 153
Goldstein, Ruby 207
Gordon, Waxey 207
Gorman, Bud 69
Gould, Joe 155, 201, 208
Gould Plan 116
Governi, Giancarlo 190
Graham, Bushy 76
Granite, Kid 98
Greb, Harry 41, 47, 113, 205, 207
Griffin, John "Corn" 135, 136, 140, 141, 193, 194
Griffiths, Tuffy 18, 41
Grill, Eddie 169
Griselle, Maurice 15, 19, 22, 81
Gross, Jack 51, 56, 57, 83, 84, 86, 195
Gühring, Ernst 67, 68, 80
Guitierrez, Luis 206

Haas, Joey 161
Hague, Frank J. 68, 159
Haile Selassie I 158
Halper, Lou 70
Hamas, Steve 71, 77, 127, 131, 140, 148, 205
Hamilton, Al 92
Hammer, Ernest 138
Hansen, Knute 14, 15, 49, 69, 70, 93

Index

Harlow, Jean 136
Harris, Cecil "Seal" 47, 137, 149, 150, 152, 159
Harris, Harold 185–187
Hart, Jack 82
Harvey, Len 82
Haukop, Johnny 9
Haynes, Leroy 93, 171–174, 177, 186
Healy, Bill 167
Hearst, Millicent 115, 161
Hearst, William Randolph 115
Heeney, Tom 49, 72, 94
Heinz, Adolph 153
Heisner, Walter 42
Hendrie, Billy 92
Herman, Tiny 47
Herz, Alfred E. 152
Hitler, Adolf 1, 182
Hoey, James J. 149
Hoff, Max "Boo Boo" 207
Hoffman, Ancil 134, 135, 137, 138, 144
Holt, Billy 123
Holyfield, Evander 208
Hoover, Herbert C. 30, 85, 93
Hope, Bob 189
Horn, Blinkey 202
Houck, Leo 41
Houghton, Eddie 161
House, Mack 44
Howard, Ron 108
Humbeeck, Jack 16
Humphreys, Joe 104, 141, 143
Hunnicutt, Michael 105, 108
Hunt, Babe 205
Huntman, Benny 175–178
Huston, Walter 124, 189
Huttick, Arthur 71, 126, 127, 130, 153

Igoe, Hype 139, 140, 195, 197
Impelletiere, Ray 42, 140, 152, 153, 154, 155, 167, 168, 205
Irwin, Toby 44, 136, 168
Isaacs, Stanley 46, 58, 118
Islas, Epifanio 12, 13, 149

Jackson, Dynamite 137, 139
Jackson, Peter 46, 195
Jacobs, Joe "Yussell" 152, 201
Jacobs, Mike 157, 158, 161, 163, 170
Jaspers, Hermann 16
Jefferies, James J. 93, 140, 203
Joh, Billy 167
Johnson, Hugh S. 140
Johnson, Jack 2, 33, 52, 53, 159, 202, 203, 206, 207
Johnson, Larry 32, 88, 139
Johnston, Jimmy 66, 67, 72, 75, 76, 83, 103, 104, 106, 112, 129, 130, 137, 148, 152, 201, 204
Jones, Billy 53
Jones, Ken 190
Jordan, Lynn 47
Journee, Paul 9, 10, 12, 14, 28, 199, 205, 206
Juliano, Billy 161

Kaliska, Bill 18
Kaminski, Joe 161
Kaplan, Phil 27
Karchi, Chris 161
Keenan, George E. 88
Kelly, Edward J. 159
Kelly, George 74
Kennedy, Joseph P. 30
Kennedy, Les 92, 93
Kerr, Muggs 83
Kieran, John 25, 40, 64, 65, 72, 73, 133, 141, 192, 197
Kilbane, Johnny 28
Kilbourne, Jack 92
Kilpatrick, John Reed 130
King Alfonso XIII 59
Kirby, Jack 60
Kirby, Tom 68
Klausner, Erwin 94, 150, 151
Klitschko, Vitali 3, 194
Klitschko, Vladimr 194
Knost, Dave 94
Kofoed, Jack 193
Kohlhaas, Hans 161
Korosi, Sandor 176
Kovacic, Giuseppe 179, 180
Kracken, Jack 157
Kugel, Hyman 36, 56

Labelle, Shirley 146
Lacri, Al 115
Laffineur, Yvan 25, 36
Laga, Robert 45
LaGuardia, Fiorello H. 140, 159
LaMotta, Jake 2, 208
Landis, Kenesaw Mountain 43
Langford, Sam 163
La Roe, Jose 16
Lasky, Art 46, 88, 90, 91, 148, 153, 154, 155, 168
Latham, Roy 132, 133
Lauer, Edgar E. 152
Laurent, Bobby 40
Lawson, James P. 163
Lazek, Heinz 168
League, Jack 97, 98
Leavelle, Tex 99
Lee, Canada 96
Lee, Johnny 96
LeFevre, Frenchy 98, 99
Legros, Fred 8
Lehman, Herbert 106
Leneve, Gustavo 76
Lenhart, Fred 32
Lennett, Kid 28
Lenny, Harry 155
Leonard, Benny 113, 140, 208
Lepore, Len 1
Lete, Jose 16
Levene, Harry 82, 83
Levinsky, Battling 18, 41 56, 75
Levinsky, King 33, 75, 79, 88, 91, 94, 95, 97, 107, 128, 131, 163, 167, 169
Levy, Lena 76
Lewis, Ed "Strangler" 1, 188
Lewis, Hank 57
Lewis, Jack 46, 47
Lewis, Lennox 208

Lewis, Nate 95
Linz, Aldo 56
Liston, Sonny 208
Lodge, Farmer 38
Lokofsky, Maurice 88
Lomazzi, Carlo 13
Lomski, Leo 75, 86, 201
Londos, Jimmy 1, 188
Lord Birkenhead 24
Loughran, Tommy 2, 18, 41, 57, 67, 75, 76, 83, 116, 129–136, 140, 149, 154, 167, 197, 199, 200, 202, 204, 217
Louis, Joe (Barrow) 2, 39, 113, 114, 121, 128, 153, 155, 157–168, 170, 171, 173, 188, 195, 197, 199, 200, 202, 215
Louis, John Henry 163
Loy, Myrna 121, 124, 189
Lynch, Charles 116, 141
Lyndell, Hyde 46

MacArthur, Douglas 85
Mackaway, Jack 92
Madden, Owney 2, 26, 27, 49, 54, 59, 147, 148, 201–203, 205, 207, 208
Mader, Eddie 161, 166, 167
Malish, Frank 97
Malloy, Mique 38, 40, 53, 55
Maloney, Jim 2, 14, 33, 57–59, 64–66, 79, 195
Mangold, Joe 87, 88
Manley, Jim 86
Mann, Nathan 161
Mansfield, Doug 17
Mara, Tim 110
Marchegiano, Perrino 119
Marciano, Rocky 2, 118, 119, 199
Marek, Max 166, 167
Marenghi, Anthony 70, 192
Marsh, Lou 69, 206
Martin, Buster 36, 37
Martin, Johnny 79, 103
Marto, Johnny 153
Masini, Ernest 86
Mastro, Earl 48
Matan, Chester 31, 87, 135, 138, 153
Mathison, Charles 74
Mays, Harold 68, 121–123, 125, 126, 127, 130
Mazurki, Mike 1, 188
Mazziol, Antonia 6
Mazziol, Bonaventura 6
McArdle, Tom 33
McAuliffe, Jack 43, 44, 46, 47, 55, 56
McAvoy, Johnny 77
McCaffery, Kid 96
McCallum, John D. 118
McCarthy, Pat 56, 57, 193
McClelland, Elmer "Slim" 48, 65
McClinton, Leon 39
McCorkindale, Don 71, 81, 168
McCoy, Kid 2, 207
McFarland, Pack 107
McGarrity, Norman 163
McGee, Willie 159

McGovern, Terry 207
McGrath, Larry 44
McGrath, Tim 45
McIntosh, Hugh 80
McIntyre, Ray 33
McKinney, Thurston 157
McLaghlan, C.S. "Red" 132, 133
McLarnin, Jimmy 140
McLemore, Henry 69
McMahon, Jess 31
McMillan, Ray 96
McNamee, Graham 140
McPartland, Billy "The Kid" 68
McTigue, Mike 18, 205
Meen, Reggie 17, 61–64, 82, 167, 195, 197
Meinert, Larry 97
Mendel, Harry 36
Merrill, Charles 30
Merriott, James 97, 167, 168
Michaels, Jack 122
Middleton, R.E. 21
Miljon, Karel 81
Miller, Davey 93
Minini, Mario 182
Mitchell, Walter, J. 107
Mitchell, William D. 85
Monckton, Walter T. 111
Mondt, Toots 187
Montagna, Frank 42
Montana, Joe 98
Monte, Joe 33 79
Montez, Mercy 98
Montgomery, Sully 40, 41, 193
Moody, Bob 121
Moody, Frank 82
Moore, Archie 39
Moore, Porter 130
Moore, Tom 46
Moppo, Jappo 47
Moret, Marcel 80
Moretti, Gene 51, 55
Morgan, "Dumb" Dan 32, 145
Morgan, Tod 27
Mosk, Stanley 190
Mosley, Shane 208
Muldoon, William 31, 72, 75, 106, 107, 203, 204
Mullally, Frederic 12, 180
Murphey, Billy 56
Mussina, Luigi 186, 187, 195, 200, 209
Mussolini, Benito 1, 126–128, 158, 164, 166, 169, 178, 181–183, 184, 189, 213, 214

Nagurski, Bronko 188
Nance, "Indian" Phil 124
Nardiello, Vincent 138
Negri, Paul 124
Negri, Rocco 124
Neidereiter, Andy 75
Neil, Edward J. 137, 141, 144, 145
Nejtek, Karel 176
Nelson, Al 18
Neusel, Walter 80, 148, 154, 164, 165, 166, 167
Nikolaeff, Feodor 16
Nilles, Marcel 15

Nolan, Nick 95
Norden, Connie 168
Norris, Bobby 18
Norris, Charles 102, 103
Nova, Lou 101, 163

O'Dowd, Bobby 98
O'Kelly, Con 9, 121
O'Kelly, Dennis 207
Olin, Bob 83, 201
Olney, Peter B. Jr. 119, 122–124, 129, 130, 134, 175
O'Neill, Joe 92
Orcutt, Eddie 196
Orlando, Guido 188
O'Sullivan, Jack 72, 79, 80, 172
O'Toole, Tommy 187
Owens, "Cowboy" Billy 34, 35
Owens, Jack 49, 97

Paccassi, Frank 54
Panoni, Vincent 144
Pantega, Julia 150
Pastor, Bob 154, 163, 166, 167
Patman, Wright 84
Patton, George 85
Pavelec, Jerry 84, 86
Pelecos, Jack 36
Pep, Willie 208
Perez, Lulu 208
Perry, Bob 44, 45
Persson, Harry 16
Petacci, Clara 184
Petersen, Soren 80
Peterson, Clayton "Big Boy" 18, 31, 95, 173, 192
Peterson, Jack 148
Petrolle, Billy 206
Phelan, John J. 106, 137, 138, 170, 203, 204
Phillips, Tug 123
Piana, Amilcare 8
Piccento, John 119
Picco, Leo 183
Pieck, Wilhelm 24
Pierce, Buddy 92
Pistone, John 209
Pius XI, Pope 111
Polozzolo, Tony 115
Poreda, Stanley 77, 86–88, 103, 167
Potgeiter, Ewart 194
Powell, Tiny 47
Pozsonyi, Laszlo 176
Prieto, Justo 149
Pryor, Sam 68
Purdy, Eddie 76, 95
Putz, Karl 176

Rachmaninoff, Sergei 25
Rand, Sally 136
Rapieri, Bruno 110
Rascel, Renato 179
Ratner, Willie 21
Rawson, Larry "Big Boy" 161
Raymond, Lew 168
Reddish, Willie 171
Redman, Jack 86, 159
Redmond, Pat 67, 68, 83

Reich, Al 9
Reilly, Tommy 39 51, 52
Renault, Jack 18, 67, 68, 82, 121–123, 125, 126
Retzlaff, Charley 47, 88, 163, 168
Reynolds, Quentin 132
Rice, Grantland 45
Rice, Joe 97
Rickard, Tex 11, 32, 72, 137, 207
Rioux, Elzear 33, 34, 35, 43, 58, 92, 99
Risko, Johnny 72, 107
Ritchie, Willie 140
Ritter, Lawrence 202
Roberti, Roberto 69, 70, 83, 93, 192
Robinson, Murray 86, 87
Rocca, Antonio 188
Rocco, Emmett 79
Rogers, Pete 49
Rojas, Quintin Romero 16
Rollini, Giulio 140
Roman, Gene 36, 70
Romero, Johnny "Bandit" 39
Rommel, Erwin 182
Roosevelt, Franklin D. 30, 93, 107, 108
Roosevelt, James 127, 159
Roosevelt, John 159
Roper, Jack 65, 66
Rosemann, Ernst 14, 15
Rosen, Charlie 36
Rosenbloom, Maxie 18, 65, 171, 201
Ross, Barney 140
Ross, Phil 123
Rossi, Al 70
Rothstein, Arnold 27, 28, 201, 207
Roxmore, Max 119, 122, 123
Ruggirello, Salvatore 12, 102
Runyon, Damon 17, 138, 152
Ruth, Babe 49, 163

Sachs, Leonard 79
Salvalaggio, Nantas 216
Salvetti, Mario 215
Sammartino, Bruno 213
Sammons, Jefferey T. 200
Sandwina, Kate 92
Sandwina, Ted 68, 77, 92, 121
Santa, Jose 12, 14, 93, 94, 124
Saunders, Jack 84
Saunooke, Chief 187
Saxe, William V. 66
Sayers, Tom 47
Schaaf, Anita 108
Schaaf, Ernie 49, 68, 75, 76, 83, 88, 91, 100–111, 115, 121, 128, 136, 137, 190, 203, 205
Schaaf, Lucy 105–107, 109
Scheuver, Remi B. 106, 107
Schlossberg, Phil 106
Schmeling, Max 2, 11, 12, 15, 17, 18, 20, 22, 51, 55, 59, 61, 64, 66, 67, 72, 82, 91, 107, 110, 111, 114, 127, 128, 130, 137, 138, 148, 152, 153, 155, 163, 168, 183, 184, 193, 196, 199–201

Schmuck, Peter 120
Schoeler, Jacob 130
Schonrath, Hans 16, 81, 82
Schulberg, Budd 190
Schultz, Art 92
Schultz, Dutch 26 27, 147
Schwake, John 94
Scott, Phil 18, 21, 82, 196
Sebilo, Leon 11, 12, 15
See, Leon 9–14, 16, 19–22, 24, 25, 27, 28, 31, 37, 38, 45, 46, 53, 54, 59, 62, 64, 65, 66, 71, 75, 76, 78, 80, 81, 83, 113, 119, 129, 180, 196, 201, 203, 205, 206
Shanks, Andy 44
Sharkey, Jack 2, 3, 18, 49, 55, 59, 61, 66, 67, 71–76, 78–80, 82, 83, 86, 100, 103–107, 110–112, 114–121, 123, 124, 126, 129, 131, 138, 140, 146, 153, 163, 173, 177, 193, 195–197, 199, 200, 202, 204–206, 207, 213, 216, 217
Sharkey, Tom 71
Shaw, Jack 36
Shawtell, Tommy 141
Shea, Leo 132, 133
Shearer, Art 46
Shires, Art 43
Sigmund, Jim 37
Siki, Battling 13
Silva, Guillermo 16
Silva, Jack 46
Silver, Jack 47, 53
Simms, Eddie 123
Simms, Frankie 47, 53
Simon, Abe 161
Sims, P. Hal 136
Sirutis, Yustin 135
Skilling, Dan 122
Skratt, Theodore J. 112, 120, 129, 139, 146, 164, 175
Slattery, Jimmy 18, 205
Smith, Al 93
Smith, Buzz 96
Smith, Ed "Gunboat" 73, 74, 77, 78, 115
Smith, Ford 97, 168
Smith, Joe (boxer from Tampa, FL) 42
Smith, Joe (manager for Tommy Loughran) 129, 133
Smith, "Little" Patsey 26
Smuts, Jan Christian 25
Snelling, O.F. 195
Snyder, Angus 45, 94
Sofio, Sonny 94
Soresi, Louis 2, 28, 104, 111, 112, 119, 120, 123, 125, 126, 128–130, 134, 145, 147–151, 155, 164, 166, 169, 170, 174, 178, 181, 201
Souto, Luiz 151
Spalla, Erminio 15
Spence, James "Young" 98, 99
Spinks, Leon 2, 3
Spohrer, Al 43
Sportiello, Felix 12
Spurgin, Jack 96
Stanley, Jack 17
Stanton, Gene 86, 92

Starace, Achille 1, 125, 126, 164–166, 178
Steinborn, Milo 187
Stillman, Lou (Ingber) 31 32
Stockings, George Joseph "Kid Socks" 60
Stookey, Byron 102, 105
Stradley, Don 197
Stribling, Guerry Boone 17, 19
Stribling, "Pa" 17, 19, 205
Stribling, W.L. "Young" 2, 17–21, 25, 30, 31, 41, 47, 54, 55, 61, 64, 66, 67, 96, 98, 134, 152, 193, 205, 206, 217
Strilich, Steve 46
Strongbow, Jules 187, 188
Suess, Artie 84
Sugar, Bert R. 158, 161, 204
Sullivan, Big Boy 96
Sullivan, Ed 189, 192
Sullivan, John L. 199
Sykes, Art 159
Sylvain, Joe 11
Szabo, Sander 1, 188

Tallent, Aaron 198
Tarling, Pat 17
Taub, Billy 210
Taylor, Bud 48
Taylor, Jack 31, 92
Tays, Alan 108
Temmes, Bill 42
Tersini, Emilia 22, 40, 81, 111–113, 115, 119, 120, 128, 130, 139, 146, 147, 148, 151, 164, 175
Thomas, Dolph 137, 139
Thomas, Dummy (Thomas Negri) 124
Thomas, Frankie (Frank Negri) 124
Thomas, Joe 12, 16, 20
Thomas, Norman 93
Thomas, Otis 27
Tippero, Dominick 109
Tolar, Jack 98
Torriani, Umberto 68, 69
Tottershaw, Jack 96
Touchstone, Bennie 47
Trafton, George 42, 43
Triner, Joe 157
Truang, Charles F. 45
Tunney, Gene 2, 26, 28, 39, 41, 51, 68, 72, 115, 121, 131, 140, 144, 159, 199, 201, 202, 206, 207
Turner, Charles 34
Turner, George 167
Tuttle, Harry "King Tut" 33, 206
Tyson, Mike 208

Udell, Larry 89, 90
Uhl, Byron H. 54
Uzcudan, Paolino 2, 13, 15, 49, 59–61, 64, 71, 75, 88, 93, 122, 125, 126, 127, 128, 131, 149, 163, 170, 197, 200, 205

Valenti, Joe 86
Valuev, Nikolay 208, 209
van der Veer, Piet 13

Van Porat, Otto 21
Vassis, Costas 92
Vermaut, Arthur 12
Villa, Francisco "Pancho" (José Doroteo Arango Arámbula) 49
Villa, Pancho (Francisco Guilledo) 27, 201
Vittorio, Emmanualle, III 182, 183
Vogt, Richard 168
Vona, Ralph 161
Von Schacht, Fred 187
Vreeland, Roger 113

Wagener, Rudi 13 14, 82, 93, 167
Wagner, Lynn 49, 192
Walcott, Joe 39, 57, 171
Walker, Al 39 52
Walker, Jimmy 27, 68, 207
Walker, Mickey 27, 59, 72, 73, 75, 88, 93, 128, 201, 204, 205
Walker, William H. 105, 138, 153, 159
Wallace, Andy 161
Walpole, Hugh 25, 26
Walsh, Davis J. 32, 36, 51, 53, 147, 192, 196
Walsh, James J. 107
Walters, Walter W. 84
Wangley, Paul 40
Warren, Billy 27
Wathey, Bill 193
Wear, D. Walker 137, 159
Weaver, Buck 35
Weinert, Charley 9
Welch, Grady 186
Welch, Suey 47
Wepner, Charlie 153
Wepner, Chuck 153
Whitney, Richard 30
Wiener, Frank 51
Wiggins, Chuck 18, 41, 42 52, 94, 195
Wignall, Trevor 196
Wilde, Jim 176
Wilkes, Ed 46
Willard, Jess 2, 3, 122, 197, 202, 206, 207, 209
Williams, Barney 152
Willis, "Cowboy" Frank 56, 57
Wilson, George 47
Wilson, Gus 115
Wilson, Hack 43
Wilson, Woodrow 85
Winston, Ed "Unknown" 103
Wolf, Al 95
Wolff, Howard 95
Woolsey, John M. 146, 148
Wooten, Jimmy 96
Wotanski, Frank 161
Wright, Bearcat 53, 54

Yuzzolino, Albert M. 130, 152

Zangara, Giuseppe 108
Zappala, Al 161
Zaveta, Frank 42
Zupan, Josef 176, 177, 185, 186

www.ingramcontent.com/pod-product-compliance
Ingram Content Group UK Ltd.
Pitfield, Milton Keynes, MK11 3LW, UK
UKHW050702160426
5217IPUK00038B/1950